Mountain Farmers

Mountain Farmers

Moral Economies
of Land & Agricultural Development
in Arusha & Meru

THOMAS SPEAR

Professor of History
University of Wisconsin at Madison

Mkuki na Nyota
DAR ES SALAAM

University of
California Press
BERKELEY & LOS ANGELES

James Currey
OXFORD

James Currey Ltd
73 Botley Road
Oxford
OX2 0BS

Mkuki na Nyota
PO Box 4246
Dar es Salaam
Tanzania

University of California Press
2120 Berkeley Way
Berkeley, CA 94720

British Library Cataloguing in Publication Data
Spear, Thomas
  Mountain farmers : moral economies of land and agricultural development
in Arusha and Meru
  1. Arusha (African people) – Agriculture – Economic aspects
  2. Meru (African people) – agriculture – Economic aspects
  3. Land use – Tanzania – History
  I. Title
  333.7'6'096782

ISBN 0–85255–736–1 (cloth)
       0–85255–737–X (paper)

Library of Congress Cataloging-in-Publication Data

Spear, Thomas T.
  Mountain farmers : moral economies of land and agricultural development
in Arusha and Meru/Thomas Spear.
     p. cm.
  Includes bibliographical references (p.   ) and index.
  ISBN 0–520–20618–5 (cloth),-- ISBN 0–520–20619–3 (pbk.)
  1. Meru (African people) -- Land tenure. 2. Meru (African people) -
- Agriculture. 3. Meru (African people) -- Government relations.
4. Arusha (African people) -- Land tenure. 5. Arusha (African
people) -- Agriculture. 6. Arusha (African people) -- Government
relations. 7. Land tenure -- Tanzania -- Meru, Mount, Region -- History.
8. Economic development -- Tanzania -- Meru, Mount, Region -- History.
9. Meru, Mount, Region (Tanzania) -- Social conditions. 10. Meru,
Mount, Region (Tanzania) -- Race relations. 11. Meru, Mount, Region
(Tanzania) -- Politics and government. I. Title.
DT443.3.M47S63 1997
967.8'26 -- dc21   96-37622
                                                              CIP

Set in 10/12 pt Ehrhardt, the Monotype revival of a seventeenth-century Leipzig face,
by Long House Publishing Services, St Vincent, West Indies
Printed in Great Britain by Villiers Publications, London N3

9 8 7 6 5 4 3 2 1

Contents

Contents

List of Maps, Photographs & Tables

Glossary

aulo	pasture (Maa)
boma	fort; German administrative post
engisaka	family homestead (Maa)
hongo	toll paid by caravans (Swahili)
kihamba	family homestead (Meru)
(i)laigwenak	age-set spokesmen (Maa); pl. of *olaigwenani*
(o)loibon(i)	diviner or prophet (Maa)
mangi	chief (Meru); also applied by Germans to Arusha
manyata	ceremonial village to which Maasai warriors withdrew following their circumcision (Maa)
(i)murran	warriors; pl. of *olmurrani* (Maa)
(ol)murran(i)	warrior (Maa)
olaigwenani	spokesman of an age-set (Maa)
olkarsis	wealthy man (Maa); a title given to chiefs by British
olngesher	age-set ceremony in which warriors are promoted to elders (Maa)
vashili	clan leaders (Meru)
vihamba	homesteads; pl. of *kihamba* (Meru)

Acknowledgements

A number of people and organizations have facilitated my research and writing over the years it took to bring this book to completion. A Fellowship for College Teachers and a Travel to Collections grant, both from the National Endowment for the Humanities, and generous research and sabbatical grants from the President and Trustees of Williams College allowed me to conduct archival and field research in Tanzania during 1988 and 1991. My work in Tanzania was conducted under the auspices of UTAFITI and the Department of History of the University of Dar es Salaam. Professor Abdul Sheriff and Dr N. N. Luanda were both extremely helpful in facilitating my research, as was the staff at the National Archives of Tanzania. Mr Chicote of the Arusha Resource Centre helped with local materials in Arusha, while Wolfgang Alpelt facilitated my work at the Lutheran Theological College Makumira.

Several people in Arusha made my work there easier and more congenial, including David and Eunice Simonson, Stanley and Marie Benson, and Erwin and Ester Kinsey. Mesiaki Kilevo and Erasto Ngira assisted with interviews in Arusha and Meru, respectively, while a number of Arusha and Meru gave generously of their time and knowledge in our interviews with them.

In the United States, I have benefited from the invigorating ideas of a number of scholars working on Maasai and related peoples, including Richard Waller, John Berntsen, Cory Kratz, John Galaty, Neal Sobania, Elliot Fratkin, and others associated in writing *Being Maasai*. I have also been inspired by another group of fine scholars who have produced rich and exciting historical work on northern Tanzania, including Isaria Kimambo, Steven Feierman, Patricia Benjamin, James Giblin, and Jonathon Glassman, while Philip Gulliver's superb ethnography on Arusha was invaluable. Derek Nurse, Rainer Vossen, and Chris Ehret gave critical advice on linguistic materials. James Brain kindly shared his personal experience in Arusha with me. Michelle and Timothy Murphy provided valuable assistance translating the *Evangelisch-Lutherisches Missionsblatt*. And Dorothy Hodgson and Patricia Benjamin generously shared reports on their ongoing work in the area.

In the course of writing, I have presented different aspects of my work to the

Department of History at the University of Dar es Salaam, the Walter Rodney Seminar at Boston University, the Conference on African Protohistory at the University of Illinois, the African Studies Association annual meetings, the Symposium on Fieldwork at Wisconsin, the Conference on the Growth of Farming Communities in Africa at Cambridge, and the African Studies Seminar and the Agrarian Studies Colloquium, both at Yale. Participants in all were as generous in their comments as in their support.

I am particularly indebted to careful and sensitive readings of the manuscript by Patricia Benjamin, James Giblin, Allen Isaacman, Sheila Spear, Jan Vansina, and the readers for the press. I have not been able to respond to all the interesting and provocative questions they raised, but they helped to make this book a better one.

Portions of Chapters 2, 3, and 9 have appeared previously in: '"Being Maasai" but not "People of Cattle": Arusha Agricultural Maasai in the Nineteenth Century' in T. Spear & R. Waller (eds), *Being Maasai* (London: James Currey, 1993), 120–36; 'Blood on the Land: Stories of Conquest' in R. Harms, J. Miller, D. Newbury & M. Wagner (eds), *Paths Toward the Past* (Atlanta: African Studies Association Press, 1994), 113–22; and 'Struggles for the Land: The Political and Moral Economies of Land on Mount Meru' in G. Maddox, J. Giblin & I.N. Kimambo (eds), *Custodians of the Land: Environment and Hunger in Tanzanian History* (London: James Currey, 1995), 213–40. I am grateful to James Currey and the African Studies Association Press for permission to republish that material here.

I am particularly grateful to Patricia Benjamin for kindly allowing me to reproduce several of her photographs and to the University of Wisconsin Cartographic Laboratory for preparing the maps. Finally, a generous grant from the William F. Vilas Trust has facilitated publication in Tanzania.

Two people have been generous beyond the call of duty and influenced my thinking greatly. Many of my ideas about Arusha and Meru history first emerged during the course of long and fruitful discussions with Mesiaki Kilevo as we traipsed the Arusha area on our way to interviews and worked long hours translating them. Working with Mesiaki, a humane and insightful student of his own society, was one of the joys of this project for me. And Richard Waller has been a font of provocative suggestions, important ideas, and enthusiastic support throughout. Always ready to read drafts, his critical comments and endless flow of suggestions have made this a far richer book than it would have been without his help.

Madison, Wisconsin

Introduction

The closing decades of the nineteenth century were traumatic ones for the Meru and Arusha peoples settled on Mount Meru in northern Tanganyika (now Tanzania) as new epidemic diseases, civil war, drought, and famine killed people and cattle in unprecedented numbers and threatened to undermine the fundamental social order. When the first two Christian missionaries then tried to settle on Meru in 1896, Arusha and Meru warriors, members of the Talala age-set, killed them to try to purge the land of evil witchcraft that had brought such social disorder. 'Talala were the Europeans of Arusha,' Eliyahu Lujas Meiliari recalled recently. 'They hated anything evil or dirty.... They killed ... witches at Kimandolu by circling around them and clubbing them to death to avoid spilling any blood....'[1]

When the British expropriated Meru land at Engare Nanyuki a half century later, Meru protested against the unjust seizure of their land, organized a political party, engaged in non-violent resistance, and took their case to the United Nations in New York. Asked later if Meru had also had anything to do with the subsequent deaths of several Europeans involved in the case, Rafaeli Mbise, a Christian evangelist who led the Meru, answered:

> I asked them if they knew about sin, really knew about sin.... I asked if they had seen people praying before they had been evicted.... Then I said they had been praying to God for help since the Europeans were not going to help them. The Lord must have heard their prayers, because he made the Europeans pay for their sins.... [D.O.] Troup drove the people away and jailed them.... So he was paying for his sins for jailing and torturing people and throwing them off the land.[2]

In between these two events, Meru and Arusha societies had been transformed. Germans and British had conquered and ruled them for half a century; many Arusha and Meru had become educated and converted to Christianity; and nearly all were involved in raising coffee. But through it all, the people of Mount Meru retained a

---

[1] Eliyahu Lujas Meiliari (AHT 8).
[2] Rafaeli Mbise (MHT 3).

1

deeply moral sense of social responsibility and economic justice. While the moral idiom had certainly changed – from witchcraft to sin – a common theme links these two accounts a half-century apart. Immoral acts bring evil upon the land until they are purged and the land cleansed. Meru and Arusha traditions and values persisted, transforming colonial ideas and institutions as they were themselves transformed by them. This book, then, is about cultural interpretation and appropriation, about the continuity of tradition and its transformation.

Mountain Farmers

Gazing out from the rooftop patio of a modern tourist hotel in Arusha today, the dry grasslands stretch endlessly to the horizon, east to the distant, snow-capped peaks of Mount Kilimanjaro, south into the Maasai Steppe, and west as far as the wall of the Rift Valley. These are classic East African savannah, formerly occupied by herds of wild game and semi-nomadic herders. As one turns to the north, however, one confronts the stark wall of Mount Meru rising sharply out of the plains to its peak at 4,565 metres.[3]

Leaving the comforts of the hotel and crossing the main road that forms the northern boundary of the town, one passes briefly through a strip of peri-urban bars and boarding houses that line the road, heading sharply uphill into a cloistered world of bananas and coffee trees so thick that one is often unable to see the houses nestled in their midst. The narrow path continues to meander upwards through the dense groves for six kilometres or so, climbing from 1,200 to 1,700 metres, until one emerges onto open maize and bean fields that continue up to the forest boundary at 1,800 metres.

This fertile well-watered band circling the southern slopes of Mount Meru is the heartland of the Meru and Arusha peoples. Increasing population over the past fifty years has slowly forced people off the mountain on to the drier, less productive plains, where their farms now extend up to 80 kilometres away; but the mountain is their home, the place where they have developed as peoples over the past two to four centuries. The first Meru were Chaga speakers who expanded from Mount Kilimanjaro during the seventeenth century to pioneer new farming settlements on the southeastern slopes of Mount Meru. Arusha were agro-pastoral Maasai who first settled on the southwestern slopes of the mountain in the 1830s during a period when struggles among pastoralists to control resources on the plains were taking place.

Meru cleared small fields in the mountain forest to raise bananas, eleusine, and beans and, over the years, slowly expanded up the mountain slopes as their families grew and they were joined by others seeking fertile land or refuge from political struggles on Kilimanjaro. Arusha, by contrast, first settled on the fringe of the plains, where they traded with their pastoral relatives and later with Swahili trading caravans on their way to

---

[3] Mount Meru is a dormant volcano whose central cone rises 4,565 metres to dominate the surrounding plains at 1,200 metres. The lower, inhabited slopes rise gently to 2,100 metres, and then sharply to the summit, giving an overall rise of 30° compared with only 8° for Kilimanjaro. The eastern wall of the cone is blown out, revealing the floor at 2,700 metres, and lesser cones, including Ngurdoto, Duluti, Oldonyo Sambu, and Little Meru, surround the base.

1.1 *Mount Meru from Arusha town* (Spear)

western Kenya from the coast, but they, too, soon set about clearing the forest and developing their own farms further up the slopes.

Settled on separate sections of the mountain, Arusha and Meru remained fairly distant from each other until they eventually came into contact, and conflict, in the mid-nineteenth century. Arusha warriors raided Meru settlements for cattle to bolster their herds, women to marry, and young men to join them in raids elsewhere. Meru subsequently joined the Arusha warriors in self-defence, and together they raided Kilimanjaro for cattle and captives.

As the century drew to a close, however, several disasters struck. A series of epidemics, droughts, and killing famines devastated people and stock throughout northern Tanzania; civil wars rent the pastoral societies of the plains; and German troops advanced threateningly up the Pangani Valley. In an effort to stem these evil afflictions, Arusha and Meru warriors killed the first two German missionaries to settle among them, and then combined to oppose the German troops sent to avenge their deaths.

German colonialists quickly established their authority over the peoples of Mount Meru in a devastating series of raids, however, and forced them to pay taxes, build roads, and construct an administrative fort on the site of modern Arusha town. The government alienated large tracts of land around the lower slopes of the mountain to European settlers, and German missionaries established missions and schools in the heart of Meru and Arusha country. Their own economies devastated, many Arusha and Meru were initially forced to work for the settlers, while others joined the missions as students and converts.

By the time the British replaced the Germans during the First World War, Meru and Arusha populations were recovering, and people were rapidly filling out the little open land still remaining on the mountain. As population continued to expand during the 1920s and 1930s, Arusha and Meru intensified their farming by replacing fields of maize and beans with bananas; shortening fallows and planting pastures with annual crops; shifting dry cattle to the plains while hand-feeding those that remained and using their manure on their fields; and raising coffee for sale. Densities continued to rise throughout the 1940s and 1950s, however, and people began to move off the mountain to settle in highland districts to the east and west, and eventually in the plains beyond.

While the mounting pressure on land fuelled Arusha and Meru agricultural development, land also provided a principled basis for their opposition to colonialism. Unable to obtain sufficient land for their needs, the presence of abundant and often undeveloped settler land surrounding them constantly offended their sense of economic justice. They tried to stave off further losses and endlessly petitioned the colonial authorities for relief, to no avail. Land shortage also set the peoples of Mount Meru against themselves, provoking struggles between elders who owned land and juniors who did not, between chiefs who controlled the spoils of the colonial system and those who were powerless, and between wealthy cattle men and poorer farmers raising food crops and coffee. By the late 1940s these tensions coalesced into popular movements directed against the chiefs and the wider colonial administration. Long-standing chiefs were overthrown and Meru carried their protest against a further round of evictions to the United Nations in a well-known case which spurred the development of the nationalist movement throughout Tanzania.

The stories of Meru and Arusha settlement on Mount Meru, their development of highly specialized and intensive agriculture, and their struggles to maintain their economic and cultural autonomy against two colonial powers are complex ones. Arusha and Meru adapted their previous economies to the new environment of Mount Meru and subsequently developed their own highly specialized agriculture within the dual contexts of their own domestic economies and a developing market economy. They also struggled to maintain their cultural autonomy, while at the same time operating within wider regional, national, and international contexts that brought Maasai, Swahili, and European influences into their own cultural repertoire. Arusha and Meru played active roles in these transformations and were at least as responsible for their outcomes as the external forces impinging on them. It is their struggles to interpret, control, and give meaning to their rapidly changing worlds that we seek to understand here.

But Meru and Arusha were two different peoples, each of whom had their own distinctive cultural values and practices while sharing broader political and economic environments with one another. This book, then, is a comparative history of two distinct peoples in order to understand the role of culture in socio-economic change. We start with the histories of Meru and Arusha settlement on Mount Meru and of the separate ways in which each people adopted similar agricultural routines. With the imposition of colonial rule, drastic restrictions were placed on their land and, in response to increasing population, both dramatically intensified those agricultural routines to bring about their own agricultural revolutions. Political tensions with the colonial authorities mounted over the Meru and Arusha peoples' refusal to work for Europeans and their continued adherence to their own agricultural and land use patterns, leading to separate political crises in the two areas in the 1940s and 1950s.

The influence of culture on Arusha and Meru responses took place on two levels. Many of their responses stemmed from common values of economic justice and social responsibility which they broadly shared with others throughout the region, while others came from each people's distinctive cultural values and practices. Thus both peoples adopted similar agricultural crops and practices when they first settled on the mountain, but developed distinctive forms of social organization in accordance with their different historical experiences. Similarly, both chose to intensify their agricultural production in response to increasing population and land shortage in the twentieth century, but they did so in subtly distinctive ways. By exploring the nature of these changes comparatively, then, the histories of the Meru and Arusha peoples can tell us much about the complex ways in which people manage socio-economic change in the context of their own lives and historical experience.

Culture and Economy in Comparative Perspective

I first began this work over a decade ago as a study of cultural economy. In simple terms, I wanted to explore how changes in the economy affected cultural factors, and vice versa. My earlier work had explored the impact of commodity trade on the peoples of eastern Kenya, and had focused on changing forms of exchange and their impact on social organization and values.[4] I now wanted to examine other types of economic change to gauge their impact, while at the same time exploring in greater depth the complex ways in which people's own values and social practices mediated such changes. Put most simply, I sought to understand how economic forces influenced social values and institutions at the same time as people's own values and practices reshaped the economic forces acting on them to produce transformations in both.

Mount Meru was a logical place on which to focus, for Meru and Arusha have both gone through a dramatic series of socio-economic changes to develop similar, highly intensive, agricultural regimes employing permanent cultivation of bananas and coffee, irrigation, hand-feeding cattle, and manuring. At the same time, however, the two peoples come from radically different cultural backgrounds, and thus have brought very different historical experiences to bear on these changes. Meru descend from agricultural Chaga, peoples who have long farmed a similar environment on Mount Kilimanjaro, but Arusha are descended from pastoral Maasai, many of whom still herd cattle on the plains today. The co-existence of two peoples of markedly different cultural backgrounds in a common environmental and economic situation thus formed a natural basis for comparison.

There was a wide range of questions to explore in seeking to understand the parallel but separate histories of the peoples of Mount Meru. Just how did these two peoples with different cultural backgrounds respond to similar environmental and economic circumstances? To what extent did each respond in a similar manner to their common environment? How, if at all, did their responses differ in accordance with their different cultural perceptions, values, and practices? Did Meru continue to adhere to Chaga social, economic, and cultural practices? Did Arusha borrow Meru farming techniques and attendant cultural forms to adapt to the unfamiliar environment, or did they devise their own techniques in accordance with their own experience? How was each affected by the penetration of commodity trade in the nineteenth century and colonial capitalism in the twentieth century, and how did each respond to the challenges these presented?

I thus started with two different sets of relationships to explore. One was the relationship between material conditions and cultural factors, how each changed, and how they influenced each other over the course of time in the case of each people. The other

---

[4] Thomas Spear, *The Kaya Complex* (Nairobi, 1978), *Kenya's Past* (London, 1981), and (with Derek Nurse) *The Swahili* (Philadelphia, 1985). Such studies of 'trade and politics' in Africa were common in the 1960s and early 1970s as historians sought to understand the impact of merchant capitalism on African societies. Our understanding of the impact of expanding commodity trade on African politics was greatly enhanced by the succeeding development of neo-Marxist approaches to African political economy and by renewed interest in exchange theory in anthropology. Such studies, however, tended to assume that economy played a determining role, and few considered seriously the reciprocal role of people's own cultural values in mediating economic change. From there the focus shifted in the mid-1970s and 1980s to underdevelopment and dependency theory, in which African historical actors were largely relegated to subsidiary roles in the development of capitalism and the world economy. Now the focus is shifting once again to seeking to understand African actors on their own terms as they struggled to adapt and give meaning to the wider forces impinging on their lives.

was the relationship between the two peoples, allowing us to compare similarities and differences in these processes between them. Each people had its own wider cultural affinities – Meru with Chaga and Arusha with pastoral Maasai – but the two also overlapped each other in their common experiences on adjacent slopes of Mount Meru. The histories of Meru and Arusha thus parallel one another as both peoples interacted with the same economic and political environment, and they intersect with one another at a number of critical junctures. But the two histories are also distinct, as each people acted within the context and terms of its own experience. In spite of the common environmental and historical forces acting on them, however, Meru and Arusha developed very differently, sometimes adapting to changes in parallel, sometimes differently, but rarely in unison.

Regional Cultural Economies

Arusha and Meru have long participated in wider spheres of social and economic exchange as people throughout northern Tanzania traded with their neighbours, married them, and migrated from one area to another. Steven Feierman and Isaria Kimambo have demonstrated, for example, the development of 'regional patterns of action' and 'commodification' accompanying the expansion of trade and Swahili culture along the Pangani valley from the mid-nineteenth century.[5] But regional patterns of action were much older than this. The first agro-pastoralists settled among hunter-gatherers at least two thousand years ago, leading to the development of a regional exchange economy, while the subsequent development of specialized agricultural, pastoral, and gathering ethnic economies was only possible through increasing interaction among different peoples within an interdependent regional economy.[6]

The development of local economies and cultures presupposed developments in regional economies and cultures. During just the last two hundred years, for example, there has been a succession of three different regional cultural economies in northern Tanzania, each with its own distinctive form of exchange, social relations, and attendant social values. The first, based on exchanges of cattle, facilitated social interaction and allowed for the exchange of agricultural, pastoral, and gathered commodities among specialized producers, and was dominated by Maasai pastoralists who controlled the bulk of the region's livestock. The second was the development during the later nineteenth century of long distance trade, pioneered by Swahili traders from the coast, introducing into the area new forms of commercial exchange along with new products, new skills, a new language, and a new religion. The third was the introduction of the capitalist economy by German and British colonialists which also brought its own forms of commodity exchange, language, and religion.

[5] Steven Feierman, *The Shambaa Kingdom* (Madison, 1974) and Isaria N. Kimambo, *Penetration and Protest in Tanzania* (London, 1991). See also James Giblin, *The Politics of Environmental Control in Northern Tanzania* (Philadelphia, 1992) and Jonathon P. Glassman, *Feasts and Riot* (Portsmouth and London, 1995).

[6] Thomas Spear, 'Introduction' in T. Spear & R. Waller (eds), *Being Maasai* (London, 1993), 1–18. See also Charles Ambler, *Kenyan Communities in the Age of Imperialism* (New Haven, 1988).

Many cultural values were thus broadly shared across the region, and changes in the regional cultural economy, in turn, were reflected in changes in local cultural economies. 'Maasai' cultural economy was based on reciprocal exchanges of cattle for rights in women and other dependants, and operated as a means by which wealthy elders throughout the region could recruit followers to ensure their own household production and reproduction. Usually such exchanges took place at the local level in the form of marriages, trading relations, or cattle partnerships, but they also took place regionally between farmers and herders to facilitate trade or complementary economic activities. 'Swahili' cultural economy focused more on trade and commercial exchanges between itinerant traders and local procurers of ivory or slaves. The preferred items of exchange were guns and cloth, which ambitious men could then use to subordinate others to them as exchanges between patrons and clients became more redistributional than reciprocal. Finally, 'European' cultural economy sought to transform the social and moral aspects of economic relations, treating labour itself as a commodity that could be exchanged directly for wages or goods, allowing individuals to accumulate capital on their own.

New forms of exchange thus followed in succession, but they did not so much supplant older forms as overlay them, producing multi-tiered patterns of exchange with people able to negotiate among them according to context. Thus it is, for example, that reciprocal social exchanges, such as marriage, continue today as a means of recruiting labour to domestic households to produce commercial crops for the international market. Conversely, people frequently use money they earn selling cash crops to invest in cattle to effect social exchanges.

While African actors have thus continually shifted their modes situationally, social scientists have found it more difficult to do so. Ethnographers have commonly emphasized local patterns of social exchange, while dependency theorists have focused on international capitalist ones. But if multiple forms of exchange coexist at any one time, it makes little sense to isolate one of them and assume that this reflects an accurate view of reality. If African actors could shift their modes contextually, we must be able to do so as well.

Many writers stress the external forces acting on African societies as the main causes of change. Thus innovation is often explained by diffusion or the borrowing of ideas from elsewhere, while social relations are seen as determined by larger economic or environmental forces. Such a focus is clearly inadequate, however, when it comes either to explaining the multitude of changes which have occurred within African societies or to understanding how and why Africans responded to external forces as they did.

Rather than pursuing such outside forces here, then, the focus will be on the strategies Arusha and Meru employed to manage changing economic conditions themselves. While such a local perspective, focusing on historical actors in their specific economic, social, and cultural contexts, is crucial if we are to understand how and why changes took place, one can no longer presume that such local contexts are, or ever were, autonomous. Regional patterns of action, the penetration of a commercial economy in the nineteenth century, the establishment of colonial rule in the twentieth, and the drive for political independence and economic development after 1950 have introduced important regional, national, and international factors into farmers' decisions, ranging from shifts in the regional economy to the imposition of government controls and taxation and the international coffee market. Local, regional, national, and international spheres of social and economic exchange are all interrelated.

The problem is how one deals with such a multitude of spheres, each with its own mode(s) of production and attendant means and relations of production, within a single frame of analysis. Much has been written in an attempt to classify African modes of production in order to demonstrate that Africa's farmers are (or are not) subsistence cultivators, peasants linked peripherally to the market economy, or capitalist farmers. But classification misses the point, because Tanzania's farmers may be, at one time or another, any or all of these, according to the context. A farmer may make a decision to plant a certain crop according to the quality and availability of family land and labour, the need for cash to pay taxes or school fees, a desire to purchase locally made iron roofing or an imported tractor, a comparison of the cost of production against government taxation and the world market price, or the need for food. One must be able to comprehend these variable strategies within a unit of analysis that takes account of varied levels of production and exchange.

Analysing how different modes of production are articulated with one another in people's lives and decisions is thus crucial. It is now well known, for example, that capitalist production in Africa relies on the domestic economy to subsidize labour costs by paying workers less than the social wage, which is then made up by the worker's family in the subsistence sector. Conversely, subsistence farmers exploit social relationships to make market investments and plough back cash gained from wages or selling crops into such social investments as titles, wives, feasts, or education. The crucial question then is not so much how we classify modes of production but how different modes are related at any one time in the context of an individual farmer's perceptions, decisions, and actions.[7]

Agricultural Development

Perhaps the most significant economic development within Meru and Arusha societies has been their dramatic intensification of agricultural production over the course of the twentieth century. Agricultural development in Africa has long been viewed as synonymous with intervention by outside experts who seek to replace indigenous practices with imported ones. Peasant farmers – usually women – using hand hoes and 'slash and burn' techniques to produce just enough food for their own consumption were relegated to the past, to be supplanted by capitalist farmers and techniques. When colonialists sought to introduce production of cash crops for export, for example, they presumed a need for European plantations, settlers, and technology. Africans were usually only included as potential producers in areas too unhealthy to attract whites. These assump-

[7] See, e.g., Juhani Koponen, *People and Production in Late Precolonial Tanzania* (Helsinki, 1988); Sara Berry, 'Social Institutions and Access to Resources', *Africa*, 59 (1989), 41–55; and Elias C. Mandala, *Work and Control in a Peasant Economy* (Madison, 1990).

tions continued into the development policies of the 1960s and 1970s, when newly-independent nations similarly sought to boost cash crop production in order to finance social and industrial development.

With the high cost, declining returns, and dramatic failures of such policies over more than 80 years, however, the experts have slowly begun to reassess their expertise and status in the light of actual African conditions and practice. African societies have traditionally enjoyed a surplus of land, but a shortage of labour. 'Slash and burn' cultivation, together with intercropping, shifting cultivation and shallow hand hoeing, preserves fragile tropical soils and conserves scarce labour; while permanent cropping, monoculture, and mechanical ploughing rapidly destroy soils or require more labour than is available. Historical crop varieties may not produce as much as modern hybrids, but they require less labour and are more likely to withstand drought and disease, producing sufficient crops in good years to produce a 'normal surplus' and in bad ones to 'cheat famine'. For farmers labouring under uncertain rainfall regimes who must produce in order to survive, risk adverse strategies that conserve resources to optimize production are more rational than maximizing ones that deplete them.[8]

It is one thing to respect African farmers' experience and expertise, however; it is another to ask who will provide the expertise for innovation as increasing population pressures and growing shortages of land and labour render historical techniques less effective. Paul Richards poses this question in his aptly titled *Indigenous Agricultural Revolutions*, in which he demonstrates the innovative potential of African agriculture as peasant 'experts' confront such challenges and resolve them within the context of their own agricultural science.[9] This is a story of such an agricultural revolution, as the peoples of Mount Meru developed progressively more intensive forms of agriculture to the point where they support up to 350 people per square kilometre today.[10]

A Tradition of Innovation and the Innovation of Tradition

The lessons of agricultural development, as with the other socio-economic changes discussed here, are clear. If we are to understand how these changes occurred and why they had the effects that they did, we must seek to understand them from the perspective

[8] For an insightful discussion of optimization vs. maximization on Mount Meru, see Louise Fortmann, 'Development Prospects in Arumeru District' (USAID/Tanzania, 1977).

[9] Paul Richards, *Indigenous Agricultural Revolutions* (London, 1985). For recent attempts to take African agricultural expertise seriously, see L. Lusco & S. Poats, 'Farming Systems Research and Extension' in A. Hansen & D. McMillan (eds), *Food in Sub-Saharan Africa* (Boulder, 1986).

[10] For comparable examples of intensification in East Africa, see F.E. Bernard, *East of Mount Kenya: Meru Agriculture in Transition* (Munich, 1972); M.P. Cowen, 'Commodity Production in Kenya's Central Province' in J. Heyer, P. Roberts & G. Williams (eds), *Rural Development in Tropical Africa* (London, 1981), 121–42; Thomas Hakansson, 'Social and Political Aspects of Intensive Agriculture in East Africa: Some Models from Cultural Anthropology', *Azania*, 24 (1989), 12–20; J.E.G. Sutton, 'Towards a History of Cultivating the Fields', *Azania*, 24 (1989), 98–113; and B.L. Turner, G. Hyden & R.W. Kates (eds), *Population Growth and Agricultural Change in Africa* (Gainesville, 1993). See Chapter 7 for a discussion of issues regarding intensification.

of the peoples involved as much as is possible. For while the analytical perspectives sketched out above are crucial in shaping our approach and interpretations, they cannot substitute for the language, actions, and rationales of the historical actors we seek to understand.

This is easier said than done, however, for Arusha and Meru voices are muted in the historical record and their actions, unexplained by their participants, often make little initial sense to us. The first problem is the sources themselves for, aside from the recent memories of living people and the traditions they maintain of the past, we usually only see Meru and Arusha historical actors obliquely through the bureaucratic language of their foreign rulers.[11] One thus must deconstruct colonial discourses to identify their biases as well as to understand the broader colonial context within which Meru and Arusha acted.

The colonial situation is a deceptive one, for behind the mask of a single historical phenomenon different people pursued different goals using different rules having different meanings. Colonizers and colonized did, of course, literally speak different languages, but they also had different cultural vocabularies and grammars. The simplest encounter could therefore have very different meanings for the respective participants. 'Work' could signify labour performed to earn wages or hoeing one's own fields to produce one's own food; economic dependence on others or a means of establishing economic and social independence through establishing one's own farm and household; the dignity of labour or slavery. Similarly, 'taxes' could represent revenue earned to promote peaceful administration and development or tribute extracted by a greater power; while 'cattle' could be a source of income, an extravagant waste, or a means of establishing social standing. Every action, every interchange, within a colonial situation must thus be looked at from the perspectives of the different actors to understand the particular meanings each gave to it.

The second problem is one of subjects. Individuals rarely appear in either the written or oral sources, so it is very difficult to get a sense of difference or variety within what often appear to be homogeneous groups. While individual colonial officers dealt daily with individual Meru and Arusha, these encounters were usually recorded as though they had taken place between a monolithic administration on the one hand, and a homogeneous people on the other. Occasionally one can identify sub-groups within Arusha or Meru society – chiefs, elders, Christians, or coffee farmers, and only rarely women or young men – pursuing their own interests, but nuances of individual behaviour are rarely discernable. Nor was the colonial administration monolithic. Local level officials had a different perspective from senior policy makers, and their views both differed from those of settlers.

The third problem is to understand Meru and Arusha voices at those times when we do hear them, for they had their own distinctive cultural idioms. Steven Feierman has

---

[11] Remarkably little has been written on Arusha or Meru apart from the extensive ethnographic studies of Arusha in the early 1950s by P. H. Gulliver [e.g., *Social Control in an African Society* (1963)] and memoirs by Kirilo Japhet & Earle Seaton [*The Meru Land Case* (Nairobi, 1967)] and Anton Nelson [*The Freemen of Meru* (Nairobi, 1967)], also dating from the 1950s. Unfortunately, the archival record is similarly thin, the victim of frequent transfers of responsibilities between different governments and mission bodies.

shown that we must understand the importance of being able to bring rain and heal the land if we are to understand the logic of peasant politics in Shambaa and the ongoing creation of peasant discourse as it shaped and was shaped by changing reality.[12] Similarly, John Lonsdale has demonstrated the degree to which Kikuyu ideas of civic virtue and the sharing of wealth influenced both Kikuyu reactions to colonialism and their construction of the 'Mau Mau' revolt against it.[13]

While both Feierman and Lonsdale are primarily concerned with peasant political discourses, I am concerned to understand the cultural logics that lay behind broad patterns of socio-economic change and the actions Arusha and Meru took to achieve this. The actions of the colonized usually speak, quite literally, louder than words, and it is frequently only through their actions that we hear them in the historical record. But how are we to interpret those actions? What are the values that informed them? Why did people do what they did and in the way that they did it?

When people resist forces intruding in their societies they frequently do so in the name of 'tradition', of defending their own way of doing things. Contrary to popular belief, however, 'tradition' is neither static nor monolithic. Rather, tradition is a contested terrain over which people debate contentious issues amongst themselves employing social ideas and values drawn from the past. Tradition provides a language for thinking about, debating, and resolving the problems of the present in an endless process of renovation, innovation, and transformation of the past. In short, tradition is a way of continuously discussing what constitutes a moral community.[14]

Arusha and Meru concepts of moral community revolved around ideals of economic justice and social responsibility, in which purposeful moral actions linked social behaviour and natural phenomena. Theirs were world views that held that everyone had a right to land and subsistence, that labour working the land conveyed rights in and responsibilities for that land, that individual wealth and power carried social responsibilities for the general welfare of all, and that anti-social or immoral acts which threatened these values brought the possibility of famine, disease, defeat, or death. In short, their views were what many writers have termed a 'moral economy' in which people enjoy a moral right to subsistence.[15]

Contrary to the views of many analysts, however – who tend to flatten the concept of moral economy to see it simply as a static or reactionary defence of subsistence and tradition against encroaching capitalism or colonialism – moral economy must be seen as comprising a dynamic set of values, like 'tradition', that continually inform people's

---

[12] Steven Feierman, *Peasant Intellectuals* (Madison, 1990). See also Mandala, *Work and Control*, 74–5.

[13] John Lonsdale, 'The Moral Economy of Mau Mau: Wealth, Poverty and Civic Virtue in Kikuyu Political Thought' in Bruce Berman & John Lonsdale, *Unhappy Valley* (London, 1992), 315–504.

[14] Glassman, *Feasts and Riot*, 19–20.

[15] The literature on 'moral economy' is extensive, but see the following important milestones: E.P. Thompson, 'The Moral Economy of the English Crowd in the Eighteenth Century', *Past and Present*, 50 (1971), 76–136; James C. Scott, *The Moral Economy of the Peasant* (New Haven, 1976); and for Tanzania, Gören Hyden, *Beyond Ujamaa in Tanzania* (London, 1980). Its origins, however, stretch further back to the substantivist school of economics in the 1950s and neo-Marxist analyses of African modes of production in the 1960s.

perceptions of and accommodations to their often changing conditions.[16] Thus, while the central values that informed Meru and Arusha moral economy were remarkably persistent – surviving the shift by Arusha from pastoralism to mixed farming in the nineteenth century or both peoples' adoption of commercial agriculture and Christianity in the twentieth century – they were also dynamic ideals that continued to inform peoples' actions even as they became modified and transformed in the process.

The importance of understanding Arusha moral economy was brought home to me one day when I was discussing with Mesiaki Kilevo why Arusha preferred to squat on Afrikaner farms in distant north Meru rather than work for English or Greek farmers closer to home. Given Afrikaners' reputation for exploiting their squatters, I could only attribute the Arusha people's preferences to the fact that Afrikaners also provided landless Arusha with land, oxen, and ploughs. Arusha squatters were thus able to establish their own farms and to accumulate enough cattle eventually to purchase land of their own back in Arusha, thus making sense of their actions within the wider terms of Arusha political economy as I interpreted it.

Mesiaki sharply disagreed with my interpretation, however. He explained that landless Arusha preferred to work for Afrikaners because their farms were far from home, and Arusha going there were not exposed to the shame of being seen as landless and having to work for others by their peers. Mesiaki's explanation was thus one that took account of the moral as well as the economic significance of land in Arusha thought.

I filed this discussion away at the time as an interesting difference in interpretation, but later I began to understand its wider import when I was trying to understand why Meru and Arusha warriors had dismembered and circumcised the bodies of the two missionaries they had killed in 1896, or why being evicted from semi-arid land in Engare Nanyuki evoked such a passionate response from Meru 55 years later. The murders, I came to realize, had been ritual ones, designed to restore moral order to a world in disarray, while possessing land for Meru had deep moral as well as economic significance.[17] Mesiaki's singular insight has thus come to inform much of my own subsequent interpretation of Arusha and Meru history and helped me to see it from the perspective of the values and experiences of those who participated in it. This was my original goal, and it is what I have tried to illuminate in the following chapters.

---

[16] See Glassman's incisive discussion of the concept of moral economy in *Feasts and Riot*, 10–25, together with Giblin's measured application of the concept in *Politics of Environmental Control*.

[17] These two phenomena are discussed in detail in Chapters 3 and 11, respectively. For recent surveys of the moral significance of land, see Parker Shipton & Mitzi Goheen, 'Understanding African Land-Holding: Power, Wealth and Meaning', *Africa*, 62 (1992), 307–25; Thomas J. Bassett, 'The Land Question and Agricultural Transformation in Africa' in T. J. Bassett & D. E. Crummey (eds), *Land in African Agrarian Systems* (Madison, 1993), 3–31; and Parker Shipton, 'Land and Culture in Tropical Africa: Soils, Symbols, and the Metaphysics of the Mundane', *Annual Review of Anthropology*, 23 (1994), 347–77.

I
Settlement
of Mount Meru

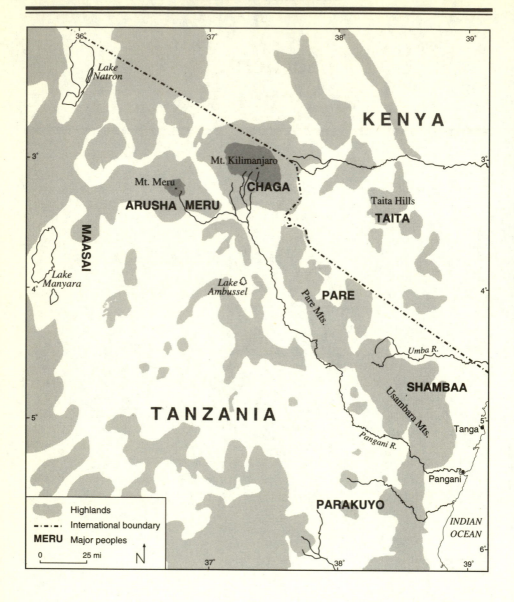

Map 1.1 Ecology and Peoples of Northern Tanzania

16

1

Mountain Farmers

Meru & Chaga
from the Seventeenth
to Nineteenth Centuries

While Mount Kilimanjaro and other highland areas of northern Tanzania have been continuously farmed for at least the past two millennia, the history of agricultural settlement on Mount Meru is much younger, going back no more than three or four centuries.[1] This is surprising, for Meru is only 80 kilometres to the west of Mount Kilimanjaro, much closer than Taita, Pare, or Usambara, among which there were frequent movements of peoples and trade. It is as fertile as Kilimanjaro, if not more so, and can easily be seen looming out of the plains to the west. Perhaps population in the other highland areas had simply not expanded sufficiently prior to 1600 to force people to look for new lands, but whatever the case, Mount Meru lay largely unpopulated until the first Meru arrived in the seventeenth century and found only isolated groups of ßakoningo hunter-gatherers living there.[2] We know little about the ßakoningo, but similar groups of hunter-gatherers long inhabited the forested highlands of East Africa until being forced to assimilate or to move when farmers cleared their forest habitat. The remembered history of Mount Meru, then, starts with the coming of the Meru.

Traditions of the First Settlers

Meru traditions generally recall that the earliest Meru came from Usambara. In the words of Anton Lucas Kaaya:

> The old men said we came from Usambara. Three men – Kaaya, Mbise, and Machame – left

---

[1] While there is archaeological evidence for early iron working settlements on Kilimanjaro and other highland areas of northern Tanzania, none exists to date for Meru.

[2] While the earliest Meru settlements can not be dated, my estimate is based on the following evidence discussed at greater length below: (1) the degree of differentiation between Meru and related dialects of West Kilimanjaro; (2) the fact that Meru traditions recall eight to nine generations (perhaps, 200–250 years) from their settlement to the 1920s, and (3) parallel evidence from western Kilimanjaro that it was a frontier district itself about that time. None of these are conclusive, but together they suggest that initial Meru settlement occurred sometime during the seventeenth century.

Usambara and went to Same. They then followed the Ruvu River as far as Sanya,... trying to find its source. They saw two mountains, Mount Meru, or Mountain of the Varwa, and Mount Kilimanjaro, or Mount Uchiru. They then followed the Firigi River, a small river that only flows in the rainy season, where they made a pact among the three of them. Then they went to Sakila [east of Meru], where they split up. Machame went east to settle in Machame [on Kilimanjaro], while Mbise and Kaaya went to the west [to Meru]....[3]

A number of other versions of the tradition collected over the last 75 years substantially affirm Anton's account, although they differ in some details. Lamireny is recalled as the overall leader in one and as an alternative name for Mbise in another; Kisarika replaces Kaaya as the leader of the Meru in another; and the precise route taken by the travellers varies in different versions.[4] Nevertheless, there is broad agreement that the earliest Meru came from Usambara with the Machame and split from them when the two settled on Meru and Kilimanjaro respectively.

In spite of such general agreement on the traditions, however, historical and linguistic evidence indicates that the earliest Meru were not from Usambara, but were Chaga speakers from western Kilimanjaro who expanded across the Sanya plains sometime in the seventeenth century. Rebmann noted in 1848 that the country west of Kilimanjaro 'belongs to Jagga [Chaga]', while Farler commented in 1882 that the inhabitants of Meru were 'of the same stock as the Chaga people'.[5] Rebmann identified this country as 'Uro', the home of the 'Ro' people.[6] The name of the mountain was then rendered as 'Mero' by Burton and Wakefield and various forms of 'Meru' by subsequent travellers.[7]

Meru today speak a dialect of Chaga that is most closely related to those spoken in western Kilimanjaro, notably Machame and Siha/Ng'uni.[8] The West Kilimanjaro

[3] Anton Lukas Kaaya (MHT 1).

[4] C. Dundas, *Kilimanjaro and its Peoples* (London, 1924), 48–50; *Arusha District Book*; Hans Cory, 'Tribal Structure of the Meru', (UDSM: Hans Cory Papers, nd); Paul Puritt, 'The Meru of Tanzania: A Study of their Social and Political Organization' (Ph.D., Illinois, 1970), 42–6; Sally Falk Moore & Paul Puritt, *The Chagga and Meru of Tanzania* (London, 1977), 91–3; Kirilo Japhet Ayo (MHT 2).

[5] J. Rebmann, 'Narrative of a Journey to Jagga, the Snow Country of Eastern Africa', *Church Missionary Intelligencer*, 1 (1849–50), map; idem, 'Narrative of a Journey to Madjame, in Jagga', *Church Missionary Intelligencer*, 1 (1849–50), 309; J.P. Farler, 'Native Routes in East Africa from Pangani to the Masai Country and Victoria Nyanza', *PRGS*, 4 (1882), 734.

[6] Meru were originally called Nrwa (pl. ßarwa), but since 'wa' shifts to 'o' in Chaga generally, this has become Nro (ßaro), transliterated by various early authors as Ro (Varo) or Roo (Varoo). Derek Nurse, personal communication.

[7] U– is the locative prefix in Swahili; U–ro thus means 'the home of the Ro people', but this soon became transformed to Mero (Meru, Méru, or Merou) by different travellers. R.F. Burton, *Zanzibar: City, Island, and Coast* (London, 1872), map facing p 1; T. Wakefield, 'Routes of Native Caravans from the Coast to the Interior of Eastern Africa...', *JRGS*, 40 (1870), map, 305; Charles New, *Life, Wanderings and Labours in Eastern Africa* (London, 1873), 393, end map; Farler, 'Native Routes', 734, 776; Joseph Thomson, *Through Masailand* (London, 1885), end map; H.H. Johnston, *The Kilima-Njaro Expedition* (London, 1886), 1; Alexandre LeRoy, *Au Kilima Ndjaro* (Paris, nd), 8, 345; Ludwig von Höhnel, *Discovery of Lakes Rudolf and Stefanie* (London, 1894), end map; Hans Meyer, *Across East African Glaciers* (London, 1891), map opp. p 1; Oscar Baumann, *Die Kartographischen Ergebnisse den Massai-Expedition des Deutschen Antisklaverei Comités* (Gotha, 1894), end map.

[8] The other West Kilimanjaro dialects are: Kißoso and Masama.

dialects developed as Chaga speakers expanded from the southern districts and began to develop their own distinctive speech patterns. While the earliest changes are broadly shared by all the West Kilimanjaro dialects, including Meru, Meru does not share those that occurred more recently among the dialects still spoken on Kilmanjaro today. Meru speakers must therefore have been present during the early stages of the development of West Kilimanjaro, but left before the later changes took place some four centuries ago to pioneer their own settlements, and develop their own dialect, on Mount Meru 80 kilometres to the west.[9]

Western Kilimanjaro in the early seventeenth century was itself a frontier area in the process of being settled by Chaga from the more densely settled southern areas of the mountain. The earliest pioneers first settled the upper regions and then moved progressively further down the slopes until they reached the plains facing Mount Meru. This was a different settlement pattern from that of the southern districts, which had been settled initially from the plains, with subsequent settlement proceeding up the slopes. Thus, as people reached the upper limits of cultivation on the southern slopes, they must have flowed across on to the upper reaches of the western slopes and subsequently expanded down the mountain to the plains.[10] A broad highland plateau extends from the base of Kilimanjaro across the plains to Meru. This plateau was much favoured by Maa-speaking pastoralists for dry season grazing. Western Chaga soon cultivated social and economic links with them and grazed their own cattle there. Once on to the plateau, then, it was an easy move across to Mount Meru looming in the distance.

The historical and linguistic evidence that the earliest Meru came not from Usambara but from western Kilimanjaro is thus in direct conflict with the traditional evidence. While Meru speak a dialect of Chaga closely related to dialects spoken in western Kilimanjaro, Shambaa and Meru are not closely related at all, and there is no evidence of Shambaa linguistic influence on Meru.[11] Meru social and political organization, religious beliefs, and material culture are also closely related to Chaga, whereas Shambaa and Meru have little in common culturally.[12] Finally, traditions from western Kilimanjaro confirm an early Meru presence there, while Shambaa traditions make no

[9] Derek Nurse, *Classification of the Chaga Dialects* (Hamburg, 1979), 52; Gérard Philippson, *Gens des bananeraies* (Paris, 1984), 102–9; idem, 'Essai de phonologie comparée des dialectes chaga' in M-F. Rombi (ed.), *Etudes sur le bantu oriental* (Paris, 1983), 41–71; Thomas Hinnebusch and Derek Nurse, 'Spirantization in Chaga', *SUGIA*, 3 (1981), 51–78; Thomas Spear and Derek Nurse, 'Maasai Farmers: The Evolution of Arusha Agriculture', *IJAHS*, 25 (1992), 481–503; Derek Nurse, pers. comm.

[10] Dundas, *Kilimanjaro*, 41–8; Kathleen Stahl, *History of the Chagga Peoples of Kilimanjaro* (The Hague, 1964), 57–67, 83–97.

[11] There are a number of reasons why the earliest Meru could not have been Shambaa speakers: (1) The two are not directly related, and thus Meru could not have developed genetically as a dialect of Shambaa. (2) There is no evidence of a Shambaa sub-stratum in Meru, such as would have been left if Meru had adopted Chaga at a later date as a result of subsequent interaction with West Kilimanjaro speakers across the Sanya plains. (3) The fact that Meru shares the earlier innovations within the West Kilimanjaro dialects, but not the later. If Meru had adopted Chaga later, they would also have adopted the later innovations that took place within West Kilimanjaro. Derek Nurse, pers. comm.

[12] Moore & Puritt, *Chagga and Meru*; Philippson, *Gens des bananeraies*, 136–213.

references to Meru at all.[13] It thus seems more probable that the earliest Meru were Chaga, with whom they share a common language and culture, than that they were originally Shambaa and subsequently assimilated to Chaga culture so completely as to leave no cultural trace of their Shambaa origins.

If this was the case, then, we must try to account for the discrepancy with the traditional evidence. The fact is that not all Meru traditions claim Shambaa origins. Two of the earliest versions collected claim that the first Meru did indeed come from Machame and Siha in western Kilimanjaro, while another traces their origins from Arusha Chini, south of Moshi.[14] Meru may simply have sought to distance themselves in subsequent versions from their numerically and politically dominant Chaga cousins by shifting earlier acknowledgements of Chaga ancestors to more distant Shambaa ones. In casting Machame as siblings, rather than as ancestors, Meru traditions acknowledge a fraternal cultural relationship with Chaga while simultaneously asserting their independence from Chaga forefathers.[15]

Alternatively, the traditions also establish the rights of the first settlers to land and office in Meru. Once Kaaya, Mbise, and their followers reached Mount Meru, Anton Lukas Kaaya's account continues,

> Mbise went west around Mount Meru until he reached Lamireny's cave near Kumu, where he hid. Today the Mbise clan still worships there during famines, droughts, or when Meru are attacked. Not everyone can go there, only girls who are virgins. They stay for seven days, and then when they come back down the mountain, the people all celebrate and it will begin to rain. I have seen it myself....
>
> Kaaya did not go with Mbise, but went to western Meru, to Midowi, on the upper Nduruma River. Kaaya started his family there and had three daughters.... Kaaya was called Kaaya from the Shambaa, 'those who remain at home'. When Machame moved, Kaaya stayed behind. When Mbise went to hide in the cave, Kaaya remained to settle....
>
> A Kaaya was always *mangi* [chief] because Kaaya came from the royal clan in Shambaa and led during the journey. People respected Kaaya because he came from the royal line, and they feared him because he was a witch. Kaaya was able to prophesy the future, so people were afraid of him; they felt they had to obey him and so made him chief.[16]

---

[13] The traditions are from Machame and Siha. Dundas, *Kilimanjaro*, 49–50; Stahl, *History of the Chagga*, 57–67, 83–97.

[14] *Arusha District Book*; B.J. Hartley, 'A Brief Note on the Meru People with special reference to their expansion problem' (nd) (TNA: 69/45/9); Krause, *ELMB*, 57 (1902), 283. Arusha Chini was an early Arusha settlement and figures prominently in Arusha traditions, as we shall see. Krause's brief reference to Meru coming from Arusha Chini may thus have been a result of confusion on his part.

[15] This hypothesis is not purely conjecture. Meru maintained their independence of Chaga during the colonial period by refusing to participate in the Kilimanjaro Native Co-operative Union and by establishing their own Citizens' Union separate from the Kilimanjaro union (see Chapters 9–11 below), and they have recently split from the Chaga-dominated Northern Diocese of the Evangelical Lutheran Church in Tanzania. Catherine Baroin, 'Le conflict religieux de 1990–1993 chez les Rwa: sécession dans un diocèse luthérien de Tanzanie Nord' (Travaux et Documents, Institut Francais de Recherche en Afrique, No. 15, 1994).

[16] Anton Lukas Kaaya (MHT 1). Again, other versions essentially agree: Cory, 'Tribal Structure of the Meru'; Puritt, 'Meru of Tanzania', 42–6; Moore & Puritt, *Chagga and Meru*, 91–3; See also C.T.S. Nasari, 'The History of the Lutheran Church among the Wameru (Varwa) of Tanzania' (B.D., Makumira, 1980), 8; N.N. Luanda, 'European Commercial Farming and its Impact on the Meru and Arusha Peoples of Tanzania, 1920–1955' (Ph.D., Cambridge, 1986), 18.

By naming Kaaya (or, in some versions, Kisarika) as the leader of the migration and first *mangi* and Mbise (or Lamireny) as the ritual expert for all Meru, the traditions effectively vest these offices in their descendants, as Anton explicitly notes. Similarly, by naming the areas occupied by the first settlers, the traditions establish the rights of their descendants to land on the mountain, rights that are further elaborated in the traditions of individual clans and lineages, as we shall see. The traditions thus clearly establish the rights of the descendants of certain early settlers on Meru to specific offices or territories, while latecomers, unmentioned in the traditions, lack such clearly defined rights.

Leaders throughout Africa frequently claim foreign origins as a means of legitimating their own claims to extraordinary power. The first Shambaa king, Mbegha, is said to have been a savage hunter from Ngulu before he became king of Shambaa and an enduring symbol of Shambaa civilization.[17] While most Meru clans recall that their ancestors came from Kilimanjaro, as we shall see, the only ones to claim special privileges also claim Shambaa origins. Kaaya's descendants became the royal clan from which the Meru chief (*mangi*) was chosen, while Mbise's were the only ritual experts who could sacrifice on behalf of all Meru. Some Kaaya even claimed to have been members of the Shambaa royal clan, thus further legitimating their claims to rule. While such claims continue to validate Kaaya and Mbise roles today, what ultimately gives them away is the fact that the term *mangi* itself, together with the institutional framework of chiefship in Meru, is Chaga, not Shambaa. We can only assume that their origins were too.

Clan Traditions, Settlement Patterns, and Social Development

The traditions of individual Meru clans reveal a more subtle and complex picture of origins than that conveyed by the 'national' traditions we have been exploring up to now. Meru clans are groups of people thought to be descended from a common ancestor, often an early settler, who share a claim to a common territory and who sacrifice together to ensure its continued fertility. Clan traditions are usually brief, containing little more than the name of an ancestor after whom the clan is named and the area he first cleared and settled. This is sufficient to establish the group's claim to land cleared by that settler. They may go further, however, and also indicate where their ancestors came from, allowing us to explore patterns of early immigration and settlement on the mountain in greater detail.[18]

Meru clans are recited in rank order of seniority (see Table 1.1: Meru Clans). While the most senior four Meru clans all claim Shambaa ancestry, none of the remaining twenty-two do. The first two clans after those of the initial settlers claim to have been

---

[17] Steven Feierman, *The Shambaa Kingdom* (Madison, 1974), 40–90. For similar traditions in Zigula, see James L. Giblin, 'Famine, Authority, and the Impact of Foreign Capital in Handeni District, Tanzania, 1840–1940' (Ph.D., Wisconsin, 1986), 36–41.

[18] Not all clans trace foreign origins; some resulted from the segmentation of other clans. Conversely, not all immigrants established their own descent groups; many were received into existing clans.

Table 1.1 Meru Clans

Clan	Origin	Settlement/*shrine*	Notes
1. Mbise	Shambaa	E. Meru, *Ung'u/ Lamireny's cave*	rainmakers
2. Kaaya	Shambaa	Kimundo *Nduluti, Nyomala*	royal clan, witches
3. Akyoo	Shambaa	Songoro *Urisho(Sura), Kivezi(Arusha)*	
4. Sumari	Shambaa Kilimanjaro Somali	Poli	
5. Nko	Maasai	Nkoaranga, Ndoombo	
6. Pallangyo	Maasai	Nkoaranga	
7. Sarajija		Sing'isi, Nkoaranga	bless homes and gardens
8. Mandola		Ulongo	
9. Isaankya	Machame	Akeri, *Msorombo*	
10. Ayo		Sura	
11. Nyiti	Kilimanjaro	C.Meru	
12. Ndosi	Kilimanjaro	Poli	
13. Mungure		Poli, Nkoaranga	
14. Nanyaro	Kilimanjaro	Akeri	
15. Kanuye/ Mafie		Ndoombo	
16. Kitomari		scattered	
17. Urio	Machame	scattered *Kimaroro*	
18. Nasari		Sura & Poli	
19. Kyungai/ Kasengye	Machame	Maji ya Chai, Sing'isi, Ndoombo *Sing'isi*	
20. Saiya		Sing'isi	
21. Kimuto		Sing'isi	
22. Vanika		Sura	
23. Ngira		Nkoanrua	
24. Nnyari	Machame	Ulonga	
25. Ilkiwuyoni	Arusha/Maasai	Ambureni	
26. Kyore			
– Sikawa	Maasai	E. Meru	iron smiths

Sources: Paul Puritt, 'The Meru of Tanzania: A Study of their Social and Political Organization' (Ph.D., Illinois, 1970), 44–46; Sally Falk Moore & Paul Puritt, *The Chagga and Meru of Tanzania* (London, 1977), 91-93; Anton Lukas Kaaya (MHT 1); Rafaeli Mbise (MHT 3); Hans Cory, 'Tribal Structure of the Meru' (UDSM: Hans Cory Papers, nd); TNA: 12844.

22

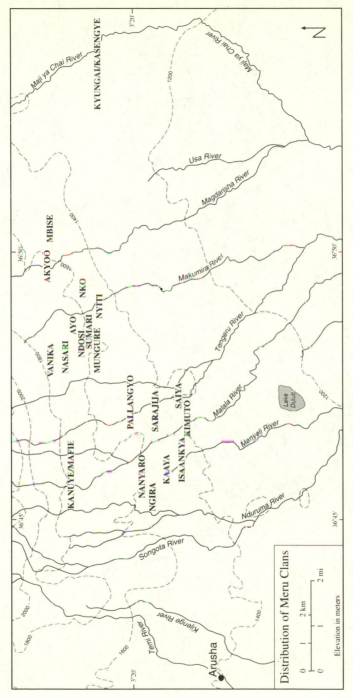

Map 1.2 Distribution of Meru Clans

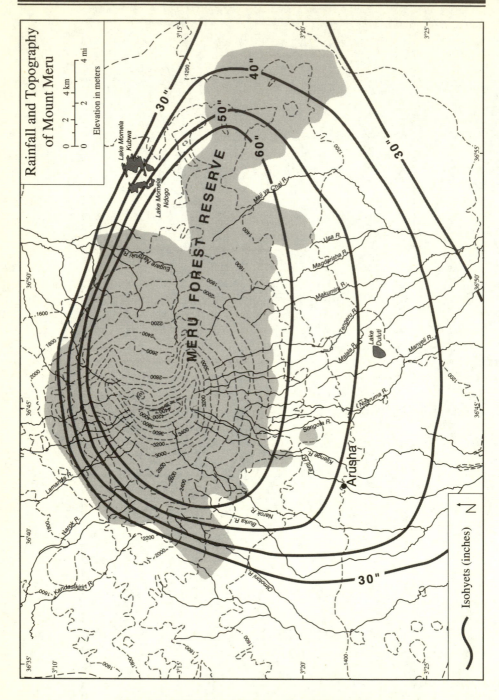

Map 1.3 Rainfall and Topography of Mount Meru
Conversion rates (approx): 30" = 750mm; 40" = 1000mm; 50" = 1250mm; 60" = 1500mm

24

founded by Maasai immigrants, indicating that Meru interacted with Maasai pastoralists on the plains from an early date. Many of the remaining clans claim Chaga – often Machame – ancestry, however, indicating that Chaga immigrants continued to play an important role in Meru society as late as the 1880s, when LeRoy reported that the wars on Kilimanjaro were causing many Chaga to emigrate to Meru.[19] The penultimate clan listed stems from neighbouring Arusha Maasai, showing the increasing influence of Arusha in nineteenth-century Meru.

The earliest settlers established their fields and homesteads 150 to 300 metres above the plains in small clearings in the dense forest on the southeastern slopes of the mountain (see Map 1:2: Distribution of Meru Clans). The core settlement areas and sacred groves where the original clan ancestor was buried for all but two of the most senior fourteen clans lie between 1,400 and 1,700 metres, while those of most of the remaining clans lie either under 1,400 metres or over 1,700 metres. Meru continued to favour the fertile and protected middle zone, away from the trade routes and pastoralists on the plains, through the end of the nineteenth century, as the first European travellers to visit Meru noted.[20]

The middle zone of southeastern Meru is extremely favourable to settlement and, most importantly, for the cultivation of bananas which dominated Meru agriculture. Meru is rich in fertile volcanic soils composed of exposed and weathered lavas that are easily worked and can sustain both annual and perennial crops year after year. Abundant rain falls bi-annually on the southern slopes and fills the rivers that cut down its slopes to supply water for irrigation dependably throughout the year. Rainfall increases with altitude, from 1,000 millimetres annually at 1,200 metres to 1,500 millimetres at 1,800 metres, and it is easily supplemented by irrigation from the many permanent rivers that continue to flow down the mountains during the dry season (see Map 1.3: Rainfall and Topography of Mount Meru).

Conditions become much less favourable, however, as one moves away from the southern slopes. Rainfall on the plains decreases rapidly from 750 millimetres to less than 500 millimetres, too little for agriculture, and many of the rivers soon run dry. Similarly, fertile mountain soils quickly give way to hard to work brown or black clays and then to powdery ash. Rainfall also declines to 500 to 750 millimetres as one moves north around the eastern slopes of the mountain until one enters a rain shadow that covers the northern slopes; permanent water supplies become much more limited and too alkaline to use in irrigation; and the soils become light powdery volcanic ash easily wind swept or dissolved in water. Expansion farther up the mountain was limited by the fact that the temperature drops with altitude and it becomes too cold for bananas above 1,700 metres or for annual food crops over 1,800 metres. The most favourable area for Meru settlement was thus that between 1,200 and 1,800 metres on the southeastern quadrant, an area roughly ten kilometres at the base by six kilometres up the slopes, that formed the core of Meru settlement.[21]

[19] LeRoy, *Au Kilima Ndjaro*, 345.
[20] Höhnel, *Discovery*, 135–7, 152–3; Krause, *ELMB*, 57 (1902), 278–80.
[21] *Arusha District Book*; D. Sturdy, W.E. Carlton & G. Milne, 'A Chemical Survey of the Waters of Mount Meru, Tanganyika Territory...', *JEAUNHS*, 45–6 (1932), 1–38; D. Conyers, 'Agro-Economic Zones of Tanzania', (UDSM: BRALUP Research Paper, No 25, 1973).

The first Meru settled in the middle reaches of this fertile and highly productive zone. Here they could raise bananas and annual crops in abundance, safe from attacks by pastoralists and insulated from influences that would later spread along the trade route south of the mountain in the 1860s. Later settlers favoured the middle banana belt as well, but as virgin land became short, many latecomers were forced into its upper reaches, while the latest immigrants had to be content with the lowest parts of the belt bordering the plains.

The first settlers carved their homesteads out of clearings in the forest and established permanent stands of bananas surrounding their houses. Such homesteads, known as *vihamba* (sing. *kihamba*), were at the centre of Meru economic and social life. Bananas provided the staple diet all year round, while one's *kihamba* was the focus of the family. One was born and raised on one's father's *kihamba* and venerated the ancestors buried there. As families expanded, older sons cut into the surrounding forest to establish their own *vihamba*, while the youngest son usually inherited his father's *kihamba*. Every man had a right to his own *kihamba*, so as land on the lower slopes became fully occupied, the next generation had to pass over their neighbours' fields to pioneer land higher up the mountain, inexorably pushing the boundaries of settlement up to its eventual limits at 1,800 metres over the succeeding centuries. In addition to *vihamba*, the first settlers also cleared open fields for annual crops of maize, eleusine, and beans and small grassy meadows where they pastured their cattle and small stock, developing in the process a complex mixed farming economy that provided a dependable and diverse diet throughout the year.

As the descendants of earlier settlers expanded up the mountain, they became dispersed into numerous separate patrilineal homesteads, each occupying its own land. Such homesteads – comprising a man, his wives, their children, and perhaps other relatives – were largely autonomous. Each had its own rights to land from clearing the virgin forest. Each also had its own labour force, consisting of its members. And each raised the bulk of its own food from the dense stands of bananas and the annual fields surrounding its homestead. Neighbours might co-operate with one another to accomplish larger tasks, such as digging and maintaining the irrigation ditches that crisscrossed the mountain or clearing the heavy forest in new settlement areas, but their assistance was only temporary.[22]

In spite of such autonomy, however, groups of related lineages continued to recognize a common social and moral identity as clanspeople, based on their putative descent from a common ancestor. Clan members worshipped together at the grave of their founding ancestor, where they sacrificed on behalf of the whole clan, and they shared liability payments given to and received from other clans. Clan elders mediated land and other disputes among members, and each clan chose its own leaders to speak for their members with representatives of other clans or the *mangi*. Clanspeople were usually too dispersed to act together in an any more concerted fashion, however. While clan territories were usually contiguous vertical slices of the mountain, reflecting the settlement patterns of their members, individual clanspeople settled far beyond their limits, but moral responsibilities and obligations to fellow lineage and clan members

[22] Puritt, 'Meru', 75–89.

transcended those of mere friends or neighbours, characterized as they were by a shared sense of moral community.[23]

All clans were considered to be equivalent, with the sole exception of the Kaaya. Clan elders met one another as equals, but they chose a Kaaya to be *mangi*. It is not clear, however, exactly what powers the *mangi* possessed.[24] The first Europeans to visit Meru complained that the *mangi* enjoyed little real power, was unable to control the warriors, and was incapable of preventing the murder of the first two missionaries to settle in Meru in 1896. Höhnel noted in 1887 that *Mangi* Matunda 'differed but little in appearance from the other Wameru....'[25] Their weakness may have been due to the growing power of the warriors in the latter nineteenth century, as we shall see, but there is no evidence that Meru *mangi* were ever more than *primus inter pares* among their fellow clan elders, their seniority based on Meru traditions and on their reputation for possessing unusual mystical powers. For not only were Kaaya generally recognized as leaders, they were also reputed to be formidable witches who could both harm their enemies and protect their allies from less powerful malevolent forces, much as Chaga chiefs were respected and feared for their mastery of the mysterious spiritual forces associated with ironworking.[26]

Table 1.2 Meru Mangi

Kaaya	
Kisarika	
Malengye	
Samana	
(Kyuta)	
Rari I	
Sola	
Rari II, or Ndemi	–1887
Matunda	1887–1896
Lobulu	1896–1900

Sources: Paul Puritt, 'The Meru of Tanzania: A Study of their Social and Political Organization' (Ph.D., Illinois, 1970), 49–51; Hans Cory, 'Tribal Structure of the Meru' (UDSM: Hans Cory Papers, nd); Anton Lukas Kaaya (MHT 1); Rafaeli Mbise (MHT 3); *Arusha District Book*.

Meru traditions list nine or ten *mangi* from the time of their initial settlement to the establishment of colonial rule in 1900 (see Table 1.2: Meru *Mangi*). Aside from the fact that Kaaya and Kisarika were reputed to have led the migration from Shambaa, however, there are no historical traditions relating to any but the last three. Most pertain to Rari II, or Ndemi, who ruled until 1887 and is said to have introduced bananas, finger

---

[23] Puritt, 'Meru', 90–6.

[24] While Puritt asserts that Meru chiefs 'controlled everything' in Meru, appointed their own councillors separate from clan elders, heard cases and passed judgements, and could demand and receive tribute from petitioners, this is contradicted by the experiences of most early Europeans (as well as by later colonial authorities) in the area, as noted below. Puritt, 'Meru,' 106–10; Moore & Puritt, *Chagga and Meru*, 113–14.

[25] Höhnel, *Discovery*, 142, 148–51; Müller & Fassmann, *ELMB*, 52(1897), 14–18.

[26] M. French-Sheldon, *Sultan to Sultan* (London, 1892), 284, 391, 400; J.C. Willoughby, *East Africa and its Big Game* (London, 1889), 116.

millet, maize, pottery, and ironworking as well as welcoming the first Arusha to settle on Mount Meru. In short, virtually all of Meru history from the time of their settlement on Meru is compressed into the reign of this one man in spite of the fact that Meru had settled on Meru at least two centuries earlier. Such compression is not unusual in oral traditions. Significant events are often clustered into one brief period to convey an overall image of great stability broken only occasionally by dramatic historical events. In this way, Meru assert the epic importance of the events of the later nineteenth century in the formation of their modern historical consciousness.

Meru and Arusha in the Nineteenth Century

The settlement of Arusha on the southwestern slopes of Mount Meru in the 1830s was certainly one of those dramatic events. While we will explore the details of Arusha settlement more thoroughly in the next chapter, our concern here is with how the coming of the Arusha affected Meru already established on the mountain. The nineteenth century was a tumultuous time on the plains. Kisongo and Parakuyo Maasai struggled over who would control the pastoral resources on the plains from Mount Meru east to the Pangani Valley and south into the Maasai Steppe, while Loogolala Maasai struggled in vain to maintain their hold on the plains around Kilimanjaro against a Kaputiei Maasai alliance expanding from the west.

Displaced by Kisongo advances against the Parakuyo, Arusha settled initially at Arusha Chini (Lower Arusha), south of Kilimanjaro, where they raised both grain and cattle. During the 1830s a number of Arusha moved west to settle at Arusha Juu (Upper Arusha) below Mount Meru. They established close ties there with the Kisongo *loibon*, Supeet, who lived nearby, and operated a flourishing market with pastoral Maasai. Their settlement thrived, and they began to expand rapidly up the southwestern slopes of the mountain. Later, with the extension of the caravan route to western Kenya in the early 1860s, Arusha Juu became a major trading centre where caravans could stock up for the long and arduous trek across the Maasai plains to the west.

Arusha also raided their Meru neighbours for cattle and captives. Arusha participated fully in Kisongo age-sets as fellow initiates and members of the same sets, and Arusha warriors, like their Kisongo brethren, frequently raided for cattle to build their herds and acquire bridewealth for marriage. Arusha also seized people. Women were taken as wives, while male captives were placed in the appropriate age-set, joined with their new age-mates in raids, accumulated cattle and women themselves, and settled in Arusha. The Arusha population grew quickly as a result, and they rapidly cleared and settled much of the southwestern quadrant of Meru.

Arusha raids began to take their toll on Meru by the 1850s, and by the 1860s Arusha were pushing back the borders of Meru settlement from the Temi to the Songota River.[27] Meru responded by building their homesteads deep in the forest and fortifying

---

[27] Krause, *ELMB*, 57(1902), 279. New reported in 1871 that Meru 'have been of late harassed by the Arusha'. New, *Life*, 393.

Table 1.3 Meru Generation and Age-sets

Meru set	Events	Arusha set	Arusha dates
Kiboroni	to Sakila?		
Kiwandai	to Sakila?		
Ulukuvai	to Meru?		
Kisavai			
Nginana			
Ulumara			
Kisaruni			
Kisetu			
Aremu (?)			
Marishari		Diyoki	*c.*1791–1811
Mirisho		Merishari	*c.*1806–26
Soori	Arusha arrive	Kidotu	*c.*1821–41
Sigoi		Twati	*c.*1836–56
Jun'uri	Arusha raids	Nyangusi	*c.*1851–71
Manguusa	Arusha to Songota	Laimer	*c.*1866–86
Talala	Meru join Arusha age-sets	Talala	*c.*1881–1905
Twati		Twati	*c.*1896–1917
Tareto		Tareto	1911–29
Kisali		Terito	1926–48
Sitimu		Nyangusi	1942–59
Steling/Seuri		Seuri	1955–74
Makaa/Rocketi		Makaa	1968–88
Kakisha		Landis	1983–

Sources: Paul Puritt, 'The Meru of Tanzania: A Study of their Social and Political Organization' (Ph.D., Illinois, 1970), 46–8, 97; Anton Lukas Kaaya (MHT 1); Rafaeli Mbise (MHT 3); Japhet Ayo (MHT 4). See Figure 2:1 for Arusha age-sets.

them with trenches, logs, and palisades with such low narrow entrances that one had to crawl on hands and knees to enter.[28]

Meru also adopted Maasai weapons and military tactics, and about 1881 took the dramatic step of joining with Kisongo and Arusha Maasai to initiate their young men into the new Maasai age-set known as Talala (see Table 1.3: Meru Generation and Age-Sets).[29] Meru may have previously had their own system of generation-sets, in which young men were periodically circumcised and incorporated into a named group, but these groups did not seem to have had any significant political or military functions.[30] Following their early encounters with Arusha, however, Meru young men increasingly developed into a warrior group, a process that was finally institutionalized with their

[28] Höhnel, *Discovery*, 142–3.
[29] Höhnel, *Discovery*, 141–51; Puritt, 'Meru', 46–8, 97–105; Anton Lukas Kaaya (MHT 1); Rafaeli Mbise (MHT 3); Japhet Ayo (MHT 4).
[30] Puritt, 'Meru,' 46–8.

initiation into Talala (c. 1881–1905) and their assumption of Maasai *murran* status. Meru were accepted into the set by the Maasai *loibon* even though they had to substitute carved wooden stools, tobacco, and goats for cattle for their fees.[31] Meru joined the succeeding two Maasai age-sets, Tuati (c. 1896–1917) and Tareto (1911–29), but by the time Terito (1926–48) was due to be initiated, the colonial ban on raiding had reduced their need for an alliance with either Arusha or pastoral Maasai. Meru joined in the initiation ceremonies, but they formed their own named set separate from that of the Maasai. Meru continued to participate in Maasai age-set ceremonies until 1959, when they broke with Arusha over the *olngesher* ceremony for Nyangusi.[32] They have continued to initiate their own sets since, though Meru Christians tend not to circumcise today, or only do so in a hospital without ceremony.[33]

Meru warriors joined their new Arusha age-mates in raiding as far as Kilimanjaro and beyond. Arusha and their Meru allies were frequently recruited as mercenaries by Chaga chiefs, and were rewarded with spoils of cattle, women, and ironwork. Rindi recruited over 1,000 Arusha-Meru warriors in his bid to take over the Moshi chieftaincy in the 1860s and he continued to employ them to raid his neighbours thereafter. Arusha and Meru warriors also served his enemy, Sina of Kibosho. Thomson tells of meeting a group of Arusha warriors traversing the high mountain track across Kilimanjaro to raid the cattle-rich area of Useri on the far northeastern side.[34]

Maasai raids were also frequently reported along the coast. While it is difficult to identify the particular Maasai group involved, Arusha were specifically named in conjunction with raids as far away as Golbanti on the Tana River, where the missionary Houghton and his family were killed in a raid on Oromo cattle.[35] Krause reported in 1902 that the main occupation of the young Meru before the German conquest was raiding for cattle:

> Armed with spears, shields and swords, they usually travelled all over the region with their neighbours, the Arusha, to the east as far as Voi and to the west beyond Mbugwe, in order to steal the treasured animals.

Trips lasted as long as nine months, and Meru captured so many cattle in the course of their raids that individual herds of one hundred head were not unusual.[36]

Meru warriors, like their Arusha counterparts, returned from their raids with so many cattle and women as spoils that they challenged the distribution of power in Meru society. Unlike Maasai, Meru warriors could marry and settle at any time, but they depended on their elders for cattle for marriage. With their new-found ability to

---

[31] Rafaeli Mbise (MHT 3); Ngole ole Njololoi (AHT 4).

[32] Minutes of Meeting of District Representatives, 30 June 1949 (TNA: 9/8/1); Ngole ole Njololoi (AHT 4).

[33] Nasari, 'Lutheran Church', 23–4; Rafaeli Mbise (MHT 3).

[34] Thomson, *Masailand*, 80–2, 126; New, *Life*, 413; Höhnel, *Discovery*, 198; Willoughby, *Game*, 112–14, 206–10; LeRoy, *Au Kilima Ndjaro*, 290–2; Dundas, *Kilimanjaro*, 80–90; Stahl, *Chagga*, 66–7, 241–6, 294.

[35] For Arusha raids, see T. Wakefield, 'The Wakwavi Raid on the District near Mombasa', *PRGS*, 5(1883), 289; C.W. Hobley, *Kenya: From Chartered Company to Crown Colony* (London, 1929), 38. For problems of nomenclature regarding the particular Maasai groups involved, see John Berntsen, 'The Enemy is Us: Eponymy in the Historiography of the Maasai', *History in Africa* 7 (1980), 1–21.

[36] Krause, *ELMB*, 57 (1902), 283–4.

acquire cattle and women on their own, however, young men no longer had to rely on their elders to marry and establish their own homesteads. They used the cattle they seized as bridewealth or loaned them to clients, while they either married the women they had captured themselves or married them to others in return for receiving the bride-wealth. Meru young men thus became free to establish their own status in Meru society.

The age-sets themselves also became a more powerful institution in Meru society than the old generation-sets had been. When a new set was about to be formed, all uninitiated men were first circumcised. They then retired for three months to their own retreat where they cut their hair short, painted their bodies and faces with white chalk, wore expensive ostrich shell bead necklaces, and gorged on meat, milk, and fat while avoiding ripe bananas, maize with beans, and green vegetables.[37] These practices, and their attendant rituals, were very similar to those of Arusha and other Maasai, and they built strong bonds of solidarity among age-mates which they carried with them back into society.[38]

Like Arusha, but unlike earlier generation-sets, each Meru age-set also chose its own leaders who mediated disputes among members and acted as spokesmen for their age-mates in issues involving other sets, thus usurping some of the responsibilities of clan leaders. Age-set leaders also acted independently of clan leaders and the *mangi* in planning and conducting raids, and they oversaw the distribution of spoils after a raid was over, giving some to those who had remained behind, but reserving the bulk for the warriors involved.[39] Clan leaders and the *mangi* thus had little power over the activities of the warriors, and they benefited little from their activities.

When Teleki and Höhnel, the first Europeans to visit Meru, arrived in 1887, they were immediately robbed of trade goods and two Wendl carbines by Meru and Arusha warriors. They were continually followed by 40 to 50 armed Meru warriors throughout their visit, and groups as large as 250 continued to extort Teleki for goods, even after he had given them 7 *doti* of *merikani* (cotton cloth), 4 strings of *murtinarok* beads, 20 rings of brass wire, 20 *mikufu* (chain rings), 20 strings of *mboro* beads, and a few charges of powder. When Teleki protested to *Mangi* Matunda, the chief replied that 'he had no influence over them', to which a warrior retorted, 'Matunda has nothing to do with the matter: we are masters here'. Matunda gave in to the warriors and bought an ox with Teleki's gifts and gave it to the warriors.[40] Ovir and Segebrock, the first Lutheran missionaries to attempt to settle in Meru, encountered a similar situation in 1896. Matunda warned the missionaries repeatedly that Meru and Arusha warriors were preparing to attack and that he could do nothing to control them, but the missionaries ignored his warnings. That night the warriors attacked, and the two were killed.[41]

---

[37] Puritt, 'Meru', 96–102; Moore & Puritt, *Chagga and Meru*, 125–8; I.R. Mbise, *Blood on Our Land* (Dar es Salaam, 1974), 3, 28–30; Cory, 'Tribal Structure of the Meru'.
[38] For Maasai, see Paul Spencer, 'Becoming Maasai: Being in Time' in T. Spear & R. Waller (eds), *Being Maasai* (London, 1993), 140–56.
[39] Puritt, 'Meru', 113–15.
[40] Höhnel, *Discovery*, 138–51.
[41] Müller & Fassman, *ELMB*, 52 (1897), 15–18. See Chapter 3 for a detailed discussion of the murder of the missionaries.

31

Meru on the Eve of Colonial Conquest

Meru had remained fairly isolated before Arusha settled on Mount Meru in the 1830s. Settling deep in the montane forest, they were relatively safe from and uninfluenced by Maasai pastoralists on the plains and, later, the trade route to western Kenya quite literally passed them by. Early descriptions of the trade route make no mention of trade with Meru, noting only that smoke could be seen rising from Meru villages in the distance.[42] Höhnel recounts in 1887 that they could find no clear paths up from the plains, even after climbing 600 feet. After marching a couple more hours, they were forced to stop for the night, still without having seen any signs of life. Meru were clearly tracking their progress, however. Teleki's scouts were set upon and robbed long before they had seen Meru themselves, and only after the party had camped for the night did Meru emerge from the woods, holding bunches of grass in their hands in the regional sign of peace.[43]

Meru were largely ignored by the many European travellers who frequented Kilimanjaro after 1848, none of whom visited Meru until 1887. The earliest descriptions of Meru were thus made from afar. Rebmann reported from Chaga in 1848 that the 'Ro' were Chaga who lived west of Machame.[44] New was a bit more detailed in his account during a visit to Chaga in 1871:

> From the accounts of the Wachaga, Meru is inhabited by a very industrious tribe, chiefly engaged in agricultural pursuits; but they are a fine, clever, bold and warlike race, though they have been of late harassed by the Arusha.[45]

Similarly, Farler noted in his description of the Pangani trade route in 1882:

> On the distant Mount Meru the smoke can be seen rising from the hamlets of the natives, who are agriculturalists of the same stock as the Chaga people. They have large plantations, and raise a good deal of grain, which they send to Chaga and sell to caravans.[46]

That was the sum of European knowledge of Meru until Teleki's visit in May 1887 was reported by Höhnel in some detail, and this together with the first missionary account provides our main picture of Meru on the eve of colonial conquest.

Höhnel commented effusively on Meru agriculture. Meru banana plantations 'covered the slopes of the mountain in every direction … nowhere else did we see such luxuriant and fruitful banana plantations'. While bananas were the chief food, Meru also grew maize, beans, eleusine, clover, some potatoes, and tobacco. They kept large herds of cattle, sheep, and goats on cultivated 'meadows' above 4,850 feet as well as 'numerous bees [who] yield better honey than we tested anywhere else in East Africa'. Höhnel estimated the Meru population at 1,000, scattered in settlements between 3,500

[42] Farler, 'Native Routes … to the Masai Country', 734.
[43] Höhnel, *Discovery*, 135–9.
[44] Rebmann, 'Narrative of a Journey to Madjame', 309.
[45] New, *Life*, 393.
[46] Farler, 'Native Routes… to the Masai Country', 734.

[sic] and 5,500 feet on the southern slopes of the mountain. Meru settlements were buried in 'primeval forest which the Wameru ... leave untouched as a protection'. They were surrounded by felled trees and were often guarded by 15 to 20 armed warriors.[47]

Armed bands of Meru and Arusha warriors were prominent everywhere Teleki and Höhnel went, and they exercised considerable power in Meru society. Some Arusha immigrants had also settled in Meru, as evidenced by the presence of the Arusha Kivuyoni clan, and Arusha and Kisongo Maasai cultural influence was readily apparent in other ways as well. Meru warriors dressed in Maasai style and carried long 'spears and shields painted white, red, and black in Masai fashion'. While most of the houses were built in the domed Chaga style and thatched with straw and banana leaves, some were built low and flat, 'exactly like those of the Masai, except that they are bigger, and instead of being finished off with earth and cow-dung, are finished off with banana-leaves'. Meru spoke Chaga, but Maasai idioms peppered their speech. And while Meru men and women usually dressed in Chaga leather garments, they often complemented them with Maasai beads and jewellery. Arusha was not the only outside influence on Meru; large numbers of Chaga refugees from the wars on Kilimanjaro were also settling in Meru, evident from the large number of Chaga clans who joined Meru in this period.[48]

The degree to which Meru were influenced by trade, however, is not clear. One would gather from Farler's and Höhnel's descriptions of how remote and inaccessible Meru were from the trade route that they did not participate in trade very much. Certainly the main trade route passed them by, and the major caravans stopped at Arusha Juu – noted prominently on all the contemporary maps – and traded with Arusha.[49] But there are suggestions that Meru traded as well. Farler noted that they traded grain to Chaga as well as to passing caravans, while Höhnel commented cryptically that Meru dealt only with ivory and slave traders.[50] Nevertheless, there was little evidence of Swahili cultural influence in Meru compared with Kilimanjaro, and trade certainly did not have the dramatic and devastating effects that it had in Chaga, Pare, and elsewhere in the Pangani Valley.[51]

Meru had thus remained relatively isolated over the course of the eighteenth and nineteenth centuries while they slowly developed as a distinctive and prosperous agricultural society. Aside from some influx of Maasai immigrants, they do not seem to have participated in the world of cattle on the plains to the same degree as Chaga, Pare, or Taita. Nor were they active participants in early regional trade. Arusha Maasai settlement from the 1830s, however, gradually forced Meru into the expanding regional system, first as Arusha raided Meru for cattle and captives, and later as Meru joined

[47] Höhnel, *Discovery*, 142–53. See also Krause, *ELMB*, 57 (1902), 279–80, 283, 436.
[48] Höhnel, *Discovery*, 143–53; LeRoy, *Au Kilima Ndjaro*, 345. See also Krause, *ELMB*, 57(1902), 279–83 and Fig. 1:1.
[49] Wakefield, 'Routes of Native Caravans', 305; Farler, 'Native Routes ... to the Masai Country', 734; Höhnel, *Discovery*, 135–9.
[50] Farler, 'Native Routes... to the Masai Country,' 734; Höhnel, *Discovery*, 152.
[51] See, e.g., Feierman, *The Shambaa Kingdom*; I.N. Kimbambo, *Penetration and Protest in Tanzania* (London, 1991); James Giblin, *The Politics of Environmental Control in Northeastern Tanzania, 1840–1940* (Philadelphia, 1992).

with Arusha to raid others. As the locus of power within Meru society shifted from control over land and kinship to that over cattle, influence and power shifted from family patriarchs, clan elders, and the *mangi*, all of whom exercised control over land, to the age-sets and the young warriors, who seized cattle and women. Long distance trade had less impact, however. Meru did not appear to sell food, ivory, or slaves in any quantity to the caravans passing by on the plains, and there was little evidence of Swahili cultural influence compared to that of Maasai. Having avoided the disruptive effects of trade elsewhere, however, Meru found themselves at the end of the century threatened by colonial domination. Before taking up that story, we must explore what had been happening in nearby Arusha over the course of the nineteenth century.

2

Maasai Farmers

Arusha & Pastoral Maasai
in the Eighteenth and
Nineteenth Centuries

While Meru settled on Mount Meru slowly over several centuries, Arusha colonized it more recently and dramatically as part of a larger restructuring of pastoral societies and the expansion of trade during the nineteenth century. Arusha were agro-pastoral Maasai from the plains who settled near modern Arusha town during the 1830s and rapidly expanded up the adjacent slopes of the mountain. Ironically, their success as mountain farmers was fuelled by their continued participation in pastoral Maasai society and by their development of Arusha as a major trading centre for caravans going to western Kenya. Arusha provided pastoral Maasai with foodstuffs and refuge in return for cattle. They initiated their young men into Maasai age-sets and raided widely for cattle and women. And they expanded their trade with pastoral Maasai to become major suppliers of the large trading caravans that stopped in Arusha prior to making the long trek across the Maasai Steppe. Unlike Meru, then, Arusha were active participants in the broader regional economy, but they successfully avoided many of the more negative effects that the Maasai wars and the expansion of trade had elsewhere in northern Tanganyika at the time.

Restructuring Pastoralism: Arusha Chini and the Early Arusha

The emergence of the Arusha was part of a general restructuring of Maasai societies throughout the nineteenth century, starting with the displacement of Loogolala and Parakuyo Maasai by Kaputiei and Kisongo Maasai during the first half of the century. Loogolala had occupied the fertile pastures north of Mount Kilimanjaro, but in the 1830s Kaputiei drove them south into the Pangani Valley, where they were challenged further by Kisongo and Parakuyo. With successive losses of cattle and access to pastures throughout the 1840s and 1850s, they were destroyed as an independent pastoral people, and individual Loogolala were forced to disperse and seek refuge among neighbouring farmers and other pastoralists.[1]

---

[1] The careful reconstructions and analyses by John Berntsen and Richard Waller of this difficult period of

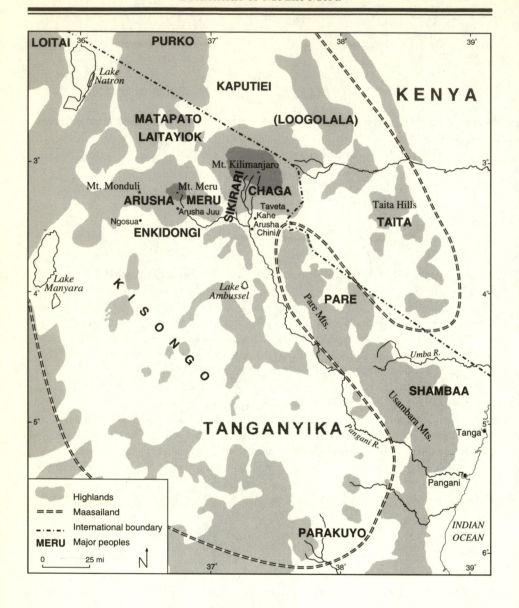

Map 2.1 Maasailand in the nineteenth century

Parakuyo Maasai, by contrast, continued to exist, but under radically altered circumstances. Parakuyo had pioneered Maasai settlement of the Maasai Steppe in Tanzania during the seventeenth and eighteenth centuries, but found themselves under increasing pressure from Kisongo Maasai advancing behind them in the early nineteenth century.[2] Kisongo drove Parakuyo from the plains either side of Mount Meru and occupied the main wells in the northern Steppe in the 1820s and 1830s. Kisongo then advanced into the Pangani Valley and the central Steppe in the 1840s and 1850s, and into the southern Steppe in the 1860s and 1870s, driving Parakuyo ahead of them.

Driven from the vital wells and dry season grazing in the plains and deprived of most of their cattle, many Parakuyo retreated into the hills and valleys south of the Pangani, where they became clients of local farmers while they regrouped and slowly rebuilt their herds. Others joined the victorious Kisongo, or trekked north into Kenya to join Laikipiak or Uas Nkishu Maasai before they too were destroyed by Purko-Kisongo in the 1870s. And still others sought refuge among Pare and Shambaa in the highlands; settled in the oasis communities of Kahe, Arusha, or Taveta in the plains; or raided along the coast to rebuild their herds.[3]

([1] cont) Maasai history have considerably enhanced our knowledge of the era. Richard Waller, 'The Lords of East Africa: The Maasai in the mid-Nineteenth Century' (Ph.D., Cambridge, 1979), 55–8, 152–5, 372–81; idem, 'Economic and Social Relations in the Central Rift Valley: The Maa-Speakers and their Neighbours in the Nineteenth Century' in B.A. Ogot (ed.), *Kenya in the Nineteenth Century* (*Hadith* 8, Nairobi, 1985), 103–20; John Berntsen, 'Pastoralism, Raiding, and Prophets: Maasailand in the Nineteenth Century' (Ph.D., Wisconsin, 1979), 128–46, 223–36; idem, 'Maasai Expansion and Prophets, 1800–1850' (unpub. seminar paper, SOAS, 1977), 1–5. See also T.O. Beidelman, 'The Baraguyu,' *TNR*, 55 (1960), 247–51. For contemporary accounts, see, e.g., J. Rebmann, 'Narrative of a Journey to Jagga, the Snow Country of Eastern Africa,' *Church Missionary Intelligencer*, 1 (1849–50), 12–23; Charles New, *Life, Wanderings and Labours in Eastern Africa* (London, 1873), 469–70; Thomas Wakefield, 'Routes of Native Caravans from the Coast to the Interior of Eastern Africa...', *JRGS*, 40 (1870), 303–38; Joseph Thomson, *Through Masailand* (London, 1885), 240–2; Justin Lemenye (H.A. Fosbrooke, trans. & ed.), 'The Life of Justin', *TNR*, 41 (1955), 31–57, 42 (1956), 19–30.

[2] Parakuyo are referred to as 'Ilumbwa' or 'Parakuyo' (rendered 'Baragui', 'Mbaravui', or 'Embarawuio' in contemporary accounts) by themselves and Purko-Kisongo, 'Wahumba' by Bantu speakers, 'Iloikop' by Kisongo, and 'Kwavi' by Bantu speakers, thus accounting for the confusing variety of references encountered in historical sources. Contemporary observers were careful to note, however, that they were Maa-speaking pastoralists, little different from other Maasai groups who each had their own prophet, clans, and age-set system. Parakuyo lived on the broad plains south of Kilimanjaro prior to the 1830s, but they were forced to withdraw into enclaves surrounded by farmers and frequently to resort to agriculture themselves following their defeats by Kisongo, leading subsequent travellers to characterize them pejoratively as agricultural 'Kwavi' and to sharply distinguish them from pastoral 'Maasai'. J. Rebmann, 'Narrative of a Journey to Madjame, in Jagga', *Church Missionary Intelligencer*, 1 (1849-50), 274–5; Richard F. Burton, *Zanzibar: City, Island, and Coast* (London, 1872), II:71; New, *Life*, 469-70, 526–7; J.T. Last, 'A Visit to the Masai Living Beyond the Borders of the Nguru Country', *PRGS*, 5 (1883), 539; Wakefield to Adcock, 11/20/82, *UMFC*, 26 (1883), 251; Thomson, *Through Masailand*, 240–2; H.H. Johnston, *The Kilima-Njaro Expedition* (London, 1886), 405–7; M. Merker, *Die Masai* (Berlin, 1910), 9. Beidelman, 'Baraguyu', 245–50; Berntsen, 'Maasai Expansion', 1-5; idem, 'The Enemy is Us: Eponymy in the Historiography of the Maasai', *History in Africa*, 7 (1980), 1-7; Waller, 'Lords', 137–44, 268–77; Waller, 'Economic and Social Relations', 114–15.

[3] Thomson, *Masailand*, 240–3; Merker, *Masai*, 7–9; Lemenye, 'The Life of Justin', 37–40; Beidelman, 'Baraguyu', 247–51; Waller, 'Lords', 305–18, 373–9; Waller, 'Economic and Social Relations', 103–17; Berntsen, 'Masai Expansion', 2-5; Berntsen, 'Pastoralism, Raiding, and Prophets', 132–43.

While some established Maasai pastoral communities were in the process of being dispersed or destroyed, new Maa-speaking agro-pastoral communities composed of refugees from the pastoral wars emerged around the fringes of central Maasailand. One of these communities formed at Arusha Chini (Lower Arusha) south of Mount Kilimanjaro.[4] Arusha Chini was a small agro-pastoral settlement at the base of the Sogonoi (or Lelatema) mountains where the Kikafu River from Kilimanjaro joins the Kikuletwa River from Meru.[5] Protected by the rivers and surrounding forest, the inhabitants of Arusha Chini grew maize, sorghum, millet, beans, cassava, bananas, sugar cane, tobacco, and potatoes on the rich alluvial soils. They also made iron weapons, collected honey, and traded with Maasai pastoralists for livestock.[6]

Arusha Chini was but one of several similar oasis communities on the plains around Kilimanjaro – all of which played critical roles in the regional economy, raising crops and trading with pastoral Maasai – and they subsequently became crucial supply and trade centres for the caravan routes that developed in the later nineteenth century. Taveta was a thriving ethnically mixed agricultural community on the Lumi River southeast of Kilimanjaro that included Pare, Chaga, and other highlands peoples together with Parakuyo and Loogolala refugees from the pastoral wars. Kahe was a smaller settlement on the upper Pangani River between Taveta and Arusha Chini, where people raised bananas, sweet potatoes, yams, beans, and maize in irrigated fields and collected salt and honey for sale on Kilimanjaro. Like Taveta, Kahe was predominantly a Chaga and Pare community, but it too had assimilated numbers of Maasai refugees and had been culturally influenced by them.[7]

Unlike Taveta and Kahe, however, Arusha Chini was predominantly a Maasai community, though its precise origins are not clear. While some contemporary observers identified Arusha as Chaga who had adopted Maasai customs and speech, others linked them with 'Kwavi', probably Parakuyo or Loogolala.[8] An Arusha tradition collected from Arusha Chini itself is emphatic that the first Arusha were 'Lumbwa' (Parakuyo) who spoke Maa and were Maasai, and not Loogolala who, the tradition claims, were not really Maasai.[9] Traditions collected recently in Arusha Juu (Upper Arusha), to which

---

[4] While the correct Maa form for the Arusha people is 'Larusa', I have retained the common English and Swahili form 'Arusha' for the sake of clarity.

[5] For locations see maps in Wakefield, 'Routes of Native Caravans', map; New, *Life*, endmap; J.P. Farler, 'Native Routes in East Africa from Pangani to the Masai Country and Victoria Nyanza', *PRGS*, 4 (1882), 776; Ludwig von Höhnel, *Discovery of Lakes Rudolf and Stefanie* (London, 1894), endmap; Oscar Baumann, *Die Kartographischen Ergebnisse der Massai-Expedition des Deutschen Atnisklaverei Comités* (Gotha, 1894), endmap; Johannes Schanz, *Am Fusse der Bergriesen Ostafrikas* (Leipzig, 1912), endmap.

[6] Thomas Wakefield, 'Routes of Native Caravans', 304; New, *Life*, 369, 459; J.P. Farler, 'The Usambara Country in East Africa', *PRGS*, 1 (1879), 93; idem, 'Native Routes', 733; Alexandre LeRoy, *Au Kilima Ndjaro* (Paris, nd.), 371, 386–90; Johnston, *Kilima-Njaro Expedition*, 424; J.D. Willoughby, *East Africa and its Big Game* (London, 1889), 195–204; Höhnel, *Discovery*, 165–7.

[7] For Taveta, see Ann Frontera, *Persistence and Change* (Waltham, 1978). For Kahe, LeRoy, *Au Kilima Ndjaro*, 371; Willoughby, *East Africa*, 94, 177–83; Höhnel, *Discovery*, 167–8; Hans Meyer, *Across East African Glaciers* (London, 1891), 198–202; M. French-Sheldon, *Sultan to Sultan* (London, 1892), 340–1.

[8] For putative Chaga origins, see New, *Life*, 459; LeRoy, *Au Kilima Ndjaro*, 390. For 'Kwavi', see Wakefield, 'Routes of Native Caravans', 304; Farler, 'Usambara Country', 93; Höhnel, *Discovery*, 165.

[9] Sabaya and Juma Nteipai Loloiliang'a (AHT 9).

many Arusha later migrated, however, are divided. Some remember Arusha Chini as a Maasai community of Parakuyo, Loogolala, or Kisongo, while others recall it as 'Kikoine'. Traditions collected earlier by Hans Cory are similarly divided. One claims that the first Arusha were 'Kikoin', or Pare from Gweno, who subsequently allied with Kisongo against Parakuyo, joined Kisongo age-sets, and adopted Kisongo customs and speech, but another asserts that the earliest Arusha were Parakuyo.[10]

In reality, the earliest residents of Arusha probably came from diverse backgrounds. All oasis communities were multi-ethnic, composed of different peoples seeking refuge from the economic disasters, political conflicts, and social misfortunes that beset the era.[11] In most, however, one culture ultimately came to predominate linguistically and otherwise. In Taveta the dominant culture was Pare; in Kahe, Chaga; and in Arusha Chini, Maasai. While people in Arusha Chini spoke both Maa and a Chaga dialect akin to that spoken in Kahe, native Maa speakers must have comprised a critical part of the original community.[12] This is clear from the pattern of linguistic borrowing that occurred. While there are a large number of Chaga loan words in Arusha Maa, they are largely restricted to the single field of agricultural terminology. More significantly, they take the form of Chaga words adopted by native Maa speakers rather than that of Chaga words retained by Chaga speakers as they adopted Maa as a second language.[13] A critical mass of emerging Arusha must thus have been Maa speakers who adopted some Chaga vocabulary and not Chaga speakers who assimilated to Maasai culture. Arusha clans and age-sets were also Maasai, and appear to pre-date Kisongo dominance of the surrounding plains.

If Arusha Chini was predominantly a Maasai community, however, it was not primarily a pastoral one. Arusha adopted a number of crops and cultivation techniques from their Chaga neighbours, an issue we will return to shortly, and they soon developed a reputation as productive farmers able to supply food stuffs in abundance. But they also continued to participate in wider Maasai culture and society and to be closely linked with pastoral Maasai, who relied on them routinely for agricultural foodstuffs, beer, and honey to supplement their pastoral diet. Economically and ethnically distinctive in their

---

[10] Mosingo ole Meipusu (AHT 1); Yohanes ole Kauwenara (AHT 2); Lodenaga Lotisia (AHT 3); Ngole ole Njololoi (AHT 4); Ngoilenya Wuapi (AHT 5); Eliyahu Lujas Meiliari (AHT 8); Hans Cory, 'Tribal Structure of the Arusha Tribe of Tanganyika' (UDSM: Hans Cory Papers), 1-3; G.A. Fischer, *Das Masailand* (Hamburg, 1885), 56-7.

[11] In addition to Taveta, Kahe, and Arusha Chini, other oasis communities included Nkuruman, Chamus, and later, Ngong.

[12] Gérard Phillipson, *Gens des bananeraies* (Paris, 1984), 95; Derek Nurse, personal communication.

[13] The distinction between borrowing by native speakers (in which isolated words are adopted from another language) and acquisition and transmission of a second language (in which numerous retentions from the first language may be carried over into the second language) is an important one that reveals much about the nature of the historical situation that produced the borrowing. In this case, the evidence is that Maa speakers, presumably Arusha, borrowed Chaga agricultural terminology; and not that Chaga speakers adopted Maa while retaining much of their previous agricultural vocabulary. The later situation would have involved more widespread phonetic changes and borrowing, including basic vocabulary items as well as more specialized cultural terms. Derek Nurse, 'Language Contact, Creolization, and Genetic Linguistics: The Case of Mwiini' (unpub. paper, African Studies Association, 1992) and personal communication.

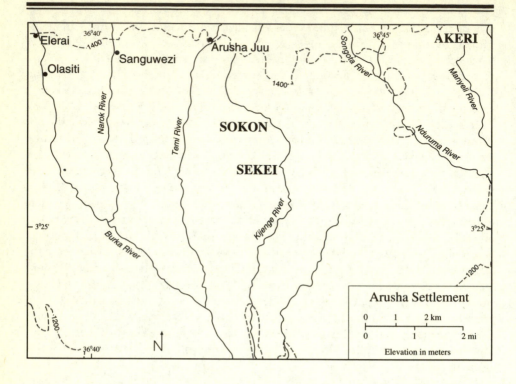

Map 2.2 Arusha Settlement

protected enclave, then, Arusha played critical roles in the larger, more inclusive regional culture and economy.[14]

From 'Little Arusha' to 'Greater Arusha'[15]

Sometime during the 1830s, when Kidotu (*c.* 1821–41) were warriors, some Arusha left Arusha Chini in the aftermath of Kisongo victories over Parakuyo on the Songonoi Plains to look for new land. They journeyed up the Kikuletwa River towards Mount Meru until they reached Olasiti on the Burka (Purka) River west of modern Arusha town.[16] They established their first settlement there and subsequently a second settlement further up the mountain at Elerai, in Boru. They also established a market at Sanguwezi on the Engare Narok River west of Ngaronaro that soon became an important livestock market where agricultural Arusha Maasai traded foodstuffs, honey, beer, and tobacco to pastoral Kisongo for livestock, milk, meat, and skins.[17]

Arusha allied with the Enkidongi lineage of Maasai prophets (*loibons*) centred at Ngosua west of the Engare Olmotoni River. Some, in fact, claim they had been recruited initially by Supeet, the principal Kisongo prophet, to dig a water furrow into the plains and raise tobacco and food crops for pastoral Maasai. Enkidongi had recently settled at Ngosua to be closer to their Kisongo clients. As patrons of Kisongo and then Arusha warriors, Enkidongi prophets ritually sanctioned their raids and received a share of the spoils the warriors gained in them. Unlike transhumant Kisongo, Enkidongi lived together in settled villages and their large settlements and herds, amassed in reward for their ritual services, soon encircled the mountain, from Monduli in the west around southern Meru and across the Sanya Plains to Kilimanjaro in the east. Arusha traded with

---

[14] Thomas Spear, 'Introduction' and 'Being "Maasai", but not "People of Cattle": Arusha Agricultural Maasai in the nineteenth century" in T. Spear and R. Waller (eds), *Being Maasai* (London, 1993), 1–18, 120–36.

[15] Rebmann and Höhnel both mistakenly translated Arusha Chini (Lower Arusha) and Arusha Juu (Upper Arusha) as Little Arusha and Greater Arusha, respectively. The terms are descriptively accurate, nevertheless. Höhnel, *Discovery*, endmap; J. Erhardt & J. Rebmann, 'Sketch of a Map of part of East and Central Africa' in Eugene Stock, *The History of the Church Missionary Society* (London, 1889–1914), II, 136.

[16] Ngoilenya Wuapi (AHT 5); Sabaya and Juma Nteipoi Loloiliang'a (AHT 9); Fischer, *Das Masailand*, 54, 56–7, 61; Fokken, *ELMB*, 60 (1905), 218; Merker, *Die Masai*, 9, 19; 'Northern Province Annual Report, 1930' (TNA: 19415/1930); 'Affinities of the Masai and Arusha Tribes', nd. (TNA: 69/45/4); Cory, 'Structure of the Arusha', 1–3; A.E. Kitching, 'Memorandum on Native Land in Arusha District', 3 Dec 1930 (TNA: 25369); *Arusha District Book*; Philip H. Gulliver, *Social Control in an African Society* (London, 1963), 10–12; B.Y. Mshana, 'Arusha Synod, Tanzania: The Identity of the Church and its Ministry to Society' (M. of Sacred Theology, Wartburg Seminary, 1976), 13–14; Alan H. Jacobs, 'Maasai Intertribal Relations: Belligerent Herdsmen or Peaceable Pastoralists?' in K. Fukui & D. Turton (eds), *Warfare among East African Herders* (Osaka, 1977), 42; Waller, 'Lords', 285–6, 314–15; Berntsen, 'Pastoralism, Raiding, and Prophets', 165–7; idem, 'Economic Variations among Maa–Speaking Peoples' in B.A. Ogot (ed.), *Ecology and History in East Africa (Hadith* 7), (Nairobi, 1979), 120–1.

[17] Mosingo ole Meipusu (AHT 1); Yohanes ole Kauwenara (AHT 2); Lodenaga Lotisia (AHT 3); Ngole ole Njololoi (AHT 4); Ngoilenya Wuapi (AHT 5); Eliyahu Lujas Meiliari (AHT 8); Sabaya & Juma Nteipoi Loloiliang'a (AHT 9); Farler, 'Native Routes', 734; Höhnel, *Discovery*, 165–6; Merker, *Die Masai*, 9; Gulliver, *Social Control*, 10; Waller, 'Lords', 314–15.

Table 2.1 Arusha Age-Sets

Tiyioki	*c*. 1791–*c*. 1811
(Kisaruni?)	(?)
Merishari	*c*. 1806–*c*. 1826
Kidotu	*c*. 1821–*c*. 1841
Tuati I	*c*. 1836–*c*. 1856
Nyangusi	*c*. 1851–*c*. 1871
Laimer	*c*. 1866–*c*. 1886
Talala	*c*. 1881–1905
Tuati II	*c*. 1896–1917
Tareto	1911–1929
Terito	1926–1948
Nyangusi II	1942–1959
Iseuri	1955–1974
Makaa	1968–1988
Landiis	1983–

Sources: P.H. Gulliver, *Social Control in an African Society* (London, 1963), 33; John Berntsen, 'Pastoralism, Raiding, and Prophets: Maasailand in the nineteenth century' (Ph.D., Wisconsin, 1979), 89. The dates accord with Berntsen's calculations, except I have indicated '*c*' (circa) for those undocumented dates prior to 1905, which he calculated on the basis of an average 20 years +/– 5 years per set.

Enkidongi at Sanguwezi, consulted with the Enkidongi prophets about raids, and joined with Kisongo to initiate their age-sets under Enkidongi guidance.[18]

With the extension of the Pangani Valley trade routes in the early 1860s, Arusha Juu also became an important source of supplies for caravans on their way to western Kenya. Arusha were known for being able to supply enough food to provision caravans of 2,000 people for the two- to four-week trek across the Maasai Steppe. Wakefield noted that Arusha Juu was rich in cattle, while Farler also commented on the large farms where Arusha grew maize, cassava, sorghum, beans, sugar cane, sweet potatoes, and yams. Arusha extracted high tolls (*hongo*) from caravans for passage. Fischer paid 200 rings of wire, 450 strings of beads, 20 rings of brass wire, and 30 pieces of clothing material, together with assorted gunpowder and lead, while Höhnel complained that the tolls were so high that caravans could barely afford to stop there on the way up country, and could only manage to do so on the trip down by trading used arms.[19]

[18] Ngole ole Njololoi (AHT 4); Ngoilenya Wuapi (AHT 5); Erhardt & Rebmann, 'Sketch of a Map'; Wakefield, 'Routes of Native Caravans', 319; New, *Life*, endmap; Farler, 'Native Routes', 734, 776; Thomson, *Masailand*, endmap; Höhnel, *Discovery*, 129–34, endmap; Baumann, *Die Kartographischen Ergebnisse*, endmap; Fokken, *ELMB*, 60 (1905), 218; P.H. Gulliver, 'A History of Relations between the Arusha and Masai' (Conference Papers of the EAISR, 1957), 2–7; idem, *Social Control*, 10–12; Waller, 'Lords', 43, 92–3; Berntsen, 'Pastoralism, Raiding, and Prophets', 161–71; idem, 'Economic Variations.' 120–1; Richard Waller, personal communication.

[19] Wakefield, 'Routes of Native Caravans', 305; Farler, 'Usambara Country', 96; idem, 'Native Routes', 731–4; Fischer, *Das Masailand*, 100, cited in N. N. Luanda, 'European Commercial Farming and its Impact on the Meru and Arusha Peoples of Tanzania, 1920–1955' (Ph.D., Cambridge, 1986), 27; Höhnel, *Discovery*, 165–6.

As Arusha agriculture and trade grew, they spread rapidly from their initial settlements on the edge of the plains up the uninhabited southwestern slopes of the mountain. The geography of Arusha is similar to that of Meru, with rainfall increasing as one ascends the fertile southwestern slopes, but decreasing as one moves around to the northwest until one finally enters the rain shadow in the north. Arusha settled the prime southern slopes first. They cleared and settled the slopes up to 1,460 metres by 1860, 1,520 metres by 1885, and at 1,680 metres by 1905.[20]

Given the small size of the initial Arusha population in the 1830s, such rapid expansion could not have occurred through simple reproduction alone. Arusha colonized the southwestern slopes of Mount Meru in less than one hundred years, less than half the time it took Meru to do the same on the southeastern ones. If we assume that geographic expansion of both peoples was due largely to population growth[21] and we take the rate of Meru population growth and expansion to be that of natural increase,[22] how do we account for the fact that Arusha increased at more than double the Meru rate? While we can not know the answer to this question for sure, it probably rests on two factors: Arusha capture and assimilation of young Meru and Chaga in raids from the 1850s and the settlement of Maasai refugees, especially women and children, in the 1880s and 1890s.

Arusha began raiding Meru during Nyangusi (c. 1851–71), when they started to expand into the western Meru districts of Sekei and Sokon Juu east of the Temi River. Over the following three decades they succeeded in pushing the boundary between them back some three miles from the Temi to the Songota River. The final Arusha victory was reportedly achieved only after Meru had wounded Meoli, the Nyangusi spokesman and war leader, who then threatened the as yet uninitiated Talala (c. 1881–1905) that he would not allow them to be circumcised until they had defeated the Meru. The Arusha youth rallied in a final decisive battle against the Meru. Thereafter, Meru youth joined Talala and subsequent Arusha age-sets in self defence.[23]

While the area between the Temi and Songota was the only actual Meru territory that Arusha seized, they raided deeply into Meru for cattle and captives. Seizing cattle for themselves allowed Arusha warriors to marry and settle earlier than if they had had to wait until their fathers allowed them to advance to elderhood and provided them with cattle for bridewealth. Arusha warriors also captured young women, who they either married themselves or gave in marriage to others in return for receiving bridewealth

[20] P.H. Gulliver, 'The Population of the Arusha Chiefdom: A High Density Area in East Africa', *Rhodes–Livingstone Journal*, 28 (1960), 18. See Figure 7:1: Arusha Expansion.

[21] If anything, the rates of geographic expansion may have lagged behind those of population growth. Existing settlement areas were more densely populated than newly settled ones, as people consolidated existing settlements before moving on. As Meru and Arusha reached the outer limits of the banana belt in the early twentieth century, average farms also started to shrink in size.

[22] Meru population was also augmented by continuing immigration from Chaga, but Meru lost population to Arusha raiding. These may have cancelled each other out, but I suspect Meru actually experienced some net decline during the latter nineteenth century.

[23] Yohanes ole Kauwenara (AHT 2); Loingoruaki Meshili (AHT 6); Eliyahu Lujas Meiliari (AHT 8); Anton Lukas Kaaya (MHT 1); New, *Life*, 393; Krause, *ELMB*, 57 (1902), 279; Merker, *Die Masai*, 19; Gulliver, 'Population', 16.

which they could then use for their own marriages. Finally, Arusha warriors seized young men, who were adopted into Arusha families and initiated into Arusha age-sets. They then joined their new Arusha age-mates to raid for cattle and captives and ultimately to marry and settle in Arusha. Meoli, the spokesman and leader of Nyangusi, was renowned not just for his bravery, but for the large number of wives and other dependants he adopted into his family.[24]

Arusha also raided Kilimanjaro and were frequently recruited as mercenaries by Chaga chiefs from the 1860s. New described five Arusha he met in Moshi in 1871:

> The Arusha wa Ju are allies of Mandara's and accompany him in most of his marauding expeditions.... In their 'get up' they were decidedly Wakuavi. Their twisted wool [hair] hung in long strings over their shorn foreheads and down their backs. The lobes of their ears were stretched as described for the Wataveta, and they wore similar ornaments. Their only clothing was a small cape made of three central pieces of the skins of new-born calves, neatly sewn together into one square piece, and nicely bound around the edges....[25]

Rindi (also known to Europeans as Mandara) had lived with Arusha in exile after being displaced as chief of Moshi in the 1860s, and had been helped by them to regain his chieftaincy around 1870. Arusha received the spoils from their raids in return. Thomson encountered Arusha warriors in 1883 on their way to raid Useri, where they reportedly captured over 2,000 head of cattle, and he noted that Rindi had recruited over 1,000 Arusha mercenaries to raid another of his neighbours. One of those neighbours, Sina of Kibosho, also employed Arusha to help train his army, though he was understandably reluctant to trust them in battle against their principal patron, Rindi.[26]

Arusha may have raided along the coast as well. So-called 'Kwavi' and 'Masai' raids were widely reported from Tanga as far north as the Tana River during the 1850s to 1890s, but it is rarely clear whether these were conducted by displaced Parakuyo, Loogolala or Arusha (all three of which were often termed 'Kwavi' indiscriminately in the sources), or Kisongo Maasai. A few accounts do speculate that they were Arusha, however. Wakefield reported one raid on Ribe in 1882, in which the warriors consumed pawpaw and vegetables and stole hoes and other agricultural implements, leading Ribe to conclude they were probably agricultural Arusha rather than pastoral Maasai. Another raid on Oromo along the Tana River in 1886 which resulted in the death of the missionary Houghton and his family was also attributed to Arusha, while warriors who may have been Arusha were also reported at Taveta and Kasigau in Taita.[27]

While most Meru and Chaga who entered Arusha society were victims of Arusha raids, many pastoral Maasai immigrated to Arusha during the 1880s and 1890s to

---

[24] Yohanes ole Kauwenara (AHT 2); Lodenaga Lotisia (AHT 3); Loingoruaki Meshili (AHT 6).

[25] New, *Life*, 413–14.

[26] Mosingo ole Meipusu (AHT 1); Ngoilenya Wuapi (AHT 5); Jonathan Kidale (AHT 7); Thomson, *Masailand*, 80–4, 128; Willoughby, *East Africa*, 112–14, 209–10, 217; Höhnel, *Discovery*, 198; LeRoy, *Au Kilima Ndjaro*, 290–2; Waller, 'Economic and Social Relations', 91–2; Berntsen, 'Economic Variations', 123–4.

[27] T. Wakefield, 'Wakwafi Raid', *PRGS*, 5 (1883), 289; *UMFC*, 29 (1886), 409–11, 590; C.W. Hobley, *Kenya: From Chartered Company to Crown Colony* (London, 1929), 38; idem, 'Upon a Visit to Tsavo and the Taita Highlands', *Geographical Journal*, 5 (1895), 555; F Jackson, *Early Days in East Africa* (London, 1930), 131–2, 156.

escape the endemic diseases and droughts that afflicted them at the time. Bovine pleuro-pneumonia, accompanied by a major drought and famine, struck Maasai herds from 1883 to 1886. No sooner had their herds recovered than rinderpest inflicted devastatingly quick and heavy losses in 1891–2 and was immediately followed by heavy human losses from smallpox. The century closed with bovine pleuro-pneumonia, rinderpest, and killing drought following one another in disastrous succession from 1897 to 1900. With heavy losses of cattle each time, pastoralists were forced to beg for food or to settle with their Arusha neighbours, relatives, and age-mates. Large numbers of women and children settled in Arusha, many of them permanently as Kisongo fathers and brothers married their daughters and sisters to Arusha for cattle to re-stock their herds. Since Arusha usually kept their cattle on small pastures high on the mountain, they were isolated from the epidemics raging across the plains and were thus a major resource for pastoralists seeking to re-stock. Pastoralists also left their children near Arusha homes in the hope that they would be found and adopted by Arusha families. Kisongo men settled in Arusha, as well, but they often departed as soon as they were able to re-stock their herds.[28]

Pastoral famine refugees were soon joined by others fleeing civil war among Purko-Kisongo. The chief prophet (*loibon*) of the Kisongo from *c.* 1866, and ritual sponsor of the warriors during the peak period of their expansion, Mbatiany, died in early 1891. Mbatiany had wandered in the bush, mad, during his last years, and had not clearly designated a heir between his sons, Senteu and Olanana. Senteu, the elder, remained at Ngosua, where he was supported by Loitai, Kisongo, Arusha, and other southern Maasai, while Olanana moved north to Naivasha and recruited supporters from the Purko and northern Maasai. With stock losses of up to 90 per cent in the rinderpest epidemic of 1891–2 and no central ritual leadership to unite them, the two sides fell to raiding one another. Senteu and the Loitai were generally dominant in the south until 1893, but then the tide started to turn against them. In 1897 the Kisongo went over to Olanana, and Senteu was finally defeated in 1902.[29]

Arusha participated actively in these struggles, initially supporting Senteu and the Loitai-Kisongo in their raids on Purko. They continued to support Senteu after Kisongo shifted to supporting Olanana, but finally switched sides and joined Olanana and the victorious Purko-Kisongo in their final raids against Loitai. Arusha also took advantage of Kisongo weakness to launch their own raids against their former allies, culminating in a bitter battle between the two at Engare Olmotonyi in which the river reportedly flowed with blood, vultures filled the air, and the two sides bitterly refused to take the oath of peace afterwards.[30] The wars had been vicious ones, prompting one Arusha to reflect:

… the Maasai are like hyenas. When you spear a hyena, it will eat its own entrails until it dies.

[28] Yohanes ole Kauwenara (AHT 2); Loingoruaki Meshili (AHT 6); Richard D. Waller, '*Emutai*: Crisis and Response in Maasailand, 1883–1902' in D. Johnson & D.M. Anderson (eds), *Ecology of Survival* (Boulder, 1988), 75–91.

[29] Berntsen, 'Pastoralism, Raiding, and Prophets', 289–93.

[30] Ngoilenya Wuapi (AHT 5); Yohanes ole Kauwenara (AHT 2); Fokken, *ELMB*, 60 (1905), 218; Richard Waller, personal communication.

The Maasai kept fighting among themselves, killing each other. Some groups disappeared, while others hid in remote areas.... Those who came here can not be traced because some of their predecessors, like the Larigon, were wiped out.... Some were wiped out, while others melted into other groups. Other Maasai exterminated them. It is a sad story that we should not really tell strangers.[31]

Severely debilitated during the wars, Kisongo refugees again flowed into Arusha, while Arusha took advantage of Kisongo defeats to settle on the plains for the first time. The breakup of the Enkidongi community at Ngosua over the disputed succession drove more refugees to Arusha, and provided additional opportunities for Arusha to seize land and cattle on the plains.

With heavy influxes of pastoral Maasai, the western districts of Arusha became rein-fused with pastoral Maasai culture. The majority of Maasai who settled in Arusha were pastoral Kisongo from the nearby plains, but they also included Sikirari and Enkidongi from Sanya and Monduli, Matapato from the Meto Hills and Longido, Laitayiok from north of Mount Meru, and Loitai from the west.[32] Their influence is still apparent in the greater prominence of Maasai culture in western Arusha today. An Arusha from Olepolos drew a sharp contrast with Arusha further east who had been more influenced by Meru:

In our family we still do not make sacrifices to our ancestors. We do not take meat to their graves or milk to the sacred groves. Newborn babies in [eastern] Arusha are called by the names of their ancestors.... Maasai do not do that. These customs have been taken from other people who settled here.[33]

Chaga captured in raids, as well as Maasai refugees, were integrated into Arusha society much as Meru captives had been previously. Boys were adopted as 'sons' by Arusha 'fathers', who then announced publicly: 'This is my son. Do not bother him. Do not take his cattle.' Young men were circumcised with their age-mates, served with them in the same age-set as 'brothers', and settled with them following marriage. Young women were married by their captors or married to others. One Arusha recalled that one of his grandmothers was Kisongo, while another was from Machame and had children in both Machame and Arusha: 'Her children were all brothers and sisters, even though some were Chaga and others were Arusha.' She continued to visit Chaga, and some of her Chaga relatives later joined her in order to escape from disturbances on Kilimanjaro at the time. Arusha genealogies are replete with similar stories; Philip Gulliver estimated that 44 per cent of Arusha lineages in the 1950s had come from Meru, 22 per cent from Chaga, and 3 per cent from pastoral Maasai.[34]

Arusha society, like other Maasai, was remarkably open to immigrants.[35] One could become Arusha by being adopted by an Arusha family, marrying an Arusha, joining an

---

[31] Eliyahu Lujas Meiliari (AHT 8).

[32] Richard Waller, personal communication.

[33] Eliyahu Lujas Meiliari (AHT 8). The implication here is that eastern Arusha adopted ancestor veneration and descent ideology from the large numbers of Meru settled among them, as noted below.

[34] Loingoruaki Meshili (AHT 6); Gulliver, *Social Control*, 12. See also Ngole ole Njololoi (AHT 4); Ngoilenya Wuapi (AHT 5); Eliyahu Lujas Meiliari (AHT 8).

[35] Spear, 'Introduction'.

Arusha age-set, or speaking Maa. Meru were initiated into Arusha age-sets even though they neither spoke Maa nor had cattle to give the Kisongo prophet for their initiation. Carved stools, goats, and tobacco were their 'cattle', and once circumcised and initiated, 'All were Arusha, even if they did not speak the language'.[36] This is not to say, however, that immigrants assimilated evenly to Arusha cultural practices or that such assimilation was one-directional. Assimilation to Arusha modes was most complete in the central districts that remained predominantly Arusha in population, but western Arusha were noticeably influenced by the large numbers of pastoral Maasai who settled there in the 1890s, and the eastern area between the Temi and Songota Rivers that Arusha seized from Meru in the 1860s and 1870s is still known for its Meru influences today.

Acceptance into Arusha society was not dependent on complete assimilation to Arusha norms, and there is little evidence that immigrants, however incompletely assimilated, suffered discrimination from other Arusha. Many Chaga and Maasai were refugees who had come to Arusha voluntarily, while Meru or Chaga captives, who were close enough to home to visit periodically, could easily have stayed there had they chosen to do so. Meru young men also chose to serve with Arusha in the Talala (c. 1881–1905), Tuati (c. 1896–1917), and Tareto (1911–29) age-sets, and participated in raids on Kilimanjaro and, subsequently, struggles against the Germans. Arusha readily discuss their foreign ancestors today, uninhibited by the fears of discrimination that characterize coastal and other societies.[37] As Gulliver noted:

> ... the patrilineal descendants of immigrants have been so completely absorbed into 'true-Arusha' lineages that such truth is no longer sociologically relevant. It is not possible to distinguish 'true-Arusha' from others in respect to their status or behaviour. Therefore the historical facts may be ignored..., and we shall assume the alleged patrilineal genealogies are correct.[38]

The demographic effects of Arusha activities went far beyond simply the number of captives, refugees, and other immigrants that were added to Arusha society. The disproportionate addition of large numbers of young women to Arusha society increased the ratio of women to men and thus probably increased the overall birthrate. The tendency of Arusha warriors to marry earlier may have also boosted the birthrate, while increasing the total number of fertile women increased the total number of births. The effect was then magnified geometrically in succeeding generations.[39] As Arusha warriors raided for cattle and women, married, and cleared the forest to settle, then, they caused the population to grow more rapidly and settlement to expand more quickly than it would have normally. Conversely, Arusha raids caused a net transfer of population from Meru to Arusha and a decline in population growth there through the loss of young women, enabling Arusha to overtake Meru in population well before the end of the century and to become the largest single Maasai section at the same time.[40]

---

[36] Loingoruaki Meshili (AHT 6); Ngole ole Njololoi (AHT 4); Eliyahu Lujas Meiliari (AHT 8); Spear, 'Being "Maasai"'.

[37] Ngole ole Njololoi (AHT 4); Loingoruaki Meshili (AHT 6); Eliyahu Lujas Meiliari (AHT 8).

[38] Gulliver, Social Control, 70.

[39] cf. Raymond Kelly, The Nuer Conquest (Ann Arbor, 1985), 59–62.

[40] The population was first estimated in 1903 at 8,365 Arusha and 5,506 Meru and in 1921 at 22,000 Arusha and 12,000 Meru. ELMB, 58 (1903), 512; Arusha District Book.

Maasai Farmers

Like other Maasai, Arusha spoke Maa, maintained close relations with pastoral Maasai, and adhered to the main tenets of Maasai culture. Unlike other Maasai, however, Arusha were not pastoralists, but were farmers. Maasai culture was an intensely pastoral one, and might have proved dysfunctional to the needs of farmers.[41] The social relations of farmers were usually rooted in land, the ancestors who had settled it, and their descendants who worked it. Those of herders, meanwhile, were focused on cattle, the elders who managed them, and the age-sets that provided social access to resources herders needed to ensure their survival. Maasai speech had a richly elaborated bovine vocabulary, but it lacked many elementary terms for agricultural practices. Maasai maintained an intensely pastoral ideology that idolized cattle and the people who kept them, while denigrating farmers who laboured on the land. Pastoralists carefully conserved natural resources, while cultivators destroyed pastures to plant crops. Pastoralism was a dignified life of leisure; agriculture, one of debased toil. Pastoral men produced while their wives laboured, but farming men laboured while their wives produced. Herders were wealthy in cattle; impoverished farmers kept only scraggy herds of small stock. Pastoralists lived in blessed harmony with God; farmers profaned God by manipulating the spirits of their ancestors.[42] A product of pastoralism, Maasai culture would seem to have been ill-adapted to the needs of agriculture.

Maasai do farm, nevertheless, and they have apparently done so throughout their history. Maasai have resorted to agriculture when they have lost stock through drought or disease; small groups of Maasai farmers like Arusha, Chamus, and Nkuruman have long existed on the plains; and prior to the 'pastoral revolution' of the seventeenth to eighteenth centuries, Maasai may have cultivated dry land grains to supplement their herds as a matter of course.[43]

In fact, the roots of Maasai agriculture are older than Maasai themselves, going back more than two millennia to their Eastern Nilotic forebears in the Sudan. All Maasai speak Maa, an Eastern Nilotic language, descended from languages centred in the southern Sudan, and it developed from proto-Eastern Nilotic through a succession of 'daughter' languages (including Teso-Lotuko-Maa, Lotuko-Maa and Ongamo-Maa), as Eastern Nilotes expanded into northern Uganda, Kenya, and down the Rift Valley over the last two thousand years. Ancestral Eastern Nilotic speakers probably practised a mixed agro-pastoral economy, for their vocabulary included words for millet, eleusine, sesame/seeds, digging, reap, field/garden, axe, grind, flour, porridge, millet beer, charcoal, fire, and hearth.[44] These terms indicate that Maasai ancestors cultivated dry land

---

[41] As indeed it appeared to Philip Gulliver, 'The Arusha: Economic and Social Change' in P. Bohannan & G. Dalton (eds) *Markets in Africa* (New York, 1965), 250–84.

[42] John G. Galaty, 'Maasai Pastoral Ideology and Change' in P.C. Salzman (ed.), *Contemporary Nomadic and Pastoral Peoples* (Williamsburg, nd), 2–6.

[43] See Spear, 'Introduction'.

[44] Rainer Vossen, *The Eastern Nilotes* (Berlin, 1982), 479–84; idem, *Towards a Comparative Study of the Maa Dialects of Kenya and Tanzania* (Hamburg, 1988).

cereals and are consistent with the archaeological record for the practice of mixed agro-pastoralism among Eastern Nilotes in the northern Rift Valley over the past two millennia.[45]

While much of this lexis is still retained by other Eastern Nilotic languages, including the language most closely related to Maa, Ongamo, Maa itself has lost it, probably in the course of the adoption of increasingly specialized pastoralism in the seventeenth and eighteenth centuries. Arusha thus had to rediscover agriculture when they resumed farming in the nineteenth century. They did this by adopting more and more specialized crops and techniques from their neighbours as they moved from the plains north of Kilimanjaro to Arusha Chini and Arusha Juu.

This process is revealed by three sets of loan words dealing with agricultural terminology in Arusha Maa. The oldest, including the general words for banana, banana plant, and bean, a bean and a banana species, and words for sugar cane, sweet potato, tobacco, field, and hoe, all derive from Central Kenyan languages. The second set, including several species of bananas, banana rope and head-pad, rubbish heap, and hearthstone, come from Central Kilimanjaro dialects of Chaga spoken around Arusha Chini. The third, and most extensive, comes from Meru, and includes words for eleven different banana species, sweet potato, yam, banana fruit, digging stick, sickle, two kinds of hoe, pestle, adze, and seed. It would thus appear that as the ancestors of the Arusha moved through southern Kenya, around Kilimanjaro to Arusha Chini, and finally to Arusha Juu, they also began adopting new agricultural techniques, picking up more specialized crops and techniques as they moved into progressively more distinctive environments.[46]

As Arusha increasingly shifted from herding to farming, they also adapted pastoral social relations and cultural norms to their needs. Arusha household economy was organized in much the same way as it was among pastoral Maasai. The basic unit of production in Arusha was a man, his wives, and their children. Wives were allocated land by their husbands, much as pastoral men allocated cattle to their wives. Each wife was thus provided with sufficient resources to provide for herself and her children, and together they provided most of the labour to raise their own food after their husbands had initially cleared the land and planted bananas. Successive wives built their houses alternately on either side of the gate leading into the homestead, like other Maasai, and wives on each side of the gate formed a division (*olwashe*) within the household. The wives and children of the right or left were considered to be more closely related to one another than to those of the other side; they often co-operated with one another; and inheritance was divided between the two sides.[47]

Arusha settled initially on the lower slopes of Mount Meru and, as families grew,

[45] While there is no direct archaeological evidence for early agriculture in the northern Rift, the presence of grinding stones and pestles provides indirect evidence for grain consumption. The issue of whether there was agriculture or not has been much debated and is still unresolved.

[46] Thomas Spear and Derek Nurse, 'Maasai Farmers: The Evolution of Arusha Agriculture', *IJAHS*, 25 (1992), 481–503.

[47] P.H. Gulliver, 'Structural Dichotomy and Jural Processes among the Arusha of Northern Tanganyika', *Africa*, 31 (1961), 19–35. Arusha clans, age-sets, and settlement areas were similarly paired.

older sons cleared and settled new lands further up the slopes, while the youngest sons inherited their fathers' fields, in accord with general Maasai inheritance patterns. Age-mates pioneered new lands together after they had retired from being warriors, and in this way, localized sections of age-sets, led by their spokesmen (*laigwenak*), developed as the main focus of local social organization.[48] This was in marked contrast to Meru, where residence was based on descent; lineages were the main form of social organiza-tion; and clan elders mediated disputes and led sacrifices to ancestral spirits. Lineages developed over time in Arusha as well, especially in the older settled areas where lineage elders assumed responsibility for adjudicating claims relating to land, but they remained shallow and never became effective means of wider social organization.[49] The only area in Arusha where descent became an important principle of social organization was that between the Temi and Songota Rivers that Arusha seized from Meru in the 1860s and 1870s. Meru cultural influences remained strong in this area, and people continued to worship at ancestral shrines, practise witchcraft and sorcery, and speak Meru, contrary to practices elsewhere in Arusha.[50]

Practices associated with warriorhood were, perhaps, the most antithetical to farming. Pastoral Maasai warriors (*murran*) withdrew to their own village (*manyata*) soon after circumcision in their teens, and they remained there until they were promoted to elders, married, and settled in their thirties. During this period, warriors performed no work, associated largely with each other, abstained from eating agricultural produce, and gorged themselves on meat prior to raiding others for cattle. While such practices developed a strong pastoral orientation and built strong bonds among age-mates, agri-cultural Arusha could ill afford the loss of labour it entailed, to say nothing of the warrior's extravagant consumption of beef.

Arusha were able to adjust *murran* seclusion and late marriage to suit their labour needs, however, as well as adapting their labour needs to the practices of the *murran*. Arusha warriors did not withdraw to their own *manyata*, unlike their pastoral brethren, and so their periods of seclusion were much shorter, confined to the immediate periods when ritual events took place and often timed to accord with the agricultural calendar.[51] Arusha warriors also tended to marry and assume elder status earlier. Their acquisition of cattle and women in raids on Meru and Chaga and their ability to pioneer new lands enabled warriors to marry and settle on their own prior to their formal promotion to elderhood, forcing the elders to recognize reality and allow them to be promoted earlier than the elders might otherwise have wished.

[48] Gulliver, *Social Control*, 71–5.

[49] With increasing land shortage and the tendency for sons to remain at home and divide their patrimony today, localized descent structures have become important vehicles for preserving claims to land, thus perhaps explaining the prominence Paul Spencer attributes to them in his re-analysis of Gulliver's data: 'Opposing Streams and the Gerontocratic Ladder: Two Models of Age Organization in East Africa', *Man*, 11 (1976), 153–75. My hypothesis is that descent played a lesser role when land was freely available and brothers became dispersed among different age–set settlements, as confirmed by Gulliver, *Social Control*, 75–100.

[50] Yohanes ole Kauwenara (AHT 2); Eliyahu Lujas Meiliari (AHT 8); Krause, *ELMB*, 57 (1902), 279; Gulliver, 'Population', 16; D.C. Flatt, *Man and Deity in an African Society* (Dubuque, 1980), 27–34; James Brain and Mesiaki Kilevo, personal communication.

[51] Gulliver, *Social Control*, 137–44; Cory, 'Structure of the Arusha', 18–19; Loingoruaki Meshili (AHT 6); Spencer, 'Opposing Streams', 154–60

Arusha labour needs were also adaptable to the needs of the initiates. Unlike shifting agriculture where peak labour demands during the rains required intensive use of all available labour for the duration of the planting season, labour demands of irrigated mountain agriculture were spread more evenly throughout the year. Bananas required little work once they had been planted, and seasonal crops were planted and harvested in succession throughout the year. Arusha farming was combined with cattle-keeping on small mountain pastures that were rotated periodically with annual crops to maintain the fertility of rich volcanic soils. Irrigation channels were simple and easily maintained by local groups of users. Labour needs were thus spread throughout the year, and they closely matched the consumption needs of the family. All grown members of the family worked, men tending the bananas and women the cattle and annual crops of grains and beans. The main variation in labour demand related to the developmental cycle of the family. Young families with only parental labour and young dependants had to work harder than mature families with plenty of labour and few non-working dependants. By the time Arusha boys became *murran*, then, family needs for their labour were not as great, and they could contribute to ongoing labour demands as needed in between their ritual activities.[52]

Being Maasai: Arusha and Pastoral Maasai

While pastoral Maasai ideology had to be adapted to their needs as farmers, Arusha had good reasons for retaining their overall identity as Maasai. Being Maasai enabled Arusha to retain strong links with pastoral Maasai on the plains. Pastoralists depended on Arusha for agricultural produce to supplement their own milk and meat during seasonal fluctuations in production or when drought periodically struck the plains. Arusha also provided honey and millet for beer, and Arusha boys herded Maasai stock. In return, pastoral Maasai provided Arusha with a ready supply of stock, milk, meat, and skins, as well as the means to enter pastoralism for those Arusha who chose to do so.

Economic relations were easily conducted among relatives, affines, and age-mates. Arusha *murran* were initiated with Kisongo into the same age-sets, and later they traded cattle with their Kisongo age-mates and married each others' daughters. Pastoral women brought milk and skins to the homes of Arusha relatives to trade for grain or honey. Arusha men placed surplus cattle with pastoral friends on the plains, often in exchange for their sons' help in herding Kisongo stock. And when deadly drought struck the plains, Arusha provided pastoralist relatives, affines, and age-mates with refuge, food, and cattle for re-stocking their herds.

---

[52] This also contrasts with the current situation. With increasing land shortage and resultant agricultural intensification from the early twentieth century, labour demands have increased considerably: cattle have been stalled, mountain pastures planted, fodder has to be laboriously carried up from the plains, and manure must be carried out on to the fields. Some of these increased demands have been offset by the use of oxen for ploughing and other labour-saving technology, and men now undertake a greater amount of agricultural labour than previously. The ideology of *murran* leisure persists, nonetheless, as I was informed one day in spite of the fact that a *murran* was hoeing a field in front of us.

Arusha–Kisongo relations varied according to circumstances and the needs of each, as shown by shifting patterns of intermarriage between the two. One pattern predominated during times of relative prosperity among pastoral Maasai, when they had a surplus of cattle relative to available labour. Under these conditions, pastoral Maasai married Arusha women in exchange for cattle, thus gaining women and children as labour, while at the same time ridding themselves of excess cattle from their herds. In the process, they also gained Arusha affines who could provide herdboys, access to agricultural products, or potential refuge in times of need. Conversely, Arusha were almost always short of cattle required for marriage or of sufficient pastures on which to graze the stock they had. In obtaining cattle from pastoral Maasai, they also gained affines with whom they could place cattle surplus to the restricted pastures on the mountain as well as social resources to move into pastoral society should they wish to do so. Since all Arusha and Kisongo warriors participated in the same age-set rituals and often shared in the same *murran* feasts, such marriage alliances were easily arranged among age-mates in the two societies.

A second marriage pattern obtained during periods of drought or cattle diseases on the plains. Such disasters rarely struck Mount Meru with the same degree of severity as they struck the plains. The mountain received much higher and more reliable amounts of annual rainfall, and the streams flowing down it provided water all year round for irrigation, assuring Arusha of adequate produce in good years as well as in most bad ones. Arusha cattle were kept in small groups on isolated mountain pastures, thus insulating them from the epidemic cattle diseases which spread rapidly among the large Kisongo herds on the plains, especially during drought conditions when herds were concentrated on restricted dry season pastures or around the few available waterholes.[53] Arusha thus usually had adequate supplies of food and cattle which they could exchange with Kisongo at times when destitute Kisongo suffered from a shortage of cattle relative to the number of people. Kisongo women and children frequently sought food and refuge among Arusha affines and age-mates during famines, while Kisongo men remained on the plains to try to preserve whatever cattle remained and to rebuild their herds afterwards with stocks from Arusha and elsewhere. Kisongo were thus able to obtain food, reduce their surplus population, and acquire a nucleus of cattle or small stock to rebuild their herds, while Arusha obtained women, wives, and agricultural labour to increase their own production at times of increased demand from their pastoral kin.

Arusha benefited regardless of the terms of trade and social exchange with the pastoral economy. During times when cattle were plentiful and relatively inexpensive, they built up social capital in the form of cattle and daughters married to pastoralists, while during the disasters that afflicted pastoralists periodically they gained women and children to expand the agricultural economy. The demands for cattle, food, women, and labour among pastoral Kisongo and agricultural Arusha were thus complementary and synchronized with each other over time, ensuring that relations between them were amicable at precisely the time when both pastoralists and highland societies were engaged in endemic conflicts among themselves.

[53] Merker, *Die Masai*, 347n.

The balance between Arusha and pastoral Maasai began to change in the 1880s, however, when disease and famine caused Kisongo and other pastoralists to become increasingly dependent on Arusha. And with the death of Mbatiany about 1891 and the combined disasters of the 1890s, open conflict broke out between them. Kisongo, Arusha, Loitai, and other southern Maasai had fought together with Senteu early in the decade, but later Arusha challenged both Kisongo and Loitai. Weakened by disease, drought, and raids, Kisongo and Loitai were forced to allow Arusha to establish their presence on the plains adjacent to Mount Meru for the first time. By the time the pastoralists recovered, German rule had been established, confirming Arusha gains, and Arusha have been pushing out to Monduli and on to the plains beyond ever since.

As Arusha started to assert their dominance over pastoral Maasai, earlier patterns of pastoral Maasai cultural hegemony began to shift as well. In contrast to pastoral ideology extolling the virtues of pastoralism, Arusha began to develop their own counter-ideology. Arusha emphasized the virtues of the lush well-watered highlands and their strong diversified economy, contrasting them with the barren plains and the vagaries of pastoral production. Farmers were prosperous, intelligent, and sophisticated in contrast to their poor and backward pastoral cousins. The counter-ideology would reach its full development in the colonial era, as many Arusha became educated Christians and coffee farmers, but its seeds may have been first sown in the changing relations between farmers and herders in the closing decades of the nineteenth century.[54]

Arusha and Meru

In contrast to the largely complementary relations that had existed through most of the nineteenth century between Arusha and pastoral Maasai, relations between Arusha and Meru were often marked by competition and conflict. Just as earlier competition among pastoralists for access to vital resources on the plains had turned to deadly conflict, with many driven out of pastoralism altogether, competition among the peoples on Kilimanjaro and Meru generated increasing conflict during the course of the century as people struggled to gain access to the same critical resources.

Arusha relations with their highland neighbours had never been very close. In spite of the fact that Arusha lived near Chaga/Meru speakers at both Arusha Chini and Arusha Juu and absorbed large numbers of them into Arusha society, there was virtually no linguistic borrowing by either Maa or Chaga/Meru speakers from the other beyond Arusha adoption of Chaga and Meru agricultural terminology discussed above. Nor did Arusha adopt other Chaga or Meru institutions. The lack of Chaga or Meru influence on Arusha is due, in part, to the fact that there was little opportunity for trade among them. Arusha had traded salt to Chaga for iron hoes at Arusha Chini, but little trade was noted between Arusha and Meru on Mount Meru.

---

[54] Galaty, 'Maasai Pastoral Ideology', 17–18. While Galaty's analysis is based on the situation today, I feel that the contrast may date from the later nineteenth century when Arusha began to exert their dominance over adjacent plains pastoralists for the first time.

Conversely, Arusha and Meru both required land and labour to work it, and they competed with one another for access to them. Fertile land in the lower reaches of the mountain was already in short supply by the mid-nineteenth century when Arusha started raiding across the Temi River into Meru territory, and they subsequently seized the districts of Sekei and Sokon Juu for themselves. Land was still available higher on the mountain, but it required labour to clear the heavy forest and settle it. It was at this point that Arusha warriors started raiding Meru for cattle and women so that they could marry, clear the land, and farm it.

The main advantage Arusha had over Meru was their military organization and skills. Arusha warriors forged strong bonds among their age-mates during their initiation, and they were driven to capture cattle and women by a combination of *murran* machismo and the need to marry and settle. They were well armed with shields and long broad spears and practised in using them. Before embarking on major raids, up to 2,000 Arusha warriors would petition the *loibon* to guide them. Scouts were then sent out to locate vulnerable herds, while the warriors feasted on meat to strengthen themselves. All then set off en masse, marching for days until they reached their target, where they lay in wait until the cattle had been brought into the kraal, struck quickly, and escaped with the spoils.[55] Arusha age-sets were so effective that by 1881 Meru adopted them in self-defence, joined the newly initiated Talala, and joined with their new Arusha age-mates to raid others themselves.

While Meru continued to initiate their young men and participate in Arusha age-sets around the end of the century, however, the union of Arusha and Meru age-sets proved to be only temporary when – in the aftermath of German conquest – Arusha power lapsed, raiding ended, and Meru no longer had any incentives to do so. Meru initiated their own sets after 1926, thus reasserting their separate identity and setting a pattern that would be repeated throughout the colonial period as Arusha and Meru continually asserted their independence of one another in local government, the missions, and co-operatives.

On the Eve of Conquest: Arusha in the 1890s

By the 1890s, then, Arusha had come to dominate Mount Meru and the nearby plains. They had adapted quickly to the highland environment and expanded rapidly by assimilating large numbers of Meru, Chaga, and other Maasai, transforming themselves from mixed farmers and herders on the plains to more intensive highland farmers within a couple of generations. Their transformation was highly selective, however. While they adopted new forms of agriculture almost completely, they were able to modify other aspects of their pastoral culture selectively to meet the very different needs of mountain agriculture.

Universal age-sets remained the primary means of social organization, though they soon became localized in specific neighbourhoods where clusters of their members

---

[55] Ngole ole Njololoi (AHT 4).

settled. Young Arusha men continued to be initiated and serve as warriors together. As warriors acquired cattle and married, they banded together with some of their age-'brothers' to clear new land on the mountain and settle in neighbourhoods where their section of the age-set became the principal means of local social organization. While men continued to recognize their affinity with members of their age-set settled elsewhere, daily interaction with their neighbours, whether members of their age-set or not, developed local ties at the expense of more distant ones with age-mates elsewhere. Sectional and neighbourhood ties thus came to supplant broader ones based on age, and embraced all those who settled in an area.[56]

During their initiation, Maasai warriors chose spokesmen (*laigwenak*) to represent their interests with the *loibon* and other age-sets, but while *laigwenak* were respected men who were able to influence their fellow age-mates, they did not exercise institutionalized authority. As Arusha warriors raided more and more widely during the later nineteenth century, however, Great Spokesmen, chosen by the senior warriors, emerged to lead the raids. The first was Meoli, who served during Nyangusi (*c.* 1851–71) and its successor Laimer (*c.* 1866–86), and who is popularly credited with the final Arusha victory over Meru by refusing to allow the emergent Talala set to be circumcised until they had defeated the Meru. Talala chose two Great Spokesmen, one for each half of Arusha. Marai represented Boru higher on the mountain, while Rawaito represented Burka. The authority of the Great Spokesmen must have been extremely limited, however. Like *Mangi* Matunda in Meru, Merai and Rawaito were powerless to control the warriors who harassed Teleki and Höhnel and later killed the Lutheran missionaries Ovir and Segebrock.[57]

The dominance of the warriors in their relations with the first Europeans to visit Meru and Arusha dramatically represented the power and autonomy they had achieved during the later nineteenth century. Previously, warriors had been dependent on their seniors for advancement to elder status that would allow them to marry and settle. They were also dependent on their fathers for the cattle that would allow them to do so. Like Maasai elders elsewhere, Arusha elders usually sought to hold back the warriors so that they might continue to exercise power and marry themselves. By acquiring cattle and women in raids and clearing their own land, however, Arusha warriors were able to marry independently of the elders and force their seniors to recognize reality and promote them after the fact.[58] Laimer (c. 1866–86) and Talala (c.1881–1905) benefited especially as the last sets to raid Meru and Chaga before German conquest put an end to such raids, while Tuati (c. 1896–1917) and all future age-sets would have to seek other means in the new German and British colonial orders for their advancement.

The localization of age-sets and focus on neighbourhood were related to the critical shift in Arusha society from cattle to land as the main source of wealth. Cattle remained

[56] Gulliver, *Social Control*, 25–53.
[57] Gulliver, *Social Control*, 150–51; Cory, 'Structure of the Arusha', 4–5; Höhnel, *Discovery*, 138–51; Müller and Fassman, *ELMB*, 52 (1897), 15–18.
[58] This paralleled the increasing power of *murran* among pastoral Maasai at the same time. Richard Waller, personal communication.

important stores of social value and sources of investment, and would continue to be so throughout the colonial period. During the early 1940s, for example, when wheat prices increased, some Arusha sold cattle and bought land, tractors, and combine harvesters to raise wheat on the plains, but when prices declined after the war, they sold the land and equipment and reinvested in cattle.[59] Land became the main means of producing wealth, nevertheless. Control over land was vested in the men who cleared it, allocated use of it to their wives, and ultimately passed control of it to their descendants, giving rise to multi-generational households under the direction of family patriarchs. As long as land remained freely available, however, younger men could escape gerontocratic control by settling elsewhere, thus inhibiting the development of deeper land-based lineages. Typically, older sons pioneered land for themselves higher on the mountain, while the youngest sons remained at home to inherit their fathers' land. Lineages thus became widely dispersed, and did not develop into significant social organizations. Arusha clans were, in fact, generalized Maasai identities which an individual inherited at birth as a personal attribute, but which had little wider political or mystical significance. As Gulliver has noted, common descent served more as a means for recruiting potential moral support during disputes than as a structural feature of Arusha society.[60]

The lack of emphasis on restrictive descent-based categories of social organization, in favour of the less restrictive category of age, facilitated the assimilation of large numbers of Meru, Maasai, and other foreigners into Arusha society. Young men, as explained earlier, were adopted as 'sons' into Arusha families and joined the relevant age-set, where they became 'brothers' (*ilalashera*) to their Arusha-born age-mates. Immigrant women's roles, in common with those of Arusha women generally, were a function of their relationships with men. Young women were married and assumed the roles of wives and mothers, little different from those of native-born women. They were allocated land by their husbands; they joined the right- or left-hand side of the household that differentiated the family internally; and inheritance passed to their sons through them.

The one disability which foreign women suffered was that they usually had no Arusha father or brothers to protect their interests. While some foreign women were married to other men by their captors, who received the bridewealth for them and so became their 'fathers', most had little recourse to help from a husband who mistreated them. Their greatest security came, perhaps, when their sons became warriors. Maasai mothers, whether foreign or locally born, played important roles in their sons' initiation; they often settled later in life with them; and, in retrospect at least, they are remembered fondly by their descendants today.[61]

Arusha retention of Maasai identity was thus far from dysfunctional to their adoption of agriculture; it was critical to their success in the highly competitive world of the highlands. This is a surprising conclusion to reach, for one would have expected inexperienced

---

[59] Luanda, 'European Commercial Farming', 165–73.

[60] Gulliver, *Social Control*, 69–126; idem, 'The Arusha Family' in R.F. Gray & P.H. Gulliver (eds), *The Family Estate in Africa* (London, 1965), 197–229.

[61] Gulliver, *Social Control*, 70, 141–4.

Arusha to have borrowed heavily from their more experienced Meru neighbours, or even to have been absorbed by them, as many Maasai who settled elsewhere were. While Arusha did develop a similar intensive agricultural economy to Meru, however, they did not follow related Meru cultural patterns, but adapted their own pastoral cultural heritage to their changing needs. Each people thus remained culturally distinctive. In Meru control of land, social relations, and religious beliefs all continued to be related to principles of descent, while in Arusha they remained related to principles of age. Arusha and Meru thus continued to pursue similar economic objectives in fundamentally different ways as each continued to order its world according to its own cultural values and perceptions.

II

Colonialism & Resistance under German Rule

3

Blood on the Land

Talala
& the Germans
1881–96

When Arusha and Meru youth joined together about 1881 to initiate the new Talala (*c.* 1881–1905) age-set, they put an end to three decades of fighting between them. The warriors of Talala – 'The Expansionists' – soon gained a considerable reputation as they raided widely for cattle and women, were sought after as mercenaries by Chaga chiefs, displaced Kisongo herders on the plains around Mount Meru, and gained increasing influence and power within their own societies.

The 1880s and 1890s might thus be seen as a period of unbridled prosperity for the peoples of Mount Meru but for events occurring on the broader regional stage that threatened to engulf them. Afflicted by successive waves of drought, disease, and struggles for survival, pastoral Maasai became embroiled in a series of suicidal civil wars that left them weak and vulnerable to attacks from others. Increasing trade in ivory and slaves throughout the Pangani Valley gave rise to predatory trading chiefs who perverted traditional social relations to prey on their own people, causing widescale political disruption and insecurity throughout the valley and adjacent highlands.

German conquest at the end of the century exacerbated earlier trends. German opposition to Senteu, the prophet of the southern Maasai, and to pastoral Maasai generally resulted in their being evicted from the better-watered pastures of the Pangani Valley and Sanya plains and ultimately in Senteu's defeat at the hands of his northern rival, Olonana. The devastatingly effective use of rifles and machine guns in brutal punitive raids enshrined the rule of violence, contributed further to the spread of disease, and entrenched in power those who benefited from it. German rule also introduced new elements into northern Tanganyika as they supplanted local authorities, seized people's land, and forced them to work for the benefit of German settlers.

Such disruptions were slow to reach Mount Meru on the western fringes of the region, however, and did not seem to affect Meru or Arusha adversely at first. Disease and famine among pastoral Maasai remained largely confined to the plains and brought numbers of Maasai women and children into Arusha and Meru societies. Arusha were also able to extend their settlements on to the plains towards Monduli during the civil wars following Mbatiany's death in 1891. Similarly, the growth of the caravan trade at

61

Arusha Juu provided new sources of wealth without precipitating the inequalities and violence it had caused in the Pangani Valley, while Arusha and Meru warriors gained considerable spoils from the wars for trade and political power on Kilimanjaro.

Disruptions in the broader regional order must have begun to impinge on Arusha and Meru consciousness from the early 1880s, nevertheless, for Talala are remembered by Meru and Arusha today not only for their successes in meeting these problems, but also for their struggles to combat evil and restore moral and social order to a world crumbling around them. Talala were seemingly driven by a deep sense of foreboding as the Pangani Valley collapsed into disorder, Maasai fought Maasai, and the spectre of German domination advanced towards them from the coast.

They were not alone, for in the 1890s broad trends developing over decades throughout the region suddenly culminated in specific crises involving political power, economic production, and social order almost everywhere. Older polities and social orders collapsed, new ones arose bloodily, famine struck devastatingly often, and new illnesses killed by the thousands. In Meru and Arusha many of these crises became encapsulated in the events of the night of 19 October 1896, when Arusha and Meru warriors joined together to kill the first two missionaries who attempted to settle among them. Our focus thus shifts radically from broad historical trends to the events of a few days as we seek to understand the cumulative effects of the dramatic changes and crises of the late nineteenth century.

Prelude to Conquest: 1884-95

While few Europeans visited Mount Meru, and Arusha and Meru had little direct experience of German colonial designs before 1895, they could not have been ignorant of events taking place along the coast and in the Pangani Valley during the previous decade. News of German treaties, forced labour, taxation, land seizures, and bloody battles fought throughout the valley spread rapidly along the trade routes to Arusha Juu or was picked up by Arusha and Meru as they travelled throughout the region.

German conquest came quickly and brutally to the coast and valley, signalled not by decades of slowly encroaching trade relations but by the sudden appearance of Karl Peters in November 1884 gathering treaties on behalf of the German East African Company (DOAG). Peters' goals to pre-empt the British and force the German government to declare a protectorate over the mainland were both accomplished by the end of 1886, and the Company then set out to establish control and exploit its new possession.

One of the first areas the Germans targeted was the Pangani Valley, building on Peters' and Karl Jühlke's treaties in the area, and its lucrative trade. Germans first attempted to establish a station at Korogwe in 1886 to interdict the main trade route through the valley. Korogwe was soon abandoned due to illness and was subsequently burned by a Pangani trader, and was boycotted and abandoned a second time after attempts were made to re-establish it the following year. Germans then attempted to establish a tobacco plantation and market at Lewa, between Pangani and Korogwe, but soon found that local people avoided the market and were willing to work only sporadically on

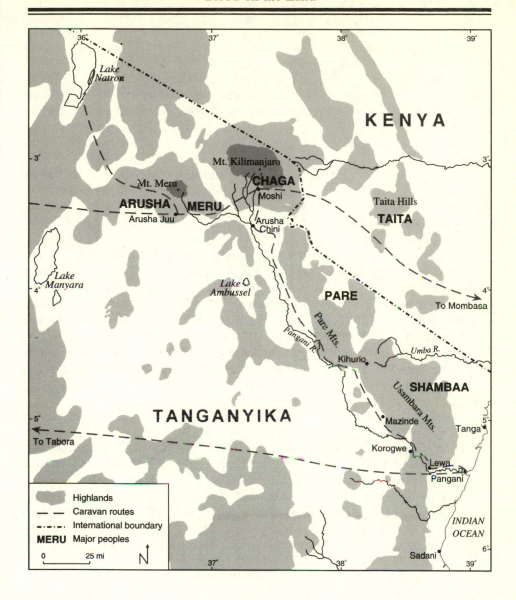

Map 3.1 Pangani Valley and Mount Meru

the plantation. The German manager resorted to contracting for slaves, but they fled the harsh labour routine. He then sought to coerce local workers, but they revolted and forced him to flee after only six months.[1]

Having failed to gain footholds in the interior, the Company forced the Sultan of Zanzibar to cede control over coastal customs revenues, and in August 1888 it sought to occupy the main coastal towns to collect them. Rapidly expelled from all but Bagamoyo and Dar es Salaam, the Company was compelled to ask the German government to finance an expedition under Hermann von Wissmann to put down the revolts. Wissmann arrived in April 1889 with a thousand Sudanese and Ngoni soldiers and proceeded to bombard the towns and pursue their inhabitants into the hinterland when they sought to escape. Massacres were common in the Pangani Valley behind Sadani, Pangani, and Tanga, and many coastal notables were publicly hanged. By mid-1890 the revolts were put down, and the following January the company ceded overall control to the imperial government.[2]

Wissmann immediately mounted a major campaign to impose German rule throughout the northeast. Proceeding up the caravan route from Pangani, he negotiated, cajoled, and forced submissions from one people after another. The first to sign was Semboja, the ruler of Mazinde, father of the Shambaa puppet king Kimweri, and patron of many of the leading trading chiefs in the area. Semboja had been impressed by Wissman's earlier campaigns, and he quickly agreed to fly the German flag in return for German recognition of his authority over West Usambara and the valley. The Germans soon allied with Semboja's opponents in East Usambara who were willing to sell land to German planters, however, and following his death in 1895, they hanged his son and installed his enemy Kinyashi on the Shambaa throne.[3]

In the meantime, Wissmann continued north to install an agent of Semboja in Kihurio and to grant flags to aspiring Pare trader-chiefs. From Pare, Wissman went on to Moshi, where the DOAG had maintained a station since 1887. He immediately became embroiled in Chaga politics by allying with Rindi against his enemy Sina of Kibosho. A combined German-Moshi expedition devastated Kibosho in February 1891, seizing 7,000 cattle and over 10,000 small stock, thus forcing Sina's submission. Most of the other Chaga chiefs soon followed suit. With Rindi's death in November, however, the Germans switched their allegiance to Marealle of Marangu, who then incited them to mount a disastrous campaign against Rindi's son, Meli, during which two Germans were killed and the remaining German troops were forced to flee to the coast. Meli was defeated the following year, but Marealle successfully involved the Germans in another alleged conspiracy in 1899 which resulted in the Germans hanging nineteen competing chiefs and leaders from Moshi, Kibosho, Arusha, Meru, and elsewhere.[4]

Arusha and Meru were not uninvolved in these events. Arusha warriors had served

---

[1] Jonathon P. Glassman, *Feasts and Riot* (Portsmouth and London, 1995), 188–90.

[2] John Iliffe, *A Modern History of Tanganyika* (Cambridge, 1979), 91–7.

[3] Iliffe, *Modern History*, 99.

[4] Iliffe, *Modern History*, 100–102; Isaria N. Kimambo, *A Political History of the Pare of Tanzania* (Nairobi, 1969), 198-214; idem, *Penetration and Protest in Tanzania* (London, 1991), 46–50; Charles Dundas in *Northern Province Book*. See also Justin Lemenye, 'The Life of Justin', *TNR*, 41 (1955), 31–57, 42 (1956),

Chaga chiefs since at least the 1860s; Rindi owed his throne in Moshi and his dominance on Kilimanjaro to their support; and Sina employed Arusha to train his warriors in Kibosho.[5] Arusha and Meru warriors participated in the combined German-Moshi attack on Kibosho in February 1891 and, after witnessing German firepower first hand, made peace with Wissmann. His ammunition almost exhausted, Wissmann retired to the coast, having successfully completed his northern campaign.[6]

While Arusha and Meru were probably aware of earlier events in the Pangani Valley as well, there was little direct German involvement on Mount Meru itself before the Evangelical Lutheran Mission of Leipzig attempted to establish a mission in Meru in October 1896. The German commander at Moshi, Captain Johannes, had conducted a brief raid in October 1895 to punish Arusha for raiding Meru, but he subsequently withdrew to Moshi, leaving the area unadministered. Two Catholic missionaries tried to set up a mission in Arusha in August 1896, but they failed to follow up on it. The same month a Lutheran missionary, Ewald Ovir, reconnoitred potential mission sites with Johannes, and seemed to be well received by the Arusha spokesman Rawaito and the Meru chief Matunda. Herr Bronsart, the head of the Kilimanjaro Trade and Agricultural Company, had built a house at Matunda's, but he was largely engaged in an ostrich farm on the plains.[7] There was thus little to indicate that Mount Meru would soon witness a bitter struggle for colonial control.

The First Mission: 1895-96

Mission expansion accompanied that of the Germans. Missionaries from the British Church Missionary Society had been among the first Europeans to visit Kilimanjaro in the 1840s and 1850s. The snow-capped mountain astride the equator continued to exercise a strong pull on their imaginations until the Rev. A.E. Fitch responded to Rindi's appeal for teachers and finally established a CMS mission at Moshi in 1885, the same year Jühlke signed a treaty with Rindi. Rindi had other than religious teachings in mind, and when Fitch refused his request for guns to use against Kibosho, Rindi blocked the mission's supplies of water and foodstuffs. The mission persevered, regard-

(4 cont.) 19-30; Charles Dundas, *Kilimanjaro and its Peoples* (London, 1924); Kathleen Stahl, *A History of the Chagga Peoples of Kilimanjaro* (The Hague, 1964).
[5] Mosingo ole Meipusu (AHT 1); Ngoilenya Wuapi (AHT 5); Jonathan Kidale (AHT 7); T. Wakefield, 'Wakwafi Raid,' *PRGS*, 5(1883), 289; *UMFC*, 29(1886), 409–11, 590; Joseph Thomson, *Through Masailand* (London, 1885), 80–4, 128; J. C. Willoughby, *East Africa and its Big Game* (London, 1889), 112–14, 209–10, 217; Ludwig von Höhnel, *Discovery of Lakes Rudolf and Stefanie* (London, 1894), 198; Alexandre LeRoy, *Au Kilima Ndjaro* (Paris, [1893]), 290–2; C.W. Hobley, *Kenya: From Chartered Company to Crown Colony* (London, 1929), 38; idem, 'Upon a Visit to Tsavo and the Taita Highlands', *Geographical Journal*, 5(1895), 555; F. Jackson, *Early Days in East Africa*, (London, 1930), 131–2, 156; Richard Waller, 'Economic and Social Relations in the Central Rift Valley: The Maa-Speakers and their Neighbours in the Nineteenth Century' in B.A. Ogot (ed.), *Kenya in the Nineteenth Century* (Hadith, 8) (Nairobi, 1985), 91–2; John Berntsen, 'Economic Variations among Maa-Speaking Peoples' in B.A. Ogot (ed.), *Ecology and History in East Africa* (Hadith 7), (Nairobi, 1979), 123–4.
[6] Iliffe, *Modern History*, 102; Dundas in *Northern Province Book*.
[7] Muller & Fassmann, *ELMB*, 52 (1897), 12, 15; Weishaupt, *ELMB*, 67 (1912), 461.

less, but after Rindi was succeeded by his son Meli in late 1891, relations again soured as the missionaries sought, unsuccessfully, to mediate between Meli and the Germans. They were subsequently ordered to withdraw by the Germans following the aborted German attack on Meli in June 1892, and in December the CMS reluctantly sold the mission to the Evangelical Lutheran Mission Society of Leipzig, then planning to open a mission field in northern Tanganyika.[8]

The people of Moshi had other ideas, and burned the Moshi mission soon after the CMS missionaries had departed to prevent their return. Deterred from reoccupying Moshi, the Leipzig mission established its first station in 1893 at Machame, and subsequently expanded into Mamba and Mwika before finally reoccupying Moshi in 1896.[9] They were precluded from establishing further missions on Kilimanjaro by the presence of French Holy Ghost missions, however; so the Leipzig missionaries decided to explore the possibility of expanding westwards to Mount Meru, where Meru spoke a related dialect to Machame, and in August 1896 Brother Ovir set out with Johannes to reconnoitre possible sites. They went first to Arusha, where Ovir was well received by Rawaito; but he decided against establishing a station there after he experienced some opposition from the warriors, discovered that Arusha spoke Maa, a totally different language from the Chaga spoken by the missionaries, and found two Catholic missionaries had already begun to erect a station there. He then visited Matunda in Meru, where he decided conditions were more propitious for establishing a station at the chief's homestead at Akeri. His recommendation to establish a mission in Meru was accepted by the home body on 7 October, and with the arrival of a long-awaited supply caravan from Tanga on 8 October, the Leipzig missionaries lost no time in mounting an expedition to Meru. The Lutherans' expansion across Kilimanjaro had been blocked by Catholic missions, and they did not wish to give the Catholics Ovir had encountered on Meru the chance to beat them to the 'bridge to the West'.[10]

On Tuesday 13 October 1896 a number of Leipzig missionaries collected in Machame to baptize Brother Müller's infant daughter Johanna. Gathered around their new harmonium in a school room festively decorated with palm fronds, they celebrated 'a feast of brotherly fellowship' and offered prayers for Brothers Ovir and Segebrock's success in establishing the new mission in Meru. That afternoon the two young Brothers said farewell to their colleagues and joined seventy porters from Moshi and Machame waiting outside to set out across the steppe for Meru. The following day Captain Johannes visited Machame to inform Müller that he intended to visit Mbugwe

---

[8] A.A. Lema, 'The Impact of the Leipzig Lutheran Mission on the People of Kilimanjaro, 1893-1920' (Ph.D., Dar es Salaam, 1973), 90–9.

[9] Lema, 'Leipzig Mission', 101–39.

[10] This account of Ovir and Segebrock's expedition is largely drawn from a report compiled from the letters of Emil Müller, Robert Fassmann, Ewald Ovir, Karl Segebrock, and Captain Johannes in *ELMB*, 52(1897), 12–19. See also Weishaupt, *ELMB*, 67 (1912), 461 and Max Schoeller, *Mitteilungen über meine Reise nach Äquatorial-Ost Afrika und Uganda, 1896–97* (Berlin, 1901), I:152–4. Cf. accounts by Lema, 'Leipzig Mission', 146–51; Paul Puritt, 'The Meru of Tanzania: A Study of their Social and Political Organization' (Ph.D., Illinois, 1970), 55–8; R. Mbise et al., 'Historia ya Kazi ya Injili Meru kuanzia mwaka 1895–1979 kwa Jubilii ya Miaka 75 (Akeri, 1979), 1–2; C.T.S. Nasari, 'The History of the Lutheran Church among the Wameru (Varwa) of Tanzania' (BD, Makumira, 1980), 26–31.

with his young wife and that he would stop in Meru on the way to witness the transfer of land to the missionaries.

Ovir and Segebrock arrived at *Mangi* Matunda's in Meru two days later on 15 October and immediately moved into the house built earlier by Bronsart. Matunda offered them beer, maize, bananas, and later a steer, to which the missionaries responded with gifts, including a pair of scissors. Their porters returned to Machame the following day, while the Brothers set out to locate an appropriate site for their station. After initially being refused use of a local 'spiritual site', they settled on a large site surrounded by maize fields on the west bank of the Malala River. Adjacent to a spectacular waterfall, it lay across the river and 500 to 1,000 metres downstream from Matunda's. They immediately moved their goods to the new site, where they set up a large tent for their supplies, erected another for themselves, and built banana bark huts to house a kitchen and their workers.

Ovir and Segebrock were well established by the time Johannes and his wife, accompanied by Lt Wilhelm Merker and thirty soldiers, arrived on Sunday 18 October. The missionaries expressed their pleasure with Matunda's welcome and refused Johannes' repeated offers to stay with him at his camp nearer the chief's home. The next morning, on 19 October, the missionaries set to work fencing the mission property and then met Matunda and the chief Arusha spokesmen – Rawaito and Masinde – at Johannes' camp in the afternoon to present Matunda with 25 *gora* of cotton for their land. Assured by the Meru and Arusha leaders that all was safe, the missionaries returned to their new station at 6.00 in the evening, while Johannes retired to his tent and wife at 11.00 pm.

At midnight Matunda visited Johannes' camp to tell him that he had just been warned by an Arusha woman that Arusha warriors were planning to attack. Johannes dismissed him as drunk, but three hours later a sentry reported that Rawaito and Masinde had visited the camp together to confirm the earlier rumours, and at 3.15 am, Matunda, Rawaito, and Masinde all came to report that Rawaito had seen three Arusha warriors nearby. Rapid fire rang out almost immediately from Johannes' soldiers as they spied a large force of warriors in the banana groves surrounding them. The warriors drew back, but then the sound of a single shot, followed by the 'shattering of boxes and trunks accompanied by frightful howling', came from the missionary camp downstream. Surrounded and unable to respond immediately to the missionaries' plight, Johannes held the warriors off while dispatching a Meru worker to investigate the disturbances. The scout returned just before 5.00 am to report that both missionaries had been slain.

Johannes cleared camp half an hour later and marched to the mission station, where he discovered that the missionaries had been speared some thirty times each and their camp had been thoroughly plundered. Rajabu, a mission worker, emerged from hiding to report:

at around 3.00 am, when the moon was low in the sky, a huge group of warriors with shields, swords, and clubs – in full war regalia – came out of the banana groves and consulted with each other near the mission station. While a small group surrounded the station in a half circle around the back, the large mass moved across the river in order to attack Captain Johannes. When the fire of his soldiers was heard, the warriors forced their way into the sleeping quarters of the two missionaries. One of them shot once, then both were stabbed.... Brother Ovir cried out, 'I am dying, but I bless you'.[11]

Three of the Chaga mission workers had also been killed, two more captured, and three had escaped. The warriors then looted the station, destroying what they did not want, and left.

Feeling threatened by the large crowd that gathered, Johannes hurriedly buried the missionaries and said 'The Lord's Prayer'. He then took a photograph of the grave, entrusted the few goods that remained to Matunda, and quickly departed for Moshi. Johannes would return within two weeks to exact a terrible revenge, but the mission would not establish a station in Meru again until 1902. When they did return, they found the whole area surrounding Matunda's deserted. The current *mangi* lived three-quarters of an hour to the east and insisted that they not settle at the old site. They opened the graves on Easter Day to discover that the missionaries' bodies had been disinterred shortly after burial, stripped naked, and dismembered before their bones were thrown into the bushes. Meru traditions note that they had been circumcised as well.[12]

'The History of Meru is Soaked in Blood'

The murder of the young missionaries seemed inexplicable to their colleagues on Kilimanjaro. Peaceable men of God who had no worldly designs on the peoples of Mount Meru had been brutally murdered for no apparent reason, while the local leaders stood helplessly by. Müller could only conclude: 'The history of Meru is soaked in blood,' and console himself with the thought:

> we still have property at Meru, rightfully gained through purchase and consecrated with the blood of our Brothers. God will certainly not let everything be in vain. We will humble ourselves under His powerful hand, which hit our hearts and our work so hard, so that He will raise us to His side.[13]

And yet, they should have been forewarned by the experience of the explorers, Teleki and Höhnel, who had visited Mount Meru nine years earlier in 1887.[14] The two travellers had been plundered by Meru and Arusha warriors immediately on their arrival, and they were continuously harassed by them throughout their visit. When Teleki had appealed to Matunda for assistance, the *Mangi* protested that he had no influence over the warriors, to which a warrior retorted: 'Matunda has nothing to do with the matter: we are masters here.'[15]

Ovir himself had also received indications earlier that the warriors did not welcome the prospect of European settlement on Meru and that their leaders were powerless to control them. When he first visited Mount Meru to lay the groundwork for the mission

---

[11] Johannes, *ELMB*, 52 (1897), 17-18.
[12] Krause, *ELMB*, 57 (1902), 216–17, 282-283; Nasari, 'Lutheran Church', 31.
[13] Müller, *ELMB*, 56 (1901), 371, 52 (1897), 19.
[14] See Chapter 1.
[15] Höhnel, *Discovery*, 138–51.

in August 1896, he had been warned by a porter that Arusha did not welcome them. Ovir chose to disregard the warning after being received by Rawaito, but he was subsequently forced to leave Arusha precipitately, nonetheless, for reasons that are not clear. After what must have been more congenial discussions with Matunda, Ovir recommended that a mission be established in Meru.

There was no mention of danger when the missionaries celebrated Ovir and Segebrock's departure two months later, but when Johannes visited Machame the next day, he and Müller openly discussed the fact that the chiefs on Meru were powerless in the face of possible hostilities, without considering whether this presented any danger to the missionaries. According to later testimony by Rajabu, Matunda himself made the same point when he welcomed the missionaries on 15 October, noting that the warriors opposed Europeans settling in the country and that he had little power to control them.[16]

When Johannes arrived on 18 October with his troops, the missionaries expressed praise for Matunda, noting that they had no reason to fear just because of the previous behaviour of the warriors. They also dismissed accounts by two 'Ndorobo' hunters concerning previous disturbances in Meru and refused Johannes' oft-repeated invitations to stay at his camp. While the missionaries fenced their plot the following day, Matunda, Rawaito, and Masinde were all with Johannes in his camp. From this as well as from reports he had received from others, Johannes later concluded that the missionaries had little cause for fear, but that night he disregarded repeated warnings from all three that the warriors were about to attack until, standing outside with them at 3.15 am, his troops spotted the warriors surrounding them and opened fire.[17]

While Johannes and the missionaries should thus have been aware of the warriors' hostility and the lack of control over them by either the Meru *mangi* or the Arusha spokesmen, they professed innocence and could only muse on the probable causes afterwards. In his letter of condolence to the mission director on 31 October, Johannes noted:

> This misfortune struck both gentlemen like a bolt out of the clear blue sky. Even I myself suspected nothing like this, which you can gather by the fact that I had taken my wife along on the expedition. The motive for the murderous attack seems, as far as I can tell at this point, to be that the people opposed the settlement of Europeans in their lands out of fear that they would be enlisted for work. The Wachagga, Wakuafi and Masai are in no way accustomed to work and they despise it as slavery.[18]

Müller made a similar point indirectly when he queried some Meru he met in Machame in 1901. After reassuring the Meru that his fellow missionaries had had no intention of forcing Meru to work, but had only wanted to bring them medicine and the Word of God, he then asked them why they had killed the missionaries. The Meru responded that the attack had been led by Arusha who did not want the Europeans to

---

[16] Müller doubted Rajabu's testimony as Rajabu did not apparently speak Machame, the Chaga dialect most closely related to Meru that the missionaries spoke with Matunda, and another mission worker, Uledi, apparently knew nothing about the conversation. *ELMB*, 52 (1897), 15–16.

[17] Müller, Fassmann, Ovir, Segebrock, and Johannes, *ELMB*, 52 (1897), 12–17.

[18] *ELMB*, 52 (1897), 16.

settle amongst them, but then noted that Meru had little against Europeans *except* work.[19]

Arusha and Meru knew what work for the Germans involved. Starting with the ill-fated Lewa plantation, Germans had employed forced labour and contracted slaves as porters, plantation labour, and construction gangs. Müller's attempt to pre-empt the Meru response by denying the mission used forced labour reveals that he probably knew that they knew about it too. Such denials would become commonplace after the mission was re-established in Meru as the missionaries struggled with the contradictions between their conscientious objection to forced labour and their belief in the efficacy of work. Further, their own need for labour, their meagre finances, and the reluctance of local people to work for others for little reward soon placed them in a similar situation to the settlers and administration.[20]

Labour, then, was certainly one reason for Meru and Arusha opposition to Europeans. Potential loss of land was probably another.[21] Germans had already established extensive plantations in eastern Usambara and the Pangani valley, and Lutheran and Catholic missionaries had obtained large tracts on Kilimanjaro when Ovir and Segebrock conspicuously fenced in their large plot and paid Matunda 25 lengths of cloth for it on their fateful last day in Meru.

Conquest was no doubt a third reason. The warriors of Talala had direct experience of German punitive expeditions. Many had witnessed Wissmann's devastating raid on Kibosho in 1891, during which the Germans and their Moshi, Arusha, and Meru allies destroyed Sina's fort and confiscated over 17,000 stock. They had seen the German rout of Moshi in 1893. And Arusha had also experienced German power directly in October 1895, when Johannes led a punitive raid against them and seized a number of Arusha cattle and Chaga-born wives. Thus, when Ovir and Johannes toured Arusha and Meru the following August, or Johannes arrived with 30 soldiers three days after Ovir and Segebrock in October, the warriors were no doubt wary and watched them closely.

As Rajabu's eyewitness account makes clear, the mass of warriors targeted Johannes' camp, while only a small group remained behind at the mission station, and they attacked the missionaries only after Johannes' soldiers opened fire on the larger group surrounding his camp. The missionary station, the more vulnerable target, was subsequently destroyed, while the warriors abandoned any attempt to attack Johannes' camp directly. They may not even have intended to attack in the first place. Just as warriors had continually shadowed Teleki and Höhnel without attacking them, they may simply have been maintaining vigilance when Johannes' soldiers, spurred by Matunda's and Rawaito's warnings, sighted them, panicked, and opened fire, thus precipitating the attack on the missionaries. Müller himself speculated that the warriors probably intended to attack the government forces and not the missionaries:

[19] *ELMB*, 56 (1901), 371.
[20] See Chapters 4 and 5.
[21] A.S. Mbise, 'The Evangelist: Matayo Leveriya Kaaya' in J. Iliffe (ed.), *Modern Tanzanians* (Nairobi, 1973), 28. For land in Arusha and Meru thought, see Chapter 9.

When one considers the conditions surrounding the attack on the 20th of October, there are grounds for the supposition that punishment of our missionaries was not the first priority [of the warriors], but [rather punishment] of the representatives of the German government whose punitive hand had already been felt in the year 1895 by the restless Arusha people.[22]

The attack on the missionaries was thus a function of broad Arusha and Meru resistance to German colonialism in which the missionaries found themselves caught up in issues regarding labour recruitment, land alienation, and colonial conquest which were larger than themselves. They may have been caught up in internal Arusha and Meru politics as well. The warriors of Talala had been notably successful during the 1880s and 1890s in gaining cattle and women in their raids on Kilimanjaro. Their elders resented the warriors' wealth and independence, but found themselves powerless to control them. Already at odds, the two groups then differed over how to respond to the additional threats posed by the Germans. While warriors sought to challenge the Germans and drive them away, Matunda, Rawaito, and Masinde sought to appease them by exchanging gifts and granting them land. Having further alienated the warriors by these acts, the elders were then powerless to control them, and they could only vainly try to warn the Germans of the impending attack in the hope of staving off further conflict.

The warriors of Talala were not simply contesting power with their elders, however. For many Arusha and Meru today, Talala was an age-set which struggled valiantly to re-establish moral order in a world in danger of collapse. In the judgment of one Arusha reflecting on the period today:

> Talala were the Europeans of Arusha.... They hated anything evil or dirty and would try to get rid of it.... Talala executed a lot of people, especially women. They killed ... witches at Kimandolu by circling around them and clubbing them to death to avoid spilling any blood.... If two uncircumcised people were caught sleeping together, they were staked down alive, one on top of the other, at the cross-roads and left to die for all to see....[23]

'Talala were the Europeans of Arusha.' The phrase is a mysterious one until one considers the rest of the statement and the reputation Europeans later gained in Arusha. Talala were engaged in a moral crusade to combat witchcraft and illicit sex. Later, European missionaries conducted similar crusades against what they saw as the moral evils of Arusha society. Like all Maasai age-sets, each Arusha set represents the *Zeitgeist* of the period during which it served as warriors. The Age of Talala, then, was one in which great moral evils threatened Arusha society, and Talala were those who fought to stem the moral crisis afflicting Arusha society.

The moral crisis had been precipitated by the profound disruptions people suffered during the last decades of the nineteenth century, known throughout northern Tanganyika as 'The Time of Troubles'. Bovine pleuro-pneumonia, drought and famine struck from 1883 to 1886, followed by rinderpest in 1891–2 and bovine pleuro-pneumonia, rinderpest and killing drought between 1897 and 1900. Famine was accompanied by increasing political violence throughout the Pangani valley as predatory raiding chiefs

---

[22] *ELMB*, 52 (1897), 19.
[23] Eliyahu Lujas Meiliari (AHT 8).

overturned established polities and raided their own followers for slaves. Pastoral Maasai bitterly fought one another in desperate bids to control depleted pastoral resources. And German troops savagely imposed colonial rule throughout the area.[24]

Uncontrollable diseases, recurring droughts, civil wars that pitted age-mates against one another, and societies where patrons enslaved their erstwhile clients were offences to social norms. All brought death, death on an unprecedented scale, inexplicable and uncontrollable. All were manifestations of a loss of social control brought on by immorality. Anti-witchcraft campaigns conducted throughout Meru and Arusha were one attempt to identify and punish those responsible.[25] Driving out the Europeans was another.[26]

That the first Europeans were seen as morally ambiguous at best, and probably evil, is illustrated in Ismael Mbise's novel, *Blood on Our Land*. In the novel, the first European to visit Meru is depicted as a stranger who initially confounded people because he was white at midday, and neither black like those who lived during the day nor a white spirit who roamed about at night. How could one tell, people asked, if he was good or bad? The stranger might be like the fatherless albino girl who killed others, or he might even be her father. The stranger also acted in morally ambiguous, if not offensive, ways. He ate greens in the market, urinated in front of women, wore trousers that obscured his sexuality, and was responsible for the disappearance of people he recruited as porters. Europeans were clearly seen as people who did not know how to behave and so threatened moral norms and the social order they upheld.[27]

When Meru and Arusha warriors killed the first missionaries to settle among them and then disinterred their newly buried bodies to strip, dismember and circumcise them, they were thus seeking more than just to stem the German advance. They were seeking to restore moral order. The presence of Europeans had already brought great hardships that could only be overcome if the forces of evil that had caused the hardships were expunged. After killing the missionaries, Arusha and Meru warriors are also said to have pursued Johannes as far as the Sanya River, where Johannes' wife dropped a doll she was carrying, and the warriors, thinking she had miscarried, abandoned the chase.[28]

[24] Richard Waller, '*Emutai*: Crisis and Response in Maasailand, 1883–1902' in D. Johnson & D.M. Anderson (eds), *Ecology of Survival* (Boulder, 1988), 75–91; Thomas Spear, 'Introduction' in T. Spear & R. Waller (eds), *Being Maasai* (London, 1993), 1–18; Steven Feierman, *The Shambaa Kingdom* (Madison, 1974), 120–204; Kimambo, *Political History*, 122–222; John Berntsen, 'Pastoralism, Raiding, and Prophets: Maasailand in the nineteenth century' (Ph.D., Wisconsin, 1979), 289–93; and James L. Giblin, *The Politics of Environmental Control in Northeastern Tanzania, 1840–1940* (Philadelphia, 1992), 45–81.

[25] Donald C. Flatt, *Man and Deity in an African Society* (Dubuque, 1980), 224–33. Cf. A.I Richards, 'A Modern Movement of Witch-finders', *Africa*, 8 (1935), 448–61 and M. Marwick, 'Another Modern Anti-Witchcraft Movement in East Central Africa', *Africa*, 20 (1950), 110–12.

[26] Arusha and Meru were right to attribute the causes of 'The Troubles' to Europeans. Bovine pleuropneumonia, rinderpest, and smallpox were all introduced to Africa by Europeans and spread rapidly along the trade routes established in response to increasing European demand for African ivory, slaves, and other products. Political violence was also a result of increased trade, especially that in guns and slaves, as traders and aspiring chiefs employed new sources of wealth to subvert older forms of political authority. See, e.g., Feierman, *Shambaa Kingdom* and Kimambo, *Political History*.

[27] I. Mbise, *Blood on Our Land* (Dar es Salaam, 1974), 9–19.

[28] Mbise, 'Kazi', 2; S.E. Nnko, 'The Interdenominational Conflicts within the Meru District of the E.L.C.T. Northern Diocese', (Diploma in Theology, Makerere, 1980), 3.

And Meru abandoned Matunda's after the murders and would not allow the mission to resettle there when it returned in 1902.

Once the warriors had killed the missionaries, however, they had to cleanse themselves. Uncircumcised men were unclean, and killing them put the warriors themselves at risk, while the spirits of the dead missionaries might return to seek revenge if their bodies were left peacefully interred and whole.[29] Uncircumcised men, aborted foetuses, and land where blood had been spilled were all polluting and thus seen as threats to the moral order. All needed to be cleansed lest they bring further death.

Arusha associated the colour red with blood, heat and fire, impurity, violence, disease, and natural disaster, all dangerous forces that had to be tamed for life to continue. White, in contrast, represented milk, semen, purity, peace, harmony, and prosperity, and thus affirmed life; while black denoted coolness, shade, dampness, earth, fertility, and birth, and thus symbolized regeneration and reconciliation. While God might embody all these elements, people had to struggle to maintain balance among them. Purity, wholeness, and unity ensured life, fertility, rain, and well-being; while impurity, brokenness, and dissent brought death, famine, drought, and sickness.

Warriors covered themselves with red ochre, were passionate and unrestrained, and killed to protect others; while prophets, elders, and spokesmen for the age-sets wore black, were calm and restrained, and were responsible for ritual healing and moral probity. Warriors, under the moral guardianship of the prophets, thus assumed the particularly difficult role of reconciling red and black elements – of maintaining peace, order, and life while necessarily employing violence, disorder, and death.[30] The warriors of Talala were therefore struggling for much more than simply their own generational interests. They were struggling to reassert the moral authority necessary for life itself.

Arusha and Meru would thus have agreed with Müller: the history of Mount Meru *was* soaked in blood. They would differ, however, over its significance. For Müller and his fellow missionaries, Meru was soaked in the blood of martyrs whose sacrifice would eventually bring redemption. For Meru and Arusha, blood represented evil and destructive forces that brought social disorder and death. Warriors who had been on raids had themselves and their spears ritually cleansed on their return. And witches were killed by clubbing them to death to avoid spilling blood. If Meru was soaked in blood, it had to be cleansed.

Talala was thus engaged in a moral crusade to purge the moral evils from within and outside Arusha and Meru societies that threatened social order and survival. Their resistance to European settlement was a moral resistance to the evils of European colonialism responsible for undermining social order. It is on these terms that Arusha and Meru traditions are most eloquent today when they recall the circumcision of the dead missionaries and the scattering of their bodies to prevent their spirits from returning or when they respectfully recount Talala's harsh 'European' morality.

Arusha-Meru resistance was, of course, also characterized by political resistance as

[29] Nasari, 'Lutheran Church', 31.
[30] Flatt, *Man and Deity*, 70–4, 90–6, 255–76. See also Paul Spencer, 'Becoming Maasai, Being in Time' in Spear & Waller, *Being Maasai*, 140–56.

they sought to retain control over their own land, labour, and sovereignty. Politically, however, both Meru and Arusha were divided, and different factions – represented by Matunda or Rawaito and the warriors – developed their own strategies for responding to the threat of German conquest. It was for precisely this reason that the moral resistance of Talala was so important, for it represented an attempt to unite people behind a single moral vision of the many evils besetting them.

The form of Meru and Arusha resistance was important for another reason. The German conquest and subsequent loss of sovereignty, land and labour came on the heels of the disasters of the 1880s and 1890s, during which cattle and people died from inexplicable diseases, Maasai bereft of united ritual control slaughtered fellow Maasai, and wealthy patrons enslaved their former clients. Internal disasters became fused with external ones as the sheer magnitude of the crises fundamentally challenged peoples' economic, social, and political security. Unable to understand a world chaotically collapsing around them, the warriors of Talala struggled to restore the moral underpinnings of social order. Their response to the unprecedented challenges from without was thus to seek to cleanse the pollution within. The threat of colonialism may have been external, but Talala's actions stemmed from their own experiences and understandings gained in the tumultuous closing decades of the nineteenth century.

4

Conquest &
Colonization

1896–1916

German retribution for the death of the missionaries was swift and ruthless. Captain Johannes launched massive punitive expeditions against both Arusha and Meru in late 1896 and early 1897, destroying permanent banana crops, burning food stores, and confiscating Meru and Arusha livestock. Johannes withdrew to Moshi afterwards, however, and colonial rule was not firmly established until, after two further expeditions in early 1900, German troops were permanently garrisoned in Arusha and a formal administration established. The German authorities then appointed their own chiefs and headmen to rule over Arusha and Meru, imposed mandatory taxes in cash and labour, and confiscated large tracts of land for Afrikaner and German settlers. Shortly after the establishment of German rule, the Leipzig missionaries returned from Kilimanjaro, establishing permanent missions in Meru in 1902 and Arusha in 1904. German colonialism, in all its political, social, and economic dimensions, was firmly established at last, and it continued until it was dislodged, and ultimately replaced, by the British during the First World War.

The German attacks destroyed the power of the warriors, eliminated the main Arusha and Meru leaders, and delivered a devastating blow to their economies. Recovery would have been difficult at the best of times, but the years 1897–1900 were anything but that, as bovine pleuro-pneumonia, rinderpest, and drought combined to deliver killing famine throughout northern Tanganyika, and as the Maasai civil wars following Mbatiany's death in 1891 reached their peak. The opening years of German rule thus found Meru and Arusha in desperate straits, struggling to replant their bananas and rebuild their herds amidst widespread social and political disorder, from which they would not fully recover until 1907. At the same time, the imposition of German rule disrupted power and authority within Meru and Arusha societies, imposed additional economic demands in taxes and labour on them, and fundamentally challenged Arusha and Meru world views.

Arusha and Meru responses to colonialism must thus be seen in terms of the various contexts, local and colonial, in which they found themselves. Colonial demands for taxes and labour, for example, imposed added burdens on their economies, but crop sales and wages also provided them with cash to rebuild their own herds devastated by conquest and disease. New forms of authority in the administration and missions were destructive of earlier forms, but also provided new means for achieving power and influence within their societies. Adherence to Christianity alienated converts from others, but also promised education and jobs as well as alternative ways of dealing with illness and the wider moral crisis induced by colonialism.

Learning 'What Death Was': 1896–1900

When the remnants of the mission party returned to Machame in late October 1896, Müller related, 'the horrors in the first moments were indescribable. The station boys cried aloud. Chief Shangali appeared immediately and expressed his regrets and his outrage. The unrest and agitation lasted deep into the night in the otherwise quiet Nkarungo.'[1] Fearing further attacks, Johannes posted ten soldiers to Machame; Shangali's warriors guarded the mission and patrolled Machame's borders; and the missionaries in Moshi sheltered in the German *boma* (headquarters).

Captain Johannes immediately began to organize a punitive expedition. Seizing the opportunity for spoils, Shangali offered his assistance, and on 31 October Johannes set out from Moshi with 95–100 soldiers and 4,000–6,000 Chaga auxiliaries. Armed with guns and rifles, Johannes and the Chaga attacked the spear-wielding warriors of Talala and the still uncircumcised Tuati (*c.* 1896–1917) on 5 November. The battle raged for three hours before the Arusha-Meru warriors broke and fled before the onslaught, leaving 500 to 600 of their dead behind. Johannes allowed the Chaga, who had lost 120 to 140 warriors themselves, to loot and kill freely until Arusha surrendered the goods they had plundered from the mission. Johannes then fined Arusha 360 lbs of ivory and Meru 720 lbs; repatriated 500 women, who he claimed were Chaga seized by Arusha and Meru earlier, to Kilimanjaro; and seized 3,000 cattle and 5,500 small stock and sent them to Machame before he returned to Moshi at the end of November.

Two months later, Johannes and his Chaga allies returned to Mount Meru to conduct further punitive expeditions from 20 January until 5 February 1897. Arusha and Meru were stripped of their remaining livestock; more 'Chaga' women were repatriated to Kilimanjaro; and looting continued until 'there was nothing more to fight or plunder'. Permanent banana plantations were cut down and maize stores burnt; 10,000 cattle were taken for distribution to Chaga allies; and Meru and Arusha were forced to pay additional reparations before the Germans and Chaga withdrew for the second time.[2]

In the aftermath of the German campaign, Arusha and Meru withdrew to home-

[1] Müller, *ELMB*, 52 (1897), 18.

[2] Max Schoeller, *Mitteilungen über meine Reise nach Äquatorial-Ost Afrika und Uganda, 1896–97* (Berlin, 1901), I:154–7; John Iliffe, *A Modern History of Tanganyika* (Cambridge, 1979), 102; John L. Berntsen, 'Pastoralism, Raiding, and Prophets: Maasailand in the nineteenth century' (Ph.D., Wisconsin, 1979), 305–6; N.N. Luanda, 'European Commercial Farming and its Impact on the Meru and Arusha Peoples of Tanzania, 1920–1955' (Ph.D., Cambridge, 1986), 39; Anton Lukas Kaaya (MHT 1); Kirilo Japhet Ayo (MHT 2); Yohanes ole Kauwenara (AHT 2); Lodenaga Lotisia (AHT 3).

steads high on the mountain and sought to rebuild their ravaged economies. The losses of cattle and permanent banana crops were serious ones, and it would take years of slow breeding and re-planting to replace them. The difficulty of recovery was compounded by the general onslaught of bovine pleuro-pneumonia, rinderpest, locusts, and drought that brought killing famine to the northeast between 1897 and 1900. With their normally abundant crops of bananas and maize reserves destroyed, Arusha and Meru experienced a rare instance of famine on the mountain.

Recovery was slow. In 1902 there were so few goats on Meru that missionaries had to bring their own from Kilimanjaro. Since goats were the small change of the stock economy – the starting point for rebuilding a herd because of their rapid rate of reproduction and low cost – Meru and Arusha could not even begin to rebuild their herds without them. A year later, missionaries reported that there was still no cattle on the mountain. It was not until 1907 that Arusha and Meru had rebuilt their herds and enjoyed a sufficiently abundant harvest to celebrate with extravagant feasts, during which wealthy men competed for influence by seeing who could slaughter and give away the most oxen.[3]

Meru and Arusha were left in peace by the Germans until December 1899, when Chief Marealle of Marangu informed Johannes that Moshi, Kibosho, Arusha, Meru, and pastoral Maasai were conspiring against them. Johannes set out to punish the alleged offenders and attacked Arusha and Meru again on 28 February 1900. The aging warriors of Talala and newly-initiated warriors of Tuati were no longer able to offer effective resistance, however. Johannes quickly arrested the main Meru and Arusha leaders – Lobolu, Matunda's son and successor in Meru; and Rawaito, Lebanga, and Maraai, spokesmen for the Arusha – and took them to Moshi, where they were publicly hanged with 15 other alleged ringleaders of the revolt. Johannes returned to Meru for the last time in July 1900 to conduct a final punitive expedition and establish a permanent garrison in Arusha town. Arusha and Meru were effectively subdued at last. When the Leipzig missionaries returned to Meru two years later, they were received peaceably, and when rumours of another insurgency swept Kilimanjaro in 1904, Germans on Mount Meru expressed confidence that they were in no danger.[4]

The conquest of Mount Meru had gone hand in hand with the conquest of the surrounding pastoral Maasai, and it coincided with the difficult period following the prophet Mbatiany's death and disputed succession between his sons, Senteu and Olonana. When Wissmann first encountered pastoral Maasai east of the Pangani River in 1891, he drove them west across the river and into the plains. Mbatiany died the same year and southern Maasai came under the prophetic leadership of Senteu at Monduli, west of Arusha. Senteu was rebuffed when he sought an alliance with the Germans in 1893, and the Germans attacked the Maasai again in 1894. Following the

[3] Kirilo Japhet Ayo (MHT 2); Fickert, *ELMB*, 58 (1903), 41; Krause, *ELMB*, 58 (1903), 94, 98; Ittameier, *ELMB*, 62 (1907), 561.

[4] Schoeller, *Mitteilungen*, I:158–160; Krause, *ELMB*, 60 (1905), 18, 37, 219; Iliffe, *Modern History*, 101–2; Kathleen Stahl, *A History of the Chagga Peoples of Kilimanjaro* (The Hague, 1964), 194–98, 272–4, 320–36; Mosingo ole Meipusu (AHT 1); Yohanes ole Kauwenara (AHT 2); Lodenaga Lotisia (AHT 3); Ngoilenya Wuapi (AHT 5).

subsequent German raids on Mount Meru in 1895–96, Senteu withdrew from the lush pastures surrounding Mount Meru to the semi-arid steppe around Ngorongoro. Reduced to hunting and scavenging, Kisongo and Loitai raided two caravans near Ngorongoro early in 1897, for which the Germans quickly retaliated.

The ongoing struggle for survival tested Senteu's Kisongo-Loitai alliance, and in July 1897 the Kisongo leader Tolito deserted Senteu to join the northern Maasai under Olonana. Continued Kisongo raids combined with endemic disease and famine throughout 1897–1900 to force Senteu's remaining Loitai to become more dependent on Arusha, but Arusha turned on them as well in the aftermath of the German raids on Meru in early 1900. Two years later, Senteu and the remaining Loitai were finally forced to make peace with Olonana, and in 1904–5 Maasai finally joined together to celebrate Talala's ceremonial advancement from senior warriors to elders. 'The Expansionists' had served valiantly for twenty-four of the most trying years of Arusha, Meru, and pastoral Maasai history; their successors, conquered before they were even circumcised, would become known as Tuati, 'Those who sacrifice'.[5]

While the factual details of the conquest related above come primarily from German accounts, Meru and Arusha remember these events differently. They recall the iniquity of Chaga allying with Germans to defeat them. They remember confronting massed fire power and being mowed down without mercy as they learned for the first time 'what death was'. They recall the unfairness of having their land taken from them and given to Afrikaner and German settlers, the shame of men being chained together like slaves and forced to build roads without tools, and the injustice of women having to carry rocks to build the new German headquarters, or *boma*, in Arusha town. They remember the hard economic times after the Germans had confiscated most of their cattle, cut down their bananas, and burned their maize stored in trees. But most of all they tell of senseless and amoral cruelty inflicted by the Germans, conveyed in one popular account of people forced to climb trees, which were then chopped down, killing those in them. The warriors of Talala had been right about the moral evils brought by Europeans after all.[6]

Boma and Chiefs: 1900–1916

The *boma* that Meru and Arusha were forced to build in 1900 was a solid statement of the imposition of a new political and moral order. Set on a small hill at the base of Mount Meru, the fortress-like building faced out over the plains below. One approached along a 'fine wide road, equal to a well-kept highway in England', that was 'carefully marked off in kilometres', the adventurer John Boyes noted on a visit in 1903.

> The road led to a place called Arusha, and as we approached it we came to our astonishment in sight of a truly marvellous building, erected in European style and surrounded by a moat....
> The *boma* was a one-storey building of stone and mortar, with a huge tower in the centre and the whole glistened bright in the sunlight, like an Aladdin's Palace transported from some

[5] Berntsen, 'Pastoralism, Raiding, and Prophets', 303–9.
[6] Arusha and Meru Historical Traditions, all.

4.1 Arusha Boma and 'Bwana Fisi' [Herr Küster]
(J. Boyes *Company of Adventurers* 170)

fairy-land and dropped down in the heart of the tropics. Emblazoned on the front of the tower were the Royal Arms of Germany, which could be seen nearly a mile off....

The station was walled off and, being furnished with a Maxim and a machine gun, made a formidable stronghold....[7]

Standing in the midst of the 'lush plantations of the Waarusha', one approached the fort along a wide straight path and entered through a heavy stone portal into an open courtyard, surrounded by stone walls, with a square, flat-topped tower in the centre and Swahili-type houses arrayed along the back wall.[8] Boyes was impressed by the amenities:

Water from neighbouring gullies was laid on throughout the building, and a plentiful supply was available for all purposes. Water-power was used for driving a lathe in the workshop, and the officer had a staff of trained Natives. The wood-work especially was particularly well done. Even the tiles on the roof were made by the Natives, and the building was made entirely from local material. The inside of the station was paved with stone; the living rooms were fitted with electric bells; and Herr Küster said he hoped to install electric light at an early date.[9]

The town itself lay below the *boma* and consisted of some thirty Indian, Greek, and Arab shops selling cloth, trinkets, soap, enamelled plates and bowls, beads, and copper wire. One even had a sewing machine out front and produced jackets and trousers for the German soldiers and 'more progressive natives'.[10] Boyes found:

Everything about Arusha was equally surprising, the streets being well laid out with fine side-

[7] John Boyes, *The Company of Adventurers* (London, 1928), 169–71.
[8] Krause, *ELMB*, 57 (1902), 279.
[9] Boyes, *Company*, 170–1.
[10] Fokken, *ELMB*, 60 (1905), 392.

walks, separated from the road by a stream of clear water flowing down a cemented gully-way. We had discovered a real oasis in the wilderness. The township was spotlessly clean and we saw Natives with small baskets picking up any litter lying about, as though the place were the Tiergarten of Berlin and not the wild interior of the Dark Continent....

Attached to the fort was a splendid kitchen garden in which grew almost every kind of European vegetable, and next to that a coffee plantation.[11]

The German administration, like the *boma*, was built on solid military lines meant to impress. German military officers served as both local commanders and district officers, alternately administering and punishing their unruly subjects. Mount Meru had been administered, largely by means of punitive raids, by Captain Johannes from Moshi. With the completion of the *boma* in 1901, colonial troops were garrisoned in Arusha under the command of First Lieutenant Georg Küster, and Arusha remained under military rule until the general transfer to civilian administration throughout Tanganyika in 1906. Even under civil rule, however, district officers continued to wield considerable power in the exercise of their authority, and they did so largely free of troublesome constraints imposed by the central government. Few remained in Arusha long enough to gain much of an understanding of the local situation. Eleven district officers served an average of sixteen months each during the period of German rule from 1901 to 1916.[12]

Table 4.1 Meru Mangi

Ndemi	–1887	
Matunda	1887–96	
Lobolu	1896–1900	Kaaya; s/o Matunda; famine; hanged
Masengye	1900–1	Kaaya; s/o Matunda; imprisoned
Nyereu	1901–2	Nasari; imprisoned
Sambegye	1902–25	Nanyaro
Sante	1925–30	Nanyaro; s/o Sambegye; imprisoned
Kishili	1931–45	Kaaya; s/o Matunda; deposed
Sante	1945–52	reappointed; resigned
Sylvanos	1953–63	Kaaya; ss/o Matunda; popularly elected; first educated Christian.

Sources: F. Longland (1931), *Arusha District Book*; Hans Cory, 'Tribal Structure of the Meru' (UDSM: Hans Cory Papers, nd.), 202; Paul Puritt, 'The Meru of Tanzania: A Study of their Social and Political Organization' (Ph.D., Illinois, 1970), 49–51; Anton Lukas Kaaya (MHT 1); Rafaeli Mbise (MHT 3).

German officers ruled through local Arusha and Meru leaders, but in the aftermath of the mass hangings of 1900 they had difficulty identifying likely leaders and persuading them to serve. The Germans initially chose Masengye (1900–01), a son of former *Mangi* Matunda (1887–96), to replace his executed brother, Lobolu (1896– 1900), as Meru chief, but Masengye was deposed and imprisoned within a year for murder (see Table 4.1: Meru *Mangi*). Abandoning the royal Kaaya clan for a nominee viewed as a

[11] Boyes, *Company*, 170.

[12] Iliffe, *Modern History*, 117–22. For German officers in Arusha, see Dülfer, *Das Deutsch-Ostafrika-Archiv*, I:80.

Table 4.2 Arusha Mangi/Olkarsis

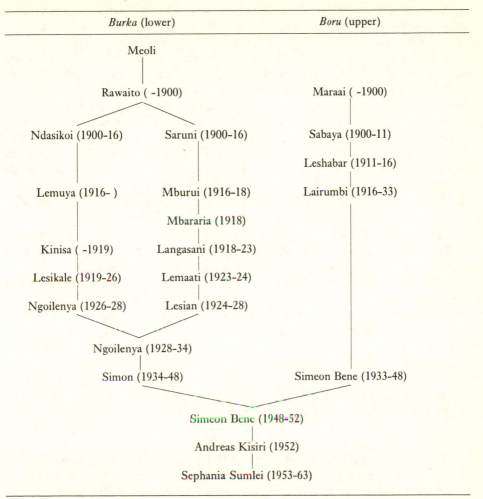

Burka (lower)	*Boru* (upper)

Meoli

Rawaito (-1900)

Ndasikoi (1900-16) Saruni (1900-16) Maraai (-1900)

Sabaya (1900-11)

Leshabar (1911-16)

Lemuya (1916-) Mburui (1916-18) Lairumbi (1916-33)

Mbararia (1918)

Kinisa (-1919) Langasani (1918-23)

Lesikale (1919-26) Lemaati (1923-24)

Ngoilenya (1926-28) Lesian (1924-28)

Ngoilenya (1928-34)

Simon (1934-48) Simeon Bene (1933-48)

Simeon Bene (1948-52)

Andreas Kisiri (1952)

Sephania Sumlei (1953-63)

Sources: Fokken, *ELMB*, 60 (1905), 39; C.M. Coke (1932), *Arusha District Book*, Hans Cory, 'Tribal Structure of the Arusha Tribe of Tanganyika' (UDSM: Hans Cory Papers, 1948), 5; Yohanes ole Kauwenara (AHT 2).

more reliable collaborator, the Germans then appointed Nyereu (1901–02) from the Nasari clan, but he too was soon imprisoned, allegedly for neglecting his duties and procuring girls for German soldiers.[13] The Germans finally found the nominee they had been seeking when they appointed Sambegye (1902–25), a member of the Nanyaro clan and favoured neighbour of the missionaries newly re-installed at Nkoaranga. Sambegye prospered as chief, taking ten wives by 1905, and he continued as chief until

[13] Leipzig missionaries, who had recently re-established the mission at Nkoaranga near Nyereu's home, were apparently better disposed toward Nyereu, however, for they slaughtered an ox at Christmas and presented a portion of it to Nyereu's wife to take to him in prison. Krause, *ELMB*, 58 (1903), 14, 139.

1925. He soon ceased being a mission favourite, however, and in 1905 Rev. Krause complained that his overt friendliness was but a mask for covert opposition: 'How could it possibly be otherwise! His friends are beer and women, and he knows these do not mix with the new teachings.'[14]

Arusha, unlike Meru, had no tradition of chiefdom, so the Germans appropriated the tradition of regional spokesmen (*laigwenak*) that had first emerged during the warriors' raids of the 1850s, and called them *Mangi* after the Meru term for chief.[15] Having hanged Maraai and Rawaito, the spokesmen from Boru (upper Arusha) and Burka (lower Arusha) respectively, however, they had to find replacements. The new Arusha spokesman for Burka was Ndasikoi, but the Germans also wished to reward their Afro-Arab ally, Saruni, and so they split Burka between the two men (see Table 4.2: Arusha *Mangi/Olkarsis*). Both men remained in office for the duration of German rule. Sabaya (1900–11) was appointed in Boru and served until his death, when he was replaced by his eldest son Leshabar (1911–16). Arusha opposed Leshabar and burned down his home, however, forcing the administration to replace him with Lairumbe (1916–33), a wealthy cattle trader associated with the Lutheran mission.[16]

The Germans also appointed local headmen to rule over individual districts below the chiefs. In Meru, these came initially from the ranks of local lineage or clan leaders (*vashili*), who normally were chosen by local clan members to mediate disputes among them and represent their interests with other clans and the *mangi*. *Vashili* became increasingly dependent on the administration, however, as they became encumbered with the unpopular tasks of raising labour and taxes.

In accord with differences in local Arusha politics, headmen were initially drawn from the ranks of local age-set spokesmen (*laigwenak*) chosen by their age-mates to mediate internal disputes and to represent their interests with other sets. As in Meru, however, their traditional legitimacy quickly broke down before the illegitimate nature of the tasks they were asked to assume by the authorities. Thereafter, headmen, like chiefs, increasingly became drawn from an emerging group of younger men associated with either the government or the mission.[17]

While there is no direct evidence to assess the impact of these changes on the nature of local leadership in Arusha and Meru, we can place them within the context of broader trends in the changing nature of power and authority in both societies. Prior to 1896, the warriors of Talala exercised an increasingly dominant role in both Meru and

---

[14] Müller, *ELMB*, 56 (1901), 371; Krause, *ELMB*, 57 (1902), 280–1; 59 (1904), 360; 60 (1905), 445–6; Ittameier, *ELMB*, 62 (1907), 560; Blumer, *ELMB*, 64 (1909), 170; F. Longland (1931) in *Arusha District Book*; Paul Puritt, 'The Meru of Tanzania: A Study of their Social and Political Organization' (Ph.D., Illinois, 1970), 49–51, 115–16; Hans Cory, 'Tribal Structure of the Meru, T.T.' (UDSM: Hans Cory Papers, nd.); Anton Lukas Kaaya (MHT 1); Rafaeli Mbise (MHT 3); Emanuel Kasengye N'nko (MHT 5).

[15] The British later termed Arusha chiefs *olkarsis* after the Maa term for a wealthy and influential man. See Chapter 10.

[16] Fokken, *ELMB*, 60 (1905), 39; Blumer, *ELMB*, 67 (1912), 111; C.M. Coke (1932), *Arusha District Book*; Hans Cory, 'Tribal Structure of the Arusha Tribe of Tanganyika' (UDSM: Hans Cory Papers, 1948), 5; Yohanes ole Kauwenara (AHT 2).

[17] Sally Falk Moore and Paul Puritt, *The Chagga and Meru of Tanzania* (London, 1977), 112; P.H. Gulliver, *Social Control in an African Society* (London, 1963), 17–23. See also Chapter 10.

4.2 Arusha chief and wives (J. Schanze *Am Füsse der Bergriesen OstAfrikas* 182)

Arusha. While neither society had a tradition of strong central authority, the military successes and increasing wealth of the warriors during the 1880s and early 1890s enhanced their status and power while eroding whatever authority the *mangi* in Meru or the *laigwenak* in Arusha had possessed previously. German conquest and rule reversed this process, for not only did Talala's crushing defeat in 1896–7 damage their self-confidence and reputation, as shown by their disintegration in 1900 but, more critically, the warriors lost nearly all their cattle as well as the means to replenish them. As power and wealth shifted to chiefs and headmen appointed by the administration, the influence of the warriors continued to wane. No future Arusha age-set attained the fame of Talala; joint activities by Arusha and Meru warriors ceased; and Meru slowly withdrew from the Maasai age-set system altogether until they refused to join with Arusha to initiate Terito in the mid-1920s.

Chiefs and headmen appointed by the Germans after 1900 saw their potential power and influence increase as a result of their newly institutionalized authority, their support from the colonial administration, and their ability to use their new-found power to gain wealth. At the same time as power and status were shifting from the warriors to the chiefs, the means of attaining them were also shifting from criteria based on age, respect, wealth in cattle and bananas, and the size of one's following to those based on education, affiliation with the government and mission, and wealth gained from wages.

While the means of achieving power were changing, the ways in which it was deployed through wealth in cattle and social investments were frequently similar, thus

83

obscuring the more fundamental changes taking place under the surface of Arusha and Meru social relations. Chiefs became known for their large cattle herds and number of wives and, following the bumper harvest of 1907, there was a spate of 'ox-hangings' around the mountain as wealthy men competed to see who could distribute the most meat to their friends and followers so that they might be 'lauded by the people'.[18] Such changes were gradual at first, scarcely noticeable during much of the German period, but they would become more prominent in the years to come.

Chiefs' newly-enhanced power and status did not come without costs, however. Chiefs and headmen were frequently unpopular with their followers as they became increasingly answerable to their German patrons, losing their own legitimacy in the process. Just as the Germans quickly abandoned appointing Meru chiefs from the royal Kaaya clan, so all chiefs came to owe their office to the whim of the government rather than to whatever influence or status they possessed locally. Increasingly, one's patrons became more important than one's clients, as chiefs came to have a share in the power of others, rather than exercising it on their own.

The German administration, like the conquest that had established it, was viewed as harsh and unjust by Meru and Arusha. They called Lt Küster 'Bwana Fisi', or Mr Hyena. The missionaries thought that his successor, Baron Ludwig Friedrich von Reitzenstein, was 'kindly' and 'well-disposed toward the natives', respected by them because he allowed 'no idling or disobedience from his chiefs or their underlings', held court according to local custom while making 'sure it was not spoiled by the long-wind-edness of the natives', and successfully built roads without resorting to the feared *kiboko* (whip).[19] The missionaries' notion of respect gained by the firm exercise of authority was not the same as that held by Arusha and Meru, however, who objected to the continued use of corvée (unpaid labour) for public works, the collection of taxes, the corruption of chiefs and, most of all, the seizure of precious land for South African and German settlers.[20] In their exercise of unfettered power and their continued reliance on military force and coerced labour, German officials must not have appeared to be very different from the predatory trading chiefs who had preceded them elsewhere in the Pangani Valley.

Taxes and 'Solid Regulated Work'

As Meru and Arusha grievances concerning taxes, chiefs, labour, and land make clear, concerns of the German administration soon shifted from political control to economic exploitation. One of their first official acts was to impose a head tax of three rupees on all adult males. The equivalent of more than a month's wages, the head tax was delib-erately designed to force Africans out of the domestic economy to work for wages for the government and private farmers.

---

[18] *Mangi* Sambegye had ten wives and Sabaya fourteen. Ittameier, *ELMB*, 62 (1907), 561; Blumer, *ELMB*, 64 (1909), 170; Weishaupt, *ELMB*, 67 (1912), 484.

[19] Krause, *ELMB*, 60 (1905), 18. See also Boyes, *Company*, 169; Fokken, *ELMB*, 60 (1905), 37.

[20] Arusha and Meru Historical Traditions.

Forced labour on caravans, public works, and plantations had accompanied German rule from the very beginning of conquest. Initially Arusha and Meru were drafted to work on the *boma* and roadworks as part of their punishment for opposing conquest, but the German administration continued to use corvée thereafter as a means of extracting labour from the local economy when the head tax alone proved insufficient. Those who were not otherwise employed by either the missions or settlers were continually threatened with mandatory labour. The ability of the missions to employ labour cheaply, for example, was related directly to the demands of the government. Brother Fickert reported in 1902 that the mission was inundated with more people seeking work than it needed due to local people's 'desire to be free of their corvée for the government, which naturally benefits us in our work'. Faced with a shortage of labour in 1907, the mission gave their workers identity cards which they could show to chiefs and government officials to gain exemption from government levies. Later the government itself introduced work cards that required all men to work at least thirty days for Europeans every three months or face mandatory government labour.[21]

Meru and Arusha took advantage of the alternatives to corvée that were offered during the early years of colonial rule but, after enjoying the bumper harvest in 1907, they became much more reluctant to enter the labour market. Nor were they inclined to accept the low wages that corvée was designed to maintain. While the missionaries paid their workers and pupils, providing cash for taxes and an exemption from government labour, they were careful to call their payments to pupils living allowances, not wages. They soon found, however, that pupils expected to be paid to attend school, and as increasing opportunities for work at better wages for other Europeans grew, students agitated for increased payments and left when their demands were not met. According to one student:

> When we work for another European, we receive our pay; with you, we earn nothing, so you may as well not hope that we will come to school. Our people made out earlier without school and were not dumb — we'll do just as well without school.[22]

The missionaries were forced to raise their allowances from 2.5 rupees to 3 rupees per month in 1906 to compete more closely with the 4 rupees the plantations were then paying.[23]

Clearly some Meru and Arusha were becoming more willing to work for wages and beginning to respond to wage rates as an incentive, but most remained reluctant to work for Europeans at all, and the plantations were increasingly forced to rely on migrant labour recruited from central Tanzania. Rev. Fokken thought Arusha and Meru were reluctant to work because they lacked economic incentive and so worked only to earn enough cash to pay their taxes:

> The young people would rather smear their bodies in red earth and oil, braid their hair, and

---

[21] Fickert, *ELMB*, 58 (1903), 41; Krause, 60 (1905), 17; Fokken, *ELMB*, 64 (1909), 86; 68 (1913), 569; Jonathan Kidale (AHT 7).

[22] Blumer, *ELMB*, 66 (1911), 363.

[23] Fokken, *ELMB*, 62 (1907), 411; 68 (1913), 571; Ittameier, *ELMB*, 64 (1909), 38; Blumer, *ELMB*, 66 (1911), 385.

walk around the countryside, go from one dance to another, and engage in other such idle activities. And why should they work? They come one or two months to work occasionally, earn a few rupees, buy a sheep with them, and put away three rupees for the time 'Bwana Mkubwa' collects the property tax. They have no further cares.

For Meru and Arusha, however, wage labour took them away from their own fields and was desirable only when they needed to recapitalize the domestic economy from 1900 to 1907. Arusha and Meru were also selective in the types of work they would undertake, as Fokken further observed when he noted that Arusha particularly hated carrying head loads, while Meru were willing to engage in the task with added compensation.[24]

Missionaries had an ambivalent attitude to work themselves. On the one hand, they preached the gospel of work as necessary to a Christian life, insisted on paying labour, and continually stressed the necessity of training their converts in good work habits. As Schachschneider complained:

> … without solid, regulated work, they lapse into the lazy life of the plantations, and only too quickly does the proverb 'Idleness is the root of all vices' show itself to be true. Such was the case with the Christian Petro.[25]

On the other hand, they feared that Meru and Arusha would become corrupted by money. Ittameier noted: 'Profits are increasing and the standard of living is rising; may our natives not forgo the eternal in favour of the earthly!'[26] A year later, his fears seemed to be realized:

> People have come into money and livestock, but this inspires greed in them and takes up all thoughts. Rupees, cattle and goats are the solutions for the large and small. Thus there exists little desire to turn the senses from the earthly to the eternal.[27]

Arusha and Meru had different views of 'work' from those held by the missionaries. Meru and Arusha were independent farmers whose primary goals were to produce enough bananas, annual crops, and milk and meat to feed their own families and provide a small surplus. Work clearing forest lands to establish one's homestead and fields conveyed rights in the land itself, unlike work clearing settler's land which brought only meagre wages. Hard-working farmers enjoyed abundant crops, increased family wealth, and gained the respect of their neighbours, while wage labour earned few rewards beyond the cash needed to pay hated government taxes or to buy newly available consumer goods.

During hard times, however, cash could be used to buy foodstuffs or to obtain cattle to rebuild one's herds. Labour supplies were thus abundant during the difficult years from 1900 to 1907, when Arusha and Meru sought cash to rebuild their economies ravaged by conquest, drought, and disease, but they declined rapidly in the aftermath of the abundant harvest of 1907 that signalled economic recovery.[28] Thereafter people

---

[24] Fokken, *ELMB*, 62 (1907), 410–11.

[25] Schachschneider, *ELMB*, 63 (1908), 326. See also Ittameier, *ELMB*, 62 (1907), 560; Fokken, *ELMB*, 59 (1904) 452; 66 (1911), 492; 68 (1913), 567.

[26] Ittameier, *ELMB*, 62 (1907), 561.

[27] Ittameier, *ELMB*, 64 (1909), 37.

[28] Fickert, *ELMB*, 58 (1903), 41; Ittameier, *ELMB*, 62 (1907), 561; Fokken, 62 (1907), 410–411; 64 (1909), 86.

sought, quite rationally, to spend as little time as possible earning whatever money they required for taxes or consumer goods while devoting the bulk of their efforts to developing their own fields.

Even though wage labour was generally seen by Arusha and Meru as an impediment to progress, then, cash did come to have increasing utility within the domestic economy during the German period. Meru and Arusha used cash to rebuild their herds in the aftermath of conquest and natural disaster, buying stock from Nyamwezi and Swahili traders in Arusha. Local accumulators similarly converted cash into stock to deploy in social investments, such as large feasts or bridewealth, to gain status and dependants. Men such as Sambegye or Lairumbe used their official positions as chiefs to acquire wealth which they used to build their herds and enhance their own personal followings of wives, children, and other dependants. Early mission adherents, such as Lazaros Laiser or Simeon Bene in Arusha, also turned their new status as educated men and as Christians into traditional forms of influence via their leadership of the Church and government.

Arusha and Meru were quick to develop other ways of earning cash as well. Women sold foodstuffs to townsmen, the missions, and the growing numbers of workers on the European farms, while the cattle trade became popular among men, especially in the western parts of Arusha bordering the plains. Coffee was first introduced as a cash crop by the mission on its own properties in 1902, and by 1907 early converts and farm workers began planting coffee themselves. Meru and Arusha were thus increasingly able to meet their needs for cash without diverting a significant amount of labour from the domestic economy, while at the same time they used cash to expand their own economy to meet their own increasing needs.[29]

It is impossible to say precisely what impact wage labour and the cash economy had on labour relations within Arusha and Meru societies. Young men were the ones most likely to work for wages, whether for government, the mission, or private employers, but since warriors had not been major contributors of domestic labour during the closing decades of the nineteenth century, their outside labour probably did not result in significant losses to the domestic economy. And as workers returned to the domestic economy after 1907, young men increasingly worked on their own farms. Wage labour or participation in the cash economy probably did not have much impact on the sexual division of labour either, as men continued to clear new fields and tend bananas while women raised annual crops and sold their own surpluses. More significant changes would follow.

The 'Iron Ring' of Land Alienation

If the threat of colonial labour demands to the domestic economy was largely deflected, however, large-scale land alienation fundamentally threatened Arusha and Meru long-

---

[29] Krause, *ELMB*, 58 (1903), 138; Fokken, *ELMB*, 59 (1904), 453; Boyes, *Company*, 170; Schachschneider and Ittameier, *ELMB*, 62 (1907), 168, 560, 562; Luanda, 'Commercial Farming,' 154; Lodenaga Lotisia (AHT 3).

term survival and would become the central economic and political issue in both societies over the course of the twentieth century. The German administration's attitudes to land were contradictory at best, favouring European settlement in some areas, while sharply restricting it in favour of African smallholder production in others. The cool and fertile highlands of northeastern Tanzania was one of the favoured settlement areas, but the conquest of Usambara had led to such an orgy of land grabbing by European speculators that the government started in 1895 to restrict alienation to leasehold grants of unoccupied land and required leaseholders to clear and develop 5 to 10 per cent of their land annually. From Shambaa, the settlers moved on to Kilimanjaro and Meru, but there was little unoccupied land on the congested mountain sides themselves, and settlers were forced to accept lower land around the bases of the mountains, rapidly ringing each with a chain of European farms and plantations.[30]

The Arusha *boma* and township were themselves placed in the midst of one of the most densely settled areas of Arusha, and Mount Meru became one of the few areas in Tanzania where the administration actively promoted European settlement through schemes designed to attract both small- and large-scale farmers. The first was the settlement of one hundred Afrikaner families who had driven their ox wagons north after the Boer War, arriving in Arusha in 1902:

> The men – strong, wide figures with long beards, crushed down hats, serious, but in many ways good-meaning facial features; the women with large bonnets; the children like small farm boys and girls at home; the heavy covered wagons; the beautiful dogs; in short, just as one has seen it so manifold in pictures.[31]

The administration welcomed the Afrikaner pioneers and gave each family 1,000 hectares on the northern slopes of Mount Meru between Oldonyo Sambu and Engare Nanyuki in the hopes that they would develop this semi-arid region on the fringes of Maasailand. They hoped in vain, however. Within a few years many Afrikaners had either moved on to Kenya or returned south, while those that remained preferred to hunt or keep livestock and cultivated only small gardens of vegetables and maize.[32]

In 1906 the government sponsored German peasants to develop small-holdings at Leganga on southeastern Meru between Usa River and Maji ya Chai. Several Evangelical Lutheran settlers had already become established west of Arusha town when the government decided to settle German refugees from southern Russia. Forty people were recruited at a cost of 7,000 marks each, and each family was given fifty hectares to grow wheat, maize, and vegetables. Far from being experienced peasant farmers, however, the recruits were poorly-educated, unskilled labourers who were unable to adjust to farming under colonial conditions, and the scheme collapsed almost immediately. The first settlers were already on their way home as the last arrived. The German-Russians were replaced in 1908–9 by Swabian Germans from Palestine in the hopes that they would adapt more readily to colonial conditions, and Leganga soon became known as

[30] John Iliffe, *Tanganyika under German Rule, 1905–1912* (Cambridge, 1969), 56–66, 118–41; idem., *Modern History*, 126–7, 142–5.

[31] Krause, *ELMB*, 6 (1905), 19.

[32] Weishaupt, *ELMB*, 67 (1912), 461; Iliffe, *German Rule*, 59–60; Luanda, 'Commercial Farming,' 46–9.

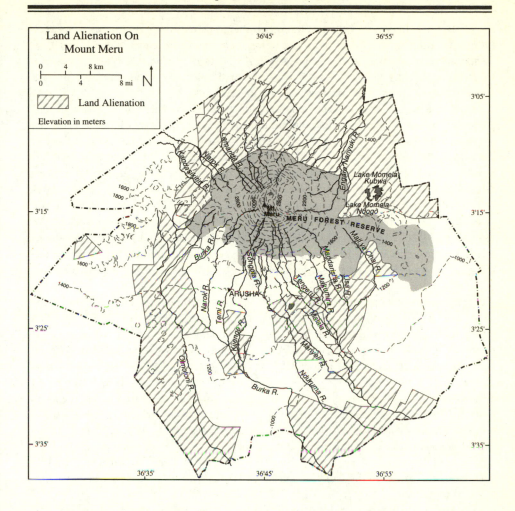

Map 4.1 Land Alienation on Mount Meru

the 'Palestiner Reservat'. The government then opened up larger grants between Nduruma and Usa River and recruited Reich Germans to develop them. By 1910, 89 farms had been allocated to Germans. Of 195,907 hectares of land suitable for crops and livestock in Arusha District, 23,700 hectares, or 12 per cent, was alienated overall, though most of it remained unsurveyed and undeveloped.[33]

The result was a disastrous restriction of land available for Meru and Arusha. Alienated land formed an almost solid band around the heavily populated slopes of southern Meru, effectively restricting Arusha or Meru expansion down the mountain and on to the plains. The administration also blocked upward movements by establishing a forest reserve above 1,600 metres, at that time the upper limits of Meru and Arusha settlement. Arusha and Meru would effectively push the northern boundary up to 1,800 metres before the British effectively closed it in the 1920s, but the implications for the future were clear: 'An "iron ring" of alienated land was clamped around the native lands on the mountain.'[34] With expansion blocked, Arusha and Meru could only turn in on themselves, occupying vacant hillsides and pastures on the slopes, while turning their political grievances outwards against the settlers and colonial authorities in the years to come.

The imposition of German rule on Mount Meru thus fundamentally challenged the Meru and Arusha peoples' social, political, and economic practices and beliefs. The hierarchical, military administration of the *boma* threatened the fluid nature of local politics – in which wealthy patrons built their influence by feasting their clients, sharing cattle with them, and marrying their daughters – and led to the rise of a new class of local leaders beholden to their colonial overlords. 'Work' for cash wages posed a threat to continued family production and values, and land alienated to German settlers challenged the social contract in which every family had a right to its own *kihamba* or *engisaka*. In short, German political economy premised on 'solid regulated work', capitalist production for the market, and authoritarian politics conflicted sharply with Arusha and Meru moral economies based on everyone's rights to sufficient land to support one's family, to the fruits of one's own labour, and to the exercise of social and political influence.

The two world views were not irreconcilably opposed to one another, however, and the peoples of Mount Meru proved adept at using colonial means to achieve their own ends. Thus chiefs used their new administrative powers to increase their local influence by acquiring numerous cattle and wives, while labourers similarly invested their wages in social as well as productive capital. In the process, new social syntheses began to emerge as people re-evaluated their own practices and beliefs in the light of new opportunities. Such simultaneous subversion of the colonial order and transformation of their own would continue throughout the period of colonial rule and beyond.

[33] Krause, Schachschneider, and Fokken, *ELMB*, 59 (1904), 395; 62 (1907), 166–8, 412; 63 (1908), 328; 64 (1909), 87; 65 (1910), 153–5; Weishaupt, *ELMB*, 67 (1912), 504; Luanda, 'Commercial Farming,' 42, 50–1.

[34] Tanganyika Territory, *Report of the Arusha-Moshi Lands Commission* (Dar es Salaam, 1947), 17. See also A.E. Kitching's analysis of the impact of German land alienation, 'Memo on Native Land in Arusha District', 3 December 1930 (TNA: 25369), as discussed in Chapter 9.

5

Establishment of the Mission

1902–16

The Leipzig missionaries on Kilimanjaro had looked forward to the day when they could redeem their 'property at Meru, rightfully gained through purchase and consecrated with the blood of our Brothers' ever since the events of 1896.[1] With the establishment of the German *boma* in Arusha in 1901, they immediately petitioned the government to be allowed to re-establish their mission in Meru. Captain Johannes felt that the situation on Meru was still too unsettled and repeatedly refused their requests to return. Following his transfer to Dar es Salaam and the safe ascent of Mount Meru by a German scientist, however, the missionaries finally gained reluctant government approval. Rev. Arno Krause and Brother Karl Fickert set out from Machame on 22 February 1902. Stopping at Arusha on the way, they arrived at the original mission site in Akeri on 24 February, but finding the area deserted, they continued on to Nkoaranga, the home of the current Meru chief, Nyereu. Nyereu's wife welcomed them with large quantities of food, while Nyereu and other elders greeted them kindly.

After returning his hosts' greetings, Krause recalled the story of his martyred brothers. He explained that he had come only to teach the Word of God, carefully re-assuring them that he did not desire stock, women, or children or intend to ask people to work for nothing. The chief welcomed the missionaries, but he insisted that they abandon their plans to resettle the site at Akeri where Ovir and Segebrock had been killed. The surrounding area had been abandoned after the murders; people were afraid to go there, he explained, and it was still subject to possible attack by Arusha. Krause reluctantly agreed with Nyereu, and he accepted the chief's offer of a lush 24-hectare site on the Mbembe River, slightly to the north of his own, in exchange for gifts worth 48 rupees. The two Germans settled in, confident of their safety, despite rumours that Arusha and Meru warriors still vowed to drive the Europeans from Meru.[2]

[1] Müller, *ELMB*, 52 (1897), 19.
[2] Krause, *ELMB*, 57 (1902), 215–18, 276–84, 397–400; Weishaupt, *ELMB*, 67 (1912), 462. Since the early history of the mission is told in some detail elsewhere, I intend to cover only the main themes here. See relevant issues of *ELMB*; C.T.S., Nasari, 'The History of the Lutheran Church among the Wameru

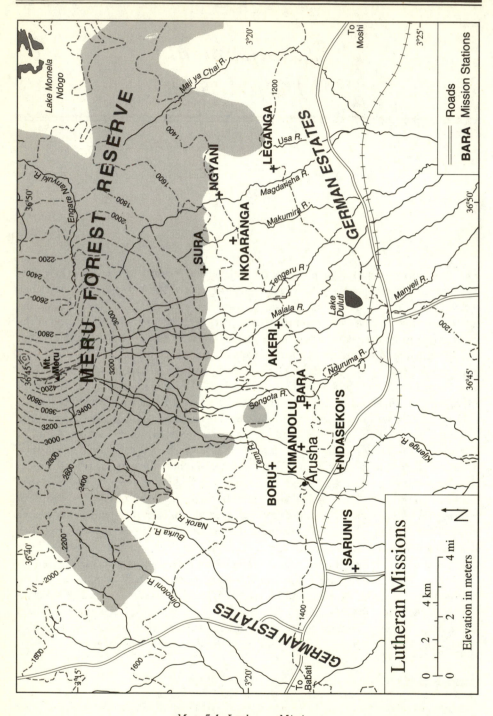

Map 5.1 Lutheran Missions

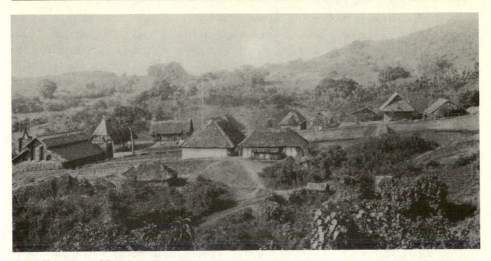

5.1 Nkoaranga Mission (J. Schanz *Am Füsse der Bergriesen OstAfrikas* 177)

Brother Fickert, the mission craftsman, immediately set to work clearing the bush, digging a canal from the river, and building a house and small chapel. There was no shortage of workers during these hard times, and by the end of June he had finished the main house, a kitchen, a barn, and a dormitory for boarding students. In the meantime, Rev. Krause settled down to learning the Meru dialect so that he could begin preaching in it as soon as possible. He started a school in April with ten pupils, most of them mission servants, and preached his first sermon in Meru at the beginning of May. By July Krause had established a boarding school and begun to hold services for 100 to 150 people on Sundays in the newly consecrated chapel. Over the course of the following year, the number of pupils at Nkoaranga grew to over 70, and Krause established day-schools at Ngyani and Akeri, thus fulfilling his promise to his dead colleagues to resume their work there. In the meantime, Fickert completed a new larger church, a stone workshop, two dormitories, a large cattle barn, and a 350-tree coffee plantation. The mission was growing rapidly, but, Krause lamented, there were still no candidates for baptism. Another year passed before the first eleven catechumens presented themselves in July 1904, and yet another before they were finally baptized in June 1905. The next two followed in 1907.[3]

Things were proceeding sufficiently smoothly by February 1903, however, to consider establishing a second station in Arusha. In spite of the difficulties of learning Maa, a totally new language, the Lutherans were still concerned that the Catholics might pre-empt them. Krause and Fickert negotiated with Chief Sabaya for a 20-hectare site in

([2] cont.) (Varwa) of Tanzania' (BD, Makumira, 1980); S.E. Nnko, 'The Interdenominational Conflicts within the Meru District of the E.L.C.T. Northern Diocese' (Dip. in Theology, Makerere, 1980); R. Mbise et al., 'Historia ya Kazi ya Injili Meru kuanzia mwaka 1895–1979 kwa Jubilii ya Miaka 75 (Akeri, 1979).

[3] Krause (and Fickert), *ELMB*, 58 (1903), 12–16, 38–41, 137–41, 316–18, 338–42; 59 (1904), 94–98, 121–3; Weishaupt, *ELMB*, 67 (1912), 462–3.

Boru, three-quarters of an hour up the mountain from the *boma*, and on 20 June 1904 Rev. Hermann Fokken and Brother Luckin arrived from Chaga with First Lieutenant Reitzenstein to lay claim to the new station. They were welcomed by Sabaya and the Arusha spokesmen with gifts of cornmeal and bananas. The chief remained friendly and visited them daily, while Fokken was careful to stress that they had no intention of exploiting people who helped them.

> We take advantage of this contact with the chief, of course, only insofar as it is compatible with our duties. It does not occur to us, for example, to demand that the chief give us a number of people to work, either for nothing or for a small tip.... we say 'the worker is worth his wage', and each person who works for us is paid for his work.[4]

Since some Arusha were already acquainted with the mission, Fokken and Luckin set to work at once. Fokken conducted his first service on 25 June, attracting 400 people, and immediately opened a school with 31 pupils, seven of them boarders. As in Meru, the two missionaries divided the work between them. Rev. Fokken slowly learned the Maa language, preached sermons, taught in the school, and established day-schools at the two other chiefs' headquarters in Burka. In the meantime, Brother Luckin built the mission complex of houses, schools, and church, imposing a formal European order of straight paths and stone houses surrounded by grass lawns and flower gardens on the rank African bush, thus echoing Fokken's attempts to instil a tidy moral order in the minds of his students. They had no trouble getting workers, and the station soon became a major building industry composed of foresters, pit-sawyers, carpenters, tile-makers, stone-cutters, bricklayers, and limestone-burners.

Fokken, like many Europeans before and after, was immediately smitten by the Maasai: 'It is a sheer pleasure to work with these young, powerful, often beautiful warriors with plaited hair.' The schools, meanwhile, suffered their ups and downs. Chief Ndasikoi looked after his school and attendance remained fairly regular, but Saruni neglected the building and drafted the students into work details, forcing Fokken to threaten periodically to close it. Within six months, Fokken had attracted his first seven candidates for baptism from the boarding school, but their paths to becoming Christians proved to be rocky ones. Four were subsequently dismissed for demanding higher allowances and not taking their studies seriously; another was held back as apathetic; and one died just before the lone remaining candidate, Paulos, was baptized in April 1907, over two years after starting his studies. Four more were baptized a year and a half later in a group that included Simeon Bene, soon to become one of the most prominent men of his generation.[5]

In spite of the flurry of activity at both missions, then, they had produced only eighteen Christians between them after nearly six years of dedicated work, and the missionaries feared they were in danger of losing some of these as their young converts

---

4 Fokken, *ELMB*, 59 (1904), 452. See also Krause, *ELMB*, 58 (1903), 318; 59 (1904), 391; Fokken, *ELMB*, 59 (1904), 450–3; 63 (1908), 246–47; Weishaupt, *ELMB*, 67 (1912), 534.

5 The other three Arusha baptized were Johannes, Eliahu, and Lukas. Fokken, *ELMB*, 59 (1904), 450–3, 540–2; 60 (1905), 37–40, 216–19, 391–4, 556–7; 62 (1907), 190–2, 382–5, 409–13; 63 (1908), 60–2, 145–9, 245–8, 374–9; 64 (1909), 84–7, 167–73.

struggled to reintegrate themselves into their communities. Krause and Fokken saw themselves engaged in a constant battle against ignorance and deceit. The mission regulars, workers and boarding pupils alike, were all paid servants of the mission, and they often refused to appear if they were not paid. Others promised to come, but they attended only sporadically if at all.[6] As Krause despaired:

> Since there is no compulsory education here, this small community stops coming for any number of reasons: sometimes it's too cold, sometimes it's raining, sometimes they go into the steppe in order to trade meat for bananas with the travelling livestock traders, etc. That they come now and then for lessons is because they hope to receive some cloth from me.[7]

'A Cabin of God in a Field of Blood'

Arusha and Meru were reluctant to join the missions because the missionaries alienated them from their families and friends. Strict separation of mission adherents from 'pagans' was, in fact, conscious mission policy as the missionaries sought to create a new society governed by new loyalties, beliefs, values, and practices. Their primary strategy was to enlist young boys, and later girls, in boarding schools, where they were isolated from their families and friends and consciously re-socialized into the missionaries' own practices and beliefs. They were taught Bible history and geography, catechism, writing, and arithmetic in the mornings, while in the afternoons they were encouraged to develop good work habits and moral behaviour by working on the mission farm. Boys were warned not to associate with their age-mates and prohibited from dancing, drinking, or joining age-set ceremonies. Girls had to forsake their dress and jewellery for plain smocks and were similarly enjoined from taking part in local social activities.[8] As one Christian recalled:

> In the early days there was an insistence on a complete separation between Christians and followers of traditional religion. Young Christian converts were told that, while they might greet their relatives and friends when they met them, they should not linger, but move down the path. On no account should they attend any ceremonies or festivities involving any non-Christian religious practice.[9]

If students left school to attend dances or family affairs, they were punished or

---

[6] Krause, *ELMB*, 58 (1903), 40; 59 (1904), 362–4; Fokken, *ELMB*, 59 (1904), 540; 62 (1907), 384, 410; Ittameier, *ELMB*, 62 (1907), 560; 64 (1909), 38; Blumer, *ELMB*, 63 (1908), 146; 66 (1911), 363, 385; Schachschneider, *ELMB*, 63 (1908), 326.

[7] Krause, *ELMB*, 57 (1902), 398.

[8] Donald C. Flatt, *Man and Deity in an African Society* (Dubuque, 1980), 288–307; Krause, *ELMB*, 59 (1904), 389; Fokken, *ELMB*, 62 (1907), 191, 410; 68 (1913), 167; Blumer, *ELMB*, 64 (1909), 170; Ittameier, *ELMB*, 64 (1909), 36; Weishaupt, *ELMB*, 67 (1912), 485; Seesemann, *ELMB*, 68 (1913), 111; Ngoilenya Wuapi (AHT 5); Eliyahu Lujas Meiliari (AHT 8).

   While the Leipzig mission sought to place Christianity within a local cultural context, according to their philosophy of *Volksmission*, they systematically challenged local values in practice. Cf. A.A. Lema, 'The Impact of the Leipzig Lutheran Mission on the People of Kilimanjaro, 1893–1920' (PhD, Dar es Salaam, 1973) and J.C. Winter, *Bruno Gutmann, 1876–1966* (Oxford, 1979).

[9] Quoted in Flatt, *Man and Deity*, 288–9.

expelled when they returned. In October 1903, almost all the students at Nkoaranga spent a night out at a community feast, leading Krause to warn them they would be punished if they left without permission again. One, Lekario, had been an excellent student, but he became sullen and defiant, before he finally ran away. Later Krause saw him at a dance, graced with jewellery and red ochre as though he had never been at the mission. Another, Mture, returned after being absent for two days but, after being punished, he ran away again. Later he returned and begged to be readmitted. Krause agreed to do so, but lowered his stipend. Nyafi was one of the earliest and brightest of the Meru students and catechumens, but he ran away a couple of years later and adopted the 'indecent ways of other natives' after his mother opposed his baptism. When he returned after a couple of weeks, Krause refused to readmit him, thus setting a pattern for students who sought to balance their own loyalties against the inflexible demands of the mission.[10]

One of the first girls to join the Arusha mission subsequently ran away and resumed her 'heathen' dress. The missionaries confiscated it when she returned, but when she prepared to run away a second time, she shed her mission frock and escaped into the night nude. Fokken despaired of getting any girls to join the mission:

> ... the girls do not want to miss their nightly dances! For they can already imagine that, just as our boarding boys are not allowed to go dancing, neither would they be granted permission for this. Nor would they be allowed to cover their upper bodies with oil and red earth and paint their faces with white earth in order to be picked up for dancing in this get-up by the young warriors any longer. If this is denied them, then they will not come to us.[11]

The missionaries also sought to prohibit polygamy, and they derided men for living off the work of their wives. Krause complained: 'When one goes through the plantations here, one meets at the most a few wives or girls tilling; the men sit together in some spot, usually drinking beer....'[12] Arusha and Meru valued polygamy because wives provided men with labour, status, and descendants, while it allowed women to share the burdens of work and child rearing. In response to Krause's admonition that they should take only one wife, a Meru man replied, 'But what should we eat?' while a wife added, 'If only one woman is with a man, she has too much work.'[13] Many opposed the missions because of the ban on polygamy. One catechumen's mother threatened: 'If you have yourself baptized and can only marry one woman, then you can no longer come to me to eat,' while a married catechumen refused baptism at the last moment in order to marry another wife.[14]

[10] Krause, *ELMB*, 59 (1904), 364–5; 60 (1905), 423; Blumer, *ELMB*, 64 (1909), 170; Schachschneider, *ELMB*, 63 (1908), 326; A.S. Mbise, 'The Evangelist: Matayo Leveriya Kaaya' in J. Iliffe (ed.), *Modern Tanzanians* (Nairobi, 1973), 30.

[11] Fokken, *ELMB*, 62 (1907), 191.

[12] Krause, *ELMB*, 58 (1903). See also Weishaupt, *ELMB*, 67 (1912), 483.

[13] Krause, *ELMB*, 59 (1904), 363.

[14] Krause, *ELMB*, 60 (1905), 17; Ittameier, *ELMB*, 62 (1907), 560; Weishaupt, *ELMB*, 67 (1912), 483. See also Mbise, 'The Evangelist', 32; B. Kaaya, 'The Planting of Christianity in Meru: Its Conflicts and Similarities with the Traditional Culture of the Meru' (Dip. in Theology, Field Work Report, Makerere, 1978), 5–7; Flatt, *Man and Deity*, 299–300.

The missionaries' assaults on Meru and Arusha values reached a climax in 1908 when young men approached the period of circumcision during which they were initiated into the next age-set. Fokken realized that circumcision was essential for advancement to warrior status and that warriorhood was the most 'treasured occupation' of Arusha and Meru young men. He also knew that the mission could scarcely disallow a practice supported by the Bible, and that as a custom, and not a religious act, it was mission policy not to interfere. Nevertheless Fokken concluded that 'Maasai-style' circumcision, together with the dancing, drinking, and feasting that accompanied it, encouraged such general immorality that the mission could not tolerate it. Inexplicably, however, he accepted 'Bantu-style' circumcision, and advocated that mission adherents be so circumcised in order to avoid the Maasai ritual. And, somewhat ironically, he never attacked female circumcision which was being conducted at the same time, and so girls continued to be circumcised in the normal Maasai fashion. Ittameier at Meru agreed with Fokken's position, and a common mission policy against Maasai circumcision for males was decreed.[15]

Most Arusha and Meru rejected Fokken's attempted compromise, however, and threatened to banish anyone who took part in the mission ceremony. In Meru the mission proceeded to circumcise its adherents before the general ceremonies to pre-empt them from doing so later. Eleven of the thirteen Christians agreed, but only four of the sixteen catechumens and fewer mission workers and pupils went along with the mission. In Arusha the missionaries waited until after the general ceremonies. All five Christians and four catechumens, two boarding pupils, and four servants chose the Christian version. Fokken had them guarded all night, lest their relatives persuade them to recant, and then exulted that eleven out of fifteen had 'turned their backs on heathendom', but this 'victory' carried a high price for both the converts and the mission. After one mother discovered her son had been circumcised by the mission, she 'cried, raged, and cursed the day of his birth'. Meru and Arusha scorned men circumcised in the mission manner as foreigners; such men subsequently had difficulty finding women willing to marry them, and they were forced to sit in meetings with the women and children. Attendance at mission schools and services plummeted, taking more than two years to recover, and then was set back again when circumcision resumed in 1910.[16]

The mission policy of separation and cultural intolerance was reciprocated by many Meru and Arusha, who ostracized and rejected those who joined the mission. One Arusha Christian recalled that early Christians

> ... were treated as rubbish. People despised them as people who were poor and lost.... They were forgotten. They were not wanted anymore because they had brought dishonour to the family. They were dogs. They were dead.... The *murran* taunted them and beat them.... When I got married people despised me. They would pass me working in my *shamba* and throw rocks at me, saying I dishonoured men by working in the *shamba* like a woman.[17]

---

[15] Fokken, *ELMB*, 63 (1908), 374–9. Neither Fokken nor Ittameier explain what they took the differences between 'Maasai-style' and 'Bantu-style' circumcision to be.

[16] Fokken, *ELMB*, 63 (1908), 374–9; Ittameier, *ELMB*, 64 (1909), 37–8; Blumer, *ELMB*, 66 (1911), 385; Flatt, *Man and Deity*, 289, 298–9.

[17] Loingoruaki Meshili (AHT 6). See also Eliyahu Lujas Meiliari (AHT 8).

Terms like these – rubbish, poor and lost, forgotten, dogs, dead, and calling men women – were about as powerful an anti-social litany as Arusha or Meru could imagine, and they echo through the accounts of the first Christians. Mission adherents were characterized by the foul smell of mission soap, in contradistinction to sweet-smelling red ochre:

> After we left [someone's house], they would wash the chair we had sat on and smear it with red ochre to remove the smell of soap. When the children saw us coming, they ran away and hid....[18]

Families opposed their children joining the missions and frequently beat them or rejected them when they came home. 'Mothers do not want to give up their girls,' Fokken observed. 'They have to work for their mothers, till the fields, gather wood from the forest, bring water from the river, etc.'[19] Women cried, shaved their heads, and mourned the loss of children who left, just as they would for children who died.[20]

The missions' attacks on polygamy, circumcision, and the celebrations accompanying initiation struck at the heart of Arusha and Meru social and moral values. Marriage was a primary means of joining and building large prosperous families, and polygamous families were notably more prosperous than others. Polygamous males had numerous offspring and large farms, and they enjoyed widespread respect. Wives in polygamous marriages shared the burdens of work and child-rearing with one another, while participating in the more vibrant social life of large families. And initiation was the high point of a young man's – and his mother's – life, allowing him to become an esteemed warrior and thereafter to advance to respected elderhood through his progressive socialization in values associated with manliness. Initiation, thus, was critical if young men were to become properly socialized adults, just as it was for young women if they were to become adult wives, mothers, and elders.[21] In becoming Christian, then, Meru or Arusha risked not just social ostracism; they risked not being considered Meru or Arusha at all.

The First Christians

In view of the events of October 1896 and the missionaries' and, subsequently, local peoples' antagonistic attitudes towards one another, it is a wonder that the missions attracted any followers at all. But conditions had changed since 1896, as Krause was well aware:

> At that time the Waro [Meru] owned livestock; but not now; at that time they had not yet felt the power of the German government, but now they do to a rather great degree; at that time they knew nothing of the value of the rupee, but now it is different.[22]

[18] Loingoruaki Meshili (AHT 6).
[19] Fokken, *ELMB*, 62 (1907), 191.
[20] Blumer, *ELMB*, 67 (1912), 112; Mbise, 'The Evangelist,' 30, 37; Ngole ole Njololoi (AHT 4); Eliyahu Lujas Meiliari (AHT 8); Mesiaki Kilevo, personal communication.
[21] Paul Spencer, 'Becoming Maasai: Being in Time' in Thomas Spear & Richard Waller (eds), *Being Maasai* (London: 1993), 140–56.
[22] Krause, *ELMB*, 59 (1904), 98.

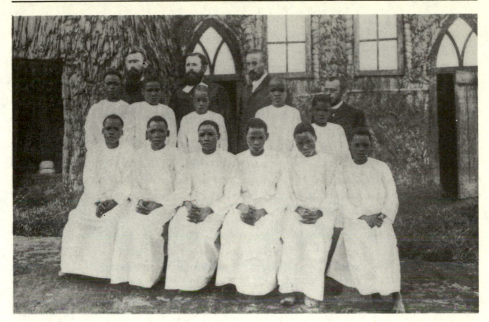

5.2 Missionaries and catechumens (J. Schanz *Am Füsse der Bergriesen OstAfricas* 172)

Meru and Arusha knew this too, and many were initially attracted to the missions by the prospect of wages, livestock, or security that would help them recover their earlier fortunes, as Krause further noted:

> The blacks look to us for many things: work in order to earn rupees so they can buy women, material, and animals; protection from their tormentors; medicine for their sicknesses; but about that which is most essential, no one has asked.[23]

Wages and material goods were among the earliest incentives. The missions had little difficulty getting workers interested in earning wages and exemption from the hated corvée until the abundant harvest of 1907 signalled Arusha and Meru economic recovery. Boarding pupils insisted on being paid competitive wages to attend school and left when they were not. Becoming a steady mission worker or pupil usually involved making a future commitment to Christianity. The missions got nearly all their early converts from these two groups, and they fired workers who were only interested in pay. The missionaries were also continually asked for gifts of cloth, food, and money, and were careful to restrict their Christmas gifts to those already affiliated with the mission. People offered to care for mission livestock, on the understanding that they could keep some of the offspring. Finally, the mission soon became the principal source for obtaining the most valuable means of earning cash of all, coffee, and Christians soon became its most prominent growers.[24]

[23] Krause, *ELMB*, 59 (1904), 362.
[24] Krause, *ELMB*, 57 (1902), 282, 398; 58 (1903), 139; 59 (1904), 362; 60 (1905), 445–6; Fickert, *ELMB*, 58 (1903), 41; Blumer, *ELMB*, 63 (1908), 146; 66 (1911), 362–3, 385; Ittameier, *ELMB*, 64 (1909), 38; Jonathan Kidale (AHT 7); Japhet Ayo (MHT 4).

All the mission students, catechumens, and converts were young men and women, people likely to be attracted to the new forms of knowledge the missions offered and the new opportunities open to educated Christians in the recently established colonial order. Three of the first Meru converts became the first African teachers in the mission's schools, and others soon followed. Of 69 adult male Christians in Meru in 1912, 38 worked for the mission, three were in seminary, and 14 worked for other Europeans. Many of the other early converts found lifelong careers in mission or government service, and Simeon Bene and Lazaros Laiser ultimately rose to become Chief and head of the Lutheran Church in Arusha respectively.[25]

Material factors were not the only ones drawing Arusha and Meru to the missions, however. Sick people unable to be cured by normal means were also attracted to the missions, and those who recovered frequently became committed Christians. Krause provided a case study:

> Another sick child was brought to us a few days ago.... The little boy was quite emaciated and so weak that he could not even stand any more; he was feverish and complained of sharp pains in his body. The sickness had already lasted more than three months, and all magic on the part of the father had produced no results.... Soon we came to realize that the boy had worms; a cure was introduced, which soon showed favourable results. In the middle of the cure the old man returned and wanted to take the boy back home... to make sacrifices to the spirits so that the spell would disappear from his body. The boy, however, did not want to return home, but stayed with us.... I used this case to show... our boarding pupils the foolishness of their superstition. I suggested to them how stupid it is to think every sickness to be a spell and how even more foolish it is to want to call help by making sacrifices to the spirits. The sick boy would certainly have died, had he stayed longer at home. The means of dealing with sickness given by God are good care, medicine, and prayer.[26]

Meru and Arusha would have agreed on the last point: care, medicine, and appeals to spirits who caused illness were indeed the components of any successful cure. While the missionaries constantly ridiculed Meru and Arusha for believing that spiritual forces were responsible for causing illness and complained that people treated them simply as healers of last resort, they employed healing prayers themselves to demonstrate the superior efficacy of the Christian faith, their popularity waxing or waning depending on whether their patients recovered or not. When a young girl was cured and sought to remain at the mission against her father's wishes, Rev. Leonard Blumer asserted: 'we had a certain right to her'.

Nor were the mission's cures that different from Meru or Arusha ones. When Krause himself became severely ill in 1906, the mission doctor doused and sweated him with baths and compresses. In a similar case, Blumer treated a pneumonia patient with camphor, baths, packing, and wine. Sweating was a common treatment, as the missionaries sought to purge the body of ill substances, thus paralleling local beliefs. The missionaries offered 'health prayers', and Christian converts continued to believe that illness had a moral as well as a physical dimension; as shown when the early Arusha

[25] Schachschneider, *ELMB*, 68 (1913), 517; Mbise, 'Kazi,' 6.
[26] Krause, *ELMB*, 58 (1903), 39–40.

Christian, Simeon Bene, wrote to Fokken that he had sinned grievously (by shopping on Sunday) and had become sick as a result.[27] At one point Fokken himself feared that he would be held morally responsible if the chapel collapsed and hurt anyone. 'We still live in a completely heathen country,' he remarked. 'Should the chapel collapse as a result of a strong storm during one of our gatherings, we would have a hard time taking responsibility.'[28] The mission's prayers were thus taken as seriously as its medicines, and Arusha and Meru could have been excused for thinking the missionaries disingenuous as they sought cures for their ailments.

In the aftermath of the environmental and political crises of the 1890s and the apparent failures of Arusha and Meru means of moral control, some of Talala's heirs were also attracted to the wider moral and social teachings of the missionaries, including the story of Abraham and his huge herds of livestock. Girls and boys fleeing to the mission to avoid unwanted marriages or unhappy homes sought escape from the old social order, while others were attracted to the new. When Krause asked his first catechumens why they wished to become Christians, the majority responded 'they found pleasure in the Word of God'. Such an answer was, no doubt, the expected one, but many also admitted to wanting work, livestock, and exemption from mandatory labour. Another convert confessed to Fokken: 'I first came to you looking for work. But now my heart has changed and I seek from you stories of God'.[29] Mission theology was strongly evangelical, stressing individual salvation and redemption from sin, and a number of Meru and Arusha responded to the call.

Matayo Kaaya was baptized in 1907 and remained a strong Christian in spite of being treated badly by the missionaries. While he admitted that his initial motive had been to gain an education, he said that his conversion had ultimately come from fundamental questions he had regarding creation, the purpose of life, and its ultimate end. He felt the new religion supplanted fear with the feeling of peace and the promise of life after death. Simeon Bene wrote to Fokken that even though people rejected him and chided him for making less money than if he worked for other Europeans, he nevertheless was joyful in his faith and urged Fokken to use his 'beautiful tongue' to spread the good word to others. Christian festivities also became popular. Christmas services in the candle-lit churches were well attended from the beginning, and when 38 white-robed Meru were baptized in a dramatic mass ceremony in 1911, 700 non-Christians attended and contributed to the feast in a dramatic reversal of earlier opposition and boycotts.[30]

Girls and women also became increasingly drawn to the missions. Few girls attended school before 1908, a fact the missionaries attributed to their mothers' need for them to work at home and the girls' desire to be free to 'carouse' at nightly dances, especially

---

[27] Krause, *ELMB*, 58 (1903), 39–40; 60 (1905), 425; Schachschneider, *ELMB*, 62 (1907), 166; Blumer, *ELMB*, 64 (1909), 170–1; 66 (1911), 384–5; 67 (1912), 113; Simeon Bene to Fokken, 19 August 1910, quoted in Fokken, *ELMB*, 64 (1910), 558.

[28] Fokken, *ELMB*, 63 (1908), 61.

[29] Krause, *ELMB*, 58 (1903), 139–40; 59 (1904), 361–2; 60 (1905), 16–17, 390; Blumer, *ELMB*, 64 (1909), 170; Mauer, *ELMB* 66 (1911), 523–4; Weishaupt, *ELMB*, 67 (1912), 535–6; Ngoilenya Wuapi (AHT 5); Loingoruaki Meshili (AHT 6).

[30] Simeon Bene to Fokken, 19 August 1910, quoted in Fokken, *ELMB*, 64 (1910), 558; Mbise, 'The Evangelist,' 31.

during the festive periods of circumcision. By 1912, however, the day-schools were composed almost exclusively of girls, more girls were being baptized, and even a few mature women were attending baptism classes.

The reasons for increased interest by girls and women are not clear, but several factors may have influenced them. Some sought refuge from unwanted or unhappy marriages. Others brought their children to the mission health clinics and were grateful when they were cured. Wives were deeply affected if they were unable to have children, the most important social role for women, and many sought – and received – spiritual aid from the missions. Women may also have felt the pervasive sense of moral crisis more deeply, as indicated by their greater attendance at healing services. Outsiders in their husband's family, women had little status or security and thus less stake in the status quo. With greater grievances and less to lose, perhaps, women felt freer to explore new ways of thinking and behaving.[31]

The mass baptism of 1911 in Meru was a sign of things to come. Only 41 Meru had become Christians between 1905 and 1910, but 147 more were baptized from 1911 to 1916. Old day-schools were revived, new ones opened, and village chapels built. Much of the credit for the upturn belonged to the first generation of educated Christians who began to assume increasing responsibility for the day-to-day operations of the missions. Day-schools were placed under the direction of African teachers and evangelists for the first time in 1908. Of the first group baptized in Meru in 1905, Luka Kaaya, Nderingo Pallangyo, and Yohana Ndosi were sent to Marangu for further training and returned to assume responsibility for the schools at Akeri, Ngyani, and Nkoaranga, respectively. Saul, an Arusha Christian educated at Mamba and Moshi, was appointed to the main Arusha school in 1905 and to the day-school at Ndasekoi's (Kimandolu) in 1908. The schools prospered under their direction. Previously, the missionaries had only visited the out-schools two half days a week; now they were under the full-time direction of resident teachers from the community who actively recruited students and patiently overcame local opposition. Many of those who went to school or converted subsequently recall fondly the influence these early teachers had on their lives.

The shift to a greater Meru and Arusha role in the missions came just as the missions themselves were undergoing the first major changes in their personnel since they had been established. Krause was invalided to Germany in 1906 and replaced by Revs. Ittameier and Schachschneider in Meru. In 1910 Fokken was transfered to Nkoaranga to replace Schachschneider, with Blumer assuming responsibility for Arusha. Fokken returned to Arusha a year and a half later, but Blumer went home on extended sick leave early in 1912 and Fokken himself left the following year, to be replaced by Roth (see Table 5.1). Each shift broke continuity as the newcomer struggled to learn the language and become familiar with the local community.

In contrast, the first Christians formed a tightly knit cohort who had been raised together on the small mission stations, isolated and subjected to ridicule by their peers, and trained at Moshi and Marangu together. Matayo Kaaya attended Marangu with Lazaros Laiser and other Meru and Arusha Christians, where they became lifelong

---

[31] Krause, *ELMB*, 60 (1905), 425; Fokken, *ELMB*, 62 (1907), 191; Seesemann, *ELMB*, 68 (1913), 519–20.

Table 5.1 Leipzig Missionaries in Meru and Arusha

Meru (Nkoaranga, est. February 1902)

Rev. Arno Krause	1902–07
Bro. Karl Fickert	1902–?
Rev. Edward Ittameier	1905–09, 1926–37
Rev. Schachschneider	1905–10, 1912–17
Rev. Hermann Fokken	1910–11
Bro. Mauer	1910–11?
Sis. Elizabeth Seesemann	1912–14?
Sis. Friederike Steinacker	1912–?

Arusha (Boru, est. June 1904)

Rev. Hermann Fokken	1904–10, 1911–13
Bro. Luckin	1904–06
Rev. Leonard Blumer	1907–30
Rev. Roth	1911–14
Mr. Eisenschmidt	1916?
Rev. Rissman	1927–29
Rev. M. Pätzig	1930–40
Rev. J. Hohenberger	1930–40

Sources: *Evangelish–Lutherische Missionsblatt*; C.T.S. Nasari, 'The History of the Lutheran Church among the Wameru (Varwa) of Tanzania' (Makumira, 1980); R. Mbise et al, 'Historia ya Kazi ya Injili Meru kuanzia mwaka 1895–1979 kwa Jubilii ya Miaka 75,' (Akeri, 1979); Donald C. Flatt, *Man and Deity in an African Society* (Dubuque, 1980).

friends. He then served as a teacher, evangelist, and pioneering coffee farmer in Akeri and West Meru until he retired in 1947. Slowly assuming responsibility for the missions during the early 1910s, these first Christians virtually took them over when the German missionaries were interned during the First World War, and they continued to exercise leadership in Meru and Arusha, socially, politically, and economically, for the rest of the colonial period.[32]

By 1910, the first generation of educated Christians had come to form their own societies, educated together and marrying amongst themselves, thus laying the foundations for influential family dynasties to come. In Arusha converts built Swahili-style houses around the mission, where they formed 'a large family, a little community of God'. As their example spread, more conversions followed, and the mission communities began to attain permanent places within the larger societies. By 1910 the Meru congregation finally had 21 men eligible for communion, the requirement for forming their own parish meeting and electing their own leaders, and in 1911 the wider Meru community turned out when it celebrated a mass baptism and two marriages. As

[32] Fokken, *ELMB*, 60 (1905), 556–7; 64 (1909), 84–5, 169; 66 (1911), 202–3, 491–3; 68 (1913), 109–10, 567; Schachschneider, *ELMB*, 63 (1908), 327; Ittameier, *ELMB*, 94 (1909), 36–37; Blumer, *ELMB*, 64 (1909), 168–70; 66 (1911), 359–64; Nasari, 'History of the Lutheran Church', 54; Loingoruaki Meshili (AHT 6); Jonathan Kidale (AHT 7); Eliyahu Lujas Meiliari (AHT 8). For the career of an early Christian, see Mbise, 'The Evangelist', 32–7.

opportunities for educated people in the church, the administration and the Meru community continued to grow, so did the Christian communities.[33]

Such Christian communities remained firmly embedded within their wider Arusha and Meru social orders, however. The German missionaries had established separate Meru and Arusha missions, each conducted in the vernacular language, and they themselves were strongly identified with the individual missions in which they served, some for lengthy periods of time. While Arusha and Meru Christians may thus have gone to school together and become brothers in the faith, they remained members of separate mission churches – and societies – as they continue to be today. Lutheran Christianity did not transcend local ethnic identities, but it did slowly become a part of them, helping to define their modern reformulations, as we shall see.

While Christians remained only a tiny minority, they nevertheless represented some of the ways Meru and Arusha sought to come to terms with the combined moral, political, and economic crises of the turn of the century. The missions provided work, wages, and education to combat economic decline as well as physical and moral means for confronting personal and social ills. Their potential benefits were largely restricted to younger men and women – those who dared to risk social alienation – while others preferred older and seemingly more secure courses to economic security and social status. Nevertheless, the first Christians introduced a new image of educated, Christian, progressive men and women in Arusha and Meru societies to counter older images of unrestrained warriors, submissive wives, and temperate elders.

The clash between Germans, on the one hand, and Arusha and Meru, on the other, was not simply a struggle for political and economic dominance, though it was indeed that. It was also a clash between two world views held by peoples who fundamentally thought about themselves, their lives, and their histories in different ways. Meru and Arusha societies were focused around land, the men who held it, the women who worked it, the children who would inherit it, and the morality that sustained it. Cattle were their preferred means of social exchange, and with them they wove expanding networks of social relations designed to keep the social system working productively. Thus, when they faced the potential loss of their land and labour, they fought to preserve them. Later, when they lost their cattle, they used whatever means they could, including wage labour, to recover them, but when wage labour threatened their own labour supplies, they ceased working for cash. The struggle over land was the one threat they were not able to counter, and that struggle would continue throughout the colonial period.

The Germans, on the other hand, put a high reliance on political and economic dominance as they sought to capture Arusha and Meru economic production for themselves, but they also sought to remould African societies in their own image. Their priorities also included land and the labour to work it, but their preferred form of exchange was cash. Africans tilling their own fields were viewed as lazy and indolent, while work for wages on the land of others was viewed as virtuous. They sought to undercut activities that underpinned the local social order, such as dancing, drinking,

---

[33] Fokken, *ELMB*, 66 (1911) 492; 68 (1913), 135; Mauer, *ELMB*, 66 (1911), 523–4; Loingoruaki Meshili (AHT 6).

and age-set initiation, while replacing them with regulated work and Christian forbearance that upheld the new.

The struggles between the Germans and Africans over political domination, economic control, and ideological hegemony were played out continually on a number of different levels. While the German army was clearly able to impose overall political control and to place its designated candidates in positions of authority, local power and influence continued to be exercised through cattle, whether given in marriage or slaughtered for feasts. The Germans could take land, but not the labour to work it, and they were never able to subordinate Arusha and Meru economies to their own. The missionaries could convert some to Christianity, but they could not control the interpretations people made of it as they continued to address their own concerns in Arusha, Meru, *and* Christian terms. The Germans may have conquered the Arusha and Meru, but the latter continued to set their own terms, however transformed, and to subvert those imposed by their colonizers. The fact that the Germans accentuated local ethnic boundaries and identities through their administration and missions virtually ensured that they would do so.

III

Colonialism &
Agricultural Development

1916-61

6

Recolonization

The Establishment
of British Rule

German rule over Tanganyika ended abruptly during the First World War, but colonialism continued in Tanganyika for another 45 years under British rule. The initial differences between German and British colonialisms were not great, partly because the two entertained similar colonial goals and partly because the British simply sought to carry on, in their best common law tradition, what the Germans had already started. While Tanganyika had been one of Germany's most important colonies, however, it was only a minor League of Nations Mandate in Britain's vast colonial empire. British ambitions were also sharply limited by the difficulties of post-war recovery and by the Depression that followed.

Mere management was not without its problems, for contradictions that were inherent in the colonial situation continually threatened the fragile colonial social order, precariously balanced between European and African interests. Those contradictions surfaced early in the British period in a number of different areas, including local administration, tax and labour policy and, most especially, in land policy. The British implemented the policy of Indirect Rule, for example, by which colonial authorities sought to integrate 'traditional' or 'native authorities' into colonial administration in such a way as to maintain the fabric of local life while at the same time allowing colonial authorities to direct and exploit it to their own ends. In doing so, they re-enforced local identities and created new pseudo-traditional authorities and laws that neither represented the old social order nor ultimately contained the newly emerging one. By continuing and extending large-scale land alienation to settlers and becoming partially under obligation to settlers' interests regarding land, labour, and crop marketing, they provoked African resistance that slowly undermined the colonial order and led eventually to its dissolution. And in introducing a market economy and encouraging Meru and Arusha to produce for the market, they inadvertently created a situation that empowered African farmers in that resistance.

The War for Northern Tanganyika

The First World War started in East Africa when three companies of German Schutztruppe, augmented by local settlers, seized Taveta just across the Kenyan border from Kilimanjaro in August 1914. Following abortive British counter-attacks on Tanga and Moshi in November, it then settled down to a series of cross-border skirmishes for the next year and a half, as the Germans sought to disrupt the Uganda Railway north of Mount Kilimanjaro, while the British raided Moshi and the Tanga railway to the south. The British War Office refused to open a front in East Africa, however, until the fall of German Southwest Africa (Namibia) in July 1915 and the arrival of 20,000 South African troops in Kenya under the command of General Smuts that December. Cut off from their supplies, meanwhile, the Germans under Colonel von Lettow-Vorbeck were preparing for a guerrilla war, in which their vastly outnumbered forces occupied the British and Belgians in a prolonged chase around East and Central Africa for the duration of the war.

In March 1916, Smuts launched a two-pronged attack around both sides of Mount Kilimanjaro designed to trap the German forces at Moshi. One division advanced from the west through Longido to Engare Nanyuki, northeast of Mount Meru, where it paused briefly to attack German forces at Oldonyo Sambu to the west before continuing through Sanya to Moshi. The other division attacked Moshi through Taveta to the east. After briefly engaging the British forces, however, the Germans retreated to Kahe, south of Moshi, where they eluded a subsequent British attack and withdrew further south along the Tanga rail line. While the main British forces pursued the Germans south to Morogoro, others turned west towards Arusha. Finding the *boma* already abandoned, they pursued the retreating Germans south to Lolkisale where, after another brief engagement in early April, the Germans escaped towards Dodoma to the south. The war for northern Tanganyika was effectively over less than a month after it had begun.[1]

The bulk of British and German forces moved through northern Tanganyika sufficiently quickly for the war itself to have little impact on the peoples of the area. In contrast to Kenya or regions further south, for example, few Meru or Arusha were impressed as carriers or served in either army, and large-scale food requisitioning was limited to the brief period troops were in the area.

The main local impact was after the troops left. Arusha and Meru took advantage of the withdrawal of German troops and settlers to loot the *boma*, occupy abandoned farms, and clear new fields in the forest reserve. When the British authorities interned all but one of the Leipzig missionaries, the first generation of Arusha and Meru Christians assumed responsibility for their own schools and churches for the first time. According to Ittameier, who returned to Meru in 1926, the experience of the Christians was reflected more generally by all Meru and Arusha, as they discovered their own worth, while Europeans had exposed their weaknesses. Henceforth, he felt, Arusha and Meru would no longer be willing to be used as objects for the colonialists' benefit.[2] The

---

[1] John Iliffe, *A Modern History of Tanganyika* (Cambridge, 1979), 240–3; Charles Miller, *Battle for the Bundu* (London, 1974), 42–167; N.N. Luanda, 'European Commercial Farming and Its Impact on the Meru and Arusha Peoples of Tanzania, 1920–1955' (Ph.D., Cambridge, 1986), 60–4; Loingoruaki Meshili (AHT 6).

[2] 'Memorandum by the Chief Political Officer on the Administration of Occupied Territory in German East Africa,' 2/17/17 (PRO: CO691/4/10666); Iliffe, *Modern History*, 252; Luanda, 'Commercial Farming,' 65–9; Yohanes ole Kauwenara (AHT 2); Ittameier, *ELMB*, 83 (1928), 202–10.

lessons would stay with Meru and Arusha for the rest of the colonial period, during which time their determination to go their own ways would lead them to be continually characterized as 'intractable', 'stiff-necked and arrogant', and 'lawless and undisciplined' by British authorities.

Re-establishment of Colonial Rule

Valuable as the lessons were, however, Meru and Arusha soon discovered that colonialism was not yet over. They had merely exchanged one set of colonial masters for another. Britain acquired most of German East Africa as a League of Nations Mandate after the war, but British resources were so limited that colonial rule was not firmly re-established until the 1920s. Local administration lapsed during the war as German officials withdrew and were replaced by only a skeletal British military administration. British military authorities further relaxed colonial rule by interning the remaining German settlers and missionaries and eventually deporting them back to Germany. The re-establishment of effective civilian administration in the aftermath of the war was slow. Many German farms remained vacant into the late 1920s before British authorities reallocated them to Greek and British settlers, and the former Leipzig mission stations on Meru remained under Meru and Arusha leadership until the American Augustana Mission assumed nominal responsibility for them in 1921.

As the British slowly restored colonial control and authority in the aftermath of the war, they adopted previous German administrative structures based on ethnicity and left them more or less intact until 1948. In Meru, the British continued to recognize *Mangi* Sambegye, while in Arusha they acknowledged the recently appointed Lairumbe in Boru (upper Arusha), but replaced Ndasikoi and Saruni in Burka (lower Arusha). Sambegye (1902–25) and his successors, Sante (1925–30, 1945–52) and Kishili (1931–45), enjoyed long tenures in Meru, as did Lairumbe (1916–33) and Simeon Bene (1933–52) in Boru. The two chiefdoms on either side of Arusha town in Burka were less stable, however, going through a number of short-term chiefs until the two chiefdoms were united under Ngoilenya (1926–34) and Simon (1934–48) and finally joined with Boru under Simeon Bene in 1948 (see Tables 4.1: Meru *Mangi* and 4.2: Arusha *Mangi/Olkarsis*).

Since the Germans had sought to identify local authority structures and work with them – unlike their policy of appointing non-local *akidas* elsewhere in Tanganyika – and the British largely confirmed their arrangements, the ground was already laid for the formal implementation of Indirect Rule in 1926. Under the terms of Indirect Rule, ostensibly 'traditional' leaders were constituted as Native Authorities responsible for settling local disputes according to 'customary law', thus supposedly insulating people from the dislocating effects of social change. At the same time, however, Native Authorities were also responsible for collecting taxes, recruiting labour, and enforcing local ordinances on behalf of the colonial administration, thus potentially disrupting the established social order.

In places like Meru the Germans and the British sought to employ pre-existing chiefly institutions, but in societies like Arusha, where there had been no chiefs, they

111

created them. In neither case, however, were the colonial chiefs 'traditional' in any real sense. They were appointed by the colonial authorities and ultimately derived their authority from them, whether they possessed 'traditional' legitimacy or not. When the Germans had been unable to appoint a satisfactory *mangi* from the 'royal' Kaaya clan in Meru, they readily appointed someone from another clan, and the British generally followed suit, even as they painstakingly recorded their transgressions. Arusha had no chiefs, only men of influence, and they had been hanged in 1900, but the Germans and the British after them simply appointed their own and called them by the Meru term, *mangi*.[3]

While chiefs were given their authority by the colonial administration and were ultimately responsible to it, they found numerous ways to use that authority for their own purposes. Long-serving chiefs soon became the wealthiest and most powerful men in Arusha and Meru societies, using the powers they gained from the colonial authorities to support their own patronage networks and to attain positions that, while ultimately dependent on the colonial authorities, were also to some extent independent of them. Under the strictures of Indirect Rule, chiefs were given powers to collect taxes, recruit labour, and try cases – thus increasing their formal authority – and frequently used these powers to benefit themselves or their favoured clients. Chiefs also frequently assumed the authority to distribute valuable new resources, such as jobs or land, and used such patronage to enhance their own social influence and standing.[4] In 1925, for example, all three Arusha chiefs were accused of extorting funds from people for their own use. The two minor chiefs of Burka, Lesikale and Lesian, were deposed and imprisoned or fined, but the powerful chief of Boru, Lairumbe, was dealt with administratively because he was deemed too important to the administration to lose.[5]

The structure of colonial authority was thus a top-down affair, but there were popular sanctions on the exercise of power that limited its effects. Colonial authorities sought to appoint men as chiefs who had influence locally, for the whole aim of indirect rule was to harness their legitimacy to the colonial chariot, but a chief's influence was dependent on his observance of local standards of patronage and generosity. Leaders were expected to protect and reward their followers, not exploit them, and thus their continuing legitimacy was dependent on their ability to shield people from colonial exploitation and to share the spoils of colonial office with them. A chief without popular respect was unable to serve either colonial or his own interests. Chiefs thus often sought to ameliorate the impact of colonial rule on the people, and colonial authorities were usually forced to accede to these limits placed on their unfettered use of power.

Tax and Labour

The British also continued German policies regarding taxes and labour. The Hut and

---

[3] Iliffe, *Modern History*, 318–41; Hans Cory, 'Tribal Structure of the Arusha Tribe of Tanganyika' [1948], 6–7, (UDSM: Cory Papers, 201). For a notable example of 'making customary law' see the discussion of the 1948 Constitutions in Chapter 10.

[4] See, e.g., P.H. Gulliver, *Social Control in an African Society* (London, 1963), 154–9.

[5] Annual Report, Arusha District, 1925 (TNA: 1733/36).

Poll Tax was set initially at shs 6/-, roughly equivalent to the German rate of 4 rupees, and was subsequently raised to shs 10/- in 1925 and shs 12/- in 1928, where it remained throughout the 1930s.[6] Intended to force people to work for settlers, the head tax was the equivalent of one or two months' wages at prevailing wage rates. Those who refused to work, or were not able to raise the required amount in other ways, were required to labour on public works.[7] As late as 1950 compulsory labour amounting to 10 days per person per year was also still being used in 'tribal turnouts'.[8]

Arusha and Meru remained reluctant to work for settlers, however, as they had been since 1907. The reasons were not hard to find, though district officials found it oddly difficult to confront them directly:

> The Arusha and Meru do not generally speaking work satisfactorily for the settlers being unreliable in coming to work and lazy.... The fact that the settlers themselves are very short of coin to pay labour regularly is a factor of some importance in the disinclination of the Arusha and Meru to seek plantation employment.[9]

The style was catching:

> Experience shows that the Arusha and Meru are not highly satisfactory as labourers – being lazy and disinclined to work regularly – the fact that these tribes occupy very fertile country and are comparatively rich in stock is the dominant reason.[10]

Working and living conditions on the plantations were notoriously bad, even by the low standards of colonial officials. Settlers' lack of capital frequently led them to withhold wages or workers' cards to force them to keep working, and when workers were paid, wages were low. During the boom of the 1920s wages climbed from shs 14/- to 20/- for six to eight weeks' work.[11] They then slipped to shs 5-12/- during the depression before climbing back to shs 15-20/- during the Second World War.[12] Few Meru

[6] Total revenue due from the Hut and Poll Tax in 1916 was shs 54,400/-; 1920: 58,700/-; 1925: 108,000/-; 1930: 121,500/-; 1935: 124,000/-; and 1940: 139,300/-. Most of the tax went into the central treasury, with only 10% allocated in 1925 (raised subsequently to 21% in 1928) to the local Native Authorities to spend on their own expenses and projects. *Arusha District Book*.

[7] Tax defaults did not become a major problem until the Depression, when they rose from 297 in 1932 to 3,987 in 1933 and 4,118 in 1934. Northern Province, Annual Reports, 1932–34 (TNA: 11681).

[8] Minutes, District Meetings, 7 April 1949, 5 May 1949, 6 Oct 1949, 5 Jan 1950, 9 March 1950 (TNA: 9/8/1).

[9] Arusha District, Annual Report, 1920-21. Settlers frequently lacked sufficient capital to bridge the harvests and became heavily indebted to their brokers in London, forcing them to constrain or withhold wages wherever possible.

[10] Arusha District, Annual Report, 1924 (TNA: 1733/42). See also Northern Province, Half-Yearly Report, 1927 (TNA: 10902); Northern Province, Annual Report, 1928 (TNA: 11681).

[11] A work card was issued to all workers to record the number of days they worked. Each card recorded 30 days' work or tasks and workers were only paid when their cards were completed. While colonial officials frequently characterized the wages received for each card as a monthly wage, workers did not work every day, and it frequently took them six to eight weeks to complete a card.

[12] N.N. Luanda, 'Commercial Farming', 117–25; Joshua S.K.M. Doriye, 'The Effect of the Plantation Economy on Indigenous Agriculture in Northern Province, Tanzania, 1930-1960' (unpub. HIS 301 paper, University of Dar es Salaam, 1973-74), 16-25; Leonard Shio, 'A Political Economy of the Plantation System in Arusha' (MA, University of Dar es Salaam, 1977), 98-106; Northern Province, Annual Report, 1934 (TNA: 11681); anon., 'Wages – Current Rates' in *Arusha District Book*.

or Arusha men were interested in such poor returns on their labour when those from raising their own cattle, coffee, or foodstuffs were much higher.[13]

The estates employed labour on different terms – permanently, seasonally, and daily for different jobs. Skilled labour was the most permanent and best paid, and it usually consisted of male workers or squatters who lived semi-permanently, often with their families, on the settlers' farms. While most permanent workers came from outside the district, landless Arusha and Meru who had to work preferred to squat on north Meru for Afrikaners who gave them land for their own cattle and crops, taught them to plough with oxen, and required less work in return than commercial farmers.[14]

Seasonal labour consisted largely of male migrants from Central Province who worked for a few months at a time during the off-season from their own farms and herds at home. Meru and Arusha generally avoided such work because of the poor pay and conditions and the fact that its timing often conflicted with work on their own farms. Day labour was employed in large numbers during the harvest to pick coffee as well as at other times for weeding and insect control and was performed by Meru and Arusha women and children on a 'casual' basis.[15] Unlike the men, Arusha and Meru women had few alternatives for earning money. They could sell foodstuffs in local markets or on the settler farms, but they did not have access to the more lucrative commodities, cattle or coffee, to buy manufactured goods that were increasingly appearing in the markets or to pay school fees for their children. Settlers also often required women to pick coffee in exchange for water rights or permission to gather fodder or firewood on their lands.[16]

While settlers preferred squatters with whom they could exchange access to uncleared surplus land on their estates for cheap and dependable labour, they could not attract sufficient labour on such terms. P.E. Mitchell, the Acting Provincial Commissioner, understood the process, if not the squatters' motives:

> ... it is invariably the fact that in the early years of European development the settler or farmer is anxious to obtain squatters. Land is plentiful and of comparatively low value, and labour is often difficult to get and more difficult to control. At first the squatter, actuated largely by the FEUDAL instincts of the African, supposes that if he lives on a man's land he must work for him, but competition for labour very soon teaches him otherwise – indeed he is usually taught by some neighbour of his master's who seduces him from his allegiance – and then there follows a troublesome stage ending usually in the triumphant departure of the squatter to

---

[13] See Chapter 7. P.H. Gulliver, *Report on Land and Population* (Dar es Salaam, 1957), 26; Luanda, 'Commercial Farming', 136–41.

[14] Shio, 'Plantation System', 98; Luanda, 'Commercial Farming', 132–6; Lodenaga Lotisia (AHT 3).

[15] Child labour became a major issue in Kilimanjaro in the late 1920s when parents and chiefs sought on moral grounds to restrict settlers from employing children, while settlers claimed that Chaga wished only to exploit their own children at lower wages. Mitchell supported the settlers, asserting 'I have yet to meet the African tribe in which morals before the age of puberty can be said to exist', but Webster resolved the dispute in favour of the Chaga, pointing out their dependence on family labour and the low pay offered by the settlers. Northern Province, Annual Report, 1927 (TNA: 11681); Question asked by Howe-Browne, 30 April 1929; PC/NP to CS/DSM, 14 May 1929 (TNA: 11908/II).

[16] Luanda, 'Commercial Farming', 127–136; AO/AD to Sr. AO/Moshi, 1 June 1936 (TNA: 9/12/14); Sr.LO to DC/AD 11 Dec 1957 (TNA: 472/ANR/1/57).

public lands, and the extreme irritation of the settler with the Government for allowing him to do so.[17]

With few squatters and local labour in short supply, settlers thus remained highly dependent on migrant workers for seasonal labour. By the late 1920s settlers employed an average monthly work-force of 8,000 to 12,000, most of whom were migrants from outside the district; and comparable figures obtained for the 1940s.[18]

Re-alienating the Land

The demand for labour was fuelled by the reallocation of German estates to British, Greek, and other settlers. One of the first acts of the British when they took control in Arusha was to intern the remaining German settlers and confiscate their farms, thus effectively halting most commercial production in the District for nearly a decade while the farms themselves became overgrown and reverted to bush. Nearly 300 Afrikaners remained north of Mount Meru, allowed to stay because they were British subjects, but only a few of these were commercial farmers. The rest remained subsistence herders and farmers or became squatters on others' land as their own holdings became fragmented and dispersed among their many children.[19] The main coffee and mixed farms south of Mount Meru had been largely German-owned, however. They reverted to the Custodian for Enemy Property for disposal, and their reallocation was extremely slow due to a general lack of settlers, markets, and government support.

While the British authorities in Tanganyika were generally opposed to settler agriculture because they felt that the soils, labour supplies, and transport were all insufficient to make settler farming viable, they were also concerned that existing commercial production be maintained. Virtually all the Mount Meru farms were eventually reallocated to settlers, but the administration was not encouraging. It limited leases to 33 years, gave no credit, did not extend the Tanga railway to Arusha until 1929, and provided no subsidies until the Second World War.[20]

The British authorities were also aware of the increasing shortage of land for Arusha and Meru farmers on Mount Meru, though they tended to interpret this as a problem of insufficient pastures for cattle on the mountain and a lack of access through the 'iron ring' of settler farms to the abundant grasslands below rather than as a shortage of cultivatable land on the mountain itself. They therefore allocated eight farms to Meru and Arusha in 1920 to provide access to plains grazing: two to Meru in Engare Nanyuki and Temi, and six to Arusha in Olmotonyi and Olkokola.[21] All were on the lower, drier

[17] P.E. Mitchell [c. 1927] in *Arusha District Book*.
[18] Arusha District, Annual Report, 1919-20 (TNA: 1733/1); Labour Statistics, 1944-50 (TNA: 9/LAB/23); Luanda, 'Commercial Farming', 136–41.
[19] Luanda, 'Commercial Farming', 80–1, 180–95; 'Land Development Survey; I: Dutch Settlement in Northern Province' [Dec 1930] (TNA: 19449).
[20] Luanda, 'Commercial Farming', 10.
[21] A.E. Kitching, 'Memorandum on Native Land in the Arusha District', 3 Dec 1930 (TNA: 26257, also 25369); Luanda, 'Commercial Farming', 272–8.

slopes and unsuitable for banana cultivation. The British were to remain fixated on the wasteful keeping of cattle as the source of the Arusha-Meru land problem and on access to the plains as the solution, and all their future attempts to address the land problem on Meru took a similar approach, restricting Arusha and Meru cultivation to the confines of the southern slopes of the mountain.[22]

Ex-German leases on Meru totalled some 41,584 hectares, of which 10,868 remained in Afrikaner hands and 1,821 were granted to Arusha and Meru in 1920, leaving 28,895 hectares for redistribution to new settlers.[23] One of the first groups to be attracted to Meru were Greeks and Cypriots, fleeing the Greco-Turkish War of 1921–2, who joined a few of their countrymen who had settled earlier. Greeks soon monopolized much of the best coffee land along the Arusha-Moshi road between Nduruma and Maji ya Chai, and 200 Greeks eventually settled around Meru. The boom in coffee and sisal during the 1920s brought British and other settlers. Acreage planted in coffee more than quadrupled during the 1920s and large sisal estates were started south of the Arusha-Moshi road. Some of the new settlers were from Kenya; others were ex-British soldiers with little farming experience; and a few were Germans allowed to return.[24]

The new settlers took up most of the ex-German leases remaining and prompted the government to release nearly 30,000 hectares of new land in the semi-arid areas south of the Moshi-Arusha road for sisal. Some 25,727 hectares of ex-German and new land were alienated between 1927 and 1929 alone and, by 1930, a total of 75,256 hectares had been alienated by the British, representing an 81 per cent increase over the German period.[25] The land boom peaked in 1929, and the resulting Depression forced many settlers into bankruptcy or the hands of their brokers, while others fled to the Lupa goldfields.[26] Recovery only came with the Second World War, when the administration finally threw its support to settlers to boost wartime production. German settlers who had returned during the inter-war years were again deported, and after the war some 30,000 hectares of ex-German land were again reallocated to promote large-scale agricultural development.

While the British were thus able to assume the colonial mantle over Mount Meru fairly easily, their ability to impose their own policies was continually contested by Arusha and Meru throughout the remaining colonial period, as we shall see in the chapters to come. Just as British power was limited by their dependence on maintaining the legitimacy of the chiefs, for example, their ability to exploit the area economically was

---

[22] See Chapter 9. This fixation on keeping cattle as a generally wasteful and self-indulgent enterprise characterized British approaches to Maasai and to pastoralists generally. Richard Waller, personal communication.

[23] LO to DC/AD, 3 Jan 1929 (TNA: 472/LAN/13); Kitching, 'Memorandum on Native Land in Arusha District'. Accurate figures of German land alienation are extremely hard to get because of the uneven quality of German records, the lack of accurate surveys, etc. Some of my figures therefore differ somewhat in detail, though not in overall scale, from those given in Luanda, 'Commercial Farming, 80–4.

[24] Arusha District, Annual Reports, 1920–7; Luanda, 'Commercial Farming', 53, 80–9, 195–209. Luanda's thesis is the fullest study of the plantation sector on Mount Meru to date.

[25] LO to CS/DSM, 19 Nov 1929 (TNA; 10079/IV); 'Land Development Survey: II: Acquisition of Land by Natives', 1930 (TNA: 26257).

[26] Northern Province, Annual Reports, 1931–3 (TNA: 11681).

limited by Meru and Arusha strategies to ensure their own economic welfare. As local populations continued to rise, land on the mountain became increasingly short and Arusha and Meru each began to intensify their own agricultural production in ways that ensured the maintenance of their own economies.

Some of those responsible for these developments were the first generation of Meru and Arusha Christians who had assumed responsibility for the missions during the war years and greatly expanded their scope in the years to follow. These people, and those who followed them, became instrumental in raising coffee and in later developing a vibrant co-operative movement that helped to ensure continued Arusha and Meru economic independence from settlers who coveted their land and labour.

Struggles over the land continued, however, as settlers and the administration continually sought to expand the plantation economy while Meru and Arusha struggled to extend their own. Such struggles frequently came to a head over British attempts to expand Arusha town; abortive appeals by Arusha and Meru to expand the amount of arable land available on the mountain; contests over political authority among colonial officers, chiefs, and popular movements; and ultimately by the British attempt to dispossess Meru from land around Engare Nanyuki that led to the Meru Land Case and anti-colonial mobilization throughout Tanganyika.

A common theme runs through all these struggles, as Meru and Arusha each sought to maintain and expand their own moral economies against the moral intrusions of settlers and colonial administrators, and it is this common theme that we will pursue in the following chapters.

7

Land, Population
& Agricultural Development

Arusha and Meru responses to the imposition of British rule focused almost exclusively on farming and land. By the 1920s their populations had recovered from the depredations of the late nineteenth century and the German conquest and began to increase rapidly. Hemmed in by the band of alienated land below and forest reserve above, however, they rapidly exhausted vacant land remaining on the mountain and were forced inward to increase their agricultural productivity to feed the growing number of people on the land. They pursued a number of different strategies to accomplish this. They cleared steep hillsides and riverbanks and planted them in crops. They planted mountain pastures with maize and beans, moving their cattle to the plains or hand-feeding them on the mountain and using their manure for fertilizer. As they expanded cultivation of annual crops into the higher and lower reaches of the mountain, they planted bananas solidly across the middle slopes, and slowly adopted iron hoes, ox-drawn ploughs, and eventually tractors, to ease their workloads. They began to produce large quantities of maize, beans, and onions for sale and later developed coffee as a major cash crop. When they seemed to reach the limits of what they could produce on the mountain, they expanded into the highlands on the northern side of the mountain and then on to the southern and western plains. This was initially to graze their cattle, but they soon began to convert those areas into annual crops and eventually bananas as well.

While Meru and Arusha occupied similar environments and followed similar courses to develop the highly productive and efficient agriculture they pursue today, the particular strategies by which they accomplished this differed significantly. Meru put their emphasis on expanding banana and coffee cultivation that provides the mainstay of the area's agriculture today, while Arusha tended to rely more on mixed farming of annual crops and cattle, shifting to a greater reliance on bananas and coffee only in the 1950s and 1960s. Each thus sought to pursue its own economic vision, facing the problems of the twentieth century with the lessons they had carried over from the nineteenth.

It was an extremely complicated process, and we shall have to explore it from a

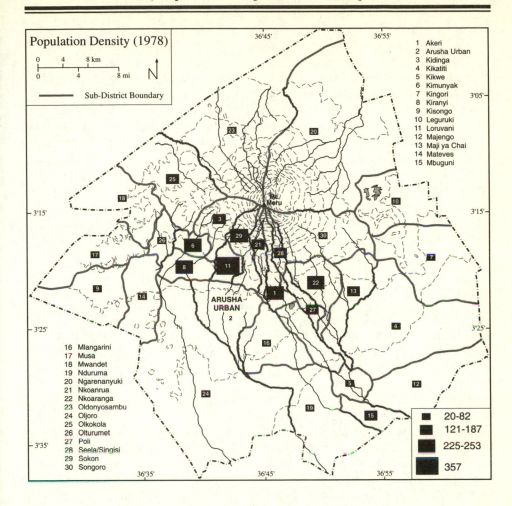

Population Density (1978)

0   4   8 km
0   4   8 mi
N

——— Sub-District Boundary

1 Akeri
2 Arusha Urban
3 Kidinga
4 Kikatiti
5 Kikwe
6 Kimunyak
7 Kingori
8 Kiranyi
9 Kisongo
10 Leguruki
11 Loruvani
12 Majengo
13 Maji ya Chai
14 Mateves
15 Mbuguni

16 Mlangarini
17 Musa
18 Mwandet
19 Nduruma
20 Ngarenanyuki
21 Nkoanrua
22 Nkoaranga
23 Oldonyosambu
24 Oljoro
25 Olkokola
26 Olturumet
27 Poli
28 Seela/Singisi
29 Sokon
30 Songoro

20-82
121-187
225-253
357

Map 7.1 Population Density in Arusha and Meru Districts

119

number of different perspectives to try to understand it all. First there were the under-lying structural factors – land shortage, population growth, and agricultural potential – that set the overall limits within which Arusha and Meru farmers made their choices. We shall explore these here to try to understand the general processes of agricultural development in this century. Within these limits, Meru and Arusha pursued a variety of options, while rejecting others, and we shall try to explore some of these as well, but the focus in this chapter remains on processes rather than on specific events. In the next chapter we will shift the focus to the human dimension, seeking to understand how Arusha and Meru made their choices and the implications these had for their societies. Finally, in the concluding chapters, we will look at the political implications of these choices in the ceaseless struggles, between Meru and Arusha on the one hand and the British administration and European settlers on the other, over land and political power,; a struggle which had as serious implications for relations among Arusha and Meru themselves as it did for the ultimate fate of colonial rule in Tanganyika.

Pioneers and the Open Frontier: 1830s–1900s

Land was freely available on Mount Meru prior to the German conquest, and as Meru and Arusha populations increased over time, pioneers pushed up the mountain slopes, clearing the forests as they went. Arusha expansion during the nineteenth century, fuelled by the infusion of Meru, Chaga, and Maasai captives and refugees, was so rapid that succeeding age-sets cleared and settled the whole southwestern quadrant of the mountain from 1,300 to 1,600 metres, an area some 16 kilometres around the base by 10 kilometres up the slopes, by the end of the century.[1]

Arusha first settled on the Burka River, west of modern Arusha town at 1,300 metres, during the Kidotu (c. 1821–41) age-set (see Table 7.1). The land was uninhab-ited, and they cleared the surrounding areas to plant bananas, eleusine, maize, and beans. During Twati (c. 1836–56), they expanded some 5 kilometres north and west, from 1,300 to 1,460 metres, while during the succeeding Nyangusi and Laimer (c. 1851–86) sets, they advanced another 1.5 kilometres up to 1,520 metres and pushed the boundary with Meru east to the Songota River. By the end of the century Talala and Twati (c. 1881–1917) had filled out the southwestern quadrant up to 1,600 metres and opened up new districts to the east formerly occupied by Meru and to the west for-merly occupied by pastoral Maasai.[2]

While Meru preceded Arusha on the mountain by a couple of centuries, Meru expansion was not nearly as rapid or as extensive as Arusha. The first Meru settlements had been established up from the plains at 1,400 metres, and succeeding generations slowly expanded up the mountain until they reached 1,600 metres by the end of the nineteenth century. Meru population thus grew only slowly during the seventeenth and

---

[1] See Chapter 2.

[2] P.H. Gulliver, *Report on Land and Population in the Arusha Chiefdom* (Tanganyika Provincial Administra-tion, 1957), 17–19. While differing over details, Patricia Benjamin's detailed surveys of upper Arusha confirm the overall trends identified by Gulliver (personal communication).

Table 7.1 Arusha Expansion

Period	Burka	Boru	Area
Kidotu (ca 1821–41)	Sombetin Sokon Chini		1,300 m S & SW of town
Twati (*c.* 1836–56)	Sinon Sekei Levolosi	lower Kiranyi	1,300–1,460 m N & S
Nyangusi & Laimer (*c.* 1851–86)	upper Sekei lower Sokon Juu	upper Kiranyi western Kirevi Loruvani Ilmwandet	1,460–1,520 m N, NE, & NW
Talala & Twati (*c.* 1881–1917)	Sokon Juu	Siwandet lower Kimunyak lower Kidinga lower Kioga	1,520–1,600 m N, NW, & W
Twati & Tareto (1896–1929)	Bangata Sasi Baraa	upper Kimunyak upper Kidinga upper Kioga Sambasha Olevolos	1,600–1,800 m E, N, & NW
Tareto, Terito & Nyangusi (1911–59)	lower Sombetin lower Sinon lower Baraa	Olorien Olturumet Olkokola Mateves Oldonyo Sambu Kisongo Musa/Likamba Mwandet Maasai Oljoro/Muriet Mangarini Nduruma	1,300–1,800 m E, NW & plains

Source: P.H. Gulliver, *Report on Land and Population in the Arusha Chiefdom* (Tanganyika Provincial Administration, 1957), 17-19.

eighteenth centuries, and it seems likely that Meru actually lost population to Arusha during the middle years of the nineteenth century until they began to raid widely and amass population themselves after 1880.[3]

While the rate of expansion of the two peoples differed, expansion followed a similar pattern among both. Early pioneers settled initially on the lower slopes, clearing enough

[3] See Chapter 1.

land for themselves and their immediate descendants to raise permanent crops of bananas, annual crops of maize, beans, eleusine, and various root crops, and herds of cattle and small stock. Permanent stands of bananas were established around people's homes, while surrounding areas were cleared for annual crops or pasture. Each household maintained its own fields for bananas, annual crops, and pasture, but people also established common pastures and could cut into surrounding forests for additional annual fields when necessary.

As families increased in size and original settlements became fully occupied, older sons moved up the mountain to clear the forest and establish their own settlements. In Meru these were usually brothers, leading to the development of linked patrilineal homesteads extending up the mountain, but in Arusha age-mates usually pioneered together when they retired from being *murran,* and localized sections of the age-sets thus became the characteristic form of local social organization.

Closure: 1900s–1920s

Arusha and Meru had thus cleared and settled from the edge of the plains to 1,600 metres by the time the Germans conquered them and put a brake on future expansion by alienating most of the land around the southern slopes of the mountain below 1,300 metres and establishing a protected forest zone above 1,600 metres. For the next forty years, further Meru and Arusha expansion would be turned largely inward as they sought to support their growing population by clearing and planting steep hillsides and river banks, planting mountain pastures in food crops, and intensifying their agricultural practices to produce higher yields per acre.

During the first decade of German rule, Arusha and Meru sought merely to recover from the devastation of conquest, when the Germans had seized their cattle, destroyed many of their banana groves, and killed thousands of Meru and Arusha while repatriating others to Kilimanjaro.[4] The abundant harvest of 1907, which Meru and Arusha celebrated with feasts of roast oxen, marked their recovery, however, and population began to grow thereafter, putting pressure on their newly constricted lands.[5] Their initial response was to bring uncultivated land between holdings, on steep hillsides, or along the banks of the rivers that plunged down the mountain – previously neglected as too difficult to cultivate or irrigate – into cultivation. By the early 1930s virtually every bit of land, no matter how steep or difficult, was cultivated.[6]

Arusha also continued to edge around the western slopes of the mountain into Sambasha and Olevolos as well as east into the lower districts between the Temi and Songota rivers seized earlier from Meru.[7] With the collapse of German authority in 1916, Meru and Arusha resumed upward expansion as well, rapidly clearing and

[4] See Chapter 4.
[5] Ittameier, *ELMB*, 62(1907), 561.
[6] DO/AD to PC/NP, 16 Sept 1930 (TNA: 69/45/9); Northern Province, Annual Report, 1932 (TNA: 11681); C. Gillman, Diaries, XVIII/97h/29.5.36 (OCRP: MSS.Afr.s.1175).
[7] P.H. Gulliver, 'The Population of the Arusha Chiefdom, A High Density Area in East Africa', *Rhodes-Livingstone Journal*, 28 (1960), 12; idem, *Land and Population*, 19.

7.1 Kihamba and annual fields (Spear)

planting up to 1,800 metres before the British reimposed a forest reserve in 1920 and struggled to defend it against further Arusha and Meru encroachments.[8]

With land at an increasing premium, Meru and Arusha were faced with difficult choices. They could work for wages on the European estates then being developed around the base of Mount Meru, as they had before their own fortunes recovered in 1907; they could move onto the plains; or they could seek to increase their own yields to support more people on the mountain itself. Most chose the third option, rejecting wage labour as demeaning and poorly paid throughout the colonial period,[9] and they

[8] See, e.g., DC/AD to PC/NP, 26 March 1927; PC/NP to CS, 4 April 1927; Conservator of Forests to PC/NP, 20 Oct 1930, et seq. (TNA:11201/I).

[9] Gulliver, *Land and Population*, 26. Given Arusha and Meru distaste for wage labour, recruiting local labour for the estates remained a perennial problem, and most labour continued to be recruited from Central Province throughout the colonial period. See, e.g., Arusha District, Annual Report, 1923 (Hallier Papers, OCRP: MSS.Afr.s.1072); Gillman, Diaries, XX/82b/10.28 (OCRP: MSS.Afr.s.1175); PC/NP to Secretary, Arusha Coffee Planters Association, 5 Jan 1928 (TNA: 11127/I); Northern Province, Annual Report, 1932 (TNA: 11681); Northern Province, Draft State of Agricultural Policy, 1955 (TNA: 9/8/2).

resisted moving to the dry, malarial, and tsetse-infested plains until the 1940s and 1950s, as we shall see.

Meru and Arusha agriculture was highly productive, and they consistently produced a surplus that was traded to pastoral Maasai, even in years of drought.[10] It was also conducive to further development. One of the mainstays of their economies was bananas (*Musa spp.*), and they grew over twenty different varieties that matured at different times and were used variously for eating, cooking, frying, baking, and making beer. Long grown in the highlands of northern Tanganyika, bananas were well suited to the fertile well-drained soils, moderate climate, and dependable rainfall of Mount Meru. They produced high yields year after year without depleting the soil, especially when grown with other crops. Nutritionally comparable to potatoes, bananas are high in carbohydrates and low in protein and provided a balanced diet when supplemented with milk, meat, beans, and maize or eleusine, as Meru and Arusha did.

Bananas thus provided Arusha and Meru with a wholesome and dependable source of food that required little work to produce. Their yields could also be improved significantly. Increasing density from 200 to 600 plants per acre raised yields to 400–500 bunches (6-8 tons), enough to feed 7–9 adults for a year. Meru and Arusha mulched their bananas, fertilized them with animal manure, and intercropped them with maize and beans to increase their yields still further. Bananas were thus close to an ideal crop for people faced with the need to feed more people on a limited amount of land.[11]

Meru and Arusha also raised annual crops of maize and beans. Maize (*Zea mays*) grew well on the well-watered volcanic soils of Mount Meru, and could produce two crops a year on the middle slopes and another on the colder, higher slopes. Arusha and Meru intercropped maize with beans (*Phaseolus vulgaris*) and other pulses to maintain soil fertility. Together the two crops comprised a complete diet, and supplemented bananas well.[12] Meru and Arusha supplemented maize and beans with other crops, such as taro (*Colocasia antiquorum*), sweet potatoes (*Ipomea batatus*), and various vegetables, planting them in succession to ensure a steady supply of different crops throughout the year.[13] Finally, they raised finger millet (*Eleusine coracana*) to make beer, a crucial ingredient in all social interactions and exchanges and an important dietary supplement and famine reserve.[14]

Annual crops were rotated with pasture. Beans, maize, eleusine, and vegetables were planted for several years in succession, with stock allowed to graze on crop residues and fertilize the soil with their manure between crop cycles, and then followed by longer fallow periods when the pastures were used solely for grazing livestock. Pastures were

[10] Arusha District, Annual Report, 1919–20 (TNA: 1733/1); AO/AD, Annual Report, 1946 (TNA: 472/-).

[11] Max Schoeller, *Mitteilungen über meine Reise nach Äquatorial-Ost Afrika und Uganda, 1896-97* (Berlin, 1901), I:161–2; AO/AD to Sr.AO, 11 April 1931 (TNA: 9/17/1); Northern Province Native Agriculture, 1945 (TNA: 9/6/5); R.E.D. Baker & N.W. Simmonds, 'Bananas in East Africa', *Empire Journal of Experimental Agriculture*, 19 (1951), 283–90, 20 (1952), 66–76; K. Shepherd, 'Banana Cultivars in East Africa,' *Tropical Agriculture, Trinidad*, 34 (1957), 277–86; N.W. Simmonds, *Bananas* (London, 1959), 129–83, 252–71; J.D. Acland, *East African Crops* (London, 1971), 9–16.

[12] Northern Province Native Agriculture, 1945 (TNA: 9/6/5); Acland, *Crops*, 20–6, 124–30.

[13] Northern Province Native Agriculture, 1945 (TNA: 9/6/5); Acland, *Crops*, 57–8, 204–5.

[14] Fokken, *ELMB*, 60 (1905), 38–9; Acland, *Crops*, 114–15.

7.2 Annual fields and pasture (Benjamin)

planted in *morua* grass and hedged to confine stock and prevent soil erosion. Cattle, sheep, and goats were thus carefully integrated into overall crop management to maintain soil fertility and provide a steady supply of milk and meat.[15]

Each household maintained its own fields and pastures, which men allocated to their wives for their own use. Men prepared the soil and planted bananas, cleared the fields for annual crops, and oversaw the herding of stock, while women planted, weeded, and harvested the annual crops, prepared them for consumption, and milked the stock.[16] The combination of perennial bananas, a variety of annual crops grown in different micro-ecological zones, and irrigation served to distribute the workload for both men and women throughout the year (see Table 7.2).

On the lower slopes of the mountain, annual fields were prepared during the short rains in November and December; maize and beans were planted in February and March; and they were irrigated, weeded, and finally harvested from April to October. Annual crops were planted later and matured more slowly higher on the mountain, with preparation and planting taking place from May to August, irrigation and weeding from

[15] A.E. Haarer, 2 July 1925 (TNA: 9/6/5); B.J. Hartley, 'A Brief Note on the Meru People with Special Reference to their Expansion Problem', 25 March 1938 (TNA: 69/45/9); Northern Province Native Agriculture, 1945 (TNA: 9/6/5); Hans Cory, 'Arusha Land Tenure' (UDSM: Hans Cory Papers, 38), 23; Gulliver, *Land and Population*, 65–6. Benjamin (personal communication) found rotation of annual crops and pasture was probably less than previously reported, at least in Western Arusha.
[16] DO/AD to PC/NP, 12 Feb 1926 (TNA: 69/233); Cory, 'Arusha Land Tenure', 23–4; Louise Fortmann, 'Development Prospects in Arumeru District' (USAID/Tanzania, 1977); Ngole ole Njololoi (AHT 4); Mesiaki Kilevo, personal communication.

Table 7.2 Agricultural Calendar

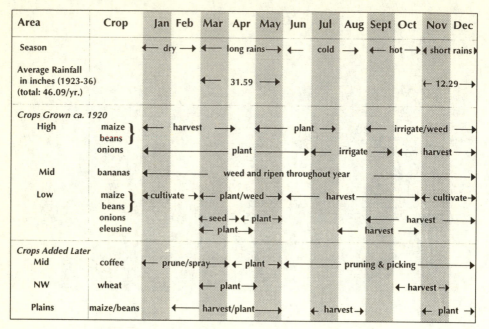

Note: Meru generally one month behind Arusha in non-irrigated areas due to heavier rainfall.
Sources: Compiled from Arusha District Note Book; D. Sturdy, 26 Feb 1930; T.C. Cairns, Agricultural Calendar, 1940 (all in TNA: 9/6/5); District Agricultural Officer, Monthly Reports, 1955–6 (TNA: 472/-).

September to December, and harvest from January to March. Eleusine was planted in March and April, and matured from April to October, while onions were planted from March to May and harvested from September to December. Bananas were tended and ripened throughout the year.

The most common tools were digging sticks made from hard olive wood which were sufficiently durable to open up the friable soils and dislodge weeds, but by the end of the nineteenth century iron hoes were increasingly used.[17] Irrigation was simple, easily maintained, and used to compensate for shortfalls in rain or to extend growing seasons as required. As people settled new districts, they dug a main channel from a mountain stream higher on the slopes and led it across the slopes above the new area. Separate furrows were then dug down through individual fields which were controlled by placing or removing small piles of earth to allow each household to flood its fields once every fourteen days. Everyone in the system helped to maintain the main channels, and each household drew its allotment in an established rotation.[18]

Arusha and Meru agriculture thus ensured a steady supply of diverse foods throughout the year and was capable of considerable development by increasing crop densities, inter-cropping, extending growing seasons, and producing multiple harvests. The rich

[17] Ngole ole Njololoi (AHT 4).
[18] Cory, 'Arusha Land Tenure,' 25; AO/AD, Monthly Reports, 1955 (TNA: 472/-); Mesiaki Kilevo, personal communication.

volcanic soils retained their fertility year after year; rainfall was dependable and abundant; and irrigation allowed farmers to compensate for variations in rainfall or extend their growing seasons as needed.

Table 7.3 Population: 1921-78

Area	1921	1928	Arusha 1931	1948	1957	1967	1978
Boru							
Loruvani	4160	4713	4954	4474	5669		12069
Kiranyi	2577	2577	2472	6452	6112	N/A	11380
Kidinga	2761	3159	3808	7646	6187		8535
Kimunyak	1614	1461	1375	6888	4982		8832
sub-total	11112	11910	12609	25465	22950	28387	40816
Burka							
Sokon Juu	1343	1369	1460	5646	6816		13972
Sekei	2412	2554	2339	4443	5161		3629
Sombetin	1757	2073	1946	4179	4940	N/A	8086
Sokon C.	1666	1832	1695	4533	6020		7132
Moivaru	1956	1904	3565	2710	3829		3804
other	1826	2044	2034				13172
sub-total	10960	11776	13039	21511	26766	38884	49795
sub-total:							
Boru/Burka	22072	23686	25648	46976	49716	67271	90611
Northwest Highlands							
Olkokola				2403	4999		8534
Olturumet							2772
Mwandet				1554	3951	N/A	6944
Musa			296	2065	4244		6087
sub-total			296	6022	13194		24337
Plains							
O. Sambu							6493
Mateves							4161
Kisongo				2218	3922	N/A	3876
Oljoro							13685
sub-total				2218	3922		28215
sub-total:							
NW/Plains			296	8240	17116	38118	52552
Total	22072	23686	25944	55216	66832	105389	143163

Table 7.3 Population: 1921-78 (cont.)

Area	1921	1928	Meru 1931	1948	1957	1967	1978
Highlands							
Nkoanrua	2015	2088	1931	3366			7499
Ndoombo	823	985	1037	1734			
Akeri	1620	1745	1627	2004			11597
Poli	1868	1622	2129	2067	N/A	N/A	7584
Nkoaranga	2130	2093	2165	2707			12382
Seela/	1330	1422	2347	2436			5651
Singisi							
Songoro	1880	1877	1898	4442			6293
sub-total	11616	11832	13134	18755	32357	36832	51006
Northeast Highlands							
Engare Nanyuki				2452			6930
Leguruki							8183
Kingori					N/A	N/A	9950
Maji ya Chai							10274
Towela				1353			1353
sub-total				3805		22786	36690
Southern Lowlands							
Majengo							3722
Kikwe				335	N/A	N/A	5678
Mbuguni				336			7229
Kikatiti							10606
sub-total				671	1223	16787	27235
TOTAL	11666	11832	13134	23231	36200	76375	114931

Note: Census tracts varied from one census to the next leading to some discrepancy between adjacent units.
Sources: 1921-31: *Arusha District Book*; 1948: *African Population of Tanganyika Territory, 1948* (Nairobi 1950) (TNA: 472/CEN/2/II); 1957: *Tanganyikan African Population Census, 1957* (Nairobi 1958) and P.H. Gulliver, 'Memoranda on the Arusha Chiefdom: Arusha Chiefdom Population 1948-57', 24 Oct 1957 (UDSM: Hans Cory Papers, 277) 13-14; 1967: *1967 Population Census* (Dar es Salaam, 1969) vol I; 1978: *1978 Population Census: Preliminary Report* (Dar es Salaam, nd) I:48, II:46-55.

Patterns of Population Growth: 1920s–1970s

With further upward expansion foreclosed, the western districts filling, and agricultural productivity increasing, population began to build up on the mountain slopes themselves. Still recovering from the traumas of the German conquest, population only increased slowly through the 1920s, but it more than doubled between 1928 and 1948 in both Arusha and Meru, and continued to expand at high rates throughout the 1980s (see Table 7.3). Arusha population was almost double that of Meru in 1921 and it continued to expand at higher rates throughout the 1920s, 1930s, and 1940s, but its rate of expansion fell dramatically behind that of Meru in the 1950s, 1960s, and 1970s (see Tables 7.5 and 7.6).[19]

As population grew, people expanded from older and more densely settled districts on the central slopes to later and less densely settled ones to the east and west (see Table 7.4 and Map 7.2).[20] In upper Arusha (Boru) this involved a shift from east to west, from Loruvani on the border of Meru – where densities already approached 150/km² in the late 1920s and remained fairly constant into the 1960s – west into Kiranyi, Kidinga, and Kimunyak, where densities averaged 50/km² in the 1920s and only approached those of Loruvani in the 1950s and 1960s. It also involved shifts up the slopes into the less densely settled upper districts. By the late 1970s, densities in all areas of Boru except Kidinga had risen to between 250/km² and 360/km². Meanwhile, in lower Arusha (Burka), population expanded from the older districts surrounding Arusha town (Sekei, Levolosi, Sombetin, Sokon Chini, and Sinon) to areas east of town (Sokon Juu, Bangata, Sasi, Moivaru, and Baraa) in former Meru territory, with average densities climbing to 140/km² in the 1970s.

Similarly, Meru were more densely settled in the older western districts bordering Arusha (Nkoanrua, Akeri, and Poli) and spread into the more thinly settled districts to the east and north over the 1930s and 1940s until they approached an average density of 60/km² in all but Nkoanrua, where density exceeded 100/km². By the 1970s densities had increased to 170–250/km² across the middle banana belt of Meru and to 60–150/km² in the higher zones.

Broader patterns of population distribution changed as well, as people began to expand beyond the southern slopes of Meru into the northern slopes and out on to the adjacent plains. Arusha population in 1920 was divided between Burka, the less densely

[19] While it is not clear whether the increase in population resulted from lower mortality, increased fertility, or some combination of the two, the incorporation of numbers of foreign women in Meru and especially in Arusha societies in the later nineteenth century would have continued to contribute to population increase in succeeding generations. For a discussion of issues relating to population growth during the colonial period, see Dennis Cordell, Joel Gregory, & Victor Piché, 'African Historical Demography' in D. Cordell & J. Gregory (eds), *African Population and Capitalism* (Madison, 1994), 14–32, and John Iliffe, 'The Origins of African Population Growth', *JAH*, 30 (1989), 165–9. For the long-term effect of assimilating women on population growth, see Raymond Kelly, *The Nuer Conquest* (Ann Arbor, 1985), 59–62.

[20] See Chapters 1 and 2 for an analysis of early Arusha and Meru settlement. The central districts also contain the oldest irrigation furrows: D.S. Sturdy, W.E. Carlton & G. Milne, 'A Chemical Survey of the Waters of Mount Meru...,' *JEAUNHS*, 45–6 (1932), 32. The history of Arusha settlement is also outlined in Table 7.1 above.

Table 7.4 Population Density, 1921-78 (persons/km²)

Area	1921	1928	1931	Arusha 1948	1957	1967	1978
Boru							
Loruvani	123	140	147	133	168		358
Kiranyi	57	57	55	143	136	N/A	253
Kidinga	45	52	62	125	101		139
Kimunyak	52	47	44	220	159		283
Average	65	70	74	149	134	166	238
Burka							
Average	31	33	37	60	75	109	140
Average: Boru/ Burka	42	45	49	89	94	127	172
Northwest Highlands							
Olkokola				34	71		121
Olturumet							62
Mwandet				18	45	N/A	79
Musa			3	18	38		54
Average			3	22	49		77
Plains							
O. Sambu							19
Mateves							48
Kisongo				25	45		44
Oljoro							50
Average				25	45		36
Average:							
NW/Plains			3	23	48	50	48

Area	1921	1928	1931	Meru 1948	1957	1967	1978
Southern Highlands							
Nkoanrua	61	65	61	106			187
Akeri	44	48	46	62			251
Poli	43	37	49	47			173
Nkoaranga	39	38	39	49	N/A	N/A	225
Seela/							
Singisi	35	38	63	65			151
Songoro	19	19	19	44			63
Average	36	37	41	58	100	114	158

Table 7.4 Population Density, 1921–78 (cont.)

Area	1921	1928	1931	Meru 1948	1957	1967	1978
Northeast Highlands							
Engare Nanyuki				7			21
Leguruki					N/A	N/A	82
Kingori							78
Maji ya Chai							123
Average						35	55
Southern Lowlands							
Majengo							40
Kikwe				5	N/A	N/A	77
Mbuguni				7			145
Kikatiti							48
Average				5		39	62

Note: As noted in Table 7.3, census tracts varied from census to census. Since the definition of areas of earlier tracts was not available, densities were calculated according to the area of 1978 tracts (after Mlay), thus leading to possible overestimation of the settled area of earlier tracts (especially in newer settlement areas) and a correlative underestimation of density. They thus do not accurately reflect true densities in terms of land actually occupied at the time, but do indicate overall trends in terms of total land available in each area. Gulliver calculated on the basis of smaller areas, and came up with correspondingly higher density figures. Patricia Benjamin's detailed surveys of western Arusha promise to correct some of these problems.
Sources: as for Table 7.3, plus P.H. Gulliver, *Report on Land and Population in the Arusha Chiefdom* (Tanganyika Provincial Administration, 1957); I.D. Thomas, 'Population Density in Tanzania, 1967' (BRALUP Research Notes, 5b); Wilfred Mlay, 'Population Pressure in Arumeru District,' (Arusha, 1982).

settled area surrounding Arusha town, and Boru, the more densely settled area higher on the mountain (see Table 7.5). During the 1920s population grew only slowly in both areas, with average densities of 31–7 persons/km² in Burka and 65–74/km² in Boru. As overall population more than doubled in Arusha during the 1930s and 1940s, however, densities increased apace, triggering the first moves off the mountain west towards Monduli to settle in Musa, Olkokola, and Mwandet and out on to the Kisongo plains.[21]

When the overall Arusha population almost doubled again in the 1950s and 1960s, however, population in Boru increased only marginally, while it nearly doubled in Burka, quadrupled in the northwestern highlands, and increased over seven-fold on the plains. With most of the northwestern highlands settled, vast new areas of the plains were opened up and densities rose everywhere, to 109/km² in Burka, 70/km² in the northwest, and 36/km² on the plains. By 1970 new land for expansion on the plains was limited, newly settled areas in the plains and northwest became more crowded, and much of the increase in population had to be absorbed on the mountain itself, pushing densities up to 238/km² in Boru and 140/km² in Burka, while those in the northwest

21 The first Arusha settlements in Musa were reported in DO/AD to PC/NP, 18 July 1934 and PC/NP to LO, 26 July 1934 (TNA: 10079/V). The reconstruction put forward here parallels that in Gulliver, *Land and Population*, 20–1.

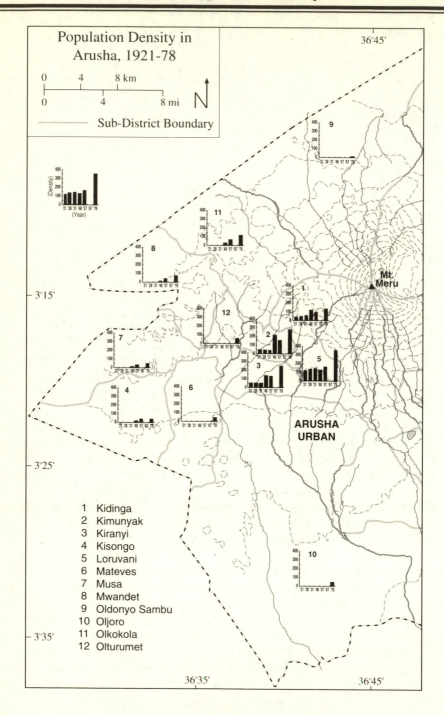

Map 7.2a Population Density: Arusha

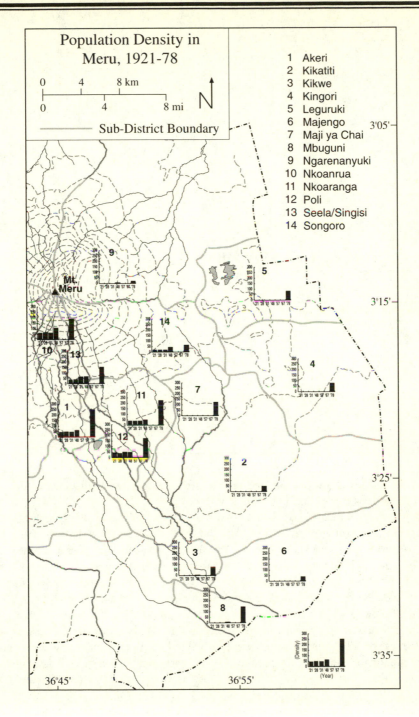

Population Density in Meru, 1921-78

0   4   8 km
0   4   8 mi   N

Sub-District Boundary

1 Akeri
2 Kikatiti
3 Kikwe
4 Kingori
5 Leguruki
6 Majengo
7 Maji ya Chai
8 Mbuguni
9 Ngarenanyuki
10 Nkoanrua
11 Nkoaranga
12 Poli
13 Seela/Singisi
14 Songoro

Map 7.2b Population Density: Meru

Table 7.5 Arusha: Distribution of Population Increase (%)

Period	Increase	Boru	Burka	NW High	Plains	Total
1921–31	pop.	13	19	–	–	18
	dens.	13	19			
1928–48	pop.	114	83	First	–	133
	dens.	114	83	settlements		
1948–67	pop.	11	81	270	614	91
	area	0	0	17	406	
	dens.	11	81	218	44	
1967–78	pop.	44	28	9	78	36
	area	0	0	0	77	
	dens.	44	28	10	0	

Table 7.6 Meru: Distribution of Population Increase (%)

Period	Increase	High	NE high	SE low	Total
1921–31	pop.	13			13
	dens.	13			
1928–48	pop.	59	First		96
	dens.	57	settlements		
1948–67	pop.	96	499	Initial	229
	dens.	96	400	settlements	
1967–78	pop.	38	61	50	50
	dens.	38	57	59	

grew only modestly to 77/km² and the settled areas in the plains nearly doubled, keeping densities there constant at 36/km².[22]

Thus, while population growth in Arusha in the 1930s and 1940s was absorbed evenly on the mountain, that in the 1950s and 1960s sparked off wide-scale shifts from Boru to Burka and subsequently into the northwest highlands and plains. These movements drove up densities on the drier northwestern highlands and plains, causing subsequent growth in the 1970s to be absorbed more evenly on the mountain and new settlement areas on the plains, driving densities in all areas to record highs.

Meru followed a somewhat different pattern of growth. Unlike Arusha, where population growth shifted dramatically from one area to another, growth was more evenly paced across the different areas in Meru (see Table 7.6). With initial population density on the mountain being half that of Arusha, and early population growth less, much of the population increase in the 1930s and 1940s as well as that in the 1950s and 1960s

[22] Again, this accords with Gulliver, *Land and Population*, 22–3. For individual histories, see Mosingo ole Meipusu (AHT 1) and Ngole ole Njololoi (AHT 4).

was absorbed on the mountain, where average densities increased from 37 to 114/km², while expansion into the northern highlands around Engare Nanyuki occurred later, but then proceeded at a more rapid pace than in Arusha. By the time densities in the northeast reached 35/km² in the 1960s, Meru began to move into the southeastern lowlands as well. With the northeast and plains both approaching densities of 60/km² in the 1970s, however, growth became more evenly spread across all areas, with densities in the highlands reaching 158/km².

Thus the initial stages of population growth in both Arusha and Meru were met by spreading out into less densely occupied districts on the mountain itself (western Boru, Burka, and upper and eastern Meru). But as densities on the mountain rose over 150/km² in parts of Arusha in the 1940s and 100/km² in Meru in the 1950s, population began to spill into the drier northern highlands and then out onto the plains until densities there rose to 36-77/km², at which point population growth recommenced on the mountain itself and densities increased to 200-360/km² in most of the older districts.

Agricultural Intensification: 1920s-1960s

With population densities increasing throughout the 1920s and 1930s and only limited possibilities for bringing further land on the mountain into production, Arusha and Meru were again faced with difficult choices. They chose to continue their earlier efforts to increase agricultural yields and found new ways of doing so by planting pastures with annual crops, hand-feeding cattle and using their manure as fertilizer, extending banana cultivation into areas previously planted in annual crops while expanding annual crop production into areas previously used for grazing, and raising new crops for sale on the market.

As all available land on Mount Meru came under cultivation, farmers began to reduce intercrop and fallow periods when stock were allowed to graze on annual fields to enable them to plant more annual crops. Forced to reduce the number of cattle they grazed on the mountain as a result, they transferred dry stock to the plains, where they were herded by neighbourhood boys or pastoral Maasai kin, and fed the remaining milch cows with crop refuse or with grass carried up from the plains by women. They then burned the remaining crop residues and carried cattle manure out onto their fields to enrich the soil and increase yields. Similarly, communal pastures were enclosed by individual farmers and planted in crops. By the late 1930s scarcely any pastures remained in the central districts and most stock was either grazed on the plains or hand-fed.[23]

Both Meru and Arusha managed their herds carefully to maximize milk and meat production while minimizing labour. While they kept an average of six to eight cows for every ten persons, only three to five of them were kept on Meru, while the rest were grazed on the plains (see Table 7.7). Cattle on the mountain were kept primarily for milk, while dry cows, bulls, and steers were grazed on the plains until they calved or

[23] A.E. Haarer, 2 July 1925; DO/AD to PC/NP, 16 Sept 1930 (TNA: 69/45/9); Hartley, 'Brief Note on the Meru'; Notes by N.R. Reid, *Arusha District Book*; VO/NP to DO/AD, 10 June 1939 (TNA: 9/6/5); Northern Province Native Agriculture, 1945 (TNA: 9/6/5); Gulliver, *Land and Population*, 65-6; Cory, 'Arusha Land Tenure', 23-4; Yohanes ole Kauwenara (AHT 2).

Table 7.7 Cattle (1949 Cattle Census)

Area	Population	Arusha Density	Cattle	Head/pers	F/M
Boru					
Loruvani	4479	133	2541	0.57	4.7
Kiranyi	6452	143	2756	0.43	1.0*
Kidinga	7646	125	6231	0.81	0.8*
Kimunyak	6888	220	1669	0.24	3.4
sub-total	25465	149	13197	0.52	1.3
Burka					
Sokon Juu	2902		322	0.11	3.8
Sekei	4443		1351	0.30	4.1
Sombetin	4174		1417	0.34	6.1
Sinon	4533		834	0.18	4.7
Moivaru	2710		1367	0.50	4.3
sub-total	21511	60	7258	0.34	5.0
NW High					
Olkokola	2403	34	1452	0.62	1.9
Mwandet	1554	18	2863	1.84	2.4
Musa	1065	18	3996	1.94	2.1
sub-total	6022	22	8311	1.38	2.1
Plains					
Kisongo	2218	25	4560	2.06	2.0
Totals	55216		34817	0.63	

Area	Population	Meru Density	Cattle	Head/pers	F/M
Highlands					
Nkoanrua	3366	106	1194	0.35	5.8
Ndoombo	1734		454	0.26	5.9
Akeri	2004	62	1081	0.54	4.2
Poli	2067	47	1079	0.40	6.0
Nkoaranga	2707	49	1413	0.52	4.5
Seela	1005	65	284	0.28	58.7
Singisi	1431	65	661	0.46	4.9
Mulala	2093	44	1385	0.66	16.5
Sura	2349	44	1326	0.56	4.7
sub-total	18755	58	8877	0.47	6.0
NE High					
Engare Nanyuki	2452	7	8008	3.26	1.0
Totals	21207		16885	0.80	

* These areas contain sub-districts on or near the plains where large numbers of male cattle were kept, thus accounting for the abnormally low F/M ratios for milking herds.

Source: 1949 Cattle Census, District Note Book (TNA: 9/6/5).

7.3 Livestock in Arusha homestead (Benjamin)

were slaughtered for meat. An average of four to six females were kept on the mountain for every male, while there were only one to two females for every male in the plains or in those districts adjacent to them. The combination of crop and cattle management was 'an extraordinary system of intensive mixed farming', producing bananas, milk, and meat for human consumption, while providing cattle with highly digestible banana fodder that was high in carbohydrates and minerals and had a productive value greater than hay, silage, or mature grass.[24]

As pastures were planted with annual crops, fields previously devoted to annual crops were planted permanently in bananas, thus extending the belt of banana cultivation across the middle slopes. By the late 1930s, Meru farms averaged 2.5 acres, of which 0.5–0.75 acre were planted in bananas. Over time bananas were further extended into annual fields that had once been pasture, as well as into lower and higher reaches of the middle belt, pushing annual cropping into regions that were either too cold or too dry for bananas.[25] Flying over Mount Meru in 1936, Gillman noted the luscious green velvet 'chess-board pattern' of Arusha gardens, the 'amazing tilling of some very steep slopes', and 'a very marked increase in area under bananas' in Meru. While Arusha appeared to lag behind Meru in banana cultivation – testimony, Gillman thought, to their continued love of cattle – it was only a matter of time before the central slopes in Arusha would become a dense patchwork of irrigated banana groves as well.[26]

At the same time as Arusha and Meru were expanding banana production and

[24] Simmonds, *Bananas*, 271, referring to a similar system on Kilimanjaro.
[25] Hartley, 'Brief Note on the Meru'; Northern Province Native Agriculture, 1945 (TNA: 9/6/5).
[26] Gillman, Diaries, XVIII/97h/29.5.36, 9 (OCRP: MSS.Afr.s.1175).

Table 7.8 Recorded Marketed Crop Production

Year	Maize (tons)	Beans (tons)	Onions (tons)	Wheat (tons)
1930		27*	21	
1931	180*	38*	17	
1932	809*	48*	54	3*
1933	140*	4*	8	1*
1934	517*	35*	36	2*
1935	329*		37	2*
1936				5
1937				39
1938				85
1939			150	200
1940			240	500
1941			260	300
1942			360	600
1943			854	448
1944	205	103	764	642
1945	414	652	1324	387
1946	206	96	1287	112
1947	1246	410	1179	129
1948	2133	484	1622	175
1949	770	729	1073	175
1950	1748	506	634	107
1951	4564	709	967	112
1952	3600	751	1063	11
1953	1224	231	1000	6
1954	2965		1399	79
1955				
1956				
1957				
1958				
1959	200		200	
1960				
1961/2	1920*	2946*	4084	
1962/3	9500*	4322*	4450	
1963/4	17310*	7028*	5000	
1964/5	10500*	6432*	5500	
1965/6	6173*	6469*	5500	
1966/7	3243			
1967/8	4274			
1968/9	2168			
1969/70	3369			437
1970/1	12712			600
1971/2	1587			2810
1972/3	6973	616		5213
1973/4	6609	1662		4934

* denotes total of European and African production. All other figures include African production only.

Sources: AO/AD to Sr AO, 7 April 1931 (TNA:472/22); Agriculture Department, Annual Reports, 1931–5 & 1945–65 (TNA: 472/22 & 472/-); Arusha District, Annual Reports, 1945–54 (TNA: 9/4/6; 472/-; 472/ANR/1); Agriculture Department, Monthly Reports, 1945–54 (TNA: 9/4/6; 9/AGR/5; 472/-); DA to CS/DSM, 18 December 1939 (TNA: 9916); 'Wheat', 1940 (TNA: 9/6/5); Northern Province, Native Agriculture, 1945 (TNA: 9/6/5); PC/NP to Member for Agriculture, 7 August 1948 (TNA: 31265); ARCU records, 1961–74 cited in Leonard Shio, 'A Political Economy of the Plantation System in Arusha' (MA, Dar es Salaam, 1977), 163.

extending annual crop production for their own consumption, they were also marketing crop surpluses to workers on the surrounding plantations. While recorded marketed crop figures for the 1920s to 1940s are notably unreliable, Meru and Arusha were already producing enough maize in the 1930s to feed the migrant workers engaged on road and estate work in the area, and by the late 1940s they were selling an average of 829 tons of maize and 412 tons of beans annually. By the early 1950s, these had risen to 2,820 and 549 tons respectively (see Table 7.8).[27]

Arusha and Meru also marketed their produce in Arusha town, where there was a high demand for milk, livestock, and vegetables, and Arusha continued to trade actively with pastoral Maasai.[28] They also developed a major new crop for sale locally, selling an average of 29 tons of onions annually in the early 1930s, increasing to 1,297 tons annually by the late 1940s. Onions, maize, and beans produced for local markets were the most valuable cash crops in Meru and Arusha, consistently outpacing coffee until the dramatic expansion of coffee production in response to rising prices in the 1950s and 1960s.[29]

High value *arabica* coffee was first introduced on Meru by Leipzig missionaries in 1902, when Fickert planted the first 80 trees at Nkoaranga. By 1907 the mission was reaping a ton and a half of beans and early Christians began to plant their own trees.[30] Interest was limited at first, given that it took several years for coffee trees to bear, and that without ready transport to Moshi there was only a limited market among local planters; but by 1923–4 Meru had planted almost 50,000 trees and Arusha had acquired their first plots when the administration transferred the Thiele farm (Farms No 183 & 194) to them.[31] Production began to pick up slowly thereafter, averaging 25 tons annually in the late 1920s, 65 tons in the 1930s, 143 tons in the 1940s, 467 tons in the 1950s, 2,037 tons in the 1960s, and 3,966 tons in the early 1970s (see Table 7.9).[32]

Coffee planting and production grew in spite of early opposition from settlers and the administration, severe droughts and low prices throughout the Depression, and high transportation and marketing costs. Settlers complained publicly that poor disease control and theft by Meru and Arusha farmers threatened their own trees, but they were privately more concerned over possible competition and ensuring local supplies of labour.[33] They were successfully able to persuade the administration to restrict further

---

[27] While the Blue Books contain annual figures for crop production from the 1920s, these are totally unreliable indices of African production, repeating the same estimated totals year after year. More accurate estimates contained in the Annual Reports of the Agriculture Department from the early 1930s lumped European and African production of maize and beans together until the late 1940s.

[28] VO/NP to DO/AD, 10 June 1939 (TNA: 9/6/5); N.R. Reid reported in 1939 that 600 cattle a month were sold for slaughter locally, while the demand for goats and sheep consistently exceeded supply: *Arusha District Book*.

[29] Northern Province, Annual Report, 1934 (TNA: 11681); Northern Province Native Agriculture, 1945 (TNA: 9/6/5).

[30] Krause, *ELMB*, 58(1903), 138; Schachschneider, *ELMB*, 62 (1907), 168, 562.

[31] Arusha District, Annual Report, 1923 (OCRP: Hallier Papers, MSS.Afr.s.1072).

[32] Case histories of individual growers, casting more light on the expansion of coffee production, will be taken up in Chapter 8.

[33] Memorandum by the Chairman of the Board of Coffee, 6 July 1927 et seq. (TNA: 11160); Memo by Combined Association of Arusha, 27 July 1929 et seq. (TNA: 11908/I); Dir. of Agriculture to CS/DSM, 17 April 1930 (TNA: 12968/I).

Table 7.9 Coffee Production

Year	Production (tons)		Trees (no. or acres)		Growers (no.)		Prices (shs/ton)	Returns (shs*/grower)	
1924			49491#						
1925		16					2540		
1926		6					2400		
1927		36				240	2380		357
1928		37				486	2340		178
1929		31			M	374	2200		103
					A	287			
1930		45			M	324	1560		96
					A	409			
1931		33				700	560		26
1932		44					806		
1933		100					515		
1934		47							
1935		85		700 a		1300	358		23
1936		49					551		
1937		43					523		
1938		82	M	.41m#	M	807	624		43
			A	.26m#	A	395			
				691 a					
1939	M	96				1100	638		73
	A	30							
1940		152.5					470		63
1941		99					672		38
1942		133					1120		105
1943		73					1972		100
1944		198							150
1945	M	54							
	A	39							
1946		161					2000		
1947		144							
1948		184							
1949		195		1150a					
1950/1		200	M	1.2m#	M	2334			
			A	.3m#	A	795			
1951/2	M	191					1254=		
	A	144			A	649		A	278
1952/3	M	208							
	A	85			A	650			
1953/4					A	651			
1954/5	M	184	M	2626a	M	3143	10600	M	621
	A	125	A	1528a	A	1819		A	728
				2.5m#					
1955/6	M	369	M	2625a	M	3000	6540	M	804
	A	182	A	2083a					

140

Table 7.9 Coffee Production (cont.)

	Production (tons)		Trees (no. or acres)	Growers (no.)		Prices (shs/ton)		Returns (shs*/grower)	
1956/7	M	341		M	3494	M	9091	M	790
	A	179		A	1050	A	8951	A	1388
1957/8	M	239					7720		
	A	101		A	1100			A	867
1958/9	M	500							
1959/60	M	769		M	3900		6300	M	901
	A	389		A	1100			A	2228
1960/1		724		M	5000	M	5720		
1961/2		782					5800		
1962/3		1182					4960		
1963/4		1819					6300		
1964/5		2067					5360		
1965/6		4015		M	6603		6020		2483
				A	3131				
1966/7		2280					5460		
1967/8		2313					5180		
1968/9		3272							
1969/70		1919					7660		
1970/1		2962							
1971/2		4910							
1972/3		4360							
1973/4		2642							
1974/5		4955		4122a					

Notes:
* Currency figures are East African shillings.
1. All figures include Meru and Arusha unless designated M (Meru) or A (Arusha).
2. Returns/Grower from sources or calculated from available data.
Sources: Agriculture Department, Annual Reports, 1928-33, 1945-65 (TNA: 471/22; 472/-); Northern Province, Annual Reports, 1928-33, 1945-51, 1956-7, 1959 (TNA: 11681; 19415; 471/R.3/2); AO/AD to Sr AO, 7 April 1931 (TNA: 472/22); T.C. Cairns, 'Native Coffee Growing,' 1940 (TNA: 9/6/5); DO/AD to AO/AD, 21 Feb 1940 (TNA: 9/12/13); AO/AD to Sr AO, 14 Oct 1941 (TNA: 9/12/13); Northern Province, Native Agriculture, 1945 (TNA: 9/6/5); AO/AD, Monthly Reports (TNA: 9/4/2/II); Arusha District, Annual Report, 1952-3 (TNA: 472/-; 472/ANR/1); misc. corres. (TNA: 19904/1); ARCU records cited in L. Shio, 'A Political Economy of the Plantation System in Arusha' (MA, Dar es Salaam, 1977), 163; S. Mbilinyi, The Economics of Peasant Coffee Production (Nairobi, 1976), 47.

expansion of African cultivation in 1927, but Meru and Arusha continued to plant regardless, and the administration was forced to relax its restrictions in 1933 following the collapse of settler production during the Depression. To continue restrictions, the Chief Secretary noted, would convey the impression to Africans that the administration did not wish them to prosper and would be impolitic, given the profits people were making.[34]

[34] Director of Agriculture to CS/DSM, 13 July 1928, citing report by the District Agricultural Officer, A.E. Haarer, 3 July 1928; DC/AD to PC/NP, 1 August 1928 and PC/NP to CS/DSM, 4 August 1928 (all in TNA: 11908/I); Circular Nos 77 of 1927 and 3 of 1933 and related correspondence (TNA: 11160); D. Sturdy, 'Native Coffee on Meru,' in AO/AD to Sr AO, 15 May 1931 (TNA: 9/12/13); Northern Province, Annual Report, 1934 (TNA: 11681). See below for further discussion of this issue.

While droughts in 1932–4 and 1939–41 and low prices during the Depression dealt severe blows to settler production, they had less effect on Arusha and Meru production. Meru and Arusha intercropped coffee with bananas on irrigated fields, thus enabling them to continue planting in spite of drought, while the settlers, located on the lower reaches of the rivers flowing down Mount Meru, had less reliable sources of water for irrigation. Similarly, settlers were highly dependent on prices to hire labour and pay their mortgages and crop advances. When prices collapsed in 1930, many laid off their work-forces or went bankrupt, leaving their trees to deteriorate from neglect.[35] Arusha and Meru, by contrast, had little capital invested in coffee, relied on family labour, and had other sources of support, allowing them to sustain production in spite of low prices. The fact that their early plantings were just beginning to bear in 1929, and continued to do so regardless of demand, made supplies relatively inelastic in relation to prices in any case. Given the collapse of settler production, many in the administration reversed normal economic rationality and argued that Meru and Arusha should, in fact, increase production in response to low prices in order to maintain their incomes. Arusha and Meru were not deceived, however; while they continued to maintain the coffee they had, they remained reluctant to expand cultivation further until prices recovered in the early 1940s.[36]

Finally, Meru and Arusha expanded production in spite of the fact that they incurred high marketing and transportation costs for their crop. The railroad was not extended to Arusha until 1929 and, in the early years, Arusha and Meru farmers sold their crops to local settlers at 30–35% less than Chaga farmers on Kilimanjaro received, while their first attempt to market their own crop directly in London in 1929 resulted in losses to the local Arusha and Meru Native Coffee Planters' Association.[37] They put their crop out to tender from local traders thereafter, but they continued to receive below market prices until they established their own marketing co-operatives in the 1950s.[38]

Meru and Arusha raised coffee because it was highly compatible with banana cultivation and because it provided increasing rates of return on land and labour. They planted coffee interspersed among bananas, allowing the bananas to provide beneficial shade to the new trees, and they mulched and irrigated coffee at the same time as bananas. The main additional labour required was for pruning, picking, and processing the beans, but these activities extended throughout the year, and they could be accomplished on small plots using family labour and inexpensive hand tools.[39]

While some in the administration approved of Meru and Arusha raising coffee, the perennial problem of land shortage was never far from most administrators' minds, and many felt that Arusha and Meru risked their well-being by growing cash crops instead

[35] Agriculture Department, Annual Reports, 1933–35 (TNA: 472/22); Northern Province, Annual Reports, 1929–33 (TNA: 11681).

[36] Northern Province, Annual Report, 1929 (TNA: 11681); Agriculture Department, Annual Report, 1934 (TNA: 472/22); Arusha District, Annual Report, 1934 (TNA: 472/22); CS/DSM to PCs, 3 March 1938 (TNA: 19904/II); T.C. Cairns, 'Native Coffee Growing', 1940 (TNA: 9/6/5).

[37] Northern Province, Annual Reports, 1933–34 (TNA: 11681).

[38] Marketing and the development of Arusha and Meru co-operatives will be considered at greater length in Chapter 8.

[39] Simon Mbilinyi, *The Economics of Peasant Coffee Production: The Case of Tanzania* (Nairobi, 1976), 35, 90–4.

7.4 Coffee and bananas in Arusha (Benjamin)

of food. The District Agricultural Officer, A.E. Haarer, strongly supported the 1927 restrictions on coffee and worked hard to persuade Meru to abandon coffee in favour of food crops, but he despaired when they doubled their coffee plantings despite his best efforts. He was even more disturbed by increased cultivation of *mbeke*, or eleusine: 'It is well known that Mbeke is not used as a food, but for fermenting banana juice and producing a strong alcoholic drink. Hence ... the increased use of Mbeke means that more bananas are used for producing drink than for food.'[40]

Not everyone was so concerned. The Chief Secretary responded that coffee was too profitable and popular with growers to restrict and that eleusine was merely a mild beer drunk by all, 'just like British country people'. If the Chief Secretary was less than impressed by Haarer's arguments, A.E. Kitching, the District Commissioner in Arusha, was enraged by them:

1. The general impression conveyed by the report... is that the Meru tribesmen have taken leave of their senses and on account of the reckless exploitation of coffee and eleusine are in imminent danger of famine. Nothing could be further from the truth.

2. There has been an increase in the cultivation of coffee during the past three years..., but the area that has been planted is still an insignificant proportion of the cultivable land. The crop is not and never will be a menace to the cultivation of food-stuffs.

3. The Meru tribesmen have always been expert cultivators of eleusine.... The crop is a very valuable commodity and is sold all over the district.... It is used for making ordinary native beer....

[40] A.E. Haarer, report dated 3 July 1928, cited in Director of Agriculture to CS/DSM, 13 July 1928 (TNA: 11908/I).

4. The whole of the Meru area is intensively cultivated and the Meru are assiduous agriculturalists. They sell annually hundreds of tons of maize and beans and thousands of bunches of bananas in the settled areas and elsewhere.

5. Mr. Haarer was camped in the Meru area for ten full days only. In this period he visited eighteen European farms... found time to visit my office on at least two occasions and opened an experimental seed station in Meru. He certainly had no time left to make an adequate inspection of the Meru area and as a result of inquiries which I have made I say explicitly that he did not do so.... His report is rubbish.

The Provincial Commissioner forwarded Kitching's response to the Chief Secretary 'with complete confidence'.[41]

While Kitching summed up the Meru position rather well, the debate was by no means ended. Kitching's successor as District Officer, R.A. Pelham, agonized that Meru cattle were being forced off the mountain, making milk 'almost unprocurable' and thereby threatening children's health. While Pelham felt that it was probably necessary to plant lucrative crops such as coffee and eleusine when land was so sparse and that Meru might even be encouraged to buy their maize from settlers, he feared that increasing population and cultivation was sure to impoverish the land until it would produce nothing.[42] The District Agricultural Officer banned further planting in 1937 to 'ensure ... no further limitation of the land required for essential food production or grazing'.[43] And D.S. Troup, the District Officer in 1947, argued that the land shortage on Meru resulted from 'the maldistribution of the land which is supporting inedible cash crops at the expense of food crops, thereby precluding the maintenance of the population increase'.[44]

They need not have worried. Meru and Arusha were well aware of the land problem, put high premiums on conserving resources and food security, and integrated cash crops in their agricultural routine precisely because they provided greater returns on land and labour than the alternatives. They adopted coffee only slowly at first, until rising prices in the 1940s and 1950s made it the most lucrative crop to grow. Similarly, they were quick to reject cotton in the 1940s because of its poor returns.[45] They also steadfastly rejected segregating coffee and bananas, as the agriculture department advocated, because, taken together, bananas and coffee produced a greater total yield than either grown separately, a fact the administration did not recognize until the late 1950s.[46] Together the two also ensured an adequate food supply as well as a cash income, a virtue underlined for Arusha and Meru by the low prices for coffee in the 1930s. Meru and

[41] DC/AD to PC/NP, 1 Aug 1928, and PC/NP to CS/DSM, 4 Aug 1928 (TNA: 11908/I).
[42] DO/AD to PC/NP, 16 Sept 1930 (TNA: 69/45/9).
[43] T.C. Cairns, 'Native Coffee Growing,' 1940 (TNA: 9/6/5).
[44] DC/AD to PC/NP, 4 Nov 1947 (TNA: 9/NA/1).
[45] PC/NP to CS/DSM, 23 July 1928 (TNA: 11160); Northern Province Native Agriculture, 1945 (TNA: 9/6/5); Agriculture Department, Annual Report, 1945 (TNA: 472/-).
[46] Commenting on the intercropping of coffee and bananas, the Northern Province Annual Report for 1959: noted: 'The indications are that the small farmer has evolved a pattern of cultivation that gives him maximum production and is best suited to his way of life and that pure stands of coffee are perhaps only advisable on the larger holdings.' (TNA: 471/R.3/2); A. Nypan & M. Vaa, 'Extension Theory and Local Theory' (Report No. 9, Section for Development Studies, Institute of Sociology, Oslo, 1974), 87–124; James Lewton Brain, personal communication.

Arusha never lacked sufficient food supplies for themselves; they continued to market surplus foodstuffs in large quantities; and they remained capable of supplying victims of drought on the plains during even the worst years.

Given the poor wages paid by the plantations (as low as East African shs 5/- per work card in the Depression and never more than shs 20/-), raising cash crops provided a far better return on labour than working for wages. Arusha and Meru could meet their needs for taxes, school fees, and consumer goods far more easily and ensure their own food production at the same time. Individual growers realized shs 100-160/- annually raising onions in the early 1940s, while coffee provided average annual net returns of shs 212/- in the late 1920s, shs 52/- through the 1930s, shs 91/- in the early 1940s, and shs 956/- through the 1950s.[47] Due to a combination of low costs, high returns from the 1950s, and compatibility with banana culture, coffee became the main cash crop, though onions, maize, and beans sales continued apace.[48] Trading in cattle was even more lucrative, allowing some Arusha to amass sufficient capital to invest in tractors and combine harvesters in the 1940s.[49] Thus, through a judicious balancing of crops, fields, labour, and investments, Arusha and Meru were able continually to increase the productivity of both their land and their labour to more than meet the needs of their expanding population, increasing their own standard of living as they did so.

Marketing crop surpluses and adopting new cash crops made new demands on the annual labour cycle and the division of labour, but were accomplished without undue risk to ongoing production of crops grown for domestic consumption. A half acre of coffee, the average amount, required about 50 hours' work spread fairly evenly throughout the year (see Table 7.2).[50] New coffee trees were planted during the long rains when there was little other work, while older trees were pruned and sprayed from January to March and the berries picked and processed from June to November. Onions were also planted during the long rains and harvested from September to November. Grown both in black cotton soil at the edge of the plains and on the high mountain slopes, onions did not displace other crops.

While the new crops did not take labour away from food crops, they did require additional labour to produce. Most of the work involving coffee except picking and processing was men's work, while women raised onions and helped pick and process coffee. As population densities rose and adult children remained at home for longer periods of time, more labour became available, and *murran* increasingly joined the active labour force.

Technological improvements also raised labour productivity. Iron hoes increasingly replaced wooden digging sticks early in the century; oxen began to be used to plough maize and bean fields in the 1920s; and the first tractors were acquired in the 1940s.[51] Since men worked with oxen and tractors, some cultivating passed from women to

---

[47] Northern Province Native Agriculture, 1945 (TNA: 9/6/5); Figure 7:9.

[48] Mbilinyi, *Economics*, 35.

[49] N.R. Reid, 1939, *Arusha District Book*; N.N. Luanda, 'European Commercial Farming and its Impact on the Meru and Arusha Peoples of Tanzania, 1920–1955' (Ph.D., Cambridge, 1986), 165–71.

[50] Mbilinyi, *Economics*, 35.

[51] AO/AR to Sr AO, 7 April 1931 (TNA: 472/22); Arusha District, Annual Report, 1923; Northern Province, Annual Report, 1937 (TNA:19415/1937); AO/AD, Monthly Report, Nov 1951 (TNA: 9/24).

men, but women had their workloads increased with the increased labour required raising annual crops, caring for hand-fed stock, and carrying fodder up from the plains. Coffee yields were also increased through the use of animal and green fertilizer, mulching, chemical sprays, and improved processing. While the average plot of coffee remained fairly constant at half an acre, for example, yields increased from 0.10 tons/ acre in 1929 to 0.17 tons/acre in 1949 and 0.73 tons/acre in 1969. By the late 1970s they had reached 1.2 tons/acre, a 12-fold increase overall.[52] With prices rising, average returns to farmers increased even more rapidly.

While Meru and Arusha were thus able to increase the productivity of both land and labour throughout the 1920s, 1930s, and 1940s to support higher population densities, this was not accomplished without considerable social and political stress, as we shall see in the following chapters. As sons were no longer able to pioneer vacant land elsewhere, they remained at home to divide and contest their patrimony, fragmenting family land into smaller and smaller holdings.[53] Tenants were among the first to suffer, as family members contested non-kin's rights to remain on family land.[54] Struggles erupted as people with land sought to circumvent the social contract guaranteeing everyone sufficient land for their needs; more land became treated as individual property; and landless individuals struggled to defend the old moral economy. In the words of one elder:

> Land is scarce nowadays, and we cannot agree to people being driven off the land which they have always cultivated because his neighbour wants to take it. What do we know about the old days? It was all different then; there was much land and people were friendly.[55]

Eventually the combination of increasing population, land shortage and fragmentation, and the social tensions they induced drove many to abandon the mountain for new land frontiers in the northern highlands and plains.

Expansion into the Northern Highlands and Plains: 1940s–1960s

As population and densities built up on the mountain through the 1930s and 1940s, Meru and Arusha were able to increase their productivity apace until densities rose over 100/km^2, or one hectare per person, at which point people began to expand into the drier, less desirable areas on the northern slopes of the mountain and out on to the plains where they had to abandon banana cultivation and rely on cattle and rain-fed production of maize and beans.[56]

Arusha first began to expand from Olevolos, Kimunak and Sambasha west along the

---

[52] D. Sturdy, 'Native Coffee on Mt Meru', 1931 (TNA: 472/ASS/12); T.C. Cairns, 'Native Coffee Growing', 1940 (TNA: 9/6/5); Figure 7:10. Patricia Benjamin, personal communication.

[53] Gulliver, *Land and Population*, 42.

[54] Gulliver, *Land and Population*, 11, 58–61, 75; idem, *Social Control in an African Society* (London, 1963), 186–258; idem., 'Land Shortage, Social Change, and Social Conflict in East Africa', *Journal of Conflict Resolution*, 5 (1961), 21–5; idem., 'A Land Dispute in Arusha, Tanzania' in *African Dimensions* (Boston, 1975), 2–14.

[55] Gulliver, 'Land Dispute,' 10.

[56] Agriculture Department, Annual Report, 1945 (TNA: 472/-).

7.5 Western Arusha plains (Spear)

Monduli spur to Musa and Likamba in the 1930s and 1940s. Drier than Mount Meru and lacking comparable water supplies for irrigation, Monduli was, nevertheless, high (1,500–1,800 metres) and cool, ideal for raising cattle, maize, and wheat. During the 1950s and 1960s Arusha spread further into Mwandet, Olkokola and Olturumet, and on to the Kisongo plains. As the northwestern highlands became increasingly crowded by the late 1960s, however, most subsequent expansion was on the plains south to Oljoro and north into areas abandoned by Afrikaners in Oldonyo Sambu.

Meru expansion lagged at least a decade behind that in Arusha, owing to lower population pressures on the mountain itself.[57] The first Meru began to filter into the northeastern slopes around Engare Nanyuki in the 1940s, where they raised cattle, maize, and beans. Meru subsequently expanded east from Nkoaranga along the Sakila ridge into Kingori, Leguruki, and Maji ya Chai in the 1950s and 1960s. Other Meru moved south into the plains, to Kikwe and Mbuguni, to raise maize and beans in the 1940s, expanding further to Kikatiti and Majengo in the 1950s and 1960s.[58] By the late 1970s Arusha and Meru had colonized the plains for 50 miles around, from Kilimanjaro International Airport in the east to Makuyuni and the wall of the Rift Valley in the west.

The decision to leave the comfortable security of the banana belt must have been a difficult one. Meru and Arusha had long been reluctant to abandon their ancestral *kihamba* and *engisaka* for the malarial and tsetse-infested plains where one was

---

[57] Northern Province, Annual Reports, 1957–58 (TNA: 471:R.3/2); Figure 7:4.

[58] AO/AD, Monthly Reports, 1953–5 (TNA: 9/4/2; 9/4/2/II; & 472/-); Northern Province, Annual Report, 1956 (TNA: 471/R.3/2).

dependent on uncertain rainfall to raise one's crops.[59] Few, therefore, made the move abruptly, and most retained their links with their natal homesteads.

The first Arusha to move off the mountain in the 1930s were herdsmen responsible for caring for stock shifted from mountain pastures to make room for crops. Arusha had long herded cattle on the Monduli spur and Kisongo plains after the rains, shifting them periodically between the plains and mountain as the occasion demanded, and during their longer stays they often planted small plots of maize and beans to supplement their diet. As land became increasingly scarce on the mountain and cattle herded more permanently on the plains, many found their stays extended and expanded their plantings. Others joined pastoral Maasai relatives or became cattle dealers.[60] Such activities were not mutually exclusive: almost everyone farmed and herded cattle, and most remained within their natal household economies, providing maize, beans, milk, and meat to highland kin in return for bananas.[61]

Raising annual crops on the plains freed relatives on the mountain to extend their banana plantations into fields previously used for annual crops. The move to the plains was thus a further stage in the development of the mountain economy, shifting cattle grazing, fodder production, and annual crops to the plains to allow for further specialization in bananas and coffee in the highlands. Whereas individual households had once integrated bananas, annual crops, and cattle at a single location on the mountain, these functions now became increasingly dispersed among family members in different locations on Meru, Monduli, and the plains, though they usually continued to function as joint economic households. A crop survey done in 1976–7 found that 65 per cent of Arusha land on the mountain was planted in bananas and coffee, 22 per cent in maize and beans, and 13 per cent in vegetables, root crops, and onions; whereas 2 per cent of land in the northwest was planted in bananas and coffee, 50 per cent in maize and beans, and 40 per cent in wheat; and 80 per cent of land on the plains was planted in maize and beans and 13 per cent in wheat.[62]

A similar dispersal followed in Meru, as elders sought out vacant plots elsewhere in the highlands and plains and placed their wives and sons out to farm them, managing the whole as a single integrated economic household. Centred on the family's *kihamba* on the mountain, a single household might include separate fields higher on the mountain for annual crops, a mixed farm in Engare Nanyuki where livestock were kept, and a holding on the plains for rain-fed maize and bean production. The same 1976–7 crop survey found that 81 per cent of Meru land on the mountain was planted in bananas and coffee and 18 per cent in maize and beans, while 7 per cent of land in the northeastern highlands and plains was planted in bananas and coffee and 91 per cent in maize and beans.[63]

[59] Northern Province, Native Agriculture, 1945 (TNA: 9/6/5).

[60] Ngole ole Njololoi (AHT 4); Eliyahu Lujas Meiliari (AHT 8); Gillman, Diaries, XII/#95/15.12.34 (OCRP: MSS.Afr.s.1175); Hans Cory, 'Arusha Law and Custom' (UDSM: Hans Cory Papers, 39), 21.

[61] Moffett to Wilson, 22 Oct 1946 (OCRP: MSS.Afr.s.592); Cory, 'Arusha Law and Custom,' 21; Chief Soil Conservation Officer to AO/AD, 30 June 1952 (TNA: 9/ADM/9); Gulliver, *Land and Population*, 21, 43–6; idem., 'Memorandum on the Arusha Chiefdom,' 17–19; idem, 'The Arusha: Economic and Social Change,' 263-4; Eliyahu Lujas Meiliari (AHT 8).

[62] Fortmann, 'Development Prospects', 24–5.

[63] Fortmann, 'Development Prospects', 24–5; Erasto Ngira, personal communication.

7.6 Meru farms on plains (Spear)

Most plains households were thus adjuncts of mountain ones, with the production of each supplementing the other, thereby insuring plains farmers from the ever present danger of drought.[64] In many ways, this was simply a further extension of earlier processes of intensification, in which pastures were replaced with annual crops, and annual crops with bananas and coffee in an ongoing extension of the banana frontier. Over time, all but the highest and coldest reaches of the mountain became devoted to bananas and coffee, annual crops supplemented grazing on the plains, and new heartier banana cultivars (such as *mkojosi*) able to survive in drier areas began to be adopted and take the place of maize on the plains.[65]

Expansion into the drier highlands and plains did not simply represent the outer extension of the banana/coffee frontier, however; it also represented a further development of earlier patterns of agropastoralism and mixed farming that had remained prevalent on the lower slopes of the mountain, especially in western Arusha.[66] Plains farmers combined extensive herding and raising beans and maize on rain-fed fields. They used oxen to clear, plough, and plant their fields; pastured their cattle on crop residues;

[64] AO/AD, Monthly Report, Dec 1953 (TNA: 472/-).

[65] A model of the successive replacement of grazing by annual crops and then bananas is explicitly developed by the Chief Conservation Officer/Tengeru in his letter to AO/AD, 30 June 1952 (TNA: 9/ADM/9). See also, Arusha District, Annual Report, 1952 (TNA: 472/ANR/1); Fortmann, 'Development Prospects,' 245.

[66] Agropastoralism and mixed farming are variants of combined crop and livestock management. Arusha agropastoralists kept larger herds and often continued to practise transhumant herding along with farming, while mixed farmers had smaller herds and tended to graze them on or near their farms. In both, however, cattle were vital for food production and security, as detailed below.

spread manure from kraals on their fields, and kept stock as insurance against possible drought and crop failure. Recent studies of western and lowland Arusha and Meru villages clearly demonstrate the advantages of agropastoralism and mixed farming over simple cultivation, with agropastoralists and mixed farmers able to till larger farms, support larger families, receive higher returns, and enjoy greater food security.[67] Agropastoralism and mixed farming in drier and lower areas thus provided an attractive alternative to the problems of land shortage on the mountain itself.

Expansion onto the northern slopes and plains offered new opportunities to many. Some Arusha who first moved to Musa were wealthy cattlemen who traded stock from central Tanganyika to Nairobi. Cashing in on the cattle and wheat booms of the early 1940s, they sold cattle and invested in ox-drawn ploughs, tractors, and combine harvesters to establish wheat farms of 200 acres or more.[68] By 1945 there were some 500 growers, producing an average of 480 tons of wheat annually and receiving annual returns up to shs 400/- a piece.[69] As wheat prices declined and maize became more profitable from 1947, however, they reduced their wheat production to an average of 135 tons/year (1946–51) before abandoning it altogether when a levy on the crop was added in 1952.[70] Commercial maize production took up the slack, so that by 1956 Arusha farmers in Musa and Likamba owned 24 tractors, were building stone houses, stores, and sheds, and comprised half the members of the commercial Tanganyika Farmers' Association recently established in Arusha town.[71]

By the late 1960s, however, opportunities for obtaining accessible land off the mountain became almost as limited as those on it. Expansion slowed and population densities rose to over 150/km[2] everywhere on the mountain and up to 350/km[2] in some districts, forcing people to consolidate their land holdings and further increase productivity. Families pursued a number of different strategies to deal with this situation. Some whose holdings on the mountain became too fragmented or small to be viable sold their remaining bits of *kihamba* and *engisaka* to neighbours or kin and moved permanently to larger holdings on the plains. Theirs became a more perilous existence, however, as rain-fed crops on the plains were prone to periodic failure, and thus these families lost the food security that Meru and Arusha had previously enjoyed. Others were able to capitalize on their combined holdings of cattle and coffee and take advantage of the increasing land sales on Mount Meru to enlarge and consolidate their family holdings, often by fractions of an acre at a time, to make them more viable.

[67] Bishnu Baral et al., 'In Search of Water: A Study of Farming Systems in the Lowlands of Arumeru District' (Working Document, Series 30, International Centre for Development Oriented Research in Agriculture, Wageningen, 1993), 36–9, 44–7; E.M. Nkonya et al., 'Arumeru District Diagnostic Survey' (Selian Agricultural Research Institute, Arusha, 1991), 33–57; Patricia Benjamin, personal communication.

[68] Northern Province, Annual Report, 1937 (TNA: 19415/1937); 'Wheat', 1940 (TNA: 9/6/5); AO/AD to DC/AD, 20 Aug 1951 (TNA: 472/NA/48); Luanda, 'Commercial Farming', 165–72, Mosingo ole Meipusu (AHT 1); Yohanes ole Kauwenara (AHT 2); Ngole ole Njololoi (AHT 4); Eliyahu Lujas Meiliari (AHT 8).

[69] Northern Province, Native Agriculture, 1945 (TNA: 9/6/5).

[70] AO/AD, Monthly Reports, 1947 and 1952 (TNA: 9/AGR/5 and 471/-); Arusha District, Annual Report, 1952 (TNA: 472/ANR/1).

[71] Agriculture Department, Annual Reports, 1948, 1952 (TNA: 471/-); AO/AD, Monthly Report, Nov 1951 (TNA: 9/24); Arusha District, Annual Report, 1952 (TNA: 69/63/21); Northern Province, Annual Reports, 1955–7 (TNA: 471/R.3/2).

7.7 High altitude farm in Arusha (Spear)

Arusha and Meru also continued to make major investments in productivity and crop diversification to increase their overall returns. Total coffee production rose to 5,000 tons annually in response to high prices as people invested in seedlings, sprays, fertilizer, and better processing facilities to enhance their yields and the quality of their crop. Raising fruits and vegetables for sale in town became increasingly popular, and many began to acquire grade dairy cattle and start commercial milk production.

Population and Agricultural Intensification

The links between population growth and increasing agricultural productivity have been much debated ever since Ester Boserup's pioneering study, *The Conditions of Agricultural Growth*, linked increases in population to agricultural development. While Boserup has been rightly criticized for failing to consider historical factors as well as differences in natural endowments and agricultural potential, Meru and Arusha are, in many respects, exemplars of Boserup's thesis, relentlessly improving the productivity of their land and their labour to achieve increasing yields and returns in response to increasing population and limited availability of land.[72]

[72] Ester Boserup, *The Conditions of Agricultural Growth* (New York, 1965). For considerations of the Boserup thesis in relation to East African conditions, see Paul Maro, 'Population and Land Resources in Northern Tanzania: The Dynamics of Change, 1920–1970' (Ph.D., Minnesota, 1974), 36–41; Mbilinyi, *Economics*; Thomas Hakansson,'Social and Political Aspects of Intensive Agriculture in East Africa,' *Azania*, 24 (1989), 12–20; B. Turner, G. Hyden, & R. Kates (eds), *Population Growth and Agricultural Change in*

Increasing population and limited availability of land were only two factors influencing Arusha and Meru choices, however. Fertile volcanic soils and abundant supplies of water enabled people to extract ever greater returns from the land. Crops such as bananas, maize, beans, and coffee were conducive to more intensive cultivation, returning greater yields for greater inputs of labour, while cattle could also be integrated into farm management to increase both food and milk production. The availability of land off the mountain was critical for the expansion of mixed farming, and the growth of local markets for food, cash crops, and cattle on the estates and in Arusha town, enabled Meru and Arusha to integrate domestic and commercial production. Arusha and Meru values played significant roles in maintaining patterns of land tenure that ensured people's continued access to resources; in their willingness to adopt new crops and agricultural routines; and in influencing people's choices among a range of alternative strategies. While such features were typical of successful cases of agricultural intensification elsewhere in Africa,[73] the conditions on Mount Meru were certainly not typical of those everywhere, and Arusha and Meru themselves pursued a variety of different responses, both intensive and extensive, to increase their productivity.

The rich volcanic soils, plentiful rainfall, and abundant supplies of water for irrigation on the southern slopes of Mount Meru provided farmers with a wide range of options to increase productivity through irrigation and fertilization, intercropping, crop succession, multi-cropping, and adoption of new crops and crop varieties, as we have seen. At the same time, however, the limited availability of such land and the sharp ecological and political boundaries between it and the forests and forest reserve above 1,800 metres and the plains and settlers' estates below 1,200 metres forced people inward to make maximum use of their endowment.

They continued to do so until economic and social pressures forced them to seek new lands in the northern highlands and plains and, in a flurry of expansionary activity, they rapidly colonized over 2000 km², two and a half times their original area. Expansion proved only a temporary expedient, however, as they soon reached the limits of available land and its productive capacity, at which point they turned back to the mountain, pushing the productivity of land and labour on Mount Meru to record levels.

While one could assert that population drove them to intensify and the fertility of the land enabled them to do so, one could also reverse the equation to assert that the fertility of the land and the success of agricultural development allowed population to continue to increase at the rates that it did without extensive out-migration, increased death rates, or lower fertility. The census and historical data do not permit sufficiently close analysis to resolve this problem of cause and effect, but there is a suggestion that

---

[72 cont.] *Africa* (Gainesville, 1993), especially introduction and conclusion; James McCann, *People of the Plow* (Madison, 1995), Chapter 3.

[73] Turner, Hyden, & Kates list the following critical elements for successful intensification, all of which apply to Meru and Arusha: favourable environment conducive to irrigation, conservation of resource base (through crop rotation, manuring, etc.), major increases in labour inputs and modest increases in capital inputs (such as animal traction or new and improved crops), continued access to land through evolving modes of customary allocation, lack of significant out-migration, significant commodity production, and development of and access to local markets. 'Beyond Intensification' in Turner, Hyden, & Kates, *Population Growth and Agricultural Change*, 401–39.

Table 7.10 Coffee: 1938–50

Area	1948 Population density	1938			1950				1938-50
		Trees	Growers	Trees/grower	Trees	Growers	Trees/grower	Growers/population (%)	Increase in Growers (%)
ARUSHA									
Boru									
Loruvani	133	53705	64	839	57006	105	543	2.3	64
Kiranyi	143	8240	20	412	12373	19	651	0.3	-5
Kindinga	125	3423	11	311	2977	18	165	0.2	64
Kimunyak	220	3374	6	562	5994	18	333	0.3	200
Sub-total		68472	101	681	78350	160	490	0.6	58
Burka									
Sokon		39457	96	411	171926	369	466	6.5	284
Sekei		10131	32	317	23692	50	474	1.1	56
Sombetin		73208	58	1262	14264	20	713	0.5	-66
Sinon		41487	40	1037	20507	29	707	0.6	-28
Moivaru		26017	68	383	96292	167	577	6.2	146
Sub-total	60	190300	294	647	326681	635	514	3.0	116
Totals		259042	395	656	405031	795	509	1.7	101
MERU									
Nkoanrua	106	79183	170	466	237808	526	452	15.6	209
Ndoombo		15443	33	468	32240	74	436	4.3	124
Akeri	62	137378	206	667	226951	415	547	20.7	101
Poli	47	65063	134	486	188533	323	584	15.6	141
Nkoaranga	49	67668	145	467	254747	410	621	15.1	183
Seela	65	10447	24	435	25587	77	332	7.7	221
Singisi	65	12682	33	384	64256	111	579	7.7	236
Mulala	44	6111	21	291	71418	192	372	8.6	814
Sura	44	16159	41	394	54304	192	283	8.6	368
Tuwela					8145	14	582		
Totals		410134	807	508	1163989	2334	499	12.4	189

Source: T.C. Cairns, 'Native Coffee Growing', 1940; District Note Book (both TNA: 9/6/5).

Arusha did begin to limit their fertility after 1948. Then again, population dynamics in this century were probably influenced by the dramatic shifts in population in the late nineteenth century that produced a relatively younger, more female, and hence more fertile population in Arusha (compared with Meru) in the early decades of this century and a relatively older, more balanced, and less fertile one thereafter.[74]

Whatever the case, remaining on the mountain always was a high priority, especially for Meru, who defined the essence of their existence in *kihamba*, the dense groves of bananas (and later coffee) that surrounded their homesteads. Bananas, as food and as cultural symbol, defined them; they remained reluctant to leave, work for others, or move into areas not conducive to their growth; and they relentlessly pushed the boundaries of the banana frontier across the mountain and out onto the plains, adopting new cultivars to do so. They were thus prone to push the limits of their environment as hard as they could, constantly increasing their productivity as they did so.

The higher densities prevailing in Arusha, however, pose a serious problem in attributing agricultural development solely to increasing population or, at least, in presuming that a certain form of development will result. If population did indeed drive agricultural development, one would expect more densely settled Arusha to have been ahead of Meru throughout the century, but colonial officers generally compared 'conservative' Arusha unfavourably to 'progressive' Meru who, they felt, planted pastures earlier, extended banana cultivation further, and adopted coffee more readily.[75]

This partly reflected pervasive European biases against Maasai. Gillman speculated that their alleged lack of progress was due to their continued love of cattle; veterinary officers constantly viewed Arusha herds as a liability and sought to limit them; and Gulliver felt that Arusha were held back by their xenophobic fear of outsiders and change, a highly ascriptive social system, and their continued adherence to pastoral Maasai values.[76] Nevertheless, Arusha supported higher concentrations of population than Meru throughout, suggesting that they pursued different strategies from those assumed beneficial by the administration.

Meru adopted coffee earlier and more rapidly and expanded banana cultivation more widely, as detailed coffee censuses conducted in 1938 and 1950 (see Table 7.10) and the 1976–7 crop survey clearly show. Twice as many Meru as Arusha raised coffee in 1938, and Meru continued to expand production more rapidly, so that by 1950 there were three times as many Meru growers as Arusha. Given that Arusha population was more than twice Meru's, individual Meru were seven times more likely to grow coffee than Arusha in 1950. Within Arusha itself, people in more densely settled Boru were less likely to grow coffee than those in Burka. There were almost three times as many

[74] The earlier censuses do not permit such fine analysis, of course.
[75] AO/Moshi to Sr AO, 26 Nov 1930, et seq. (TNA: 472/ASS/12); Sturdy, 'Native Coffee on Mt. Meru'; Northern Province, Annual Report, 1934 (TNA: 11681); T.C. Cairns, 'Native Coffee Growing', 1940 (TNA: 9/6/5 and 9/12/12); Agriculture Department, Annual Report, 1933–35, 1945 (TNA: 472/22 & 472/-).
[76] P.H. Gulliver, 'The Conservative Commitment in Northern Tanzania: the Arusha and Maasai' in P.H. Gulliver (ed.), *Tradition and Transition in East Africa* (London, 1969), 223-42. See also idem, 'The Arusha: Economic and Social Change' in P. Bohannan & G. Dalton (eds), *Markets in Africa* (New York, 1965), 250–84.

growers and trees in Burka in 1938 as in Boru, and over four times as many in 1950. Given population differences, farmers in Burka were three times more likely to raise coffee than those in Boru. Ironically, then, coffee growing had an inverse relationship with population density, with the most coffee raised in the least densely settled areas of Meru and Burka and the least grown in the most densely settled ones of Boru.[77] Not until coffee prices began to sky-rocket in the mid-1950s was coffee widely adopted in the most densely settled zones.

While fewer Arusha grew coffee, individual Arusha holdings, yields, and returns tended to be larger than those in Meru, especially in the early days. Thus, Arusha who did grow coffee tended to do so on a larger scale. The same phenomenon can be seen historically. Individual holdings everywhere averaged over an acre (at 600 trees per acre) in 1938 but, as the number of growers and trees planted over the period grew dramatically, average holdings went down in size, and they continued to shrink until they reached less than half an acre by 1969. Earlier growers were therefore likely to be wealthy men from less densely settled areas in Meru and Burka who had access to sufficient land and labour to add coffee to their existing repertoire of crops. Only later, with rising prices, did coffee come to provide sufficient returns to take the place of other crops in the more densely settled zones among farmers with less resources.

If bananas and coffee were not the immediate answer to Arusha living in the most densely settled areas on the mountain in the 1940s, cattle and more intensive mixed farming were. Meru and Arusha both continued to keep cattle, as we have seen, and they kept the most cattle precisely in those areas were population was most dense and coffee-growing least developed (cf. Tables 7.7 and 7.10). Arusha in the most densely settled older sections of eastern Boru, for example, kept more cattle per person than those elsewhere on the mountain, while those in the less densely settled areas of Meru and Burka kept fewer stock.[78] It seems likely, then, that better integration of cattle and crops was initially more effective in meeting the needs of an expanding population in Arusha.

Arusha farmers had long employed cattle in agricultural production. Cattle were fed on crop residues and pastured on fallow fields. Wealthy cattle owners were usually wealthy farmers as well, exchanging their cattle for wives and dependants to open up new farmlands. With the decrease in available pasture on the mountain and the moves into the drier western areas from the 1930s, the roles of cattle in overall food production were increased. As non-productive cattle were shifted to the plains, milch cows were hand-fed on the mountain and their manure applied to crops. At the same time, dry land farmers on the plains used oxen to clear, plough, and plant their fields; they rotated pasture and crop land; milk provided an important component of people's diet; and cattle provided vital insurance against the ever present possibilities of drought and crop failure. Cattle also provided needed capital as many Arusha in Musa undertook large-scale mechanical cultivation of wheat and maize. More intensive mixed farming

---

[77] *contra* Gulliver, 'Conservative Commitment', 226–7.

[78] Given more intensive herd management being pursued in all areas of the mountain, many cattle were kept on the plains of course, but these were the less productive part of mountain herds, as detailed earlier. Thus, people keeping more cows on the mountain also kept more off the mountain.

thus provided an attractive alternative to Arusha facing land shortage on the mountain.[79]

Given the different experiences and conditions in Arusha and Meru, then, people pursued different strategies to meet their increasing needs. Cattle had always played a larger role in Arusha moral economy than in Meru, and they continued to be a major source of social wealth for extending marriages and social relations generally. Far from impeding Arusha economic progress as claimed, however, cattle and pastoral culture were also critical elements in their overall ability to sustain high population densities. Just as cattle and continued participation in pastoral society in the nineteenth century had allowed Arusha to expand rapidly, so their herds allowed them to diversify production, resources, and capital in the twentieth century.

Arusha had herded cattle with pastoral Maasai long before the Germans restricted their land and access to the plains, and the two had long enjoyed a complementary economic relationship, as we have seen. Arusha links with pastoral Maasai continued to serve them well in the twentieth century, enabling them to graze their cattle on the plains and to obtain land there for expansion. Arusha continued to herd their cattle with pastoral kin, but they increasingly evoked claims of kinship to obtain land in Monduli and Kisongo from their pastoral partners as well. Wealthy Arusha cattle owners then used their cattle to recruit dependants to help them clear and work it.[80]

With their experience as cattlemen, Arusha also quickly learned from Afrikaner farmers how to break oxen and used them to open up farms on Monduli and the plains. There they raised maize and wheat as their main cash crops until high prices in the mid-1950s persuaded them to invest in coffee on Mount Meru as well. Arusha coffee growers represented a smaller but wealthier group than their Meru counterparts, and many of them maintained farms on both Meru and Monduli along with herds of cattle on the plains to diversify their production as much as possible.[81] Such a strategy was undoubtedly successful, even if it confounded British officers who generally favoured the Meru approach. One officer, however, bucked administration orthodoxy to enthuse that the Arusha were 'a dynamically progressive people' with 'a dynamically expanding economy' arrayed around a highly developed, intensively cropped core of bananas and coffee at the centre, surrounded by a region of ploughed fields of maize and beans in the process of conversion to bananas, and an outer circle of grazing being converted to cultivation.[82]

---

[79] Baral et al., 'In Search of Water', 36–9, 44–7; Nkonya, 'Diagnostic Survey,' 33–57; Patricia Benjamin, personal communication.

[80] Pastoral Maasai, on the other hand, frequently resented what they saw as Arusha 'land grabbing' at their expense. See Reuben ole Kuney, 'Pluralism and Ethnic Conflict in Tanzania's Arid Lands: The Case of the Maasai and Waarusha' (13th International Congress of Anthropological and Ethnological Sciences, Mexico City, 1993) and John Galaty, 'The Eye that Wants a Person, Where Can it not See? Inclusion, Exclusion and Boundary Shifters in Maasai Identity' in T. Spear & R. Waller (eds), *Being Maasai* (London, 1993), 174–94.

[81] Many of the same people, for example, were listed as officers of the wheat and coffee associations. Hans Cory, 'Tribal Structure of the Arusha Tribe of Tanganyika' (UDSM: Cory Collection), 60-61; Sturdy, 'Native Coffee on Mt. Meru'; Luanda, 'Commercial Farming', 165–72; Mesiaki Kilevo, personal communication.

[82] Chief Soil Conservation Officer to AO/AD, 30 June 1952 (TNA: 9/ADM/9).

Faced with the common problem of increasing population and limited land, then, Arusha and Meru pursued different strategies according to their own cultural backgrounds, economic strategies, and natural endowments. Arusha initially emphasized mixed farming of cattle and annual crops over bananas or coffee, but later moved to bananas and coffee as they were forced back on to the mountain in the 1960s. With more land available on the mountain, Meru focused on bananas and coffee earlier to achieve the same goals. Thus, while both were faced with similar problems, pursued parallel strategies to meet them, and ultimately developed similar responses, their individual paths were rooted in their respective histories and the ways each constructed and interacted with its environment. Increasing population on a limited amount of land may have forced Meru and Arusha to intensify their agriculture, but it did not dictate how they did so. Those were choices Arusha and Meru made in the context of their own values, skills, and resources. If they were acting in historical context, however, the roles they played would change them profoundly as well, as we shall see in the following chapters.

8

Christians, Coffee, Culture & Class

Our analysis of agricultural development so far has focused on the interplay between land shortage, natural resources, population growth, and local values, to account for the continued intensification of Meru and Arusha agriculture. Such an approach can help us understand, broadly, why and how these changes took place, but it tells us little of how individual Arusha and Meru perceived the need for change and responded to it or what impact these changes subsequently had on them. These are difficult questions, and we shall attempt only a partial answer here by focusing on the activities of one group of people – educated Christians – who pioneered the expansion of education and the development of coffee farming in Meru and Arusha societies.

We have already seen some of the choices all Arusha and Meru faced – whether to work for European settlers, colonize new land elsewhere, or develop further their own agricultural potential – and observed that they generally favoured developing their own farms and herds whenever possible. We have also seen how they increased agricultural productivity by converting pastures to crop-lands, integrating cattle into their overall agricultural routines, expanding banana cultivation across the central slopes while extending mixed farming to the edges of the mountain and out on to the plains, and producing onions, maize, beans, and coffee for sale. And finally, we have seen what impact these developments had on people's labour as they sought to reap ever greater returns from their shrinking holdings. It remains for us to explore in greater detail just who effected these changes, how they did so, and what impact they had on their societies. While all Meru and Arusha innovated, and it is thus invidious to focus on the activities on just one group, most analysis of agricultural innovation on Mount Meru has focused on the group of educated Christians, and it is the only group that emerges with any clarity from the historical record. Invidious or not, therefore, it is this group which commands our attention.

In some ways, the colonial era witnessed the rise of a new class in Arusha and Meru societies, a class defined by education, Christianity, and relative material affluence in contradistinction to an earlier class defined by seniority, gender, number of dependants and clients, and wealth in cattle. The leaders of Tareto (1911–29) were elderly

158

polygamous males who were guardians of ancestral knowledge and maintained large families, herds of cattle, and circles of clients. By the time of Nyangusi/Sitimu (1942–59) or Seuri/Steling (1955–74), however, leaders increasingly tended to be younger, educated, monogamous Christian men who commanded new and, to many, foreign forms of knowledge, who often preferred coffee over cattle, and who exercised their power in such new institutions as schools, the church, co-operatives, and the State.

It is a mistake, however, to see this change as a wholesale rejection of old values for new, for members of this new class acted in many ways like their predecessors, and they continue to coexist with them today. They too respected age, and as church elders they gathered large flocks of dependants around them. They valued large families; relied on their families for household production; and inaugurated family dynasties whose modern cement houses were clustered together on the family's *kihamba* or *engisaka*. They also valued ancestral land and fought hard to retain it. In short, many of their goals were similar to those of the earlier generation, even if their social and economic means of attaining them were new.

Christians and the Community

The first Christians in Meru and Arusha were a beleaguered lot, estranged from their friends and relatives by mission practice, their new faith, and popular disdain. Over time, however, Christians slowly became a significant force in Arusha and Meru societies as they pioneered the development of schools, coffee and other cash crops, and co-operatives, while slowly assuming political leadership within the colonial state and, later, in opposition to it. They were thus able gradually to transform themselves from social pariahs to pillars of society by seizing new cultural values and economic opportunities.

The Leipzig missionaries had set the tone of the early Church. 'A cabin of God in a field of blood', it was to stand against prevailing society and values to inaugurate a new society founded on Christian faith, education, and the work ethic. Children were isolated from their families and friends in mission boarding schools, where they took part in Bible studies, reading and writing, arithmetic, and disciplined work, while prohibited from dancing or being initiated with their age mates. Arusha and Meru responded in kind: cursing converts, treating them as children, or mourning them as if they were dead.[1]

The missions thus gained adherents only slowly at first, and those who did join were more often in search of wages, education, medical cures, or escape from home than salvation. Over time, however, small Christian communities grew, clustered around the mission stations at Nkoaranga and Boru, employed by the missions, and marrying amongst themselves. As such, however, they remained isolated from the larger communities until the first graduates of the Leipzig seminary at Marangu returned in 1908 to assume responsibility for the out-stations. In Meru, Nderingo Pallangyo was posted to Ngyani, Yohana Ndosi to Nkoaranga, and Luka Kaaya to Akeri, where he was soon joined by Matayo Kaaya and Marko Mwenda, while Saul was appointed to Kimandolu in Arusha.

---

[1] See Chapter 5.

Previously visited by the missionaries only twice a week, these out-stations now came under the full-time leadership of local teachers and evangelists who lived in the community, taught school daily, and conducted Sunday services locally. As out-stations, schools, and village chapels proliferated, people found that they no longer had to abandon their families, friends, and daily routines to go to school or become Christian, but could attend school and participate in the Church in their own communities. The number of pupils, especially girls, and converts rose accordingly, and the barriers between Christians and non-Christians began to drop. By the time the British captured Arusha from the Germans and expelled the German missionaries in 1916, a core of Meru and Arusha converts were poised to adopt the 'orphaned church' as their own.[2]

European control of the missions from 1916 to 1926 was minimal at best. While the British initially allowed the German missionaries to stay '... to maintain order amongst the terrified natives', they soon interned all but Blumer, who was allowed to stay by virtue of being Estonian. Unable to supervise the local schools and churches closely, Blumer encouraged each congregation to appoint an elder to lead services, give religious instruction, and conduct baptisms and weddings. With no outside funds coming in, each also had to pay its own teachers and become self-supporting.[3]

The British Governor, Sir Horace Byatt, granted initial oversight of the Leipzig mission to the Church Missionary Society, while opposing successive applications by the Church of Scotland, the Seventh Day Adventists, and the American Augustana Lutheran Mission to assume active control. The Scottish Presbyterian missions were too far away, Byatt thought; he deemed the SDA 'undesirable'; while he opposed turning over 'extensive missionary enterprises in this country, together with their considerable trade connexions, to an influential American interest....' Besides, he added, American and German nationality was so intermingled that it would not be clear where ultimate control lay.[4]

Local Christians held out for continued Lutheran affiliation, however, and the Leipzig missions were subsequently placed under the guardianship of the Augustana Mission in 1921 under the leadership of Rev. Richard Reusch, a Russian who had previously served with the Leipzigers. They then reverted to Leipzig control in 1927 after the Germans were allowed to return to Tanganyika, but the German missionaries were detained and deported for a second and last time in 1939.[5] The Augustana Mission again assumed control, but it had no one available in Tanganyika to staff the mission during the war years. Rev. Zakariah Urio was appointed to oversee the African church

[2] Cf. David Sandgren, *Christianity and the Kikuyu* (New York, 1989), Chapter 3.

[3] Raum to ELM, Leipzig, 20 August 1916 (PRO: CO 691/III/541–543); Arusha District, Annual Report, 1919–20 (TNA: 1733/I); A.A. Lema, 'The Impact of the Leipzig Lutheran Mission on the People of Kilimanjaro, 1893-1920' (Ph.D., University of Dar es Salaam, 1973), 211.

[4] Byatt to Secretary of State, 22 Jan 1917 and 17 Feb 1920 (PRO: CO 691/IV/190 and XXX/359). In fact, the Augustana mission was of Swedish and Norwegian origin, not German, as Byatt implied. Gustav Bernander, *Lutheran Wartime Assistance to Tanzanian Churches, 1940-1945* (Lund, 1968), 26; Elmer Danielson, 'Transition in Tanganyika' in J. Gould (ed.), *A Different Kind of Journey* (Helsinki, Finnish Anthropological Society, 1991), 28–9.

[5] Arusha District, Annual Report, 1925 (TNA: 1733/36); DO/AD to PC/NP, 26 May 1926 (TNA: 69/351); Misc. corres. (TNA: 12207).

in Meru, while Rev. Lazaros Laiser assumed the same role in Arusha, both serving until 1958 when the Evangelical Lutheran Church of Northern Tanganyika became independent of mission control.[6]

From the initial lapse of European control in 1916, then, responsibility for the mission increasingly fell to local evangelists, teachers, and pastors. One of the first Meru to lead the local church was Luka Kaaya. Luka grew up in Akeri and joined his neighbour Yohana Ndosi as one of the first boarding students at Nkoaranga in 1902. He eagerly joined the first catechism class in 1904, was one of the first eleven baptized at Nkoaranga the following December, and then went to Marangu with Yohana and Nderingo Pallangyo, for further training. The three graduated at the end of 1907 and returned to Meru to take responsibility for the day-schools at Akeri, Sura, and Ngyani, respectively. Luka built a new schoolhouse at Akeri, enrolments rose to 60 to 70 students, and over 100 attended Sunday services. Nderingo and Yohana enjoyed similar successes at Ngyani and Sura. Luka's son, Anton Luka Kaaya, later attended Marangu himself, taught school for a number of years, then worked as a medical aide, and finally was ordained as a pastor and served in Meru, Sonjo, and Karatu until he retired.[7]

Matayo Leveriya Kaaya was also raised in Akeri and spent his youth herding sheep and calves on the communal pastures high on the mountain. He remembered taking food to Ovir and Segebrock before they were slain, and he later enrolled in school at Nkoaranga in 1903 at the age of 15. He was baptized in 1907 and first worked as a teacher and evangelist under Luka Kaaya at Akeri before going to Marangu for further training and serving in Akeri and West Meru until he retired in 1947. While initially attracted to the mission by the prospect of learning to read and write, Matayo became a devout Christian, and he encouraged his students to abandon belief in ancestral spirits and the practice of polygamy. His students and potential converts, however, came from the community and continued to live there after being baptized, eating and dressing like their non-Christian neighbours and living with them.[8]

A similar group of teacher-evangelists emerged in Arusha. Simeon Bene was baptized in 1908 and taught for a number of years at Boru before becoming a clerk for Chief Lairumbe in 1924. Simeon succeeded Lairumbe as Chief of Boru in 1933, and when Boru and Burka were consolidated in 1948, he became Chief of Arusha, a position he held until 1952.[9] Lazaros Laiser started school at Boru in 1909 under Simeon's tutelage. Baptized in 1911, he attended Marangu with Matayo Kaaya and went on to a

[6] Anderson and Rother to PC/NP, 15 Aug 1940; Magney to CS/DSM, 16 Sept 1940; Rother to PC/NP, 17 Oct 1940; DC/MD to PC/NP, 30 June 1942; PC/NP to CS/DSM, 3 July 1942 (all in TNA: 69/351/6); Northern Province, Annual Report, 1941 (TNA: 19415); Bernander, *Wartime Assistance*, 25–3; Elmer Danielson, *Forty Years with Christ in Tanzania, 1928–1968* (New York, 1977), 53–7, 74–80, 121–33, 155–60.

[7] Schachschneider, *ELMB*, 63(1908), 327; Ittameier, *ELMB*, 64 (1909), 36–7; Anton Luka Kaaya (MHT 1); N.N. Luanda, 'European Commercial Farming and its Impact on the Meru and Arusha Peoples of Tanzania, 1920–1955' (Ph.D., Cambridge, 1986), 155–8.

[8] A.S. Mbise, 'The Evangelist: Matayo Leveriya Kaaya' in J. Iliffe (ed.), *Modern Tanzanians* (Nairobi, 1973), 27–41.

[9] See Chapter 6. Yohanes ole Kauwenara (AHT 2); S. ole Saibull & R. Carr, *Herd and Spear* (London, 1981), 115–17; J. Stanley Benson, 'A Study of Religious Beliefs and Practices of the Maasai Tribe and the Implications on the Work of the Evangelical Lutheran Church in Tanzania' (M. Sacred Theology, Northwestern Lutheran Seminary, 1974), 29.

distinguished career as a pastor and head of the church in Arusha until his untimely death in an automobile accident in 1958. A close friend and ally of Simeon, he modelled church organization on Arusha political structures and appointed Christian *laigwenak* to mediate disputes among Christians and to represent their interests in local government. Lazaros pioneered the extension of the mission to pastoral Maasai and Sonjo, and he actively shielded the Lutheran church from competition by other missions.[10]

A number of other Arusha followed in Simeon and Lazaros's wake. Eliezer Kisululu and Lotokorduaki were early Arusha teachers and evangelists. Eliezer's son, Mesiaki Kilevo, became one of the first Arusha graduates, married Lazaros Laiser's daughter, and subsequently became the first president of the Arusha Synod, formed when the Northern Diocese was split between its Chaga/Meru and Arusha/Maasai branches in 1973.[11] Loingoruaki Meshili grew up herding cattle for his father, who opposed his going to school, but after his sister was beaten by her teacher, Loingoruaki volunteered to take her place. He grew to like school and later became a teacher himself.[12] Eliyahu Lujas Meiliari shaved his head while still a *murran* in a vain attempt to join the German police, but he was then too ashamed to return to Arusha when he was unsuccessful, and so he went to school, was baptized, and became a teacher in Kidinga and Kisongo.[13]

While the early converts, teachers, and evangelists were all raised in the cloistered world of the missions, they had to accommodate themselves to their non-Christian neighbours when they started to live and work among them. Their attempts to forge connections across the cultural divide that separated the early Christian community from non-Christians posed potential conflicts with the Leipzig missionaries. Arusha and Meru Christians were freer to pursue their own policies after the Germans were evicted, and as educators they soon found the means of fusing their own skills and values with those of the local communities in which they resided.[14]

Their success can be gauged by the surge of converts and new schools established under their leadership between 1916 and 1926. The number of Meru converts more than tripled during the period, and the number of out-stations in both areas doubled. There were eight day-schools in addition to those at the mission stations when the Germans departed, with an average attendance of 40 each. By 1926 these had grown to a total of 19, 12 in Meru, with an average attendance of 83 each, and another 7 in Arusha, attended by 52 students each. Overall school attendance increased five-fold to 1,621.[15] The rising demand for education continued after the Leipzigers returned, with

[10] D.C. Flatt, *Man and Deity in an African Society* (Dubuque, 1980), 290; Benson, 'Religious Beliefs,' 29; Hans Cory, 'Tribal Structure of the Arusha Tribe of Tanganyika,' c. 1948 (UDSM: Hans Cory Papers, 201), 58–9.

[11] Saibull and Carr, *Herd and Spear*, 106–8; Mesiaki Kilevo, personal communication.

[12] Loingoruaki Meshili (AHT 6).

[13] Eliyahu Lujas Meiliari (AHT 8).

[14] Fokken, *ELMB*, 66 (1911), 494; Schachschneider, *ELMB*, 68(1913), 539; H. Mason & M.J. Davies, 'The Meru Problem,' enclosed in DC/AD to Member for Local Government, 12 March 1955, 15 (OCRP: MSS.Afr.s.1513); Anton Nelson, *The Freemen of Meru* (Nairobi, 1967), 71–2.

[15] The out-stations established in Arusha prior to 1916 were Kimandolu, Kidinga, Salei and Sasi, while those established 1916–26 were Olorien, Selian, and Olgilai. The earlier ones in Meru were Akeri, Ngyani, Boli, and Sura, and the later ones, Mulala, Nkwourue, Sinisi, Ndoombo, Nkure, Ikara, Amheseni, and Utona. Weishaupt, *ELMB*, 67 (1912), 502–3, 537; Schachschneider, *ELMB*, 68 (1913), 539; DO/AD to PC/NP, 26 May 1926 (TNA: 69/351).

another sixteen schools added between 1927 and 1939 and the first students proceeding to further education at Old Moshi Secondary School. By 1945 there was a total of 39 regular primary schools and 149 two-year 'bush schools', all run by local Christians. Another surge occurred under the leadership of Zakariah Urio and Lazaros Laiser during the Second World War and after, with church membership rising to 15,000 in Meru and 7,000 in Arusha under the guidance of 15 local pastors and 90 evangelists by 1962.[16]

While the first generation of teacher-evangelists had converted in their teens or twenties and had assumed their positions in the church with only a few years of education, the second generation were raised in Christian households, were better educated, and frequently went on to become teachers, evangelists, and ordained pastors. They also increasingly became seen as symbols of independent authority throughout Meru and Arusha as they assumed responsibility for the missions after the evictions of the German missionaries in 1916 and again in 1939. Returning to Meru to reassume control of the Nkoaranga mission in 1926, Rev. Ittameier found that local Christians were no longer amenable to European domination of the missions; while Elmer Danielson – who became Superintendent of the former Leipzig missions after the Second World War and oversaw their development into an autonomous church – discovered that people's human dignity had been awakened during the war years and that Christians had become the vanguard of a movement towards greater independence from both mission and government control.[17]

Coffee, Co-operatives, and Control

Teaching school was one way in which educated Christians began to gain status in the wider community. Developing coffee and farmers associations was another. The first coffee growers were drawn from the same generation of early Christians responsible for the expansion of schools and the church. Luka Kaaya was not only the first teacher-evangelist posted to Akeri, he also pioneered coffee production there, and he soon became one of the largest and most prosperous producers. He helped form and lead the first coffee growers' association in Meru in 1928 and was the first to introduce hand-operated wooden pulpers in 1936. His sons followed in his footsteps. Anton became a successful pastor and coffee farmer, enabling him to retire to a modern cement house equipped with electricity and telephone in the midst of a large family compound. Sangito inherited his father's coffee farm, developed a maize farm lower on the slopes, was one of the first tractor farmers in eastern Meru, and became general manager of the Meru co-operative in the 1950s and 1960s.[18]

[16] *Arusha District Book*; Leuschke to DO/AD, 13 Dec 1939; Pätzig to DO/AD, 16 Dec 1939 (both in TNA: 9/EDU/10); Headmaster Old Moshi to DO/AD, 26 July 1948 (TNA: 472/-); Danielson, *Forty Years with Christ*, 218.
[17] Ittameier, *ELMB*, 83(1928), 202–10; Danielson, *Forty Years with Christ*, 54, 99, 130, 138.
[18] Anton Luka Kaaya (MHT 1); minutes, 6 Oct 1932 and 12 Dec 1932 (TNA: 472/ASS/12); Nelson, *Freemen*, 121–2; Luanda, 'Commercial Farming,' 155–7;

Luka's fellow pupil and teacher, Yohana Ndosi, was the first to plant coffee at Sura in upper Meru, where he was posted in 1913. By 1931 he had five acres of coffee and shortly thereafter built himself a large cement house.[19] Another early student, Japhet Ayo, was baptized in 1913 and was the first Meru to plant coffee in Nkoaranga, where he worked as an orderly at the mission hospital. He later succeeded Luka Kaaya as President of the Meru Native Coffee Planters' Association. His son, Kirilo Japhet, achieved fame by going to New York to present the Meru Land Case to the United Nations in 1952, and he later became a medical assistant, a leader in the co-operative, a founder of TANU and its first chairman in the Northern Province, and a member of Parliament after Independence.[20]

The early Christians in Arusha were little different. Simeon Bene rose from poor origins and an early career as a teacher to become the wealthiest man in Arusha. He planted coffee in Boru, had some 2,000 cattle on the plains, and owned a large wheat farm in Engare Olmotonyi. He used his power as chief and his wealth to enlist others as clients, providing land to his fellow Christians who moved into Musa and Likamba in the 1930s and 1940s to become wheat farmers. Simeon's son, Lemburio Simeon Mejeoli, attended school at Boru and Marangu and taught at Boru for a number of years before becoming an agricultural instructor in 1944. Simeon gave him 400 acres of land in Engare Olmotonyi along with 200 cattle to buy a tractor, disc plough, and harrow. Lemburio later bought a reaper in partnership with a European farmer and went on to operate a chain of shops and a fleet of buses.[21]

Lazaros Laiser was another early Arusha coffee farmer. He founded and led the Arusha and Meru Native Planters' Association and joined with other wealthy Christians to establish a wheat farm in Musa. Like Simeon, Lazaros staffed his farms with in-laws and church associates, offering them land in return for their support.[22] Another wheat farmer, Andrea Kipuyo, grew up tending his father's large herd in Oldonyo Sambu, but left to attend school when he was 15. After teaching for some years, he became treasurer of the Arusha Native Authority and later served as deputy chief under Lairumbe and Simeon. In 1932 he got 100 acres of land in Likamba from Simeon and, after unsuccessfully experimenting with maize, he hired a plough and planted wheat. Later he bought his own team of oxen, together with a lorry that he hired out to others. He encouraged poorer Arusha to settle on his land to provide labour and became the first president of the African section of the Tanganyika Farmers' Association.[23]

The evangelists had a strong motive for growing coffee. Many of them had joined the church initially in search of education and wages, and they had been rejected by

---

[19] Luanda, 'Commercial Farming,' 157–8.

[20] Japhet Ayo (MHT 4); Kirilo Japhet Ayo (MHT 2); minutes, 6 May 1933 and 2 Nov 1933 (TNA: 472/ASS/12); MNCGA, Annual Report, 1938–39 in AO/AD to Sr AO, 24 April 1939 (TNA: 9/12/13); K. Japhet & E. Seaton, *The Meru Land Case* (Nairobi, 1967).

[21] See Chapter 6. Luanda, 'Commercial Farming,' 171–2; Benson, 'Religious Beliefs,' 29; Mosingo ole Meipusu (AHT 1); Yohanes ole Kauwenara (AHT 2); Lodenaga Lotisia (AHT 3); Ngole ole Njololoi (AHT 4).

[22] Flatt, *Man and Deity*, 290; Cory, 'Tribal Structure of the Arusha', 58–9; Saibull & Carr, *Herd and Spear*, 106–8; Benson, 'Religious Beliefs', 29; Mesiaki Kilevo, personal communication.

[23] Luanda, 'Commercial Farming,' 168–70.

Table 8.1 Expansion of Coffee Production, 1920–69

Decade ending	Production (tons)	Growers	Area (acres)	Tons/ grower	Acres/ grower	Tons/ acre	Shs./ grower
1929	30	660	c.300	0.045	0.45	0.10	100
1939	100	1200	700	0.083	0.58	0.14	70
1949	200	3100	1150	0.064	0.37	0.17	c.200
1959	800	5000	4700	0.16	0.94	0.17	1500
1969	3000	10000	4100	0.30	0.41	0.73	c.2400
average increase/ decade	220%	100%	90%	60%	0	60%	120%

Source: calculations based on Table 7.9.

their families and peers in the process. Church wages remained low, however, and they needed money to care for their own growing families and send their children to school. Like most early teachers, Matayo Kaaya was paid only shs 6/- a month by the mission to feed and care for his nine children. He and his wife had no choice but to continue to farm, supplementing their food crops with a modest cash income from coffee.[24]

Other Meru and Arusha increasingly followed the Christians' example, with the number of growers doubling on average each decade from 1920 to 1969 (see Table 8.1). Coffee's initial appeal during the 1920s was quickly offset by the low prices prevailing throughout the 1930s, such that smallholders could ill afford to sacrifice productive and more remunerative food crops to coffee. The earliest growers thus tended to come from Meru and Burka, where land was not as restricted as in Boru, and they planted larger quantities of coffee to increase their incomes.[25] As prices and returns to growers recovered during the 1940s and then increased rapidly in the 1950s and '60s, however, it became economic for farmers with more limited acreages to interplant coffee with bananas and other food crops, and coffee soon became the cash crop of choice for large and small farmers alike.

Overall acreage planted in coffee also doubled each decade, but coffee remained a smallholder crop overall. Since the number of growers was also doubling, average holdings remained close to a half acre per grower, as coffee farmers continued to cultivate their own food crops intermixed with coffee.

While the number of growers and total acreage both doubled every decade, overall production more than tripled, as farmers increased their yields by mulching with banana leaves, fertilizing with manure and greens, careful pruning, spraying for diseases and pests, and improved processing. As yields increased from improved cultivation, so did the quality of the crop, and the combination of increasing yields, improved quality, and rising prices caused individual farmers' returns to more than double every ten years on average.

[24] Mbise, 'The Evangelist,' 27–40.
[25] See Chapter 7.

165

Increasing returns certainly fuelled the coffee boom, but it was also driven by the low capital and labour costs involved and the compatibility of coffee with bananas.[26] Coffee culture easily blended in with prevailing Meru and Arusha agricultural practices, and the costs of sprays and improved cultivation techniques were more than offset by increased yields, improved quality, and rising prices, making coffee an extremely lucrative and popular crop by the 1960s.

As Meru and Arusha adopted coffee more generally, Christians took the lead in forming farming associations and defending farmers' interests against increasing government intrusion. Arusha and Meru coffee farmers joined together in 1928 to form the Arusha and Meru Native Coffee Planters' Association under the leadership of Lazaros Laiser in Arusha and Luka Kaaya in Meru. Its board and those of its successors were dominated by a small group of Christians that included Simeon Bene, Eliyahu Latawuo, Petros Sirikwa, Eliezer Kisululu, Simon Kireya, Markos Maki, Lolo Laidesoni, Lesale Lekaronga, and Filipo Songare in Arusha and Japhet Ayo, Yohana Ndosi, Marko Mwenda, Fanuel Ruben, and Anaeli Uvetie in Meru.

The first task undertaken by the AMNCPA was to market members' crops more effectively. The first growers had sold their coffee cheaply to local settlers, but in 1929–30 the AMNCPA attempted to sell the crop directly in London, unfortunately with disastrous results. The final sale price was insufficient to cover freight expenses, brokerage fees, and advances paid to Meru and Arusha farmers, leaving the new association shs 900/- in debt.[27] The following year the association put out members' coffee to bid with local dealers. Individual members then dealt directly with the successful bidder, but remained free to sell their coffee to other dealers if they wished. The successful bid in 1930 was 65 per cent of the London price.

The joint bid/individual sale procedure continued in effect for over twenty years, in spite of the fact that members' expenses were higher than those of the Kilimanjaro Native Planters' Association (KNPA) and the prices they received were 30–35 per cent lower than those obtained by Chaga. Unlike Chaga, individual members also had to pay shs 1/- to the government to register their trees, and an additional tax to the association to cover its expenses, but they preferred the arrangement because they received direct and immediate payment for their crop.[28]

Meru and Arusha refused to affiliate with the KNPA in 1931 as a result, and the AMNCPA itself split into separate Arusha and Meru associations under the leadership of Lazaros Laiser and Luka Kaaya, respectively.[29] The two associations then successfully undermined the District Officer's attempt in 1933–5 to control them by trans-

---

[26] See Chapter 7.

[27] Misc. corres. (TNA: 9/12/13 and 472/ASS/12).

[28] D. Sturdy, 'Native Coffee on Mt. Meru' in AO/AD to Sr AO, 15 May 1931 (TNA: 9/12/13 and 472/ASS/12); Agriculture Department, Annual Report, 1931 (TNA: 472/22); AO/AD, Notes of meetings with AMNCPA, 31 May 1932, 6 Oct 1932, 12 Dec 1932 and 6 May 1933 (TNA: 472/ASS/12); Northern Province, Annual Reports, 1933-34 (TNA: 11681).

[29] The history of these associations is somewhat confused because government correspondence continued, mistakenly, to refer to the old AMNCPA as well as to the Arusha Native Coffee Growers' Association or Arusha Planters' Association and the Meru Native Coffee Growers' Association or Meru Native Planters' Association.

forming them into a combined co-operative society that would hire a European manager, implement spraying and crop regulations, process coffee centrally, and market its coffee directly in London. While these were all functions undertaken by the Kilimanjaro co-operative, most Meru and Arusha farmers were wary of potential government interference and refused to join the proposed co-op. The administration was forced to turn to the Native Authority to impose compulsory registration and controls, while growers continued to fund spraying through the association and to process and market their crops individually.[30]

Fears of government interference were not unfounded. Arusha and Meru had already struggled with the government over restrictions placed on their right to grow coffee and the imposition of regulations regarding cultivation and controls over marketing. The administration first undertook to discourage further planting of coffee by Meru and Arusha in 1927 as the result of a compromise struck with settlers who wished to ban all African production. The government also undertook to rigorously enforce rules for controlling disease, as a result of which agricultural officers found themselves in the untenable position of seeking to work with farmers to control disease while at the same time enforcing sanctions on them against further planting. Arusha and Meru continued to plant regardless, forcing the administration to abandon the restrictions in 1933.[31] Two years later the administration tried to ban further planting in Arusha in the aftermath of a dispute over coffee borer control, and in 1937 it refused to sanction any more land for coffee in either area 'owing to the pressure of population and the declining fertility of the soil in the food crop areas'.[32] None of the restrictions were effective, however, and the administration's attempts to impose them continued to foster an antagonistic relationship with the people of Mount Meru.

Relationships were further strained by administration attempts to control diseases and regulate cultivation. While Meru and Arusha generally co-operated with policies to control diseases and continually improved cultivation on their own, they resisted any attempt to control land use. The Arusha and Meru Native Coffee Planters' Association and its successors regularly obtained sprays against antestia, thrips, and heiliea for their members through a levy on their crop.[33] Growers even agreed to uproot 95,000 trees infested with white borers in 1933, despite the administration's dubious legal rights to force them to do so.[34] Arusha and Meru conducted their own experiments to improve

[30] Sr AO to AO/AD, 5 Mar 1931 (TNA: 9/12/13); AO/AD, Notes of meetings with AMNCPA, 6 May 1933 and 2 Nov 1933 (TNA: 472/ASS/12); Northern Province, Annual Report, 1934 (TNA: 11681); AO/AD to DO/AD, 27 July 1935, 20 Aug 1935, and 3 Jan 1936; DO/AD to PC/NP, 13 Nov 1935; DO/AD to Sr AO, 18 April 1936; DO/AD to PC/NP, 2 Sept 1936 (all in TNA: 9/12/13); DO/AD to PC/NP, 13 Sept 1935 and reply 20 Sept 1935 (TNA: 472/AGR/7); T.C. Cairns, 'Native Coffee Growing,' 1940 (TNA: 9/6/5).

[31] Circular No. 77 of 1927, 20 Dec 1927, and related correspondence (TNA: 11160); Circular No. 3 of 1933, 12 Feb 1933 (TNA: 472/ASS/12).

[32] Cairns, 'Native Coffee Growing'; Agriculture Department, Annual Reports, 1934–35 (TNA: 472/22).

[33] Sturdy, 'Native Coffee on Mt. Meru'; Northern Province, Annual Report, 1933 (TNA: 11681); Cairns, 'Native Coffee Growing'.

[34] AO/Moshi to Sr AO, 26 Nov 1930 et seq.(TNA: 472/ASS/12); Agriculture Department, Annual Reports, 1933–5 (TNA: 472/22).

cultivation, introducing manure, coffee pulp, and green manuring in the early 1930s with dramatic results. Yields doubled, increasing from four and a half to nine bags per 400 trees; manure was found to be an effective control for thrips and other leaf diseases; and all quickly became accepted practice.[35]

Land use was another matter, however. Agricultural officers continually railed against farmers growing coffee intermixed with food crops because they felt that it contributed to poor maintenance and lowered yields. They were right about the yields; but Meru and Arusha farmers continued to intercrop coffee and bananas, because bananas provided valuable shade for the young trees, they were unwilling to restrict food crop production, and together bananas and coffee provided better returns overall than either grown separately.[36] Similarly, the administration's attempt to regulate coffee cultivation in the aftermath of the failure of the 1927 restrictions failed, largely because it sought to control farmers' activities in minute detail. The regulations mandated minimum acreages, crops coffee could be grown with, spraying and other disease controls, and precisely how coffee should be hoed, irrigated, pruned, picked, and processed. They were so detailed that the administration was incapable of enforcing them and neither Meru nor Arusha were able or willing to comply with them.[37]

The most contentious and enduring conflicts, though, resulted from ongoing government attempts to mandate and control how Arusha and Meru marketed their coffee. In the aftermath of the failure of the 1933 regulations and the District Officer's attempt to impose a co-operative in 1935, the administration tried in 1937 to establish a Native Coffee Board that would be responsible for controlling coffee production and marketing. Meru and Arusha refused to deal with the Board, and in 1947 the administration sought to impose the ordinance on them unilaterally, to no avail.[38] The government subsequently repealed the 1937 ordinance and replaced it with one mandating the establishment of a marketing board that would regulate planting, cultivation, harvesting, and processing as well as marketing. But Meru refused to sell their coffee to the Board, threatening to uproot their trees instead, while both Meru and Arusha representatives on the Board rejected compulsory marketing through the Board on principle. Meru rioted when the Native Authority attempted to impose a tax to finance regulation, and the rules were subsequently abandoned in 1952 as too difficult to implement.[39]

After years of struggling against increasing government attempts to control the industry, Arusha and Meru finally agreed to form their own officially sanctioned

[35] Agriculture Department, Annual Reports, 1933-34 (TNA: 472/22); Cairns, 'Native Coffee Growing'.

[36] Sturdy, 'Native Coffee on Mt. Meru'; Agriculture Department, Annual Report, 1930/31 (TNA: 472/22); Northern Province, Annual Report, 1959 (TNA: 471/R.3/2).

[37] Director of Agriculture, 'Note on Cultivation, Preparation, and Marketing of Native Coffee', enclosed in Circular No. 3 of 1933, 12 Feb 1933 (TNA: 472/ASS/12).

[38] PC/NP to CS/DSM, 24 Sept 1947 et seq. (TNA: 25038). On the administration's attempts to control and regulate African production and marketing generally, see D.M.P. McCarthy, *Colonial Bureaucracy and Creating Underdevelopment* (Ames, 1982).

[39] African Agricultural Products (Control and Marketing) Ordinance No. 57 of 1949 (TNA: 9/12/15); PC/NP to Member for Agriculture, 16 April 1952 and DC/AD to Member for Agriculture, 14 Jan 1953 (TNA: 25639); Arusha Native Coffee Board (TNA: 42294); DO/AR to AO/AD, 19 Sept 1955 (TNA: 9/12/2/II).

co-operative societies in the 1950s, and assumed control for spraying, crop regulations, breeding, grading, and marketing themselves. Arusha formed the Arusha (later Koimere) African Farmers' Co-operative Society in 1950, while Meru formed the Meru Growers' Co-operative Society (later Meru Co-operative Union) in 1955 under the leadership of Bonifatio Urio and Sangito Kaaya, the sons of a pastor and an evangelist. Later the two merged to form the Meru Arusha Co-operative Union in 1965.

The Meru co-operative was an immediate success. Meru hired an American adviser, Anton (Ax) Nelson, who promptly negotiated reduced broker's commissions to accord with the lower ones paid by Europeans. The Co-op developed improved cultivation techniques, acquired sprays and insecticides for its members, and established its own nursery and demonstration farm at Makumira. It provided inputs to members on credit against their crop, established its own retail stores and credit union, and developed roads and transport. Finally it graded and marketed members' crops, though Meru remained reluctant to develop central processing facilities. As quality and yields improved, incomes doubled and redoubled in its first six years.[40]

Culture, Community, and Class

There is no doubt that the Christians put their imprint on Meru and Arusha societies as they attended co-operative meetings dressed in coats and ties and opened them with prayers. Joyous daytime processions following Christian marriages contrasted with the night-time processions meant to hide the bride, characteristic of Arusha weddings. Maasai dress and separation of the sexes in meetings gave way to families in Western dress sitting together in church. And most importantly, education and Christianity became hallmarks of leadership and status.

But Arusha and Meru also made their mark on Christianity, making it uniquely their own. The split in the Church between Arusha and Meru missions echoed that within the Arusha and Meru Native Coffee Planters' Association, revealing the degree to which distinct cultural factors continued to distinguish Meru and Arusha from one another. The Leipzig missionaries had stressed use of local languages, so that Meru and Arusha, quite literally, had separate holy writs. Missionaries like Fokken and Blumer in Arusha or Krause and Ittameier in Meru, together with African church leaders like Lazaros Laiser or Zakariah Urio, dominated their churches for long periods and left their distinctive marks. The result was the creation of distinctive and separate Arusha and Meru Lutheran churches, a split that was confirmed in 1973 with the formal bifur- cation of the Northern Diocese between the two.

The Leipzig missions in Meru and Arusha had spawned their own distinctive com- munities, set apart from as well as by their local communities. As Arusha and Meru each became split into competing moral communities, each acquired its own exclusive social membership and institutions, moral values, religious beliefs, and rites of passage, as symbolized most dramatically in the enforced division between properly circumcised

---

[40] Nelson, *Freemen*, 90-137, 158–86; Japhet & Seaton, *Meru Land Case*, 62–3.

murran and improperly or non-circumcised students. When the first generation of separated Christians assumed control of local schools and churches and re-entered their communities, however, the barriers between Christians and non-Christians started to fall. And with the expulsion of the German missionaries and the assumption of local control by Arusha and Meru Christians, local communities began to enter the churches just as the churches began to enter their communities. Education became a commodity valued by many, and the churches continued to provide most of it even after the Native Authorities began to open their own schools in the late 1940s.

Christians' leadership in raising and marketing coffee furthered the standing of Christians in their wider communities, and they played key roles in the farmers' associations and their struggles with the administration over control of production and marketing. Like the schools, however, the coffee growers' associations did not belong only to Christians. Christians may have had an important role in establishing and running them, but they participated in them together with other Meru and Arusha. Such joint social encounters spread to other institutions as well, including both local governments and their oppositions.

These encounters were not just a one-way street running from Christians to non-Christians, however. While educated Christians assumed roles that depended on literacy and contacts with the administration and outside world, non-Christians continued to draw on existing resources (such as cattle, kinship, and status) to gain power and influence in the new situation. The alternate strategies are symbolized in the careers of Simeon Bene – who became the most powerful and wealthy man in Arusha as Chief from 1933 to 1952 – and Sante, his non-Christian counterpart in Meru, who drew on more traditional bases of authority and used his position to counter the increasing influence of Christians. Christians may have become important for mediating many of the new forces impinging on Arusha and Meru societies – Christianity, education, government, market economy – facilitating interaction between local and regional modes of action, but the new forces and regional modes were not necessarily dominant.

As such, educated Christians were the heirs to a long tradition within northern Tanganyika of active participation in both local and regional cultural systems going back to pastoral Maasai hegemony in the early nineteenth century and of increasing 'Swahili' cultural and commercial influence during that century.[41] Arusha and Meru had long participated in both local and regional systems, with economic resources, cultural values, status, and power drawn from one and employed in the other. Similarly, Christians drew on new resources and forms of knowledge to gain power and status in local institutions, just as people within those institutions drew on local resources to gain power and influence in regional ones.

Many observers and analysts, from early colonial officials to modern politicians and scholars, have stressed the 'progressive' role of Christians vis-a-vis their 'conservative' counterparts, depicting them as an emerging class of commercial farmers and incipient capitalists. Observers have differed, however, in their interpretations. Some in the administration wrote approvingly of the emergence of 'yeoman' farmers who employed

[41] Thomas Spear, 'Introduction' in T. Spear & R. Waller (eds), *Being Maasai* (London, 1993), 1–18.

hired labour and tractors to develop large 'modern' wheat farms on the plains,[42] while others — some colonial agricultural officers, latter-day dependency theorists, or architects of *Ujamaa* in the 1960s — criticized the growth of capitalist farmers who forsook solid self-sufficiency for the ephemeral gains of the market, or who dominated the co-operatives and exploited their fellow farmers for their own selfish gain.[43]

Proponents and opponents alike thus see the Christians as the core of a distinct new class of 'progressive' or 'capitalist' farmers who sought to 'maximize' commercial production and employed wage labour, in marked contrast to their non-Christian brethren. The dichotomy between the two groups was not, however, so clear-cut. Most coffee farmers did not abandon self-sufficiency in favour of fully commercialized agriculture; far from it. Coffee, like cattle or other cash crops, became an integral component of the overall household economy, but rarely a dominant one. Arusha and Meru coffee farmers continued to raise their own food crops, often preferring them to purely cash crops because they could either be consumed domestically or sold as needed. Time and again farmers chose *not* to maximize commercial production of one crop in order to retain an optimal level of production of all the crops they required. Hand-fed cattle consumed labour, but they provided milk and fertilizer, enhancing both human nutrition and crop yields. Total coffee production was reduced by interplanting coffee with bananas, but overall yields of coffee and bananas were greater than either grown separately. And successful coffee farmers continued to invest in mixed farms on the plains to ensure their own food production and in livestock to facilitate social exchanges. Commercial production, like livestock, then, augmented food production, and became one of a number of integrated strategies to optimize productivity in the face of rising population and limited land so as to continue to realize household self-sufficiency.[44]

If Meru and Arusha cash farmers were rarely maximizers, neither did they employ wage labour to any extent. Most farmers, whether they raised coffee or not, continued to rely on family labour, and they raised large families to provide it, thus accounting for continued population increase.[45] They adopted new crops, such as coffee or onions, only if they were compatible with family labour processes and they had sufficient family labour to do so. They also adopted new techniques, such as iron hoes or ploughs, or altered existing divisions of labour to enhance the overall productivity of family labour.

In spite of overall land pressure, few became landless and even fewer became wage

---

[42] Northern Province, Annual Reports, 1955–56 (TNA: 471/R.3/2.

[43] e.g. Cairns, 'Native Coffee Growing'; P. Puritt, 'The Meru of Tanzania: A Study of their Social and Political Organization' (Ph.D., Illinois, 1970), 181–3; G. Hyden, *Beyond Ujamaa in Tanzania* (London, 1980). Co-operatives were shut down throughout Tanzania in 1974, ostensibly because they had become dominated by capitalists. Similarly, Kirilo Japhet was expelled from Parliament because he was considered a capitalist farmer under the terms of TANU's leadership code.

[44] See Chapter 7. See also Louise Fortmann, 'Development Prospects in Arumeru District' (USAID/Tanzania, 1977) for an insightful discussion of maximal vs. optimal levels of production; Bishnu Baral et al., 'In Search of Water: A Study of Farming Systems in the Lowlands of Arumeru District' (Working Document, Series 30, International Centre for Development Oriented Research in Agriculture, Wageningen, 1993); and E.M. Nkonya et al., 'Arumeru District Diagnostic Survey' (Selian Agricultural Research Institute, Arusha, 1991).

[45] Nkonya, 'Arumeru District Diagnostic Survey', 36.

labourers. Those without sufficient land preferred to become tenants raising their own crops on land belonging to others, and the prevailing moral economy generally favoured their claims to sufficient land for their needs.[46] The one exception to the limited availability and use of non-family labour was in the northern highlands and on the plains. Landless Arusha had long squatted on Afrikaner farms north of Mount Meru, where they provided some labour or crop payment in return for the use of cattle, oxen, and land to farm. Arusha who later developed maize and wheat farms in Musa and Likamba needed larger labour forces to clear and work the land than their families could provide, and they frequently settled landless clients on the land, allowing them their own plots in return for labour. Andrea Kipuyo maintained 30 of his 100 acres for squatter clients, raising wheat on the rest.[47] Thus, where non-family labour was employed, it was usually that of tenants or clients who obtained land for their own use in return for labour under modified forms of existing patron-client relations. For just as Arusha and Meru were hesitant to work for European settlers for wages, so were they reluctant to work for one another on less than a social basis.

Arusha and Meru Christians and coffee farmers thus continued to operate within the terms of an older moral economy that fused, rather than severed, social and economic relations, while at the same time they transformed those relations in new ways to develop innovative new agricultural practices. As culture has mediated economic change, it has both affected the path of change and been transformed itself in the process.

[46] P.H. Gulliver, *Report on Land and Population in the Arusha Chiefdom* (Tanganyika Provincial Administration, 1957), 11, 58–61.
[47] Ngole ole Njololoi (AHT 4); Leonard Shio, 'A Political Economy of the Plantation System in Arusha' (MA, Dar es Salaam, 1972), 128–9; Luanda, 'Commercial Farming,' 165–9.

IV

Politics of
Land & Authority

9

Struggles for the Land

Political & Moral Economies of Land

Given the increasing pressure on land during the 1920s–1950s, it is not surprising that land became *the* focus for conflict and struggle among Arusha and Meru, European settlers, and the administration, all of whom entertained different ideas concerning land and its uses. For Meru and Arusha, the main issues involved increasing access to land deemed crucial for their economic and social survival, controlling its use, and increasing its productivity. Settlers, by contrast, sought to obtain land and control conditions of production, labour, and marketing to protect themselves from potential competition from Arusha and Meru, all of which depended on the support of the administration to achieve. The administration, in turn, sought to increase commercial production at the same time as maintaining an increasingly fragile political order but, faced with the irreconcilable conflicts involved, it was often forced to temporize.

It acceded to settler demands to restrict African coffee production in 1927, for example, but abandoned controls six years later in the face of Arusha and Meru intransigence. With land, it acknowledged Meru and Arusha needs, on the one hand, but avoided challenging settler control over alienated lands, on the other. In the end the conflicts over land – its possession, use, and meaning – were irreconcilable, and hastened the end of colonial rule in Tanganyika.

The Land Problem and its Solutions

It is the enduring irony of the land situation on Mount Meru, that while all the outside authorities historically involved in the area – German, British, *and* Tanganyikan – claimed to give priority to African peasant production, they all consistently favoured the settlers and empowered them to spread their tentacles around the mountain to choke the lifeblood of Meru and Arusha societies, their land. The Germans made Meru one of their primary settlement areas and first fastened the 'iron ring' of land alienation around the base of the mountain; the British maintained and extended German policy in spite of increasing evidence of land shortage and extreme political

175

pressure from Meru and Arusha for land; and the settler farms on Meru were among the only ones in the country that were *not* nationalized by the independent Tanganyikan government.

Members of the British administration were aware from the very beginning of their administration of the shortage of land for Meru and Arusha on Mount Meru. The district annual report for 1919–20 emphasized: 'All land not already occupied is required for expansion of the two native tribes mentioned'.[1] At the peak of land alienation in 1928, the Provincial Commissioner, G.F. Webster, emphasized in his annual report 'serious congestion does... exist and is a factor in the alienation of land ... to non-natives'. The following year he added that Arusha and Meru 'have felt land shortage acutely during 1929, especially so on account of the drought and consequent lack of grazing. There was a considerable amount of interracial friction owing to native cattle going on to European farms.' As many settlers exploited the situation to collect rent from Arusha and Maasai for grazing and water, Webster warned that very little more land could be recommended for alienation.[2]

Webster's warnings prompted the Secretary of State for Colonies to query what was being done about the situation and the Governor, Sir Donald Cameron, subsequently requested that the Assistant Secretary for Native Affairs, A.E. Kitching, investigate it.[3] Kitching had served as an Assistant District Officer in Arusha in 1920–1, and later as District Officer in 1926–8, prior to being named Assistant Secretary. He thus knew the area well, and summed up the impact of German land alienation on the Meru and Arusha so incisively and dramatically, that it is worth quoting at length:

> The two tribes were relatively small units when the German Government entered their lives, but they were well placed. They were secure from molestation by other tribes. They occupied land almost unexampled by its fertility and their irrigation channels placed them beyond the vagaries of seasonal rains. Immense plains were at the disposal of their cattle and there was an abundance of agricultural land available for further expansion.
>
> These fair prospects were quickly brought to nought by the German Government. An extensive system of land alienation to non-natives was inaugurated and proceeded in the most reckless manner. The station site was carved out of native holdings and in the vicinity of the station other holdings were allocated to the native levies who had accompanied the German forces. A township was allowed to spring up around the station and made further sequestration necessary. Two large mission stations and several small sites for Mission schools and two small farms were alienated in the heart of the native area and a belt of farms was carried right around the mountain. In the south the boundaries of these farms ran cheek by jowl with native cultivation, and entailed the expropriation of many natives.
>
> The German Government, realizing too late the effects of its land policy, ultimately decreed that no more Crown land should be alienated... but the damage had been done and when British Officers took over the district they found the Arusha and Meru cramped and penned within an area which was barely adequate for their immediate needs and practically incapable of extension to meet future requirements.
>
> In the north the encroachments of the two tribes into the primeval forest had been

[1] Arusha District, Annual Report, 1919–20 (TNA: 1733/1).
[2] Northern Province, Annual Reports, 1928 and 1929 (TNA: 11681).
[3] Secretary of State for Colonies to Cameron, 18 Aug 1930 (TNA: 26257) and Cameron's minutes thereon.

rightfully stopped by the demarcation of a Forest Reserve. In the south, extension was only possible on two narrow fronts between farms and then only for a short distance on account of tsetse fly. In the east a block of farms had been placed between the Forest Reserve and the Meru tribesmen and had deprived the latter of an outlet which would have sufficed for many years. In the west, farms had been demarcated and alienated on both sides of the Ngare-ol-mutonyi river and had deprived the Arusha of access to essential pastures beyond the river. In every quarter, normal tribal expansion... had been hopelessly compromised.[4]

While the British provided some amelioration of the situation, Kitching continued, they had not known the full extent of the problem before they re-alienated most of the German farms themselves:

The straits in which the Meru and Arusha tribesmen had been left by the German Government were not fully apparent when the district was taken over in 1916. There were no survey maps or other means of identifying accurately land which had been alienated and many European farms were derelict and unoccupied and were used at will by the tribesmen. Notwithstanding these handicaps, the situation was quickly appreciated and when the question of the liquidation of enemy properties was raised in 1920, the requirements of the two tribes received special consideration with the result that farm numbers 150, 174, 177, 178, 183, 193, 194, and 207... were retained for native use.[5]

The aim of granting Meru and Arusha the eight farms on the edges of the plains had not been to increase the amount of arable land available on the mountain, however, but merely to provide access for their cattle to the plains below.

Despite the fact that he felt the 'conditions of congestion of population ... are probably without parallel in East Africa...', Kitching was not prepared to recommend correcting earlier oversights by restoring land to Arusha and Meru:

It is clear... that a remedy will not be found by further purchases of alienated land... for the purpose of providing additional pastoral or agricultural land. The acquisition of farms with this view benefits only the few natives who are sufficiently fortunate to acquire holdings... and the needs of the population are too large and land too expensive for any substantial relief to be found in this fashion.[6]

He also considered agricultural expansion on to the plains hopeless, as they were too dry, barren, and infested with tsetse, the only possible exception being west along the ridge towards Monduli where some Arusha were already beginning to take up residence. He therefore recommended that more farms be acquired to give Arusha and Meru cattle greater access to the plains, just as in 1920.

Kitching's memo was important as it established the pattern for the administration's analysis of the land problem on Meru for years to come and prompted the Government to request that the Land Settlement Officer, F.J. Bagshawe, conduct a comprehensive survey of land distribution and use on Mount Meru. After months of further study, Bagshawe adopted Kitching's recommendations almost verbatim. He argued that Meru and Arusha both had plenty of land, as noted below; the problem was that most of it was on the plains without easy access from the mountain through the ring of European farms.

[4] A.E. Kitching, 'Memorandum on Native Land in Arusha District,' 3 Dec 1930 (TNA: 25369, also 26257).
[5] Kitching, 'Memorandum on Native Land'.
[6] Kitching, 'Memorandum on Native Land'.

Table 9.1 Land and Population of Arusha and Meru (from Bagshawe Report)

	Arusha	Meru
population	23,686	11,812
arable land on mountain (acres)	25,000	15,000
grazing land on plains (acres)	128,560	138,800
total land available (acres)	153,560	153,800

The solution was thus to provide a few more corridors that would allow Arusha and Meru to move their cattle on to the plains, and he recommended the acquisition of seven farms for that purpose, two for Meru to gain access to the east and south and five for Arusha to escape to the west, together with developing better water supplies for Meru and Arusha cattle on the plains. Webster subsequently added two farms on Monduli to provide water for Arusha settled there.[7]

The land problem in Meru and Arusha was not Bagshawe's only concern, however. He had also been delegated to investigate the situation north of Mount Meru, where Afrikaners claimed that fragmentation of land among their children had already forced many of them off the land, and they were agitating for 50,000 additional acres to join the 59,986 acres they already had into a solid block of alienated land across the north side of the mountain from Oldonyo Sambu in the west to Engare Nanyuki in the east. While Bagshawe echoed administration perceptions that the Afrikaners were ignorant 'back velders' who over-bred, whose wasteful pastoral life was more comparable to Maasai than to productive European settlers, and who had more than enough land overall for their 458 members, he nevertheless suggested that an additional 50,000 acres could be spared from Meru grazing territory for the 80 Afrikaner men who were landless. The administration rejected Bagshawe's recommendations, however, noting that the Afrikaners had more than enough land for their needs if it were only more equitably distributed between the few large landowners holding 1,000–3,000 acres each and the landless *by-wooners* (squatters) settled on their estates. Given the greater need in Meru, it could not countenance more land being transferred from productive Meru peasant farmers to 'back velders' who, it felt, would only destroy the land. Why should the government support poor whites, it asked, when hardworking settlers got little aid?[8]

Bagshawe's recommendations, as modified by the administration, were forwarded to London for approval. Arguing that Arusha and Meru should not be required to pay for land that 'was taken from the tribes by the German Government and alienated to European settlers without justification and without proper regard for the future', the

---

7 'Land Settlement Survey; II: Acquisition of Land by Natives' [Dec 1930] (TNA:26257); LDO to PC/NP, 28 Dec 1930; LDO to CS/DSM, 28 Dec 1930; PC/NP to CS/DSM 7 Jan 1931; Governor to Secretary of State for Colonies, 29 Jan 1931 (all in TNA: 25369).
8 'Land Development Survey; I: Dutch Settlement in Northern Province' [Dec 1930] (TNA: 19449); PC/NP to CS/DSM, 6 Jan 1931 (note minutes by SNA, 20 Jan 1931; CS, 23 Jan 1931; and Governor, 24 Jan 1931) (all in TNA: 19449); Governor to Secretary of State, 29 Jan 1931 (TNA: 25369).

administration requested that the government finance the estimated £17,500 required to acquire the nine farms. The Secretary of State approved the purchase, but denied the financing, forcing the administration to turn to the Meru and Arusha Native Authorities to finance the purchase themselves by levying an annual surtax of shs 2/- per person to pay for it. The two farms in Monduli, recently acquired by settlers, were dropped from the final sale, and Arusha were required to relinquish a fifty-yard strip along the eastern border of Arusha township in return.[9]

The land problem was far from solved, however. By 1938 a new study of the land problem in Meru by the Agricultural Officer, B.J. Hartley, lauded the productivity of Meru agriculture while also stressing their critical need for more land. He recommended that they be given 60,000 additional highland acres immediately as well as any settler farms that might revert to the government in the future.[10] Arusha and Meru themselves were mounting vehement protests against the earlier land purchases and refusing to pay the surtax, noting that the government had taken the land from them in the first place and then burdened them with a super-tax to buy it back. The Provincial Commissioner, F.C. Hallier, was sympathetic to their cause. Noting that the mountain was badly congested and that people were being forced to rent land and water from settlers that was once theirs, Hallier continued:

> No matter how we might argue, the native feels that we took away his land (it matters not to him whether we did it or the Germans) and that it is nothing short of rank injustice to expect him to buy it back while we continue to draw revenue from land that was once his. We should not allow the above problem to rest or drift; early and vigorous action is required, otherwise I see trouble, real trouble, such as is evident in other parts of our Colonial Empire.[11]

Hallier went on to conclude that the loan had been ill-conceived in the first place and should be forgiven to relieve Meru and Arusha from the burden of extra taxation. Arusha and Meru were being forced to repurchase land which had been taken from them initially, he argued; the government had negotiated the purchases without their knowledge; and even though they were paying for it, title deeds were in the name of the government. By forgiving the loan the government would thereby avoid further trouble and be fully compensated by the greater production that would take place.[12]

The Governor, Sir Mark Young, visited Arusha the day after Hallier drafted a second memo to the same effect and was immediately presented with another petition

[9] Governor to Secretary of State, 29 Jan 1931, and reply 7 April 1931 (TNA: 25369); Notes, 27 July 1932 (TNA: 69/602); Minutes, 23 Nov 1932 (TNA: 19449); P.E. Mitchell, 'Purchase of Land in Arusha District,' 2 Mar 1933; Governor to Secretary of State, 21 Apr 1933 and reply, 30 May 1933; CS/DSM to LO, 6 July 1933; PC/NP to Treasurer, 13 Jan 1934; Financial Arrangements, 22 Sept 1938; The Question of Title, 22 Sept 1938 (all in TNA: 25369); Agreement between H.R. Gilbert, District Officer of Arusha, and Arusha Elders, 5 Jan 1934 (TNA: 69/602).

[10] B.J. Hartley, 'A Brief Note on the Meru People with Special Reference to their Expansion Problem,' 25 Mar 1938 (TNA: 69/45/9, also 69/602, *Northern Province Book* and *Arusha District Book*).

[11] F.C. Hallier, 'Political and Economic Problems of the Moshi and Arusha Districts,' 2 Aug 1938 (TNA: 69/602).

[12] Hallier, 'Political and Economic Problems'; idem, 'Memorandum on the Purchase of Farms 134, 187, 208, 209, 210, 173, and 328 for the Arusha and Meru Tribes,' 12 Aug 1938 (TNA: 25369, also 69/602). See also P.E. Mitchell, 'Memo on purchase of farms,' 29 Aug 1938 (TNA: 25369).

by Meru and Arusha protesting the surtax. People were unable to pay the extra shs 2/- and the native treasury had gone deeply in debt making up the shortfall, they protested, when what people really needed was more land 'to meet the needs of future generations'. Young responded with a sermon on how young men should obey their elders, stop stealing cattle, cease wandering about Maasai land attending feasts, and engage in serious work herding, farming, or working for wages, while all should adopt anti-erosion measures recommended by the Agricultural Department. Then, almost as an afterthought, he added that the government had deferred its decision on their request for a remission of the loan and that it was 'making every effort' to find more land.[13] After considering various ways of reducing the payments, the administration finally decided to remit the loan in its entirety to avoid further political unrest. Young returned to Arusha six months later and, after reminding Arusha and Meru how much the government had done for them, announced his decision.[14]

In the meantime, however, both Meru and Arusha had become embroiled in further land disputes with settlers and the government. Meru had earlier purchased a leasehold farm on their own; the lease was expiring and they could not afford to convert it to freehold.[15] Meru were also threatened with further alienations in Engare Nanyuki, while Arusha were being evicted from their farms in Arusha town and faced the potential loss of another 2,000 acres south of town.[16] In response, Hallier was already petitioning the government to provide more land to Arusha and Meru. He proposed to move pastoral Maasai from northern Maasailand to southern Maasailand, thus 'anchoring' these 'anachronistic highwaymen', and granting the land east of the Rift to Arusha and Meru, thereby allowing the government to alienate further Arusha land south of the railway.[17]

Thus, while the administration seemed to respond sympathetically to Meru and Arusha needs with a genuine sense of the injustices they suffered, it continued to do nothing about their increasing need for arable land on the mountain. It focused on cattle instead, just as it had in 1920, in spite of the fact that Bagshawe's and Hartley's figures showed that Arusha and Meru had little more than one acre of cultivable land per person on the mountain itself. That it continued to respond in this way resulted as much from political pressure from settlers as from the justice of the Meru and Arusha case. Settlers constantly complained to the administration about Arusha and Meru cattle trespassing on their farms as they were taken to and from the plains, and the attempt to provide wider cattle corridors was an explicit attempt by the administration

[13] Petition by the Wa-Arusha and Wameru, 13 Aug 1938; Notes on a speech by the Governor, 13 Aug 1938 (TNA: 25369).
[14] Minutes by Financial Secretary, 31 Dec 1938; Governor to Secretary of State, 19 Jan 1939 and reply, 14 Feb 1939; Governor's Speech to Arusha, 20 Feb 1939 (all in TNA: 25369).
[15] Asst. LO/NP to LO/DSM, 9 Oct 1934 (TNA: 22519).
[16] LO/DSM to CS/DSM, 24 Jan 1935, two letters (TNA: 13017); Northern Province, Annual Report, 1927 (TNA: 11681); Dep. PC/NP to PC/NP, 9 May 1930 (TNA: 26147); DO/AD to LO/DSM, 24 Sept 1930 (TNA: 69/AR/II); DO/AD to PC/NP, 17 Jan 1931 (TNA: 12516); PC/NP to CS/DSM, 8 June 1934 and reply, 20 Oct 1934 (TNA: 12516); DO/AD to PC/NP, 17 Aug 1934 (TNA: 12516/II); PC/NP to CS/DSM, 1 Oct 1934 (TNA: 12516/II); Northern Province, Annual Report, 1934 (TNA: 11681); PC/NP to CS/DSM, 8 July 1938 (TNA: 69/602).
[17] CS/DSM, Minutes of a meeting with Capt. Hallier, 21 Oct 1937 (TNA: 25369, also 69/602).

to forestall such complaints in the future. In addition, most of the land acquired was undeveloped semi-arid land on the lower slopes that had little appeal to the majority of settlers raising coffee and mixed crops. Its sale realized substantial profits for K.V. Painter, the wealthy American settler who had paid too much for it in the first place, and enabled the administration to avoid confronting the more powerful British and Greek farmers who sought to protect precious coffee land on the mountain.

The administration was not unsympathetic to settlers. Cameron believed that white settlement was justified to promote the greater economic welfare of the colony as long as the lands in question were not required for 'native' use. In 1935 the government issued a Confidential Circular clarifying its responsibilities regarding land. The government pledged to retain as much 'native' land as possible, while considering alienation to 'non-natives' only when broader territorial interests were served. This apparent commitment to African rights was quickly qualified, however:

> While we seek to safeguard native rights, no one simply by virtue of being a native, has the right to land which neither he nor the community to which he belongs has occupied continuously in recent times.... Where there is congestion of native population in one area and ample room for expansion in another, there is a moral though not a legal obligation resting upon Government to [grant] all such expansion; but it must be strictly controlled, for otherwise Government will lose the power, which is its duty to maintain, of utilizing selected portions of the unoccupied land for the benefit of others whose claims are equally worthy of consideration on public grounds. If, for example, area A is thickly populated by an agricultural community of natives and area B is lightly populated and suitable for the growing of valuable crops, a native of A has no more right, legal or moral, than a good settler to occupy the best land in B, provided:-
> (i) the land in question is not required for the clearly foreseeable expansion needs of B;
> (ii) there is other cultivatable land available for the expansion needs of A.[18]

In upholding the rights of settlers 'whose claims are equally worthy of consideration on public grounds,' the administration thus quickly closed the door on Arusha-Meru aspirations it had so recently nudged open.

The constraints on protecting Africans' rights were further tightened in 1937 when Hallier inquired whether the administration was bound to allow settlers to convert ex-German leaseholds to freehold in view of the likely need of Meru and Arusha for the land in the future. Under the original terms of the German leases, leaseholders could apply for the right to purchase their land freehold if they made certain improvements on it, and settlers were attempting to hold the administration to the original terms. The Land Officer responded that the government was 'morally bound', if not legally, to issue freehold Rights of Occupancy on ex-German leaseholds without regard to 'extrinsic factors such as congestion of native population, or need of land for future expansion, which in the case of an ordinary application for a Right of Occupancy would probably determine, *per se*, ... that the Right of Occupancy could not be granted.'[19]

---

[18] Confidential Circular No. 13945/155, 20 Nov 1935 (TNA: 13401/II); Cameron to Secretary of State, 25 Feb 1926 (PRO: CO 691/83). The later reference, regarding Cameron's early thoughts regarding land use, was brought to my attention by Richard Waller.

[19] LO to PC/NP, 18 Nov 1937 (TNA: 472/LAN/13).

The administration's sense of its moral obligation to the settlers contrasted oddly with its legal obligations under the terms of the League Mandate to protect African interests. Few people in the administration even liked settlers. Clement Gillman, a British engineer in Tanganyika for some twenty years, was a seasoned and critical agricultural observer. He much admired the skills of both Maasai pastoralists and Arusha-Meru farmers, but was scathing in his criticism of the settlers. Noting that little of their huge farms was cleared or planted, Gillman called Lower Nduruma 'an other [sic] very good example of how the term "settlement" is used by the Kenya-type shouters as a suitable disguise for their land-speculation schemes. The area is semi-desert of the worst.' They were apparently not very attractive people either:

> I met the Usa Gang in a two hours' talk: General Boyd Moss, the gentleman 'settler' from high up the mountain, who produces nothing. Russell his shouting A.D.C., a few ugly looking penniless youngsters, a few innocent Greeks, dragged in to fill the room,... and a German or two to make a background.

Afrikaner farms in Engare Nanyuki consisted of '10 or 12 ramshackle and incredibly filthy farms with litters of children...' Only one farmer impressed Gillman: he had built a stone barn for his horses while he was content to live in a thatched house himself.[20] Those in the district administration were more tactful, if no less critical:

> The task of administering the tribes in the neighbourhood of Arusha proper is not made any easier by the presence of between four and five hundred European settlers, many of whom seem to regard Tanganyika as the happy hunting ground of Empire builders and to lose sight of the fact that the greater part of the Territory is held in trust for the native and not for the benefit of his would-be exploiter.[21]

Nevertheless, settlers had political clout and members of the administration remained sympathetic to their needs.[22] They depended on the administration to recruit labour for them, both directly by the district officers, chiefs, and labour officers, and indirectly by setting tax and wage rates. They also sought to protect their markets and labour supplies by restricting African production, controlling marketing and prices to maintain a two-tier pricing system that favoured European growers, and restricting the crops Africans could grow, ostensibly in the interests of controlling disease and theft.[23] They were also not above acting directly if their appeals to the government failed. They conspired with one another in land auctions to keep rents low, and when Asians bid against them, they either bribed the Asians to withdraw or beat them up.[24] They fought constantly with Africans and with each other over water rights, claiming expansive water

[20] Clement Gillman, 'Tanganyika Diaries,' 10/78/9-22.10.28, 75-78 (RH: MSS.Afr.s.1175).
[21] Annual Report, Arusha District, 1925 (TNA: 1733/36).
[22] There was, for example, a rowdy attempt made to join Kenya in 1928 that put the administration on warning regarding their handling of settlers. Northern Province, Half-Yearly Report, 1928 (TNA: 10902).
[23] For the restriction on African coffee growing, see Circular No. 77 of 1927, 20 Dec 1927 and related correspondence (TNA: 11160). For arguments relating to controlling disease and theft, Dir. of Ag. to CS/DSM 17 April 1930 (TNA: 12968/I); misc. correspondence (TNA: 9/12/14); Dir. of Ag. to CS/DSM, 30 Feb 1934; PC/NP to CS/DSM, 24 March 1934; PC/NP to Sr AO/Moshi, 13 July 1934 (TNA: 11908/II).
[24] DO/AD to PC/NP, 4 April 1928; K.C. Patel to PC/NP, nd and reply, 20 April 1928; PC/NP to LO/DSM, 20 April 1928; CS/DSM to PC/NP, 11 May 1928 (all in TNA: 69/205/AR).

rights against other users and arbitrarily blocking furrows to others' farms to get water for themselves.[25]

While the central administration often acceded to political pressures from settlers in the interests of 'broader territorial interest' and political harmony, administrators in the district were forced to deal with the daily consequences of implementing policy, and those were not good. Meru and Arusha generally resisted any actions by settlers or the administration that intruded on their economic autonomy, leading them to become renowned in administration circles as especially 'truculent', 'intractable', 'arrogant', and 'undisciplined' peoples.[26]

Colonial labour demands constantly provoked resistance, as we have seen. Few Meru or Arusha were willing to work for settlers, especially in poorly paid seasonal labour, and they generally refused to show up for corvée unless they approved of the project for which it was used.[27] They also resisted colonial attempts to control their labour on their own fields. While some claimed that the land problem on Meru was caused by people growing coffee at the expense of food crops, Meru and Arusha continued to expand coffee production because it provided better returns on their labour than either producing food crops exclusively or working for settlers. The claim was not unrelated, of course, to settler demands to restrict African production of coffee in order to limit competition and make African labour more readily available to themselves, but African coffee growers rejected it out of hand, as did many members of the administration.[28]

Struggles for the Land

The administration's persistent unwillingness to provide additional arable land on the mountain fuelled continual Meru and Arusha resistance to colonial rule. Land and labour provided the foci of Arusha and Meru resistance from the time they killed the first two Europeans – who they felt threatened to seize their land and force them to work – at the onset of colonization to that near its close when Meru took their case against expropriation to the United Nations. Meru and Arusha were notably reluctant to work for settlers, preferring to develop their own holdings, and they were largely successful in forcing the settlers and the administration to look elsewhere for labour. As their populations continued to grow, however, pressure on available land became acute, and they repeatedly appealed to the administration for more land. And when the administration continually failed to heed their appeals, they simply occupied undeveloped or abandoned settler estates, claiming the land as their own by virtue of the labour they had invested in clearing it and of the permanent crops they had planted, thus forcing the settlers to accede to a *fait accompli* or the administration to acquire the land for them.[29] Settlers complained constantly about Arusha and Meru trespassing on their land, while

[25] See, e.g., the numerous cases in TNA: 69/246/6, 472/112, and 472/WAT/25.
[26] These are all words one finds with disarming frequency in the colonial files.
[27] Minutes, District Meeting, 6 Oct 1949 (TNA: 9/ADM/11).
[28] DO/AD to PC/NP, 16 Sept 1930 (TNA: 69/45/9). James Lewton Brain, personal communication.
[29] PC/NP to CS/DSM, 7 March 1941; reply 5 April 1941; de la Mothe to PC/NP, 28 April 1941 (all in TNA: 69/238); Arusha District, Annual Report, 1954 (TNA: 472/ANR/1).

Meru and Arusha used almost any excuse to present appeals for more land to the administration, and rarely a year went by when either went unnoted in the annual district reports.

The struggle for land in Meru focused on re-acquiring alienated land on or near the mountain. Aside from the two farms given them by the British in 1920, Meru had been able to buy a 1,000-acre leasehold farm that contained valuable salt licks and grazing in Engare Nanyuki for shs 20,000/- in 1925, but the lease came due in 1937 and Meru could not afford to purchase the freehold, necessitating government intervention.[30] They were also allotted two other farms in the early 1930s as a result of the Bagshawe Report, for which they were assessed an annual per-capita surtax of shs 2/-. These were both lowland farms designed primarily to provide pastures in north and south Meru, however, and lacked cattle routes from the mountain. Trespassing and squatting on European farms thus continued unabated, and Meru joined with Arusha to protest against the surtax in 1938, leading to its eventual cancellation.[31]

Given their higher population density, their greater need for land, the restrictions posed by land alienated to settlers, and the presence of Arusha town in their midst, land issues arose even more persistently in Arusha, a fact recognized by the British administration when it allocated six ex-German farms to Arusha initially to provide access to plains grazing. These did not, however, abate the need for arable land on the mountain. Arusha offered to pay a thousand cattle (worth shs 80,000/-) in 1928 to buy Farm 187, two hundred intensively cultivated acres east of the Engare Olmotonyi, to gain arable land and access to grazing and the ridge to Monduli to the west, but the administration withdrew the offer to sell when the owner granted Arusha rights of passage over uncultivated areas of the farm.[32]

Five more farms were acquired for Arusha in 1934 to provide additional access to grazing, as recommended by Bagshawe, but Arusha were assessed an additional shs 2/- in tax to pay for them. Only four years later, Hallier noted increasing congestion on the slopes. At the same time Arusha were refusing to pay the surtax, while complaining bitterly that they were having to pay for land taken from them in the first place and forcing the Native Treasury into deficit. Given that the Native Authority itself had not been able to pay its two-thirds share of the debt, Hallier recommended that it be forgiven.[33] Arusha presented a petition to the Governor to the same effect, noting their need for land 'to meet the needs of future generations', and the government eventually agreed to forgo the loan, though no additional land was forthcoming for another decade.

Not only did Arusha not receive the land they needed, they were constantly faced with threats of further expropriations in and around Arusha town. The Germans had

[30] Notes on meeting, 23 Nov 1932 (TNA: 19449); Asst LO/NP to LO/DSM, 9 Oct 1934 (TNA: 22519). Ironically, this farm, on which they owned formal freehold, was the very one from which they were evicted in 1951.
[31] 'Land Settlement Survey; II: Acquisition of Land by Natives'; Bagshawe to PC/NP, 28 Dec 1930 (TNA: 26257); Northern Province, Annual Reports, 1932–3 (TNA: 11681); CS/DSM, Financial Arrangements, 22 Sept 1938 (TNA: 25369).
[32] PC/NP to CS/DSM, 25 Oct 1928 (TNA: 12826); PC/NP to CS/DSM, 6 March 1929 (TNA: 26226).
[33] Hallier, 'Political and Economic Problems'; idem, 'Memorandum on the Purchase of Farms'; Notes by Financial Secretary, 31 Dec 1938 (TNA: 25369).

placed the town in the midst of the most densely populated part of Burka. When the British occupied Arusha, approximately three-quarters of its 1,100 acres were still occupied by Arusha farmers, and Arusha continued to live and farm within the town into the 1940s.[34] Thus virtually any development within the town involved the expropriation and displacement of Arusha farming there. In 1927 a new township was laid out with considerable difficulty as there were a number of Arusha homesteads in the proposed commercial area, and many Arusha had to be forcibly dispossessed and compensated.[35] Development in town surged after the railroad was extended to Arusha in 1928–9, causing more Arusha to be evicted, even as the Depression caused many developers to default on their mortgages and Rights of Occupancy, leaving the town littered with half-finished buildings. Expropriations continued nonetheless, with 331 acres seized from Arusha at a cost of shs 29,466/- in 1931 alone.[36]

Arusha tenaciously resisted expropriation of their farms on the basis that they had cleared the land with their own labour or that they had established their farms before the town was founded, and, when forced to leave, they insisted on being granted comparable land elsewhere in addition to compensation for their houses and crops. The Germans had merely offered compensation for the land, and the British continued to ignore Arusha prescriptive rights until the 1930s, when they belatedly acknowledged them and refused to permit future expropriations unless comparable land was offered. Since little or no such land was available elsewhere, however, future development of the town was legally stymied.[37]

Arusha were ever alert to attempts to take their land, and were adept at sabotaging such attempts. In 1928 European residents applied for an unoccupied piece of land outside of town for a cricket ground, but no sooner had they started to clear it than the chief sent people to build and settle on the site. While Webster admonished the chief for his action and cited the episode to demonstrate 'how very suspitious and jealous the

---

[34] I estimate that Arusha occupied over 800 acres, based on unspecified expropriations in 1927 and 1928–9, 331 acres taken in 1931, and 436 acres in 1945–6, as detailed below. Descriptions of Arusha farms in town are found in: Krause, *ELMB*, 57(1902), 279; Müller, *ELMB*, 57(1902), 458; John Boyes, *The Company of Adventurers* (London, 1928), 169–72; Fokken, *ELMB*, 60(1905), 392; Gillman, Diaries, VIII/65/16.11.24; PC/NP to CS/DSM, 13 May 1930 (TNA: 12516); Map D⁵23, 6 May 1930 (TNA: 12516/II); Dep. PC/NP to PC/NP, 9 May 1930 (TNA: 26147); Northern Province, Annual Report, 1931 (TNA: 11681). For a detailed discussion, see T. Spear, 'Town and Country: Arusha and its Hinterland' (SOAS, 1994).

[35] Northern Province, Annual Report, 1927 (TNA: 11681).

[36] Northern Province, Annual Reports, 1928–31 (TNA: 11681); DO/AD to PC/NP, 27 Jan 1931 (TNA: 12516). Rights of Occupancy were issued contingent on occupiers erecting buildings of a certain value within a fixed number of years. Many forfeited their Rights during the depression, despite repeated extensions of the time period.

[37] PC/NP to CS/DSM, 13 May 1930 (TNA 12516); DO/AD to PC/NP, 17 Aug 1934; PC/NP to CS/DSM, 2 Oct 1934 (TNA: 12516/II); CS/DSM to PC/NP, 10 April 1942 and reply, 28 April 1942 (TNA: 12516/III). The administration also generally acknowledged that Arusha owned their land individually: e.g. Dep. PC/NP to PC/NP, 9 May 1930 (TNA: 26147); CS/DSM to PC/NP, 20 Oct 1934 correcting PC/NP to CS/DSM, 8 June 1934 (TNA: 12516). There were several ex-German farms within and adjacent to the township that the government could have acquired, but it held off doing so because it felt the owners were asking too high a price or it was not politically expedient to do so: PC/NP to CS/DSM, 12 May 1930 and 2 July 1930 (TNA: 26417).

Waarusha are of their tribal lands,' the grant was held in abeyance nevertheless.[38] In 1930 a number of Arusha claimed they had never been compensated for land seized by the Germans, and in the absence of German records to the contrary, the administration agreed to pay.[39]

The administration could only resolve its legal dilemma by seeking to justify dispossessing Arusha on other grounds. Officials claimed that African farms were unhygienic and therefore had to be cleared for health reasons. Webster noted in 1930 that Arusha in town

> ... live in tribal style: They plant a grove of bananas, and in the centre of this they build beehive shape huts of banana leaves. The huts are the home of the owner of the bananas and of his family. The same huts shelter the family cattle. Sanitation is unknown and at the present season of year conditions about the huts are filthy.[40]

Since bananas were thought to harbour mosquitos, the Township Authority passed rules calling for uprooting any standing crops within 440 yards of any habitation, thus rendering Arusha farming in town illegal, but it was unable to enforce the new rules against Arusha prescriptive rights.[41] European residents complained that Arusha rented rooms to tenants and leased their houses to Somali butchers and other 'alien natives', thereby voiding their claim that such land was essential to their livelihood, but the government dismissed these claims out of hand.[42]

The Township Authority sought permission to evict 25 Arusha in 1943 on the grounds that farming was illegal within the township, Arusha homesteads posed a threat to health, and the presence of 'tribal natives' in town was prejudicial to 'tribal discipline'. In their stead they proposed to build a European golf course, playing fields for two Asian communities, and a public park and garden, ostensibly to separate Arusha settlements from town 'for health reasons'.[43] When the Governor refused to dispossess Arusha without comparable land being provided, the Authority resolved to solve the problem once and for all by expropriating all 128 remaining Arusha of their 435.6 acres in exchange for four small settler farms totalling 184 acres. The administration balked at acquiring the farms, however, and the District Commissioner proposed simply offering the Arusha sufficiently generous compensation (shs 200/- a acre) to entice them to sell voluntarily. The Provincial Commissioner added that land was available at Oljoro, though the chiefs denied it, and that Arusha should simply be left to find their own land. In the end, Arusha were offered shs 182,360/- for their land, houses, and

[38] PC/NP to CS/DSM, 18 Oct 1928 (TNA: 10058/I).

[39] Dep. PC/NP to PC/NP, 9 May 1930 (TNA: 26417); DO/AD to LO/DSM, 24 Sept 1930 (TNA: 69/AR/II); Northern Province, Annual Report, 1931 (TNA: 11681).

[40] PC/NP to CS/DSM, 13 May 1930 (TNA: 12516). The fact that the administration refused to install sewers anywhere in town until 1957 made issues of sanitation relative.

[41] Northern Province, Annual Report, 1933 (TNA: 11681).

[42] PC/NP to CS/DSM, 12 June 1930 and minute by A.E. Kitching, 10 Oct 1930 (TNA: 10068); PC/NP to CS/DSM, 8 June 1934 and reply 20 Oct 1934 (TNA: 12516).

[43] DO/AD to PC/NP, 10 Dec 1943; PC/NP to CS/DSM, 8 May 1944 and 19 July 1944 (TNA: 12516/III). The necessity for such a 'cordon sanitaire' was an integral part of public health policy throughout the colonies at the time and provided a convenient excuse to provide expansive residential neighbourhoods and sports facilities for Europeans. Spear, 'Town and Country'.

crops and all but two were successfully pressured to accept the terms, but Arusha elders mounted a strong protest to the Governor against the evictions nonetheless.[44]

The problem was not limited to the land within the township, however. The Germans had established the boundaries of the town at a mile and a half radius from the *boma*, but the British demarcated less than one-quarter of that. As the town grew and development plots became exhausted, there was constant pressure to expand the town's boundaries into the surrounding Arusha farms.[45]

When the government initially offered to exchange grazing land for land bordering the township in 1930, the offer was rejected by the Arusha chiefs, who claimed they could not turn anyone off town land without causing hardship. Seizing the opportunity to acquire additional land, however, they offered to buy the grazing land instead. The District Officer, R.A. Pelham, felt that the offer had been badly timed, and cynically recommended that the administration wait until water was short and rinderpest, then starting, had taken its toll. Noting that land near the township belonged to small-stock owners, while it was the chiefs and other wealthy cattle-owners who wanted the grazing land, he also suggested that wealthy Arusha buy the land near town from their fellow Arusha and then exchange it with the government for grazing land elsewhere. Webster squashed these attempts to blackmail the owners or divide Arusha along class lines, however, by noting that the government was neither willing to buy the land nor to finance it. Later, under the terms of the Bagshawe Report, the administration simply insisted that Arusha give up the land bordering town as a quid pro quo for receiving grazing land elsewhere, crediting them with shs 20,000/- against the cost of the newly acquired land.[46]

The government relocated the main road from Moshi to Arusha and Namanga in 1949, taking 1,800 acres and 120 houses from 500 Arusha north of town. At the same time, the administration expropriated another 120 acres for a Tanganyika Packers plant east of town. Cash compensation only was offered in both cases, but Arusha angrily removed the survey pegs for the road, refused to accept compensation for the meat plant, and continually protested against both expropriations.[47]

No sooner had the administration carried out the final evictions of the remaining

---

[44] CS/DSM to PC/NP, 27 June 1944 and reply 19 July 1944 (TNA: 25369); DC/AD to PC/NP, 13 Dec 1944; PC/NP to CS/DSM, 25 Jan 1945 and reply, 19 Feb 1945; PC/NP to CS/DSM, 14 April 1945 and reply 3 May 1945; PC/NP to CS/DSM, 19 May 1945, reply 8 June 1945, and related memos; Certified Agreements, 4 July 1945 – 1 Feb 1946; PC/NP to CS/DSM, 15 April 1947 (all in TNA: 12516). Elders of the two Native Courts of Burka and Ilboro to H.E. the Governor, 7 Jan 1946 (TNA: 69/602).

[45] Dep. PC/NP to PC/NP, 9 May 1930 (TNA: 26147); Address by European Members to H.E. the Governor, 27 July 1931 (TNA: 12516); DO/AD to PC/NP, 17 Aug 1934; PC/NP to CS/DSM, 2 Oct 1934 (TNA: 12516/II); Arusha Township Taxpayers to CS/DSM, 18 Dec 1934 (TNA: 12516/II).

[46] DO/AD to PC/NP, 26 Aug 1921 and reply, 2 Sept 1931 (TNA; 69/45/4); Agreement between H.R. Gilbert, DO/AD, and Arusha Elders, 5 Jan 1934 (TNA: 69/602). The fact that individual Arusha displaced from town were rarely the ones who benefited from land grants on the plains shifted the conflict from one between the British authorities and Arusha to one between wealthy Arusha cattlemen, often the chief and his allies, who benefited from such transfers, and poorer Arusha farmers, who did not, as Pelham sensed.

[47] Minutes, District Meetings, 6 Jan 1949 – 8 Dec 1949 (TNA: 9/8/1); Northern Province, Annual Report, 1950 (TNA: 19415); Arusha District, Annual Report, 1952 (TNA: 472/-).

Arusha in town in 1945–6 than the Township Authority requested a major extension of the boundaries of the town as 'absolutely essential for the future planned development of the Township.' The Provincial Commissioner reluctantly concurred, noting, however, that the proposals were 'embarrassing' following as they did so closely on the heels of the expropriations.[48] The issue dragged on for some time, with the administration caught between the request to add more than 1,100 acres to the town, thus doubling its size, and the need to find equivalent land elsewhere to settle displaced Arusha, as the District Commissioner noted in 1950:

> If we are to act in accordance with the 1930 White Paper on Native Policy ... it will be necessary to find land for them of equal extent and value elsewhere.... Furthermore, as native opinion is more critical than ever, especially in this district where recent development affecting native interests has been so great, e.g. Tanganyika Packers, Namanga/Taveta Road, farm leases for production purposes, etc – and subversive interests are fanned by the Kilimanjaro [Citizens'] Union and the immigrant Wa-Kikuyu, it is all the more vital to be scrupulously just and impartial....

> The crux of the extension problem is, of course, the problem of finding any land of equal value and extent elsewhere for settlement of those dispossessed from the Town areas; for failure to have a settlement plan would undoubtedly result in the creation of a body of dispossessed and disgruntled natives. Land to be acceptable cannot be in the lowland plains, yet all other land would appear to be unavailable.[49]

While several ex-German estates remained around the town, suggestions to acquire them were either dismissed as 'not practical politics at this juncture,' or they were found to be already densely settled by Arusha.[50] The administration tried to keep the proposals for expansion secret, but the word soon got out and Chief Simeon kept the pressure on with frequent petitions to the Provincial Commissioner and Governor.[51] Arusha adamantly refused to participate in land surveys and censuses in the affected areas and the Government Anthropologist, H.A. Fosbrooke, voiced a quiet dissent against 'expropriating a self supporting peasantry to make room for a rapidly expanding non-productive urban population'.[52]

As part of the proposal, a new town plan was drafted in 1948 that called for expanded housing for Asians and Europeans and extensions to the commercial and industrial areas, in addition to a new club, a hospital, five government buildings, and some

[48] Executive Officer, Arusha Township Authority to PC/NP, 22 March 1946; PC/NP to CS/DSM, 26 March 1946 (TNA: 12516).

[49] DC/AD to PC/NP, 6 July 1950 (TNA: 472/-). See also Minutes, District Meetings, 9 March 1950, 29 April 1950 (TNA: 9/ADM/11).

[50] Minutes, District Meeting, 29 April 1950 (TNA: 9/ADM/11); DC/AD to PC/NP, 7 April 1952 (TNA: 472/-).

[51] The administration was reluctant to publish the plan as late as 1952 for fear of the 'political repercussions' of showing Arusha land included within the expanded township, and so deliberately published it only in sections: DC/AD to PC/NP, 2 July 1952 and reply 12 July 1952 (TNA: 472/-). PC/NP to DC/AD, 8 March 1950; Olkarsis Simeon Laiser to H.E. the Governor, 14 Sept 1951 and 18 March 1952; Olkarsis Simeon Laiser to PC/NP, 28 Nov 1951 (TNA: 472/-).

[52] DC/AD to PC/NP, 10 Nov 1952 (TNA: 472/-). Fosbooke to DC/AD, 14 Dec 1950 (TNA: 472/NA/48).

twelve schools, sports grounds, and centres for different European and Asian communities. Housing and facilities for Africans were noticeably absent on the grounds that they could settle outside the township, thus putting additional pressure on Arusha land.[53] The Governor strongly supported the proposals in order to bring the 'struggling, dusty town' 'up to the standards of a model modern East African town,' but the pressures on land were too great.[54] A committee formed to investigate the proposals in 1951 accepted the overall need for expansion, but suggested also increasing the density of development to make better use of available land. Even so, four members of the committee, including the District Commissioner, B.J.J. Stubbings, opposed any outward expansion, and the Provincial Commissioner eventually blocked it on political grounds in 1953.[55] The boundaries were only expanded after two estates, totalling 7,134 acres, adjacent to town were acquired in 1957, and Arusha displaced were given an average of shs 2133/- plus three acres of land for every acre they abandoned.[56]

Access to water also became an issue as settlers sought to limit Arusha and Meru use above them, while allowing little or none to pass through their farms to the pastures on the plains below. Afrikaner herders in Engare Nanyuki were accustomed to spew water out over the flats for grazing, exhausting all the water in the furrow and leaving the plains and cattle below parched, while a farmer in south Meru blocked a main furrow to supply his own 'hippo pool'.[57] Similar struggles affected just about every furrow flowing down the mountain.

Political and Moral Economies of Land

Since land and water were both at the crux of Meru and Arusha economies and both were severely threatened by colonialism, it is not surprising that conflicts over access to and use of them should have provoked resistance. And yet, the government was not unaware of their problems. A distinguished group of colonial servants – Webster, Kitching, Hartley, Hallier, and Fosbrooke – had spoken eloquently on behalf of Meru and Arusha needs, but their entreaties were rarely heeded and Arusha and Meru

---

[53] Minute from the Town Planning Officer to the Member for Local Government, 22 Feb 1950; Executive Officer, Arusha Township Authority to PC/NP, 22 April 1950; Chief Town Planning Officer to Executive Officer, Arusha Township Authority, 22 April 1950; Executive Officer Arusha Township Authority to CS/DSM, 25 April 1951 (TNA: 472/-).

[54] Note by H.E. the Governor on his visit to Arusha, 12–18 Jan 1950 (TNA: 472/-).

[55] The committee proposed to increase the density of development by promoting two-storey development in the medium density (ie. Asian) district, reducing low density (European) lots from one to three quarters of an acre, redeveloping the police lines and prison for housing, requiring employers to house their African employees, and providing piped water and sewers to all. 'Memo on the Expansion of Arusha Township Boundaries,' in President, Arusha Township Authority to H.E. the Governor, 15 Oct 1951; 'Supplementary Memo on the Expansion of Arusha Township Boundaries' (TNA: 472/-); PC/NP to Member for Local Government, 23 Sept 1953 (TNA: 12516).

[56] Northern Province, Annual Reports, 1957–59 (TNA: 471/R.3/2).

[57] DO/Masai District to DO/AD, 31 March 1927, 13 July 1927, 6 Feb 1934, and 9 March 1944; DO/AD to PC/NP, 15 Feb 1935; DO/AD, notes, 21–4 Aug 1935 (all in TNA: 472/112/21).

received little redress for their grievances. Their failure was partly due to differences in perspective between district and central administrators. District administrators confronted daily the negative impact land policy had on Arusha and Meru societies and on the administration's deteriorating relations with them, as evidenced by Hallier's fear of 'real trouble' developing if 'vigorous action' was not taken to address their grievances. Hallier was right; nothing was done, and twenty years later real trouble did develop. Dar es Salaam and London, on the other hand, were far removed from such tensions and more readily appreciated issues regarding territorial production and finance than those regarding disgruntled 'natives'.

But the failure to resolve struggles over the land was not simply a matter of different administrative perspectives; it was an issue of the fundamentally different meanings land had for the different participants and of the power each could bring to bear to impose its own interpretation on the others. The reasons for the irony noted earlier – that despite their alleged preference for African farmers, all the outside authorities involved on Meru promoted settlers' interests at the expense of African ones – thus lie in differences in the significance attached to land by administrations, settlers, Arusha, and Meru as well as in contradictions inherent within colonialism itself.

For the government, land was basically an economic issue, though it also had strong political overtones. Land was the main economic resource of the colony and members of the administration believed that it had to be demarcated, owned, invested in, and worked to achieve worthwhile commercial results. The government thus believed that European settlers could best develop commercial production in the interests of the colony as a whole, in spite of abundant evidence to the contrary. One had only to compare the orderly rows of European coffee displayed across the landscape with the untidy, overgrown farms of Africans to appreciate that. Thus while local officials may have been aware of the frequently precarious state of settler agriculture, the progress being made by African farmers, or the potentially disruptive conflicts between the two, their opinions carried little weight against perceived economic necessity.

In the end, then, settlers had more political clout than African peasants, even if they were seen as *déclassé* by the Oxbridge men in the administration and as potentially disruptive threats to the colonial order. The complaints of the settlers were heard in the European clubs of Arusha, Dar es Salaam, and London, and they were acted on so long as they did not threaten to upset the uneasy colonial order between Africans and Europeans. The administration was continually unwilling, for example, to re-allocate ex-German leasehold farms against settler opposition for either Arusha and Meru settlement or township expansion, even when they lay vacant or were occupied by settlers without leases. Meru and Arusha complaints, by contrast, were usually dismissed unless they threatened that order. Thus, the administration tried to ameliorate settler demands it knew would excite African opposition, such as enforced labour or alienating still more land; and it reversed policies, such as the restriction on African coffee, that threatened to undermine its authority.[58]

Settlers also saw land in economic terms, but ones that required political access to

[58] Memo of Combined Association of Arusha to H.E. the Governor, 25 July 1929 (TNA: 13417).

190

realize. Few settlers had the capital necessary to develop their farms, and their dependence on outside capital made them extremely vulnerable to international markets and financiers. Many were perennially in the hands of their bankers or brokers, and many ceased production or went bankrupt during the Depression. Starved of capital, they depended on government to obtain cheap labour, restrict competition from African producers, and protect their investment in land. Settler welfare was thus assured at the expense of that of Africans, who literally paid for settler production with government mandated taxes, low wages, loss of land, and restrictions and controls placed on their own commercial production.

Land thus had economic and political significance for settlers; it had social significance as well. Being a European settler in the colonies was to belong to a certain economic class, a petty colonial aristocracy, whose boorish behaviour and pursed-lip racism oddly still fascinate people today in novels and films.[59] It was a life that had largely ceased to exist in England, at least for those who became settlers, and it could only be sustained by maintaining an illusion of wealth based on racial supremacy and cheap labour, despite the fact that most settlers were perpetually indebted to their banks and brokers. Their social superiority and economic status rested on maintaining the artificial distinctions that separated 'them' from 'us': race, land, and alleged productive superiority. While the myth of race was rarely questioned, land and production both had to be fought for to maintain their holdings and their competitive advantages against African producers.

Arusha and Meru sustained, in many ways, more complex ideas about land than either the administration or the settlers. Land did, of course, have singular economic significance for people who relied on it to produce virtually all of their economic needs, alimentary as well as social. Land, and the cattle which grazed on it, were the source not only of food, but also of wealth in disposable food surpluses, beer, and cattle; and wealth was the source of social influence and political power. Given the centrality of land in Meru and Arusha economic, social, and political life, it could not help but have had great moral significance as well. Land, specifically *kihamba/engisaka*, lay at the core of people's moral being and differences over the moral significance of land lay at the base of their opposition to colonialism.

Both Meru and Arusha held that everyone had the right to as much land as they needed, and if such land was not available at home, then one had the right to clear forest land and thereby claim ownership. As population increased during the late nineteenth century, the boundaries of Arusha and Meru cultivation had been pushed inexorably up the mountain sides, until by the turn of the century they were approaching the upper limits for bananas and annual crops. Expansion had been slowed, or maybe even reversed, during the 1890s by disease, drought, and conquest, and local economies did not recover until 1907. It was precisely during this period of retrenchment in the local economy, as in so many areas of East Africa, that German authorities alienated vast tracts to settlers. Unlike Kilimanjaro and Usambara, little of the alienated land was

[59] As the romanticized film of Karen Blixen's memoirs, *Out of Africa*, or Ralph Lauren's colonial pornography advertising 'Safari' perfume shows.

191

on the mountain itself, and most had probably not been previously cultivated by Meru or Arusha, but its closure drastically restricted access to the plains for cattle, for raising annual crops, or for future expansion. By the 1920s, Arusha and Meru economies had recovered and their populations were growing rapidly, but confined by the 'iron ring' of alienated lands below and the forest reserve above, 'conditions of congestion ... without parallel in East Africa' developed that were readily apparent to most observers.

Land shortage produced a sense of economic, political, and moral crisis in Meru and Arusha societies not unlike that of the 1890s. Economically, people were forced to intensify production to maintain their standard of living. They enclosed and planted mountain pastures, pushed the limits of cultivation up steep hillsides and down river banks, and began to grow crops such as coffee that provided higher returns on land and labour.

The shortage of land also produced political tensions between government chiefs, who asserted their right to distribute new lands; wealthy men, who sought to accumulate land and were often the beneficiaries of their largesse; elders who sought to conserve land for themselves and their offspring; and landless juniors seeking land on which to settle and farm, as we shall see in the next chapter. It produced tensions between the generations as well, especially between members of Talala, who had benefited from the free-wheeling expansion of the 1880s and dominated land and cattle as the ruling elders of the 1920s, and their sons and grandsons who became increasingly dependent on them as the frontiers for expansion closed and they had to rely on their fathers for cattle and land in order to marry and settle.

Shortage of land on the mountain contributed to a growing moral crisis in Arusha and Meru societies as well. Not only did each Meru or Arusha have a right to land, he or she had the right to a particular kind of land, known as *kihamba* or *engisaka*, land that was well-watered and suitable for growing bananas on the central mountain slopes. One built one's house in *kihamba/engisaka*, raised one's family there, and surrounded it with the dense groves of bananas that sustained life. It was the central focus of people's lives.[60] One's right to *kihamba* or *engisaka* was thus fundamental to the social contract. If sufficient access to *kihamba/engisaka* were not available 'to meet the needs of future generations,' sons would fight their fathers, brothers and age-mates would fall out among themselves, and wives would leave their husbands. Individuals would starve and the social order would disintegrate.

As land became increasingly short, however, it was just such *kihamba/engisaka* that was threatened. Bananas would not grow readily on the higher slopes or on the plains. Thus even if one got land in other areas, one could not realize a full social life there. As suitable forest land and pastures on the mountain disappeared, each *kihamba/engisaka* shrank in size until it could no longer accommodate all the family claimants to it. At the same time, rights to *kihamba/engisaka* became increasingly individualized, as people sought to protect what land they had, even at the expense of their relatives. For those excluded from *kihamba/engisaka*, the social contract was broken. Some abandoned their homes for the mission, which had land and a society of its own. Others left to squat on

---

[60] P. H. Gulliver, *Report on Land and Population in the Arusha Chiefdom* (Tanganyika Provincial Administration, 1957), 26–7.

Afrikaner farms in north Meru, where they were shielded by distance from the shame of being landless and having to work for others.[61] Land bound people together; its absence threatened to tear them apart.[62]

The moral crisis within Meru and Arusha societies was reflected in what they felt was the immorality of the wider colonial order. Settlers claimed ownership of land cleared by the labour of others. Settlers also owned vast tracts of land, far more than they could develop and use, but like the proverbial dog in the manger, they jealously prevented anyone else from using it. While Arusha and Meru recognized individual ownership gained from clearing and productively working the land, one could scarcely refuse to share one's land with others if it was more than one needed. It was a moral obligation that transcended any individual right to property. But when settlers agreed to share land or water, which they possessed in over-abundance, with those who had none, they charged for it. Similarly, the government had taken land without paying compensation, but it insisted that Meru or Arusha pay a surtax to buy it back. In spite of government claims that it was 'making every effort' to find more land, it continued to hold numerous settler estates that had been abandoned by their lessees; it felt 'morally bound' to sell estates to European leaseholders without feeling similarly obligated by the terms of the League of Nations mandate to help Meru or Arusha reclaim farms when they came on the market; and it was somehow continually able to find more land to alienate without being able to locate additional land for Arusha or Meru.[63]

The centrality of land to Arusha and Meru life thus put them in fundamental opposition to settlers who threatened their land and to the administration that backed them. The fact that administrators and settlers viewed land differently meant that they could not meet Meru and Arusha demands without dismantling colonialism itself. That was something they were not prepared to do at the time, and Arusha and Meru did not yet have the power to force them to do. That would change by 1950, when the eviction of Meru from North Meru and the attempts to uphold the chieftaincy in Arusha erupted in overt resistance and rang the death knell for colonialism in Tanganyika.

[61] Mesiaki Kilevo, personal communication.
[62] Gulliver paints a similar picture, though he characterizes the Arusha responses as xenophobic: P.H. Gulliver, 'The Conservative Commitment in Northern Tanzania: The Arusha and Masai' in P.H. Gulliver (ed.), *Tradition and Transition in East Africa* (London, 1969), 231–2. For an impassioned Meru account, see I.R. Mbise's novel, *Blood on Our Land* (Dar es Salaam, 1974).
[63] Gulliver, *Land and Population*, 27–30.

10

The Politics
of Land & Authority

The struggles over possession and use of land remained the central political issues for both Meru and Arusha throughout the colonial era. If the colonial period opened with Arusha and Meru defending their land against anticipated seizure by the missionaries, it was brought to a close by Meru protests and appeal to the United Nations against British seizure of land in Engare Nanyuki. It is all too easy, however, to interpret Arusha and Meru politics as simply undifferentiated protests against land alienation and the colonial authorities. The struggle for land was not just between Arusha and Meru, on the one hand, and the settlers and administration, on the other; it also opened up fissures developing within Arusha and Meru societies themselves as people adopted different strategies to counter land shortage and colonialism, just as it created conflicts within the government and among the settlers. With no immediate solution to their need for arable land in sight, Meru and Arusha turned inward and became divided among themselves in struggles over allocation and use of land, political power, and cultural values during a series of increasingly bitter political disputes in the late 1940s and early 1950s.

The struggle for land thus became part of larger struggles among people pursuing alternative strategies for relieving pressure in the face of government unwillingness to meet their needs. As conditions changed, new rights and responsibilities inevitably over-laid and conflicted with older ones, challenging people's well-being and sense of justice. Family patriarchs sought to maintain the viability of established family hold-ings as younger men and women, who would previously have pioneered elsewhere, remained at home to claim ever shrinking shares of their patrimony. Over time promi-nent fault lines opened up along generational lines between elders who controlled access to resources and younger men who found themselves increasingly without such access. Increasingly, such struggles came to focus on the roles of government-appointed chiefs, who asserted new rights over land available for expansion and allocated it to wealthy allies and clients at the expense of others who were less well endowed. Unable to attack the colonial regime directly, people increasingly attacked the chiefs, thereby undercutting their legitimacy and indirectly challenging colonial authority itself. The first such challenges were mounted in Arusha, starting in the 1930s.

The Politics of Pseudo-Traditionalism

Given the logic of Indirect Rule, much of the protest was directed against government-appointed chiefs as the only representatives of the administration to whom ordinary people could gain ready access. In choosing to rule indirectly through local Meru and Arusha authorities both the Germans and the British sought to establish 'hegemony on a shoe-string' by appropriating local leaders' 'traditional' legitimacy and co-opting it to their cause.[1] Such a strategy was somewhat of a Faustian bargain for both the colonial rulers and their appointees, however, as several critics have noted.[2] Colonial administrators sought to establish their own authority over people and to extract substantial new resources from them through appointing chiefs able to exercise 'traditional' authority and yet be answerable to the new administration. Since chiefs had not existed in Arusha prior to the imposition of colonial rule and had enjoyed only limited powers in Meru, however, this inevitably involved a substantial expansion of chiefs' authority and power, straining the limits of whatever legitimacy they had previously had. Colonial authorities were thus ultimately restricted in the demands they could make on chiefs lest they undermine the very legitimacy on which they depended to maintain order.

Conversely chiefs themselves frequently employed the new powers and support they enjoyed to increase their own wealth and power, but they could not overly exploit people without losing the popular support on which their position and power were based. Chiefs were thus obliged to employ their new-found wealth and power generously in order to maintain ideals of reciprocity on which their positions and power vis-a-vis the colonial authorities rested. Finally, popular protest, non-co-operation, or withholding of taxes, labour, or crops threatened the positions of both chiefs and colonial authorities, thus restricting the demands they could place on independent-minded peasants. The trick for colonial authorities and chiefs alike was to maintain the illusion of central power and the legitimacy of chiefs' authority in order to ensure orderly administration and a smooth flow of extractions without inciting political unrest which threatened their goals, powers, and careers.[3]

It was a difficult illusion to maintain, and many administrators and chiefs failed to do so, as the short terms of both in the early colonial years attest. But a working understanding was soon established whereby administrators moderated their demands and chiefs walked a fine line between carrying out administrators' demands and maintaining reciprocal relations with the people on which their own effectiveness rested.

The chiefs' position was an unenviable one, but their privileged access to the colonial

---

[1] This elegant formulation is Sara Berry's from her *No Condition is Permanent* (Madison, 1993), Chapter 2.

[2] Most notably, Steven Bunker, *Peasants against the State* (Chicago, 1987); Steven Feierman, *Peasant Intellectuals* (Madison, 1990); John Lonsdale, 'The Moral Economy of Mau Mau' in Bruce Berman & John Lonsdale, *Unhappy Valley* (London, 1992), 315–504; and Berry, *No Condition is Permanent*.

[3] P.H. Gulliver, *Social Control in an African Society* (London, 1963), 156–9. For a dramatic depiction of the collapse of this illusion, see Wole Soyinka, *Death and the King's Horseman* (New York, 1975).

state allowed them to capitalize on the new resources it offered and to divert some of its power, in turn, towards their own ends. Established colonial chiefs such as Lairumbe (1916–33) and Simeon Bene (1933–52) in Arusha or Sambegye (1902–25), Sante (1925–30, 1945–52), and Kishili (1931–45) in Meru exercised more power than pre-colonial leaders had. All became wealthy men, accumulating large herds of cattle and extensive landholdings, which they deployed to develop widespread networks of allies, kin, and clients, thereby enhancing their own wealth and power as well as their useful-ness to the colonial administration. At the same time, however, the more wealth and power chiefs accumulated, the more they were able to stand up to the colonial authori-ties to protect their own and their clients' interests. The 'rational' modes of colonial bureaucrats thus became articulated with the 'patrimonial' or 'affective' ones of chiefs, each appropriating and enhancing but also moderating the power of the other.[4]

The resources available to chiefs were never sufficient to incorporate all within their networks, especially in an era of declining availability of land, or to shield their clients from all the demands of colonial authorities. At the same time, chiefs increasingly came to represent those authorities in the eyes of the people and so faced increasing opposi-tion from Meru and Arusha challenging those authorities. Ordinary Arusha and Meru soon learned, however, that they could not challenge chiefs' authority or legitimacy directly without incurring a defensive reaction from a colonial administration that was ever sensitive to 'agitators' who did not respect 'traditional authority', but they could often do so obliquely by accusing chiefs of corruption or other abuses of power. Thus, all three Arusha chiefs were accused of extortion and malfeasance in 1925, at a time when the British were in the process of consolidating their power and re-alienating ex-German estates in the face of increasing Meru and Arusha needs for land. Lesikale was deposed; Lesian was fined and subsequently deposed; but Lairumbe was simply admonished because he was deemed too important to the administration to lose.[5]

Lairumbe was a cattle trader and nephew of Maraai, one of the Arusha leaders hanged by the Germans in 1900. He was appointed chief of Boru by the Germans early in 1916, and soon gained a reputation among British authorities of being a forceful chief, with 'considerable ability and strength of character' who enjoyed the support of both conservative elders and educated Christians, including Simeon Bene, an early Christian, who became his clerk, advocate, and ultimately, successor. Lairumbe was given senior status over the other two Arusha chiefs, and when Lesian was deposed and his chiefdom abolished in 1928, Lairumbe received part of his territory.[6]

Lairumbe also had enemies, however, and four years later he was charged with being 'a great robber, thief, and a despiser of the elders' after two members of the Molelian clan were killed in a dispute over rights to an irrigation furrow. Six Lukumai clansmen were convicted of the crime and sentenced to death, but Molelian used the event to protest against Lairumbe's alleged favouritism towards Lukumai and Kivuyoni clans-men and to raise long-standing grievances against Lairumbe concerning cattle, land,

[4] The terms refer to concepts developed by Max Weber, *From Max Weber*, H.H. Gerth & C. Wright Mills (eds) (London, 1948), and Goren Hyden, *Beyond Ujamaa in Tanzania* (London, 1980), respectively.
[5] Northern Province, Annual Report, 1925 (TNA: 1733/36).
[6] Yohanes ole Kauwenara (AHT 2); Annual Reports, Northern Province, 1927 & 1928 (TNA: 11681).

water furrows, witchcraft, and murder.[7] Though the charges were a potpourri of grievances, they combined popular issues regarding land and cattle, that were sure to mobilize
popular support, with colonial issues concerning witchcraft and murder, that attracted the
attention of colonial authorities. Mass meetings called to settle the dispute attracted
crowds up to 1,000, substantially weakening the chief's support. The Provincial Commissioner, G.F. Webster, predictably aligned with Lairumbe against the Molelian
'trouble makers', suggesting spitefully that they be rusticated to an area without milk,
beer, or bananas if they continued to intrigue against the Native Authority.[8]

Lairumbe's position was secure for the time being, but as popular protests began to
mount against government restrictions on coffee growing and land issues, the administration began to doubt his continuing effectiveness. Complaints about his high-handed
actions continued to surface over the next couple of years, leading Webster to complain
that he was getting too old and 'neglects his duties and gives all his attention to his
considerable herds of cattle and to his beer pots'. Lairumbe was finally persuaded to
resign in 1933, and when Arusha were equally divided between two potential successors, both educated Christians, the administration tipped the choice to the 'mainstay' of
Lairumbe's administration, Simeon Bene. After seventeen years in office, Lairumbe
retired a wealthy man.[9]

Lairumbe's successor, Simeon Bene, came from a poor background, and as one of
the second group of Christians baptized in 1908, he had been shunned by his family and
age-mates as a child. He worked with Rev. Blumer as a teacher and became a lifelong
friend and ally of Lazaros Laiser, the leader of the Arusha Christians. He also married a
daughter of Maraai, thus enhancing his standing with the reigning Talala elders, and
served nine years as Lairumbe's clerk.[10]

By the time Lairumbe retired in 1933, Simeon had overcome his earlier status to
become a popular choice to replace the aging chief. As chief, he soon overcame his
poverty as well, becoming sufficiently wealthy in cattle, coffee, and land to be able to
build a modern-style house and buy a car.[11] As a Christian, however, he could not use

[7] The men were convicted under British law, but the administration worried that the murders might set off
a feud if bloodwealth were not also paid, as required by customary law. In a particularly creative interpretation, the Arusha District Officer, R.A. Pelham, posited that under the terms of customary law the
Lukumai would have to pay bloodwealth to Molelian only if they were released from jail, not if they were
hanged. The Arusha response is not known. PC/NP to DO/AD, 19 March 1930 and reply 27 March 1930
(TNA: 69/45/4).

[8] Arusha District, Annual Report, 1929 (TNA: 11681); Blumer to PC/NP, 2 Dec 1929 and reply 4 Dec
1929; Petition by IlMolelian Elders, 5 Dec 1929 and 10 Dec 1929; IlMolelian Elders to Baker-Smith, 9
Dec 1929 (note minute by Kitching); IlMolelian Elders to Asst. Superintendent of Police, 10 Dec 1929;
PC/NP to CS/DSM, 17 Jan 1930 and reply 24 Jan 1930 (all in TNA: 69/45/4).

[9] Annual Reports, Northern Province, 1931, 1932, and 1933 (TNA: 11681); Anon. to Superintendent of
Police/Arusha, 31 March 1932 (TNA: 69/45/4); PC/NP to DO/AD, 2 May 1932 and 11 May 1932
(TNA: 69/47/AR/4); PC/NP to CS/DSM 26 April 1933 and reply 18 May 1933 (TNA: 13368/I).

[10] Yohanes ole Kauwenara (AHT 2); S. ole Saibull & R. Carr, Herd and Spear (London, 1981), 115-17.

[11] Simeon borrowed shs 1,100/- for the house in 1938 and 7,000/- for the car in 1951. His official salary at
the time he applied for the loan for the car was shs 540/- per month, but he had 6,000/- for a down
payment and sufficient outside income to gain approval of the loan. At contemporary exchange rates, his
salary was $77 a month, and the car cost $1,860. DO/AD to Manager/Standard Bank, 2 Sept 1938;
PC/NP to DC/AD, 26 July 1951 (TNA: 69/47/AR/5).

his wealth to marry more wives, and so he recruited clients and dependants with grants of cattle and land. As western Arusha cattlemen expanded towards Monduli and began raising wheat during the late 1930s and early 1940s, Simeon became their main patron, making large land grants to his friends and allies.[12] As with Lairumbe however, the British began to worry as to whether Simeon was not accumulating too much power. By 1947 the District Commissioner, D.S. Troup, was complaining that the administration had 'passed from the hereditary authority into the autocratic and often incompetent hands of the few' in which 'the influence of Christian Native Authorities is very strong and the confusion of politics with Christianity, to the detriment of the district, is only too apparent'.[13]

Arusha politics thus revolved largely around issues of patronage and protection, as competing factions manoeuvred to gain access to the limited resources available from the colonial state through their chiefs, while at the same time trying to limit the demands it made on them regarding taxes, labour, land, and the cultivation and marketing of coffee. The focus of these manoeuvres was the chief, the only representative of the state within the purview of local politics, and tactics ranged from seeking alliances with the chief to attacks on his integrity and withholding of taxes, labour, or crops.

Making Customary Law: The Arusha Constitution of 1948

Internal unrest in Arusha mounted during the late 1930s and '40s over the land surtax, the evictions from Arusha town, land allocations in Musa, and the administration's ongoing attempts to control the cultivation and marketing of coffee. Ironically, the administration's response to this unrest brought about by the changes of the twentieth century was to attempt to restore the politics of the nineteenth century, by drafting a new 'traditional' constitution. The Arusha constitution was the first major attempt by the British to restructure local administration since German times. It was devised by the government anthropologist, Hans Cory, in conjunction with the district administration. Cory's mandate was to discover the 'traditional' basis of Arusha society before colonial intrusion fifty years previously and to suggest how it could be adapted to meet the needs of the 'modern' world, but in doing so he ended up fabricating an utterly new entity. As such, it was a notable example of the ways in which colonial authorities sought to legitimate their rule in terms of tradition, while fabricating and perverting those terms to 'make customary law'.[14]

Cory immediately set out to research and draft an extensive ethnographic study of Arusha society. It was a wide-ranging study, touching on everything from pre-colonial history to the role of the chief, the age-set system, the clan system, and Arusha relations

---

[12] Arusha District, Agricultural Annual Report, 1951 (TNA: 472/-); Arusha District, Annual Report, 1953 (TNA: 472/ANR/1). AHT 1,2,4,8; Luanda 'European Commercial Farming', 165–73; 'Wheat' (*c.* 1940) (TNA: 9/6/5); Mesiaki Kilevo, personal communication.

[13] DC/AD to PC/NP, 4 Nov 1947 (TNA: 9/NA/10).

[14] Martin Channock, *Law, Custom and Social Order* (Cambridge, 1985).

with pastoral Maasai. It was fundamentally flawed, however, by Cory's functionalist assumptions that a prescriptive system had existed fifty years previously; that it had survived, dormant but intact, during the intervening years of colonial rule; and that he could rediscover that system and resurrect it as a viable means of restoring 'tribal unity and confidence' in spite of transformations of people's economic and social institutions in the meantime. In short, Cory sought to turn back the clock and reify his understanding of Arusha 'tradition'.

These assumptions made sense because Cory believed that cultures were ultimately racially determined. Thus if he could identify what was genetically innate in Arusha culture, he could strip off the historical accretions to restore a durable biologically-determined core. He started by seeking to distinguish the respective Bantu and Maasai components of Arusha culture by examining their putative origins. Dismissing a tradition that claimed 'Lumbwa' (Parakuyo Maasai) origins, Cory accepted another that claimed Arusha were originally Bantu speakers from northern Pare who allied with pastoral Maasai and adopted their age-sets and language after settling at Arusha Chini early in the nineteenth century.[15]

If this was so, Cory reasoned, then there must be a residual Bantu cultural core underlying the Maasai veneer acquired over the past 150 years. Turning next to the chiefship, Cory realized that the *mangi* was purely a German creation based on the Meru model, and thus represented a break in Arusha development, but he claimed to discover in the charismatic war leaders of the late nineteenth century (such as Meoli, Maraai, and Rawaito) an earlier institutional model for chiefship, which he called *olkarsis*, that combined original forms of Bantu chiefship with subsequent forms taken from Maasai age and descent systems. Cory then transformed his reconstruction into an elaborate institutional complex for a unified Arusha chiefship, complete with a written constitution; a consolidated executive; a legislative council; an advisory council (*Engiliwata Olosho*) representing local councils, the clans, and educated Christians; and multi-tiered systems of civil and criminal courts.[16]

Similarly, Cory recognized that the local district headmen, or *jumbes*, appointed by the chief were also German innovations, but he found in the Arusha institution of age-set spokesmen, or *laigwenak*, an indigenous model for local district administration. While Cory recognized that spokesmen were chosen by each local section of an age-set to mediate disputes within the section and to represent its interests informally with other age-sets, he proposed that the spokesmen of all the age-sets in an area be formally constituted as an advisory council (*Engigwana em Balbal*) to the local headman appointed by the chief. He then extended the concept of spokesmen to the clans, never significant institutions in Arusha society, and to 'non-traditional' Arusha (i.e., Christians) to give them representation along with the district councils on a chief's advisory council.[17]

In the end, Cory transformed the fluid and adaptable forms of Arusha social and

---

[15] Cory, 'Tribal Structure of the Arusha Tribe of Tanganyika', 1948, 1–3, 42 (UDSM: Cory Papers, 201).

[16] Cory, 'Tribal Structure of the Arusha', 6–7, 45–6; D.S. Troup, 'Memorandum on the Reorganization ... of the Arusha' (TNA:472/NA/40).

[17] Cory, 'Tribal Structure of the Arusha', 14–41, 43–4; Troup, 'Memorandum'; Gulliver, *Social Control*, 159–63.

political life into a static array of formal institutions, each with its own pseudo-traditional name, rules, and procedures for selection, which the colonial authorities then faithfully recognized as though they were truly authentic. The whole Byzantine apparatus was a nightmare of functionalist theory transformed into bureaucratic fact that had the new Assistant District Officer, Charles Meek, running endlessly among meetings of the two central and twenty-six district councils to keep it going. Functionalists liked it, nevertheless, because it appeared to give institutional form to social function; colonial bureaucrats, because it presented a tidy chart of institutional responsibilities and reasserted the legitimacy of 'traditional' authorities.[18]

The Anti-Chief Movement and Arusha Citizens' Union

While the administration congratulated itself that the experiment was a splendid success in restoring legitimacy to 'traditional' institutions, few Arusha considered the new structures either 'traditional' or legitimate. Arusha boycotted the new institutions, and the elabourate hierarchy of courts and local councils soon lapsed through disuse. In their stead Arusha utilized other bodies, ranging from established social networks to the church and newly-formed co-operative and Citizens' Union, to challenge the authority of the chief and the reconstituted Native Authority. The dominant issue continued to be acquisition and allocation of land, but disputes over circumcision, a levy placed on commercial crop sales, newly-implemented Native Authority rules for coffee, and compulsory inoculation and dipping of cattle brought together a broad coalition of Arusha opposed to the chief and ultimately led to the chief's resignation, revision of the 1948 constitution along more democratic lines, and the election of a new chief supported by the Citizens' Union.[19]

The struggle over land continued to dominate Arusha politics and caused a pervasive distrust of government among Arusha. Phillip Gulliver, the government anthropologist who conducted extensive fieldwork in Arusha later in the 1950s, noted that Arusha viewed Europeans as powerful and alien people who sought to destroy the Arusha way of life. Settlers had stolen Arusha land through cunning and force; maintained extensive and largely undeveloped estates, while Arusha did not have enough land; and were unwilling to allow Arusha to use their land or water except by paying exorbitant fees. Government aided and abetted the settlers in continually alienating more land to them. The Forestry Department was among the worst offenders, seizing the best expansion land on Meru and Monduli, monopolizing it for its own profits, and forcing Arusha to bribe the forest guards to obtain firewood. The Native Authority under the direction of the chief was not viewed much more favourably; it was seen as an arm of the administration which co-opted and bribed Arusha to co-operate.[20]

[18] Troup, notes dated 22 Dec 1947; Troup, 'Memorandum on the... Structure of the Arusha,' and periodic reports by C.I. Meek and D.S. Troup thereafter (all in TNA: 472/NA/40); Meek, 'A Practical Experiment in Local Government' in *Arusha District Book*.

[19] Arusha District, Annual Report, 1952 (TNA: 472/ANR/1); Northern Province, Annual Report, 1952 (TNA: 19415); Gulliver, *Social Control*, 154–63.

[20] P.H. Gulliver, *Report on Land and Population in the Arusha Chiefdom* (Tanganyika Provincial Administration, 1957), 27–30.

The post-war boom further exacerbated conflicts over land, especially around Arusha town. Pressures on the town to expand led to continual expropriations of Arusha land, as we have seen. The colonial authorities seized 1,800 acres in 1949 to re-locate the main Moshi-Arusha-Namanga road and another 120 acres for a Tanganyika Packers plant outside of town. Township authorities pressed for an additional 1,000 acres to double the size of the town on the heels of evicting all the Arusha remaining in town a few years before. Ex-enemy farms continued to be reallocated to Europeans, while none could be found for Arusha.[21] A small expansion area was opened in Nduruma Chini for those evicted from town, but the land was too dry to settle.[22] Arusha distrust of the administration made it virtually impossible for colonial officers to gain Arusha co-operation for their activities.

The struggle over land exacerbated divisions within Arusha society as well. Arusha had started moving across the spur to Monduli in the 1930s, occupying most of the arable highlands of Musa and Likamba by the late 1940s. Most of the Arusha who moved were wealthy cattle-owners who used their cattle and relations with pastoral Maasai to gain access to land and to capitalize large wheat and maize farms ploughed with oxen and tractors. They also attracted clients and dependants who they allowed to cultivate their own crops in return for labour. By the early 1950s little open land remained and squatters began to contest the large farmers' claims based on traditional rights of squatters to land they had cleared and settled. The wealthy farmers were often powerful clan and family heads closely allied with Chief Simeon, however, who also owned large herds and land in Musa and who supported the grants to his friends. Arusha society thus became increasingly divided between wealthy cattlemen and wheat farmers allied with Simeon, who benefited from allocations of new land, and poorer farmers on Mount Meru who did not.[23]

Other disputes introduced different divisions. A controversy over circumcision pitted Arusha Christians against the newly reconstituted Native Authority after Pastor Lazaros Laiser protested to his friend and fellow Christian, Chief Simeon, in 1948 that Christians could not observe the closed period of circumcision or adopt the name of their age-set, as these would imply their acceptance of the pagan rites associated with them. After consulting Simeon and his councillors, the District Commissioner, D.S. Troup, insisted that circumcision was a political, not a religious, issue, and that the age-sets comprised an integral part of Arusha local government. And when the Superintendent of the Lutheran mission, Elmer Danielson, countered that it was a matter of conscience, Troup hinted conspiratorially that he had reason to believe that the Christians' objections were not purely conscientious. Troup never elaborated on his suspicions, however, and the Christians subsequently agreed to undergo circumcision in the hospital following the *eunoto* ceremony.[24]

---

[21] See Chapter 9 for details on land struggles.

[22] Dept. of Agri., Annual Report, 1951 (TNA:472/-).

[23] Arusha District, Annual Reports, 1953–4 (TNA: 472/ANR/1).

[24] Lazaros Laiser to Olkarsis Simeon, 1 Sept 1948; D.S. Troup to Rev. D. Swanson, 9 Sept 1948; E.R. Danielson to D.S. Troup, 8 Oct 1948 and reply 23 Oct 1948; D.S. Troup to Dr Reusch, 2 Feb 1949; E.R. Danielson to D.S. Troup, 5 April 1949 (all in TNA: 472/NA/40).

The issue of the crop cess (or levy), by contrast, pitted Arusha's coffee and wheat farmers against the Native Authority and the colonial administration. Arusha commercial farmers formed the Arusha African (later Koimere) Farmers Co-operative Society in 1950 to regulate and market their crops. The following year the Native Authority imposed a tax on all coffee (8¢/lb) and wheat (1¢/lb) purchased by the co-operative. The co-operative refused to pay the tax on the grounds that it discriminated against its members while non-members could avoid the tax by selling on the local market. Interestingly, the dispute also divided the colonial administration, pitting the District Commissioner, who supported the Native Authority *qua* authority, against the Agricultural Officer, who saw the cess as discriminatory and likely to reduce coffee and wheat production in favour of less valuable crops. The cess was also opposed by the Co-operative Officer, who saw it as discriminating against the most progressive Arusha and threatening the viability of their new co-operative: '… it is … not justifiable to penalize a progressive marketing organization based on the free cooperation of the people … whilst leaving untouched the produce of those growers who have not shown the same advanced spirit'. The Agricultural and Co-operative Officers were right. Arusha wheat farmers shifted to untaxed maize; the co-operative refused to purchase coffee; and farmers avoided marketing their crops through the co-operative. As with many issues, however, the District Commissioner saw the issue as essentially one of authority, insisting that to drop the cess 'would be interpreted as a "Victory" for those who have opposed the Native Authority and myself'. Nevertheless, Arusha pressure forced the administration to drop the cess as unworkable the following year in favour of a more acceptable increase in the head tax.[25]

Another issue in the early 1950s pitted cattle-owners against the administration over the inoculation and dipping of cattle. This was a particularly contentious issue in the western part of Arusha, where the wealthiest cattle-owners lived and herded their cattle on the adjacent plains. Simeon and many of the members of the Tribal Council were among them, and the Council accordingly opposed both schemes, noting that rinderpest inoculations had been given in the midst of a prolonged drought when the cattle were particularly weak. Three dips were built in 1952, but Arusha adamantly refused to use them. The following year the administration was also encountering considerable opposition to its use of forced labour on a conservation scheme in nearby Olkokola and noted: 'Politically it would be suicidal to force the [dipping] scheme on a unwilling public.… Propaganda and persuasion continue to be used in an effort to overcome Waarusha opposition.' It was not successful and the scheme was ultimately dropped in 1956.[26]

[25] Ironically, the DC rejected a suggestion from the Member for Local Government that they shift the tax to cattle as 'too political'. Arusha District, Annual Reports, 1951–2 (TNA: 472/-); AO/AD, Monthly Reports, Sept–Nov 1951 (TNA: 9/24); Comm. for Co-operative Development, 'Notes on Arusha Native Authority Cesses on Produce', 25 Sept 1951; Comm. for Co-op. Development to Member for Agriculture, 18 Oct 1951; DC/AD to PC/NP, 26 Oct 1951; Member for Local Government to PC/NP 15 Nov 1951 and reply 1 Dec 1951; DC/AD to PC/NP, 7 Feb 1952 (all in TNA: 32847/1).
[26] AO/AD, Monthly Reports, Sept–Nov 1951 (TNA: 9/24); Arusha Citizens' Union to DC/AD, 8 Sept 1952, and Engiliwata Olosho to DC/AD, 12 Sept 1952 (TNA: 472/NA/40); Arusha District, Annual Reports, 1951–53 (TNA: 472/- and 472/ANR/1); Northern Province, Annual Report, 1956 (TNA: 471/R.3/2).

The divisions that increasingly rent Arusha society were complex ones, and frequently overlapped. Pastor Lazaros Laiser, for example, was a leader of the Lutheran Church, a prominent coffee farmer, and a leader of the co-operative who opposed Chief Simeon Bene over both circumcision and the cess, but Simeon had also been his teacher at mission school and the two remained close friends, political allies, and fellow wheat farmers in Musa. Similarly, many of the coffee farmers were Christians and small-holders, while most of the western cattlemen and wheat farmers were more traditional, but many of the Musa wheat farmers also grew coffee on Mount Meru and were members of the co-operative. People were thus less divided by class than by the particular strategies they pursued within the limits of the colonial situation to attain wealth and power. Arusha elders in the west tended to base their influence on cattle and the extended social networks created exchanging them. For them, political power was a function of wealth, but they also allied with the chief and employed political relations to further enhance that wealth, just as the chiefs themselves did. Christians in the east, by contrast, had often been born poor and had become further marginalized when they became Christians, but used their education and links with the church and their fellow Christians to develop new sources of wealth through coffee smallholdings and farmers' associations, which they then sought to convert to political power.

These many interwoven strands came together in a controversy over Chief Simeon's replacement in 1952, when the newly formed Arusha Citizens' Union successfully overturned the administration's choice and installed its own candidate. In the midst of the disputes over land, the cess, and dipping, during which Simeon was accused of colluding with the colonial administration, Simeon announced that he was resigning after serving 28 years in government, 19 as chief. The administration was already grooming his deputy, Andreas Kisiri, to replace him, and it quickly pushed his election through the Tribal Council. Pent-up grievances against the authorities, which Simeon had been able to contain with his wealth of experience and contacts, poured out against his former deputy. Opponents of land alienation, the cess, and dipping combined to form the Arusha Citizens' Union (*Raia wa Arusha nzima*) and call for new elections.[27]

The Citizens' Union drew its inspiration and early support from the Kilimanjaro Union formed earlier on Mount Kilimanjaro (thus bringing the administration's usual charge against outside agitators), but its members were largely drawn from the local church and co-operative. Lazaros Laiser served as Secretary and Lotisinyayoki Ilmolelian as President. It immediately assaulted the government with a barrage of petitions, noting that the Tribal Council represented only its own interests and not those of the people. The Union took its own polls that showed 81 per cent in favour of its candidate, Sephania Sumlei, over Andreas. When informed by the District Commissioner that ordinary citizens were not allowed to vote, they replied:

> Why then are we called to meetings where we cannot express our views? Why is tax collected when there is no freedom of speech? Why do we dance for the Government but do not receive justice?

---

[27] Arusha District, Annual Report, 1952 (TNA: 472/-); Northern Province, Annual Report, 1952 (TNA: 19415).

Having made their points about free speech and taxation without representation, they appealed directly for Democracy (*Jamhuri*).[28]

The administration responded by hastily staging Andreas's installation with full colonial pomp. First, the Tribal Council formally convened to elect him and inform the Provincial Commissioner, waiting in the wings, of their choice. Then he was confirmed by the P.C. before a full police guard of honour and presented to an assembly of all Arusha. Speeches by the Provincial Commissioner, *Olkarsis* Simeon, Andreas, and the Chairman of the *Engiliwata Olosho* admonishing the people to respect the new chief concluded the formal ceremonies, after which tea was served to the invited visitors.[29]

Subsequent meetings of the Citizens' Union attracted 600 to 1,000 people, and petitions to the government continued unabated.[30] While the administration privately acknowledged that Andreas's election was 'undoubtedly unpopular' with a 'large majority', publicly it stone-walled while local government ground to a halt. After three months of vociferous activity, Andreas resigned, but a newly selected Tribal Council was in deadlock for six weeks over his successor. The administration thereupon changed the constitution to allow for popular elections with universal male suffrage, and Sephania Sumlei, the Lutheran Inspector of Schools and Union candidate, defeated Andreas, garnering 81 per cent of the popular vote, just as the Union had predicted. Following his modest installation, he appointed a number of Christians, teachers, co-operative members and businessmen to the Council; replaced the produce cess with an increase in the head tax; and initiated an extensive social development programme.[31]

The crisis was over for the moment, and the following year the administration reported enthusiastically:

He has steered a middle course between the somewhat conservative attitude of the Tribal Council... and the more vocal and less conservative outlook of the Arusha Citizens' Union. The very fact that the Chief has administered through the Council and without consultation with the Union has strengthened the hand of the former at the expense of the latter. The Council has been by no means a docile body, and has remained very much a curb on the action of the Chief on behalf, it can be said, of a majority of the Tribe.... The Citizens' Union has not been the power in the land which it had become in 1952 as a result of the absence of a properly elected Native Authority. It was noticeably less vocal, but as the year ended, there

[28] Arusha Community to CS/DSM, 13 March 1952 (TNA: 32593 and 69/47/AR); Raia wa Arusha nzima to PC/NP, 14 March 1952 (TNA: 69/47/AR and 472/NA/40); Laigwenak Lembalbal to DC/AD, 16 March 1952 and Raiya wako watiifu wa Arusha to DC/AD, 22 March 1952 (TNA: 472/NA/40); Asst. Supt. of Police (CID), Moshi to Senior Supt. of Police i/c Special Branch, DSM, 4 July 1952 (TNA; 472/NA/40); Arusha District, Annual Report, 1952 (TNA: 472/-). On the call for 'democracy' see also later letter by J.S. Lomayani to DC/AD, 19 May 1952 (TNA: 472/NA/40).
[29] DC/AD, 'Arrangements for the Installation of Olkarsis Andreas' (TNA: 69/47/AR).
[30] For ACU membership, numerous petitions, and minutes of meetings, including those between the ACU, the Tribal Council, and the District Commissioner, see TNA: 472/NA/40 and 32593. Lazaros Laiser took the minutes on all occasions.
[31] Arusha Citizen's Union to Gov., 3 July 1952, 3 Nov 1952 & 18 Nov 1952; PC/NP to MLG, 13 Aug 1952; CS/DSM to ACU, 21 Nov 1952 (all in TNA: 32593); DC/AD to PC/NP, 17 July 1952; DC/AD to Gov., 5 Nov 1952 (both TNA: 472/NA/40); PC/NP to MLG, 18 Dec 1952 (TNA: 32593); *Olkarsis* Zephania to DC/AD, 8 Jan 1953 & 13 Jan 1953 (TNA: 472/NA/40); Arusha District, Annual Report, 1952 (TNA: 472/-).

were indications of growing opposition to the Chief arising out of his refusal to bow down to the Union's attempt to usurp his functions.[32]

While the administration was clearly still playing the politics of pseudo-traditionalism, the Citizens' Union continued to exploit the land crisis until the government finally agreed to revise the constitution further on more democratic grounds in 1957.[33]

The issues surrounding the chieftaincy dispute were complicated ones, but in general they revealed the degree to which a chief, once seen as progressive, was out-flanked by popular politicians because he had become too closely involved with the colonial authorities in the operation of a pseudo-traditional form of authority that rep-resented few besides himself and his wealthy allies. New centres of power were devel-oping around the church and co-operative, and new strategies were being devised that drew as much on Christian and liberal values of democracy as on Arusha ones regard-ing the responsibilities of wealth. Ten years later the British were gone, and the newly independent government abolished chieftainship. Simeon, on the other hand, remained the very image of a modern Arusha *olkarsis* well into his 80s, walking nine miles daily dressed in a blue suit, starched white shirt, and blue and white tie to oversee his large herds of cattle and visit his 61 great grandchildren.[34]

The Politics of Chiefship in Meru

Colonial politics developed along similar lines in Meru. Sambegye was a friend and neighbour of the missionaries at Nkoaranga when he was first appointed chief by the Germans in 1902, but he did not remain popular with them for long as he became increasingly wealthy and expanded his influence by taking ten wives and hosting large beer parties. He retired in 1925 in favour of his son Sante. Barely out of his teens when he became chief, Sante was soon accused of extorting fines to pay for a car and rumours spread of his having an affair with an Indian woman, causing the British to depose and imprison him in 1930.[35]

Neither Sambegye nor Sante were members of the 'royal' Kaaya clan, which the British were intent on restoring in keeping with the new dictates of Indirect Rule. Before choosing Sante's successor, then, they diligently researched the genealogies of earlier chiefs and nominated three Kaaya. Ndesaulo Kaaya was an educated Christian and coffee farmer; Lukas Kaaya was one of the first converts, had served as a clerk in

---

[32] Arusha District, Annual Report, 1953 (TNA: 472/ANR/1).

[33] 'The Development of Rural Councils in Arusha' (TNA: 352); Arusha District, Annual Report, 1954 (TNA: 472/ANR/1); Northern Province, Annual Reports, 1955–58 (TNA: 471/R.3/2); P.H. Gulliver & H.L. Snaith, 'Report on the Constitutional Changes in the Local Government of Arusha Chiefdom', 1957 (UDSM: Cory Papers, 279).

[34] S. ole Saibull & R. Carr, *Herd and Spear* (London, 1981), 114–15.

[35] Anton Lukas Kaaya (MHT 1); Krause, *ELMB*, 60(1905), 445–6; Ittameier, *ELMB*, 62 (1907), 560; K.R. Gilbert, 'Summary of Events in Chief Sante's Cases', Sept 1930; DO/AD to PC/NP, 16 Sept 1930; Sworn Statements taken by R.A. Pelham, DO/AD, Sept 1930; PC/NP to CS/DSM, 26 Sept 1930; Asst. DO/AD to PC/NP, 25 Nov 1930 (all TNA: 69/45/9); DO/AD to PC/NP, 11 April 1931 (TNA: 69/47/AR).

the district office and as an assistant to Sante, and was the President of the Meru Native Coffee Growers' Association; while Kishili was a son of the former chief Matunda and illiterate. Meru preferred Ndesaulo, but he preferred to work on his farm and refused to accept appointment, and so the British appointed Kishili, with Ndesaulo as his deputy.[36]

This compromise seemed to contain the tensions emerging within Meru society until Ndesaulo died in 1944. Soon thereafter Sante's followers, Christians and coffee growers centred around the mission at Nkoaranga, accused Kishili of misappropriating funds, accepting bribes, placing curses on his opponents, and victimizing Christians. The District Commissioner held a Baraza to investigate the charges, and 1,400 people, evenly split between Kishili and Sante, debated the issues for over five hours without resolution. The British were forced to withdraw their support for Kishili and to replace him with his predecessor Sante, now redeemed in their eyes as the 'one outstanding figure among the Wameru who might make a success of the Chieftainship....'[37]

The brief alliance between Sante and the 'progressives' ended, however, when Sante subsequently sacked the popular headman of Akeri, Baradau Seyato. Seyato was a wealthy coffee farmer, prominent in the church and Coffee Growers' Association, who had allied with Sante to depose Kishili, thus providing him with valuable support in Kishili's stronghold of Akeri. Following his removal, however, Kaaya from Akeri joined with Nkoaranga coffee farmers in opposition to Sante, ushering in a prolonged period of unrest.[38]

The District Commissioner, D.S. Troup, attributed the breakdown of chiefly authority to the increased political activities of 'wealthy coffee growers and a rising movement of young Christians ... tending to interest themselves politically without giving consideration to the best interests of the community as a whole'. The dissidents were not without potent issues, however. Land and water continued to be critical issues, and disputes with Europeans over them were increasingly directed against Sante, who represented the government in people's eyes and was widely accused of supporting the settlers. Meanwhile, the continuing attempts of the colonial administration to impose centralized coffee marketing, a cess on coffee sales, and extensive crop regulations via the Native Authority led Meru to form the Meru Citizens' Union and boycott administrative activities.[39]

The almost total ineffectiveness of local government led the administration to propose drafting a new 'traditional' constitution in 1948, similar to that recently adopted in

---

[36] While Meru generally expressed their preference for an educated chief and supported Ndesaulo or Lukas, the District Officer did not give his reasons for finally settling on Kishili. It is tempting to assume he preferred the more 'traditional' candidate, but he did offer the post first to Ndesaulo and was anxious that Ndesaulo support the new chief as his deputy. DO/AD to PC/NP, 11 April 1931 (TNA: 69/47/AR).

[37] DC/AD to PC/NP, 9 Feb 1945 and 22 Feb 1945 (TNA: 69/47/AR); DO/AD to PC/NP, 1 March 1945; PC/NP to CS/DSM 7 March 1945, minute by CS/DSM 12 March 1945, reply 14 March 1945, and further correspondence 7 April 1945 (all in TNA: 69/47/AR/3 & 32893).

[38] N. N. Luanda, 'European Commercial Farming and its Impact on the Meru and Arusha Peoples of Tanzania, 1920–1955' (Ph.D., Cambridge, 1986), 279.

[39] DC/AD to PC/NP, 4 Nov 1947 (TNA: 9/NA/1). See also Northern Province, Annual Reports, 1946–7 (TNA: 19415); H. Mason, 'The Meru Problem,' 1955 [OCRP: MSS.Afr.s.1513(r)]. For the struggles over coffee, see Chapter 8.

Arusha. Hans Cory was again the architect, but the assumptions he made in Meru were diametrically opposed to those he had made in Arusha earlier. There he had attempted to restore ancient institutions which, he thought, had been lying dormant for years and remained viable in spite of their subsequent transformations. In Meru, by contrast, he rejected historical precedents on the grounds that Meru social institutions had been largely supplanted by Arusha age-sets in the nineteenth century and were in the midst of being transformed once again by an emerging majority of Christians and wealthy coffee farmers. Thus, he based representation on the tribal and parish councils on age-set membership, with equal representation awarded to literate and non-literate members. His focus on age-sets was badly misguided, however, for descent had long been the guiding principle of Meru social organization, and their adoption of Maasai age-sets in the late nineteenth century had barely survived into the colonial era.[40]

The architecture barely mattered, for the new constitution was doomed from the start. While Cory consulted with a number of Meru who represented both Sante and his opponents, the final draft was hurriedly adopted by Sante, his headmen, and representatives of the age-sets without being considered by the people at large. The Citizens' Union representatives on the drafting committee refused to co-operate until Sante was removed and popular elections held. Tensions rose further when Focsaner, a settler, threatened to evict a large number of long-standing Meru squatters from his land. Disturbances broke out, and eleven of the dissidents were arrested, convicted, jailed, and eventually deported from the district.[41] The administration then implemented the new constitution, but Meru refused to participate, leaving Sante to rule alone. When the Governor visited Meru a year later, he was greeted by a 'small riot'.[42]

Troup attributed the administration's failure to the fact that 'Meru are afflicted by every disease of the mind and the spirit that follows a semi-absorption of Western ideas...' First, the Arusha age-set system had obliterated their own institutions and caused them to decay.

> Then came the introduction of half-comprehended European methods and ideas and a missionising influence which in this area appears to have been wholly bad.... The people appeared actively to dislike and distrust their European officers and were much given at Barazas ... to mouthing those democratic shibboleths that concern rights, while omitting those that concern duties.

For Troup, 'A small intransigent and fanatical group of Meru' had sabotaged 'tradition' and the rot of European influence was setting in. For Meru, however, anti-colonial politics was breaking out of the pseudo-traditional channels into which it had been

---

[40] H. Cory, 'Proposals for the Adaptation of the Meru Age-Grade System to Modern Requirements' (TNA: 43200); D.S. Troup, 'Memorandum on the New Constitution of the Meru Tribe' in PC/NP to CS/DSM, 17 Aug 1948; CS/DSM to PC/NP, 22 Sept 1948; PC/NP to CS/DSM, 6 Oct 1948; DC/AD to PC/NP, 28 Nov 1948 (all in TNA: 25369).

[41] Those deported included Mbaruk Orongai, Rueben Human, Marko Mwenda, Seyaki Mukware, Lukiyo Lakunya, Martin Lingusua, Alfraeli Sablaki, Andrea Mukware, Baradau Seyato (the ex-headman), Kitoi Weria, and Ndetayo Mako Mbise. Luanda, 'European Commercial Farming,' 281; Emanuel (Makiya) Kasengye N'nko (MHT 5).

[42] Minutes, Meeting of District Reps. (TNA: 9/8/1); Mason, 'The Meru Problem'.

diverted and was beginning to flow into more 'democratic' ones that would soon lead to Dar es Salaam, Nairobi, London, and New York, as we will see in the next chapter.[43]

The Politics of Tradition and the Tradition of Politics

While colonial authorities thus sought to harness the legitimacy of 'traditional' authorities to the power of the colonial state, Arusha and Meru developed new political vehicles hitched to enduring values of wealth, responsibility, and rights to land to counter them. Rejecting the state's version of 'traditional' authority when chiefs ceased to exercise power legitimately, people organized around new institutions – the church, farmers' organizations, and Citizens' Unions – to reassert moral authority. Attacks on the chiefs may have been made by coffee farmers and Christians and directed against colonial policies regarding land alienation, taxes, labour, and cultivation rules, but they were usually framed in terms of responsibilities regarding equitable distribution of wealth and land or protection from witchcraft. Thus chiefs were accused of selling land whenever the administration expropriated it, or of practising witchcraft when people disagreed with their politics.

Such enduring moral values were not the only ones cited, however. Protestors were also quick to draw on complementary liberal values, such as freedom of speech, no taxation without representation, justice, and democracy, in their denunciations of what they saw as the illegitimate exercise of authority. 'Why is tax collected when there is no freedom of speech?' they asked, 'Why do we dance for the Government but do not receive justice?'

Administrators like Troup continually denounced the 'agitators' and 'fanatics' given 'to mouthing those democratic shibboleths that concern rights, while ignoring those that concern duties' in support of the pseudo-traditional authorities they had created. In creating those authorities, however, they neglected the responsibilities that men of wealth and power bore and subordinated them to their own bureaucratic and authoritarian structure. The protestors, by contrast, spoke of the duties of those in power to ensure the commonweal, and readily drew on their own as well as new values to make the point. For while colonial discourse may have constantly reiterated respect for 'traditional' authority, colonialism also introduced potentially subversive discourses based on liberal democracy and Christianity that complemented people's own concepts of justice and virtue. Colonial administrators thus got both 'traditional authorities' and the 'fanatics' wrong. The former, in their unbridled exercise of colonially delegated authority, were not traditional, and the latter, in their appeal to the democratic responsibilities of wealth and power, were. Arusha and Meru values, institutions, and traditions were both more flexible and more enduring than colonial authorities – with their reified notion of tradition – thought.[44]

---

[43] Troup, 'Memorandum on the New Constitution'; DC/AD to PC/NP, 28 Nov 1948 (TNA: 25369). See also Northern Province, Annual Reports, 1948, 1949 (TNA: 69/63/A/19 & 69/63/A/29).

[44] For insightful discussions of these and related issues, see Feierman, *Peasant Intellectuals*, and Lonsdale, 'Moral Economy of Mau Mau'.

11

The Meru Land Case

Just when the politics of pseudo-traditionalism was breaking down under the assault of new forces emerging in Arusha and Meru societies, a major conflict over land erupted in Meru. In an attempt to appease settler demands for ranching land north of Mount Meru to develop a beef and dairy industry, the British evicted Meru from the lands northeast of Mount Meru and attempted to resettle them on lands between Meru and Kilimanjaro previously occupied by Maasai. Meru responded with a concerted passive resistance campaign, during which they refused to co-operate in their eviction or to accept the new lands and compensation they were offered. They eventually took their case to the United Nations, where it was heard by the Trusteeship Council and the General Assembly. While Meru lost their case at the UN, they organized a successful political movement in the process that forced Chief Sante from office, replaced his administration with a popularly elected one, established a successful co-operative, and eventually recovered the lands they had lost. Their resolute stand against the colonial authorities rapidly became a rallying cry for the nationalist movement throughout Tanganyika.

The case was a long and extensively documented one, and it raises a host of different questions. Why, for example, after the long and tortured struggle over land in Meru and in the unsettled state of Meru politics did the British choose to mount a further assault on Meru land? Why did they not anticipate Meru resistance, especially in the light of the bitter struggles then building up in Kenya? And why was their policy once again so contrary to the experience of seasoned administrators? Conversely, why did Meru choose to make their stand in the semi-arid northeast, well away from the coffee belt where most Meru lived and where tensions were highest? And what did the land case reveal of the ongoing development of local politics on Mount Meru?

Interestingly, the Meru case made little impact on nearby Arusha. While Arusha suffered even greater pressure on land than Meru and some of the early proposals also called for widespread redistribution of Arusha land, the final recommendations did not affect Arusha adversely, and they did not join Meru organizing against them. Embroiled in their own disputes with the colonial authorities in the late 1940s and early 1950s over circumcision, the crop tax, dipping, the chieftaincy, and the expansion of Arusha town, Arusha remained focused on the politics of authority. Meru and Arusha may both have suffered many of the same grievances against the colonial authorities, especially those regarding land, but they each continued to perceive those grievances and to act against them independently of one another, as regional and national politics continued to be framed in terms of local issues and values.

The Arusha-Moshi Lands Commission

The British had long been aware of the problems of land on Mount Meru and nearby Kilimanjaro, as we have seen, and finally resolved to tackle them once and for all in 1946. The last major land enquiry had been the Bagshawe Report in 1930, which recommended that a few more farms be allocated to Meru and Arusha as corridors to move their cattle from the mountain to the plains. But population density had continued to build up since then and a subsequent study by Harley in 1938, as well as ongoing protests by Arusha and Meru themselves, made it clear that shortage of land remained a serious issue. At the same time, Bagshawe had recommended that 50,000 acres be made available for landless Afrikaners north of Mount Meru, a recommendation the administration had rejected, and they too continued to agitate for more land.[1] Deferred by the war, a full-scale enquiry was finally ordered in 1946 under the chairmanship of Judge Mark Wilson.

By 1946, however, the British were concerned with more than simply resolving the problems of landless Arusha, Meru, and Afrikaners. They were also aggressively seeking to develop Tanganyika economically in order to meet their own post-war needs for agricultural foodstuffs and raw materials, thereby reopening the old debate over the merits of African versus European settler production. African production was the obvious choice elsewhere in Tanganyika, but in the northeast, with its substantial settler population, Europeans held a stronger hand. Settlers were rapidly expanding coffee production in the aftermath of the Depression and the war; they were developing extensive new mixed farming areas southwest of Meru; and they pushed for the establishment of a commercial beef and dairy industry. The administration generally supported the settler case. It reallocated German estates (comprising nearly one-quarter of all the alienated land in Arusha District – some 75,000 acres in all) seized during the Second World War to other settlers, in spite of the lessons it had supposedly learned after doing the same thing after the First World War. New lands were alienated in Oljoro southwest of Arusha town, and settler leases were extended from 33 to 99 years to encourage development.[2]

The administration was not, however, uniformly committed to settler production. Chaga had already developed a major coffee industry on Kilimanjaro and were poised to overtake the settlers in productivity, and Meru and Arusha were on the verge of

---

[1] See Chapter 9.
[2] United Nations, Trusteeship Council, *Report of the United Nations Visiting Mission to the Trust Territories in East Africa*, Distr. General, T/1142, 12 December 1954, 48–50.

expanding their production of this increasingly lucrative crop. Officials were divided on the merits of African cash crop production, as we have seen. Some, like Kitching, supported it as a logical response to land shortage, while others, such as Pelham or Troup, saw it as cutting into production of badly needed foodstuffs.[3]

Unfortunately, however, the commission's terms of reference were set in Dar es Salaam, with only minimal input from local officials who might have given more prominence to Meru and Arusha concerns. The final terms called for the commission:

1. To examine and consider the present distribution of alienated land and tribal lands in the Moshi and Arusha Districts (Kilimanjaro and Meru mountains areas), and to make comprehensive plans and recommendations for the redistribution of such lands with a view to:

   (a) improving the homogeneity of alienated and tribal lands respectively; and
   (b) affording relief to congestion of the native population in tribal lands, with particular reference to the question of providing them with adequate means of access to other areas suitable for the grazing of stock, the cultivation of annual crops, and eventual settlement.

2. To advise the government as to the availability or otherwise of land in the areas in question for further non-native settlement after adequate provision has been made for the present and foreseeable future requirements of the Chagga, Arusha, and Meru tribes.[4]

What strikes one initially is that the emphasis was on the *re*-distribution of African and settler land to make each more homogeneous. The settlers from north Meru were demanding a homogeneous block of alienated land from northeastern Meru to northwestern Kilimanjaro to avoid African cattle trespassing on their land and supposedly infecting their herds with disease. While the administration had rejected such claims in the Bagshawe Report, it now enshrined them within the basic terms of reference as it became committed to developing beef and dairy industries in the area.

Secondly, the terms called for relief of African population congestion only in terms of access to *other* lands suitable for grazing, cultivation of annual crops, and eventual settlement. Little had changed since the First World War, when the British had transferred several farms to Arusha and Meru to open up access to the plains, and 1930, when Bagshawe made a similar recommendation. The assumption remained that the land problem on Meru was caused by surplus cattle on the mountain, and its solution was to move them off.[5] There was to be no question of increasing the amount of arable land available on the mountain by transferring settler farms to them, as Hartley and others had recommended earlier.

Finally, the draft terms called for advice on the availability of land for further alienation, and were only amended later at the Provincial Commissioner's suggestion to add '... after adequate provision has been made for the present and foreseeable future requirements of the Chagga, Arusha, and Meru tribes', leaving little doubt where the

---

[3] See Chapter 7.
[4] The draft terms are contained in CS/DSM to PC/NP, 31 May 1946 and 18 June 1946 (TNA: 69/9/3) and were finally published as amended as General Notice No. 595 in the official *Gazette*, 21 June 1946.
[5] Later Wilson was to extend the terms of reference to include the plains surrounding Arusha and Moshi districts, thus making this point even clearer. Wilson to Battershill, 10 Sept 1946 (OCRP: Wilson Papers, 4/2).

sympathies of the central administration lay. All in all, then, the report was thus strongly biased in favour of the settlers before it was even written.[6]

The Arguments: Views from the Districts

Wilson sat as a one-man commission and received numerous submissions from officials as well as a few from settlers, Meru, Arusha, and Chaga themselves. European settlers were represented by a single memo from the Tanganyika Coffee Growers' Association which, predictably, strongly supported their interests. They noted that while the most congested slopes of Kilimanjaro were also the heart of the European coffee-growing area, this arrangement actually benefited both settlers and Chaga. The patchwork of European and African farms, they argued, provided labour for the Europeans and work for the Africans.

Turning to Mount Meru, the TCGA memo suggested that the Afrikaner farms at Oldonyo Sambu revert to Arusha to relieve their congestion, while the already extensive European mixed farming and coffee districts south of Meru be extended, providing Meru with only a few corridors to the plains below. Further, Engare Nanyuki, northeast of Meru, should be converted to a homogeneous European block for mixed farming and ranching after the government provided water and cleared it of tsetse.[7]

The few African submissions were diametrically opposed to that of the settlers, as might have been expected. Chaga chiefs called for all alienated leasehold as well as undeveloped freehold and mission land to be returned to Chaga at no cost and funds provided to improve land below the Arusha-Taveta road. They argued that a Chaga's *kihamba* represented 'the essence of his very living', conferring on him his home, his family, and his membership in the tribe, whereas a detailed census showed that 11,000 men aged between 18 and 20 were then without *vihamba* and another 81,400 more would need it over the next ten years. 'It is,' they noted coyly in closing, 'the duty of good government to see to it that her subjects prosper....' The Moshi Native Coffee Board also informed Wilson that it planned to replace 12 million coffee trees with selected stock to improve production and required five propagation centres of 20–25 acres each to raise the seedlings.[8]

The only written submission from Arusha or Meru came from the Tanganyika

---

[6] A point made by Wilson himself when he noted that he felt bound by the Commission's terms even while he himself doubted the validity of demarcating separate homogeneous areas for African and European farmers. *Report of the Arusha-Moshi Lands Commission* (Dar es Salaam, 1947), 44–5.

[7] 'Memo, by the Tanganyika Coffee Growers Association on the Proposed Redistribution of Alienated and Tribal Lands on and around Kilimanjaro and Mount Meru Prepared for Submission to the Arusha-Moshi Lands Commission', 27 Sept 1946 (OCRP: Wilson Papers, 4/3); CS/DSM to PC/NP, 28 Oct 1946 (TNA: 69/9/3). For a personal view critical of the settlers, see Elmer Danielson, *Forty Years with Christ in Tanzania* (New York, 1977), 142–4.

[8] 'Memorandum from Chaga Chiefs', 26 Jan 1946 (OCRP: Wilson Papers); 'A Memorandum to the Commissioner, Moshi-Arusha Land Commission by a Committee Appointed by the Chagga Chiefs Council, Moshi', 7 Sept 1946; Exec. Officer, A.L.B. Bennett, MNCB to Sec'ty, Arusha-Meru Lands Commission, 27 July 1946 (both in TNA: 69/9/3).

African Association. Alienation had not been a problem in German times because the Germans had allowed Africans to graze their stock freely, the TAA memo noted, but the situation had deteriorated markedly when British settlers demanded payment for grazing and sought to monopolize the main water springs for stock, making Meru and Arusha 'more than slaves' now. The TAA called for the restoration of all alienated lands on the fertile southern, eastern, and western slopes of Mount Meru, leaving only the Afrikaner farms north of Meru in settler hands, and for the limitation of grants to non-natives to a single grant of 100 acres each.[9]

If the settlers' and Africans' proposals were fairly predictable, those from members of the administration were more varied and developed in greater detail. F.C. Hallier, the former District and Provincial Commissioner, reflected the position of many officials. While he acknowledged the 'dangerous congestion of people and stock' on Mount Meru, he recommended against transferring European estates on the mountain to Arusha or Meru as they would only become overpopulated at the cost of losing valuable European production. Hallier also rejected the 'fantastic' TCGA submission, however, noting that Oldonyo Sambu had already been turned into a 'dust bowl' by Afrikaner over-stocking. Afrikaners were as unlikely to abandon it, he thought, as Arusha were to find it a solution to their problems. The answer, then, was to shift Arusha, Meru, and their stock to Maasai, with whom they were closely related.[10]

Officials on Kilimanjaro were more sympathetic to Chaga interests, however. A long memo by the Assistant District Officer, H.F.I. Elliott, and the Agricultural Officer, R.J.M. Swynnerton, carefully detailed Chaga needs and forcefully argued that individual Chaga farms, especially on the densely settled southern slopes, had become too small to support the families living on them. Elliott and Swynnerton calculated that Chaga would eventually require all the alienated lands to meet their needs over the next 20 to 50 years, and they recommended immediate reversion of leasehold land, acquisition of freehold as it became available, and opening up the plains to settlement. In response to the usual settler objections against reversion of alienated lands to Africans, they countered that Chaga were better farmers and conservationists than settlers. Chaga coffee was already nearly as productive as European and would outstrip it as soon as they had replaced their older trees. The Moshi District Officer strongly supported Elliott and Swynnerton's conclusions. He also noted the value of Chaga contributions to the war effort and stressed the degree to which future political progress was dependent on a just and equitable solution of the contentious land problem. Finally, he refuted other submissions critical of Elliott and Swynnerton in detail.[11]

In marked contrast to the Elliott-Swynnerton memo, the submissions from officials in Arusha were distinctly less sympathetic to African needs. The Provincial Veterinary

9 Tanganyika African Association, Arusha Branch, to Sec'ty, Arusha-Moshi Lands Commission, 7 Oct 1946 (TNA: 69/9/3).

10 'Memorandum by Lt. Col. F.C. Hallier (Retired P.C.) Presented to the Arusha-Moshi Lands Commission' (OCRP: Hallier Papers); comments by F.C. Hallier to 'Memo, by the Tanganyika Coffee Growers Association' (OCRP: Wilson Papers, 4/3).

11 H.F.I. Elliott, ADO, & R.J.M. Swynnerton, AO, 'Memorandum: Land Distribution In Moshi District', 20 Aug 1946 and DO/MD to Wilson, 24 July, 24 Aug and 13 Nov 1946 (all in TNA: 69/9/3).

Officer, I.M. Pullon, focused on the stock population on Meru and the problems of trespass, fouling of water, destruction of pasture, and spread of disease as Meru and Arusha moved their stock from the mountain through the settler farms to the plains. Noting that there was insufficient stock on the mountain to fulfil human nutritional needs, while there was too much for available grazing, he advocated opening the plains to stock and settlement by clearing them of tsetse and providing water.

In contrast, Pullon stressed the value of settler agriculture, noting that the

> ... value of products from the alienated lands vastly eclipse the value of native products produced from a similar area, and go not only to increase the funds which are in part devoted to the improvement and well being of the tribesmen, but to increase the food stuffs available to those tribesmen, and their opportunities of wage earning, which increase their material well being.

In order to maintain balanced land holdings while avoiding African-settler conflicts in the future, he advocated that each block of Arusha, Meru, or alienated lands should stretch from the forest to the plains, taking in all the ecological zones of the mountain. Pullon's recommendation thus called for the wholesale redistribution of land right across the mountain into alternating wedges of Arusha, Meru, and European lands and later became known, somewhat derisively, as the Japanese flag plan as a result. Short of such wholesale redistribution, he asserted, homogeneity in the existing areas was essential for ease of administration and control of livestock disease and marketing. Finally, he added, the government itself required an additional 15,000 acres for township expansion and for stock routes, demonstration farms, and dairy farms to develop the livestock industry.[12]

The District Agricultural Officer, T.C. Cairns, echoed many of Pullon's points short of the flag proposal. He was also highly critical of Arusha-Meru agriculture, noting that the use of manure for bananas and pastures instead of annual food crops, conversion of pasture to food crop production, and planting steep hillsides all resulted in serious soil deterioration and erosion. Agricultural improvements would not be enough to relieve the situation, given the extent of overcrowding, however, and so many Arusha and Meru would simply have to move to the plains then occupied by pastoral Maasai.

In spite of what he saw as the poor quality of most European agriculture, Cairns repeated Pullon's claims about its superior value and added that it would contribute to the further development of the dairy, poultry, and pig industries. Thus, Cairns concluded:

> ... it is evident that the lands occupied by the tribesmen in the upland areas of the district are overpopulated both by human beings and stock and cannot long continue to support their present numbers to say nothing of their natural increase.... The simple solution of gradually handing over to the landless natives the areas at present occupied by non-natives is not so simple as it would appear and would... have serious economic results and upset the local balance of agriculture.... The solution proposed by the Tanganyika Coffee Growers Association has much to commend it, but although drastic measures will no doubt be required the

[12] I.M. Pullon, 'A Memorandum on the Land and Livestock Problems of the Arusha District', 7 Oct 1946 (TNA: 69/9/3).

problem in the Arusha district with the exception of finding land for the landless [Afrikaner] people of Oldonyo Sambu is not too acute...[13]

Unlike most officials, then, Cairns was much more sympathetic to the Afrikaner case than he was to Meru or Arusha ones.

The only other submission from Arusha District was a note from the Assistant District Officer, R.H. Gower, on inheritance of land, in which he briefly commented on the general shortage of land. While he noted that Arusha were able to overcome it by expanding on to Monduli, Meru expansion to the northeast was blocked by settler farms.[14] The protection of Meru and Arusha interests was thus left solely in the hands of the Commissioner.

He was not sympathetic. While Wilson did not make his ideas known directly, the rhetorical nature of the questions he asked Arusha and Meru chiefs is indicative of his thinking:

Isn't land congestion in Arusha caused by people using their former grazing lands to grow cash crops for money?

Wouldn't congestion be relieved if some moved to the plains?

Why are cattle daily moved back and forth from plains? Couldn't they stay in plains?

Will people sell cattle to keep numbers down or do they keep them for prestige?[15]

The implication of these questions seems clear: Meru and Arusha should stick to growing food crops, limit their cattle, and shift them to the plains. He had responded similarly to the Elliott-Swynnerton memo on Kilimanjaro, querying whether complete reversion of alienated lands was politically practical, economically desirable, or necessary:

Is not the present scarcity of land on Kilimanjaro due largely to the Chagga desire to grow cash crops (coffee) and so get ready money, thereby using up much of the available 'vihamba' land which formerly produced food for man and beast?

Are Chagga claims actuated by greed and land hunger rather than economic pressure? Does not land now go to the influential and not to the landless men?[16]

Wilson's mind, like the commission's terms of reference, seemed to be set. This was not to be a report in response to African needs, but to those of settlers.

The Report: View from the Centre

Wilson was true to the task and his final report supported the settlers' and central administration's positions while disregarding the more detailed submissions from district

---

[13] T.C. Cairns, 'A Memorandum on Land Distribution and Agriculture in the Arusha District', 5 Nov 1946 (TNA: 69/9/3).

[14] R.H. Gower to Sec'ty, Arusha-Moshi Lands Commission, 7 Oct 1946 (TNA: 69/9/3).

[15] M. Wilson, 'Questions for Arusha-Meru Chiefs', 9 Oct 1946 (OCRP: Wilson Papers).

[16] Wilson's comments are included with his copy of the Elliott-Swynnerton memo (OCRP: Wilson papers, 4/3).

officers, whom he openly accused of bias. Wilson opened with a summary of government land policy in which he acknowledged the general 'paramountcy of native interests' established in 1935, but also noted that settlers had been 'conducive to the early and large-scale economic development of the Territory, on which the political and social advancement of the inhabitants appears to depend'. He also observed that government policy regarding land use was changing to promote large-scale economic development. The Central Development Committee had first proposed an exchange of land in the Sanya Corridor between Mounts Meru and Kilimanjaro to promote block development and the alienation of further blocks along the railway in 1940.[17]

Turning from policy to the situation on the ground, Wilson acknowledged that the extensive alienation of land around Mount Meru by the Germans had resulted in 'an "iron ring" of alienated land ... clamped around the native lands on the mountain', thereby precluding subsequent attempts to provide relief to overcrowding on the mountain. Later the British had shown 'no proper appreciation of the future needs of the Arusha and Meru tribes and the re-alienation of the majority of farms so thoughtlessly demarcated by the Germans proceeded without protest. An unparalleled opportunity for readjustment was lost.... The farms had been sold and the ring was once more in place.' While the British belatedly discovered their mistake and provided some farms to Meru and Arusha to allow them access to the plains in 1934, this was 'merely a palliative measure'.[18]

In spite of such errors, however, Wilson concluded that the main causes of increasing population congestion on Meru were the product of general changes unrelated to alienation occurring over the past 20 to 25 years. Population was now unchecked by war, famine, disease, or local customs, as it had been previously. The growth of a cash economy enticed people to raise cash crops in order to buy new consumer goods appearing in the shops, he felt, leading to widespread 'land grabbing' and accumulation heedless of the traditional social obligations that went with wealth. While such behaviour was, of course, expected of European farmers, Wilson felt it could not be tolerated in a situation in which land was so restricted and *kihamba* had such social significance. The implications were clear: only settlers could develop the colony by growing cash crops, while Africans should restrict themselves to raising their own food and providing labour for others.[19] Indirect rule was as much an economic policy as it was a political one.

Wilson's conclusions flowed logically from the above. While he rejected wholesale redistribution of land (such as Pullon's Japanese Flag plan or the TCGA's proposal to clear out the Afrikaners and resettle Arusha at Oldonyo Sambu) as too impractical politically, and accepted the need to provide additional access for Meru and Arusha to the plains, he concentrated on the further expansion of productive European enterprise. Meru and pastoral Maasai were to be evicted from the northern part of the Sanya Corridor between Engare Nanyuki and Kilimanjaro in order to develop a homogeneous, disease-free European ranching zone, while displaced and other landless Meru were to be offered land in Chai and Ongadongishu to the south. No further mountain land was

[17] *Arusha–Moshi Lands Commission*, 8, 19.
[18] *Arusha–Moshi Lands Commission*, 14–18.
[19] *Arusha–Moshi Lands Commission*, 22–5, 42.

to be allocated to Chaga, Meru, or Arusha, with the possible exception of some under-utilized mission holdings. Rather, they were to be encouraged to settle permanently on the plains through the development of government resettlement schemes and the provision of water, anti-tsetse, and anti-malaria services. They were also admonished to improve their conservation techniques, de-stock the highlands, and abandon keeping cattle for prestige in favour of more productive uses.[20] It was a familiar and, by then, tired litany that recalled previous efforts to solve the land problem.

Wilson's proposals, especially the most controversial one regarding the removal of Meru from Engare Nanyuki, were predicated on the availability of suitable agricultural land on the plains, but he admitted that neither he nor the government possessed detailed information on the topography, climate, soils, prevalence of disease, water supplies, or agricultural resources of these areas. The same applied to Engare Nanyuki itself; touted as an area unsuitable for African agriculture but ideal for European ranching, the area was virtually unknown. Wilson was, as would soon become apparent, flying blind without instruments, guided only by dubious political, ethnographic, and geographical assumptions.[21]

While the report was published in 1947, its implementation was delayed until 1949 while the administration considered it and made final arrangements for the transfer of land. There was no shortage of official responses in the meantime. Moshi officials were frankly astonished. Swynnerton complained that Wilson had ignored population densities on Kilimanjaro and consequently failed to address real Chaga needs. He had wrongly accused Chaga of 'land grabbing', failed to understand 'the African mentality', indiscreetly published the views of officials and so stirred up settlers, and accepted TCGA arguments regarding superior European production in the coffee heartland in spite of evidence to the contrary.[22]

The District Commissioner, J.F.R. Hill, was equally disturbed. Wilson failed to address urgent Chaga needs or to consider the political repercussions of inaction, Hill wrote. He had misrepresented Chaga responses to land shortage, maligned officials as hopelessly biased, ignored the weakness of the European coffee industry, and caved in to 'vested interests'. 'The Commissioner,' he concluded, 'has made a very feeble bite at the cherry.'[23]

---

[20] *Arusha-Moshi Lands Commission*, 31–6, 39–40, 65–90.

[21] *Arusha-Moshi Lands Commission*, 10, 90–2. Wilson had, in fact, tried to get geographic information, but much of what he was given was superficial or outdated, and critical water surveys he ordered were not completed in time for his report. (OCRP: Wilson Papers).

As for his ethnography, Wilson was prone to accept uncritically the most preposterous explanations of African behaviour. Wilson's report is peppered with such statements, taken as fact, as this explanation of squatting on settler farms:

The African is imitative and gregarious and curious. When Europeans move into an uninhabited area he likes to move in too – if only to see what is going on. And there are always pickings to be had. The African has long since realized that the European settler, whether one likes him or not ... brings with him potentialities for profit and opportunity which are not to be despised and he acts accordingly. (*Arusha-Moshi Lands Commission*, 16)

Such European folk ethnography, of course, was rarely accurate and took no account of colonial economic demands for land, labour, and taxes.

[22] R.J.M. Swynnerton, 'Notes on the Report of the Arusha-Moshi Lands Commission', 3 June 1947 (TNA: 69/9/3).

[23] J.F.R. Hill, 'Note on Land Commission Report', June 1947 (TNA: 69/9/3).

The Provincial Commissioner, T.C. Revington, was more diplomatic in conveying his subordinates' concerns to Dar es Salaam. After lauding the report as an excellent one that gave a fair picture of the local land situation, he made an exception for central Chaga, where he continued to support full reversion of all leasehold estates to Chaga and bemoaned the Commissioner's dismissal of the problem of overpopulation, as this was 'the cause of all the present difficulties'. Given the likely opposition to the anticipated moves, he stressed that the government would have to bear the considerable costs of money and staff involved and emphasized that 'propaganda … based on a sound psychological approach to the African should be undertaken ASAP…' if the report were to be implemented successfully.[24]

Arusha officials were less critical and focused more on the problems of implementation, given the difficult political situations regarding the Native Authorities then prevailing in both Meru and Arusha. The Assistant District Officer, R.H. Gower, complained that Wilson had been unduly swayed by the assertions of the Veterinary Department and leading settlers that only Europeans would adhere to dipping, pointing out that Meru were already doing so. Furthermore, Engare Nanyuki was such 'forbidding country' that Gower rightly predicted that no Europeans would be able to make a living there, while Meru were able to do so successfully employing hand cultivation. Finally, given the extreme political difficulties of convincing both Meru and settlers to move, Gower suggested moving the boundary between the two further north, thus lessening the overall disruption to either and dramatically reducing the cost.[25] The Provincial Commissioner, in forwarding Gower's comments, noted that the report causes 'great dislocation to both native and non-native farming at a very high cost and will cause dissatisfaction and political irritation to all parties. I agree with the solution proposed by the District Commissioner.'[26] This was simply a pragmatic suggestion, however, and Troup followed it up with a further memo reasserting that the root of the problem was caused by Arusha and Meru growing cash crops at the expense of food.[27]

Given the range of views presented to Wilson, it is difficult to understand why he came down so strongly in support of the single brief submission from the settlers while virtually ignoring the more informed ones of the district administrators, especially since the TGCA's superficial assertions were so effectively countered by the officials. For that, one must look behind the scenes into the largely undocumented manoeuvres of the central administration in Dar es Salaam.

We have already noted the degree to which the terms of reference of the commission had been biased in favour of settler production from the start, focused as they were on the creation of homogeneous blocks of alienated land, the movement of Meru and Arusha off the mountain, and the alienation of additional land to settlers. We have also seen how Wilson appeared to be strongly predisposed towards the settlers, accepting

[24] T.C. Revington, 'Comments on the Report of the Arusha-Moshi Lands Commission', 11 June 1947 (TNA: 69/9/3).
[25] DC/AD to PC/NP, 17 May 1947 and 25 Aug 1947 (TNA: 69/9/3). See also Minutes, Meeting of District Reps., 5 Sept 1947 (TNA: 9/8/1).
[26] PC/NP to CS/DSM, 29 Aug 1947 (TNA: 69/9/3).
[27] DC/AD to PC/NP, 4 Nov 1947 (TNA: 9/NA/1).

their assertions uncritically while criticizing the alleged bias of the district officials. The TCGA submission was essentially a political statement, rather than a detailed planning document, but its biases accorded well with those of the administration, and the Chief Secretary discussed it extensively in private meetings with the settlers and the Provincial Commissioner.

In addition to these essentially political concerns, there was the larger issue of economic development. The central administration was committed to large-scale economic development after the war, and their concerns were enthusiastically echoed by the technical officers in the Agriculture and Veterinary Departments. The differences in positions between the agricultural officers in Arusha and Moshi are instructive. In Moshi Swynnerton strongly supported Chaga interests, largely because they had shown they could produce coffee as well as the settlers, whereas in Meru, Cairns still felt settlers were more productive. Administrative officers in both areas, by contrast, daily faced problems of political unrest brought about by the land problem, and so either wholeheartedly supported African needs (in the case of Elliott and Hill in Moshi) or sought at the least to ameliorate the impact of land redistribution (in that of Gower in Arusha).

Once again, then, the administration responded as it had so many times before. In asserting that the problem of land congestion among Meru and Arusha was caused by coffee growing and over-stocking, it was responding more to settler complaints over competition and cattle trespass than to Arusha and Meru ones for more agricultural land. Careful students of mountain agriculture, like Swynnerton, who realized that cash cropping and stall-feeding were integral parts of Chaga (as they were of Arusha-Meru) responses to land shortage, were ignored, while unsupported assertions to the contrary were elevated to fact. At the same time, however, a new factor had entered the equation. The administration's commitment to large-scale agricultural development accentuated its tilt towards the settlers, notwithstanding Swynnerton's arguments to the contrary . It would thus appear that Wilson and the administration responded more strongly to political pressure from settlers and to their own commitment to large-scale economic development than to the concerns of district level administrative officers deeply worried about the potential political consequences of further exacerbating the land problem.

These conclusions are supported by the subsequent acts of the government. The administration appointed a sub-committee of the Land Settlement Board to consider Wilson's recommendations and the responses in detail. The sub-committee was heavily dominated by settlers and those sympathetic to their interests, so it was not surprising that their recommendations for land redistribution on Mount Meru were even more favourable to the settlers than Wilson's. They reduced by two-thirds the number of settler farms in the Usa area to be reallocated to Meru, while confirming that Meru should be removed entirely from the northern areas and that Meru, Arusha, and Chaga should bear the full £125,000 cost of the operation. To lessen the sting slightly, they allowed some Meru to stay in Leguruki and opened up Kingori just to the south for resettlement, thus cutting down on the number of Meru who would have to move and lessening the distance the rest would have to do so.[28]

---

[28] 'Report of a Sub-committee of the Land Settlement Board Appointed to Consider the Recommendations made in the Report of the Arusha-Moshi Lands Commission, and to Submit Observations and Comments'

The Governor forwarded their recommendations to the Colonial Office for approval, but the Colonial Secretary had strong reservations about the apparent neglect of African interests. He refused to accept the TCGA's assertion that reversion would hurt production and doubted whether 'the proposals go as far as they should to secure the return to the indigenous peoples of those areas of fertile and well-watered land originally alienated by the German Government....' Accordingly, he recommended that 'estates suitable for native occupation', including a number of coffee farms, should be 'released forthwith', that no further leases should be allowed, that other alienated land should revert as needed, and that the government should pay the full costs of the moves as it had profited from the original sales.

The Governor responded with the standard *ad hominem* attack on African cash farming:

> The switchover of the Chagga from food crops to cash crops is a major cause [of land shortage] and the land hunger on the mountain is likely to grow progressively worse as the more advanced elements of the tribe obtain by devious means (as they are already doing) the good land under food crops, for commercial exploitation in the large blocks for their personal profit.... Similar considerations apply in the case of the Warusha and Mameru [*sic*] tribes, although not to the same extent.

Land reversion would, he added, create upheaval in European districts 'which contribute so heavily and so vitally to the prosperity of the Territory through their production of food and export crops'. The Wilson report had, he averred, allocated more than enough land to Arusha and Meru on the lower slopes, while Chaga would have to learn to respond to other opportunities, such as the 'almost unlimited openings for skilled workers in connection with the Groundnut Scheme' then under development in southern Tanganyika. Finally, he noted that it had been the Crown Agents, not the government, that had benefited from the sales of land originally.

The Colonial Secretary finally acceded, with the proviso that Africans not have to pay for land returned to them and that Meru be compensated for the land they lost in north Meru.[29] It was now up to the district administrators, who had rightly feared the political consequences of the report, to implement it.

'Blood on Our Land':
The Removal of Meru from Engare Nanyuki

The final White Paper of the Lands Commission called for the creation of a homogeneous European ranching district stretching across north Meru (Oldonyo Sambu to

[28 cont.] (OCRP: Wilson Papers, 4/1); Land Settlement Officer to Co-ordinating Secretary, 11 Feb 1948 (TNA: 37154); Governor to Colonial Secretary, 24 March 1948 (OCRP: Wilson Papers, 5/6). The subcommittee's members were Maj. S.E. du Toit and Mr W.H. Baldwin, both settlers; R.A.J. Maguire of the Agricultural Department; N.R. Reid, the Director of Veterinary Services; J.P. Moffett, the Secretary to the Wilson Commission; A.M.B. Hutt, the acting Chief Secretary; and the Provincial Commissioner.
[29] Governor to Colonial Secretary (Confidential No. 61), 24 March 1948 and reply (Confidential No. 188), 19 July 1948; Governor to Colonial Secretary (Confidential No. 996), 21 Oct 1948 and reply (Confidential 319), 26 Nov 1948 (all in OCRP: Wilson Papers, 5/6).

Engare Nanyuki) and the Sanya Corridor between Meru and Kilimanjaro to northern Kilimanjaro (Engare Nairobi). Meru inhabiting the northeastern slopes of Mount Meru at Engare Nanyuki and Leguruki were to be moved to land acquired for them in Kingori, with further lands made available to them in Chai and Ongadongishu in the south.[30]

The move was complicated by the fact that the land from which Meru were being evicted was not ordinary reserve land, but two former European farms (31 and 328) which Meru had purchased and held under freehold tenancy. These farms, in turn, gave Meru access to extensive range lands normally occupied by pastoral Maasai that stretched north to the Kenya border and known as the Northern Meru Reserve. They thus faced not only considerable loss of land, but land which had already been alienated from them once and which they had subsequently taxed themselves heavily to repurchase from the government and held in freehold titles.[31]

The determination that Meru would be moved was announced to them by the District Commissioner, D.S. Troup, in June 1949. Coming only six months after the constitutional crisis and deportations, their response was predictable. Meru accused Sante of selling precious land to the Europeans for personal profit, thus costing him whatever legitimacy he had left. By all accounts, Sante only approved the moves reluctantly and under pressure, and his Tribal Council actively disapproved them, but he could not avoid public responsibility without actively joining the opposition, which he did not do.[32] The crop tax and renewed threats against Meru squatters on Focsaner's farm added further fuel to the fire. Sante's administration collapsed while the opposition openly conducted mass meetings and raised funds for appeals. Meru was ripe for rebellion.[33]

Meru complained to the government that the new lands, bought with their own cash and labour, were not as good as those they were being asked to give up. Their holdings in Engare Nanyuki and Leguruki contained a varied mix of lands, including highlands

[30] Tanganyika Territory, Arusha–Moshi Lands Commission, *Redistribution of Lands in the Arusha District* (Dar es Salaam, 1949). Generally unheralded in comments on the Land Case is the fact that pastoral Maasai were also evicted from Sanya to make room for Europeans in the north and Meru in the south. Maasai lost the Northern Meru Reserve, parts of Kingori, and a 5,000-acre farm bordering Engare Nanyuki which they had bought in the 1930s.

[31] The exact figures regarding the amount of land actually transferred were widely disputed. The administration calculated that Meru gave up an estimated 5,800 acres at Engare Nanyuki and Leguruki together with an additional 78,000 acres available to them in the Northern Reserve in exchange for 11,000 acres of previously alienated land in Kingori and an additional 159,000 acres available in Chai and Ongadongishu. [Tanganyika, Legislative Council, *The Meru Land Problem*, 1952; PC/NP, 'Aide-memoire: Implementation of Arusha-Moshi Lands Commission Report up to 31 December, 1951', 23 Mar 1953 (TNA: LAN/15/A).] Meru already occupied parts of Kingori and the Chai Reserve, however, and considered the land theirs. (United Nations, Trusteeship Council, *Official Records*, 11th Session, 431st–432nd and 451st–452nd meetings, 30 June 1952 and 21–2 July 1952.) The quality of the respective lands was also in dispute, with the British claiming that Kingori was superior to Engare Nanyuki, and Meru claiming the reverse. Future events proved the Meru right.

[32] Northern Province, Annual Report, 1951 (TNA: 19415); Legislative Council, *Meru Land Problem*; Kirilo Japhet (MHT 2); Anton Nelson, *The Freemen of Meru* (Nairobi, 1967), 30.

[33] Northern Province, Annual Report, 1951 (TNA: 19415); District Agricultural Officer, Annual Report, 1951 (TNA: 472/-).

suitable for coffee and bananas, riverine lands for irrigated agriculture, scattered pockets of fertile land for rain-fed crops, and extensive salt pans and rangeland for cattle. The resettlement areas, by contrast, were hot semi-arid lowlands, lacked water supplies, and were infested with tsetse flies and malaria, making them unsuitable for either agriculture or herding. In response to Meru complaints, Troup proposed that 735 acres of salt pans be excised from the land to be transferred, and promised that the government would provide water in the resettlement areas, clear them of tsetse, and provide health clinics to care for the new settlers. When government finance proved unavailable, however, he had to resort to forced 'tribal turnouts' to clear the bush and complete the water supplies. Later the government would claim that the land at Kingori was actually superior to that at Engare Nanyuki.[34]

Meru opposition to Sante and to the plan intensified throughout 1950 and 1951. Their appeals to the Governor and Colonial Secretary were rebuffed, and when a United Nations Visiting Mission visited Arusha in September 1951, they presented it with a petition against the move. In an attempt to preclude UN action, the administration rushed through an ordinance allowing them to evict Meru forcibly from Engare Nanyuki.[35]

Meru continued to refuse to co-operate when British officials arrived to enumerate holdings and arrange compensation, however, and they rejected all offers to move voluntarily. On 17 November, the British moved into Engare Nanyuki with force. According to the official British report, 25 Meru were arrested over the course of the next twelve days, and while Meru watched from the hillside, police emptied their houses and burned them to the ground. They then transported some 400 cattle and 1,200 sheep to Kingori, and dug up buried food stores and destroyed them. The stone church and other community buildings were similarly destroyed, and roads from Meru were blocked to prevent people from returning. One man died during the exercise and a woman lost her child in childbirth.

Two weeks later, the British conducted a similar exercise in Leguruki, but Meru there were more co-operative, and the evictions were completed by 12 December. In the end, the administration asserted that 330 men and their families, about 1,000 people in all, had been moved with 'patience,... humanity, and yet firmness shown by all officers concerned...,' while the 429 buildings demolished 'were very primitive structures, poorly built, easily put together, and costing very little to replace'. 'The move was,' the official report concluded, 'completed with a minimum of hardship.'[36] Meru saw it differently.

Meru had been preparing for this day for some time as members of the Meru Citizens' Union expanded their protests against Sante, the 1948 constitution and deportations, the crop tax, and the evictions of squatters from Focsaner's estate. The Citizens'

[34] For the government view, see DC/AD to PC/NP, 28 Oct 1949 and 29 Nov 1949 (TNA: 472/LAN/54); Meeting with DC, 17 Dec 1949 (TNA: 9/8/1); Legislative Council, *Meru Land Problem*. For the Meru view: Trusteeship Council, *Official Records*, 11th Session, 451st–452nd meetings, 21–2 July 1952; Kirilo Japhet & Earle Seaton, *The Meru Land Case* (Nairobi, 1967), 12–13; Nelson, *Freemen of Meru*, 25–7, 49.

[35] Nelson, *Freemen of Meru*, 36.

[36] Legislative Council, *Meru Land Problem*.

Union (also known as the *Umoja wa Raia Wameru* or Freemen of Meru) was led by
Gamaliel Sablak, the former Chairman of the Tribal Council who had resigned in protest against Sante.[37] It was affiliated with the Kilimanjaro and Arusha Citizens' Unions,
but was an independent organization that pursued its own issues. While it was formed
in protest against the chief and government policies, it was more than just a protest
organization. Closely linked with the Meru Coffee Growers' Association, the Union
also sought to promote development, and it levied a tax of 2¢ on everyone to pay for
students to study abroad.[38]

Members of the Union were also active in Engare Nanyuki, where local people organized their own Committee of Four, consisting of Emanuel (Makiya) Kasengye N'nko,
Rafaeli Mbise, Moses Isak, and Munya Lengoroi, to lead their protests. Emanuel was
the former headman of the area who had resigned in protest when he was ordered to
enumerate the people and cattle preparatory to their eviction. He had been born in
Mulala in 1911, attended school at Nkoaranga for six years, and moved to Engare
Nanyuki as an evangelist and teacher in 1932. Since he was well known to the British
officials, he adopted the alias Maasa wa Makiya.

Rafaeli Mbise was also a Christian and a member of the Citizens' Union's committee. Born in 1914, he had eight years of education, edited the local Christian magazine,
moved to Engare Nanyuki to open a primary school in 1938, and succeeded Emanuel as
evangelist in 1945. Rafaeli served as the committee's secretary under the alias Mangi
Lienago, and his detailed written reports of meetings and the evictions were later to
confound the British representative at the United Nations. Moses Isak and Munya
Lengoroi were less well known, and for that reason they often signed the committee's
petitions, using their own names.[39]

In addition to organizing and raising money locally, the Committee of Four made
contact with the Kenya African Union in Nairobi and with the Fabian Society in
London. They launched a barrage of petitions to the Legislative Council, the Governor,
and the Colonial Secretary protesting against the impending move. They petitioned the
Chief Secretary personally in Dar es Salaam, and they protested directly to the District
Commissioner and Provincial Commissioner at meetings held in the district.

Indefatigable in their protests, Meru were non-violent in their actions. They refused
to co-operate in the enumeration of people and livestock, to move voluntarily, to assist
the British in moving them, or to accept compensation or resettlement afterwards. On
the appointed day of their eviction, they withdrew to a nearby hillside and observed the
destruction of their village through binoculars, while Rafaeli took detailed notes of
everything that they saw. No one physically confronted the British; those arrested were

---

[37] The MCU's Committee included Gamaliel Sablak (Chairman), Munya Lengoroi, Imanuel Malya, Yohane
Meriumu, Jonathan Gideon, Afraeli Leena, Elifasi Ndesaulo, Malalo Lemuree, Abraham Menyamu,
Moses Sindili, Ndetaiywa Lasheri, Masinde Mafunga, Sumuni Orongai, Seti Mekivawo, Rafaeli Mbise,
and Kirilo Japhet (Secretary). Japhet & Seaton, *Meru Land Case*, 22n.

[38] Kirilo Japhet (MHT 2).

[39] Nelson, *Freemen of Meru*, 38; I. Mbise, *Blood on Our Land* (Dar es Salaam, 1974); Rafaeli Mbise (MHT
3); Emanuel Kasengye N'nko (MHT 5); Danielson, *Forty Years with Christ*, 147.

11.1 *Engare Nanyuki* (Spear)

commonly charged with trespassing, and one who was arrested for inciting the crowd was actually admonishing them not to be rude.[40]

They also had bicycle messengers able to elude the police and carry letters quickly from Engare Nanyuki to Meru and Arusha. They smuggled out photographs and Rafaeli's notes and wired messages to Chief Koinange in Nairobi, Fenner Brockway in London, and Ralph Bunche at the United Nations in New York. The story of the evictions thus broke in the world press on 20 November, much to the embarrassment of the administration, which scrambled to find the source. Police arrested Rafaeli and deported him to Nkoaranga, but the news continued to flow out as Amos Karoiya took up Rafaeli's pen.[41]

The Meru story of the evictions was far from that later propagated by the British authorities as entailing 'a minimum of hardship'. Engare Nanyuki is shaped like a huge bowl, with Meru farms scattered along the river curling through its bottom. Meru observing the scene from the surrounding hillsides thus had a panoramic view when seven European officers, 66 to 120 armed African police, 100 Kenyan labourers, and the District Commissioner in full ceremonial dress entered the valley early in the morning of 17 November and ordered them to abandon their land and dwellings. As the Meru withdrew, police surrounded the village to prevent people from returning to their homes, and labourers began to empty the houses of their meagre possessions and load them on lorries bound for Kingori. After their homes had been emptied, bulldozers knocked them to the ground, after which workers put torches to the remains. As the

[40] Rafaeli Mbise (MHT 3); Kirilo Japhet (MHT 2); Nelson, *Freemen of Meru*, 40–1.
[41] Rafaeli Mbise (MHT 3); Kirilo Japhet (MHT 2); Nelson, *Freemen of Meru*, 38, 43.

11.2 *Burned church at Engare Nanyuki* (Spear)

burning continued for thirteen days, the flames and smoke from the thatch and wood dwellings curled up through the bowl, lighting the night-time sky and the workers scurrying among the remains below.[42]

Once the houses were levelled, police rounded up the cattle, sheep, and goats and drove them to Kingori. They then burned the dispensary, school, and finally the sturdy stone church overlooking the plains that Meru had painstakingly built in 1938. As Meru picked up the few possessions they had managed to save and trudged back to central Meru to join their relatives or squat on European farms, they could still see its stone walls standing starkly against the sky. The memory would haunt them in exile, and its walls remain a silent sentinel to the events of November 1951 to this day.

The destruction of Engare Nanyuki completed, the British moved on to attack Leguruki. By the time they finished there twelve days later, Meru had seen all they had worked for ploughed into the ground and reduced to charred smoking remains. Police then arrested any Meru still remaining for trespassing and blocked the roads from central Meru to prevent them from returning. In marked contrast to the administration's figures, Meru reported that 2,993 people had been evicted, 64 of whom subsequently died, and that 2,190 cattle driven into the bush had also died, as had 8,984 sheep and goats, 325 donkeys, 333 dogs, 479 cats, and 1,896 chickens. The survivors would have to turn elsewhere for help now.

---

[42] For vivid descriptions of the removals from the Meru point of view, see Trusteeship Council, *Official Records*, 11th Session, 451st–452nd meetings, 21–2 July 1952; Japhet & Seaton, *Meru Land Case*, 19; Nelson, *Freemen of Meru*, 40-6; Mbise, *Blood on Our Land*; Danielson, *Forty Years with Christ*, 146–7; Kirilo Japhet (MHT 2); and Rafaeli Mbise (MHT 3).

The Meru Land Case and the United Nations

The Citizens' Union had first petitioned the United Nations Visiting Mission before the evictions in September, and it subsequently tried to persuade the British authorities to delay the evictions until the full Trusteeship Council had an opportunity to hear their case. The British not only refused their request, but quickened the pace to attempt to pre-empt the Meru appeal. Meru persisted regardless. They placed pots at every crossroad to collect funds to send a representative to New York, and all who passed were expected to contribute, even babies still in their mothers' wombs.[43]

On 9 June 1952 they were finally granted a hearing before the Trusteeship Council provided they arrived before the end of the month, when the British representative, John Lamb, had to leave to be knighted by the King. Pushed for time, Meru chose to send Earle Seaton, a black lawyer from Bermuda who practised in Moshi, to represent them, while Kirilo Japhet, the secretary of the Citizens' Union, rushed to get a passport and tickets.

Kirilo Japhet was a second-generation Christian. His father, Japhet Ayo, had been baptized in 1913 and became a pioneer coffee farmer in Nkoaranga, where he served as treasurer of his church and President of the Meru Native Coffee Planters' Association. Kirilo completed eight years of school and was studying at Marangu Teachers' Training College when his German teachers were deported and the college closed during the Second World War. He then taught school himself for a while before training as a medical assistant and returning to Nkoaranga to work in the mission hospital. He quit work there in 1948 to work full-time as Secretary of the Citizens' Union, and so he was well versed in Meru politics by the time it came to go to New York.[44]

Seaton arrived in New York just in time for the Council to hear him on 30 June. In the meantime, the administration did not make it easy for Kirilo. They delayed his passport and told him repeatedly that he should not bother to go to New York as the Council had already met and decided the Meru case. Seaton was thus left to present the Meru case alone until Kirilo arrived on 17 July, when the Council agreed to hear him as well. Together the two laid out the Meru case against their removal from Engare Nanyuki some 8,000 miles away.[45]

Seaton and Japhet were well paired. While Seaton capably laid the Meru case before the delegates in careful lawyerly prose, Kirilo followed with an impassioned and detailed plea for justice. Together they recounted the history of the case in precise detail, convincingly undermining the generalized assertions of the British representatives.[46]

[43] Kirilo Japhet (MHT 2); Rafaeli Mbise (MHT 3).
[44] Kirilo Japhet (MHT 2); Nelson, *Freemen of Meru*, 64–6.
[45] Kirilo Japhet (MHR 2); Japhet & Seaton, *Meru Land Case*, 27–8.
[46] The text of the original Meru petition is in United Nations, *Petitions*. Seaton and Kirilo's verbatim testimony before the Trusteeship Council, together with British responses and questions from delegates, is contained in Trusteeship Council, *Official Records*, 11th Session, 431st–432nd and 451st–452nd meetings, 30 June and 21–2 July 1952. Some of Japhet's testimony is also reprinted in Japhet and Seaton, *Meru Land Case*.

Seaton started on 30 June by reviewing the history of the land from its initial occupation by Meru to the German alienation and the repurchase of farms 31 and 328 by Meru. He then detailed Meru relations with the authorities following the publication of the Wilson Report, noting that while they had first been informed of the projected removals on 7 June 1949 by the District Commissioner, D.S. Troup, they were subsequently told by the Acting D.C., W.A. Forbes, on 17 June 1950 that they would not have to move from those lands they had acquired by purchase. Troup returned on 9 February 1951, however, to inform them that they would indeed have to move. It was at this point that Meru began to take the threat seriously, and submit their petitions to the Governor, the Colonial Secretary, and the UN Visiting Mission, but the government rebuffed their appeals and declined to delay the evictions pending the hearings before the Trusteeship Council. Citing figures far higher than those mentioned by the colonial authorities, Seaton then detailed the actual losses suffered by the 3,000 people living in Engare Nanyuki and Leguruki.

Seaton moved on to dispute the merits of the British case. He criticized the development of homogeneous blocks and the transfer of large blocks of land to European settlers as contributing to racial segregation, contrary to the government's stated policy stressing the 'paramountcy of native interests'. Noting that Wilson himself had called the ability of Afrikaner farmers into question, he queried whether they would develop the lands along modern lines, as Meru were already doing. Seaton then questioned why Meru were only being offered the same amount in compensation as they had paid for the land over twenty years previously. Finally, he contrasted the poor quality of land at Kingori with that at Engare Nanyuki and stressed the deep attachment of Meru to land in which they had invested so much of their time, money, and labour.

Lamb was quick to counter Seaton's statement. The British Representative indignantly denied that the scheme was racial, averring disingenuously that farms would be allocated to anyone with the knowledge and capital to run them. Only later did he admit under questioning that these were likely to be Europeans and that the administration did indeed intend to separate European and African farmers to avoid conflict. He stressed that Meru were receiving much more land, and of better quality, than they were giving up and that the redistribution and subsequent development would benefit all the people of Tanganyika. In response to Seaton's query about adequate compensation, Lamb doubted if Africans could possibly have improved the value of the land they had bought previously (in spite of the fact that Europeans were renowned for speculating in undeveloped land), and he belittled the losses Meru had suffered during the evictions. Finally, he charged that the protests were mounted by a small group of political agitators for their own purposes, and hence were not representative of Meru at large (notwithstanding the fact that the official Native Authority under Sante was then in disarray).

Lamb dealt in generalized assertions throughout and frequently replied to detailed evidence, such as that regarding Forbes's statement or the lack of consent by Meru authorities, with unsubstantiated assurances that he was sure that was not the case. But Seaton had the details to refute him. He cited British statements justifying racial separation and provided details of popular meetings during which Meru supported the petitioners and made the arrangements for Seaton and Kirilo to represent them in New York.

Kirilo testified during the second set of hearings in July. Speaking in Swahili, which Seaton translated, he first detailed the difficulties he had in obtaining his passport from the Tanganyikan authorities to apologize for his delay in addressing the Council. He then fleshed out Seaton's history in greater detail, noting that Meru had killed the first German missionaries because they feared the loss of their land. After the Germans had indeed taken much of their land, Meru had been compelled to pay for the two farms at Engare Nanyuki which had been taken from them, but they had been told at the time that the land would then be truly theirs. Now it was being taken from them once again. Kirilo recounted the contradictory messages from Troup and Forbes, the protests by the Chief and Native Authority over repossession of the two farms and the poor quality of land at Kingori, and the intention of the government to hand over the land in huge blocks to a few wealthy Afrikaners who already had extensive land holdings in Oldonyo Sambu. He recalled the tragic events from 17 November through to 12 December, again detailing the extensive personal losses suffered by Meru in Engare Nanyuki and Leguruki. Closing with a number of other cases where European settlers had taken Meru land, Kirilo pleaded with the Council to recognize their desperate need for land.

With Lamb gone, the British delegate on the Council, Sir Alan Burns, responded to Kirilo's statement. He immediately disputed Kirilo's account of his difficulties with the colonial authorities, while at the same time criticizing him for not coming while Lamb was still in New York. Otherwise, he merely reiterated Lamb's earlier assertions. When Kirilo produced notes of the meeting with Forbes, Burns denied them out of hand, asserting 'it is most unlikely that a tribe would take written records of a meeting between the District Commissioner and themselves. I have never heard of such a thing happening.'[47]

Unfortunately for the Meru, however, the Trustees and their allies dominated the Trusteeship Council and, with the exception of the Soviet delegate, the Council members generally voiced their support of the British authorities. The draft resolution was offered by New Zealand before Kirilo had even spoken, and it was adopted soon after he had finished. While regretting the failure to obtain clear consent from the Meru in advance, the use of force, and the destruction of Meru property, the Council generally acceded to the British *fait accompli* before they forwarded the Meru petition and the New Zealand resolution to the General Assembly for approval.[48]

Following their testimony, Kirilo and Seaton returned to London, where they met with members of the Fabian Society. Fenner Brockway arranged an interview for them at the Colonial Office, but to no avail. Seaton then returned to Moshi, where he informed Meru of the disappointing results of their petition and collected more money

[47] The notes were, of course, Rafaeli Mbise's. The Meru account of Forbes' statement is supported by the fact that Forbes was still questioning the legality of the removals three years later. W.A. Forbes, 'Correspondence Regarding Wameru Lands', 26 Oct–15 Dec 1953 (OCRP).

[48] The text of the resolution is in United Nations, Trusteeship Council, *Resolutions*, 452nd meeting, 22 July 1952, 468 (XI). The debate concerning it is in the *Official Records* for this 452nd meeting.

for the hearings in the General Assembly to come. In the meantime, Kirilo met with a number of other East Africans in London, including Julius Nyerere; Mbiyu Koinange, Fred Kubai and Munyua Waiyaki from Kenya; and Semakula Mulumba of Uganda.[49]

Kirilo and Seaton returned to New York in November for the meetings of the Fourth Committee, meeting as a committee of the whole General Assembly. Kirilo summarized his earlier testimony and was questioned extensively by the delegates before the Committee considered the Trusteeship Council's draft resolution. Before they could do so, however, a second draft resolution was submitted by Indonesia together with eight other Asian, Latin American, and African nations condemning the moves and calling for Britain to return the land they had seized to the Meru. This was countered, in turn, by a resolution offered by Canada, the Netherlands, Norway, and Sweden which condemned the moves, but did not require Britain to return the land. Given the much larger representation of the Third World and Soviet bloc in the General Assembly than in the Trusteeship Council, the Indonesian resolution passed overwhelmingly (32-17-3) and was forwarded to the General Assembly for action.[50]

There too, however, a counter-resolution was offered by the Canadian group. While both resolutions condemned British failure to obtain Meru consent, their use of force, and their destruction of Meru property – and called on Britain to provide generous compensation for Meru losses as well as training for Meru in modern agriculture and range management – the Canadian alternative accepted the removals as a *fait accompli* and, in the face of British statements that they would refuse to withdraw in any case, accepted their occupation. Voting was again along regional lines, with Afro-Asian, Soviet bloc, and most Latin American nations supporting the more critical Fourth Committee resolution, and European and some Latin American nations supporting the Canadian version. Neither could muster the two-thirds majority required to pass, however, and so both were defeated, leaving Meru with no official response whatsoever. The British had won by default.[51]

Kirilo paid a last visit to the Trusteeship Council before returning home in July 1953. He noted that Meru were still waiting for the United Nations to give them their land back. He would, of course, discourage people from resorting to force and anarchy, as Kenyans were doing, but what, he asked the members of the Council, should he tell his people? The silence of the delegates was deafening.[52]

While Meru had thus lost their case before the United Nations, the fact that the Indonesian resolution had garnered a majority of votes and that even the Canadian resolution had condemned British actions provided Meru with a moral victory and fuelled Meru militancy in disputes over land and local government to come. It also made the colonial authorities aware that their subsequent actions in Meru would be closely scrutinized by the next Visiting Mission, and made them somewhat more amenable to Meru

---

[49] Japhet & Seaton, *Meru Land Case*, 46–7; Kirilo Japhet (MHT 2).

[50] United Nations, Fourth Committee, *Official Records*, 7th Session, 286th–291st Meetings, 29 Nov – 3 Dec 1952, 259–304; *Resolutions*, A/C.4/L.242–5 and A/2342.

[51] United Nations, General Assembly, *Official Records*, 7th Session, 410th Meeting, 21 Dec 1952, 465–72; *Resolutions*, A/2342, L/2342, and A/L.141.

[52] United Nations, Trusteeship Council, *Official Records*, 12th Session, 476th Meeting, 7 Aug 1952, 260–61.

demands. It thus served to set the tone for the ensuing end game of colonial politics in Meru.

The Meru Citizens' Union and 1953 Constitution

By the time Kirilo returned from New York in July 1953, the Citizens' Union had finally forced the administration to abandon the politics of pseudo-traditionalism and to recognize it as representative of Meru opinion. Local administration in Meru had become increasingly ineffective following *Mangi* Sante's reinstatement in 1945. After the implementation of the Wilson Report it had broken down entirely as people simply refused to co-operate with either the chief or the colonial administration. The Citizens' Union became the only effective political body in the area, but it refused to deal with the administration as long as Sante remained chief and its members remained in exile. The administration finally bowed to the inevitable, and in late 1952 it brought back those deported during the 1948 controversy over the constitution, demanded Sante's resignation, and invited the Citizens' Union to help draw up a new constitution.[53]

Representatives of the Citizens' Union met with the District Officer, Michael Davies, and the Government Sociologist, Henry Fosbrooke, over the next five months and slowly worked out a new form of government more akin to British local councils than to colonial native authorities. The reconstituted Native Authority was to be composed of a chief, popularly elected and confirmed periodically by the Council, and a representative Council chosen directly by the people.[54]

Popular elections followed in May 1953. There were two candidates for Chief, Sylvanus Kaaya and Rafaeli Mbise, but little separated the two. Both were second-generation educated Christians and members of the Citizens' Union, and both had been at Engare Nanyuki at the time of the evictions, Sylvanus as a medical assistant and Rafaeli as an evangelist. Sylvanus was also a member of the royal Kaaya clan from heavily populated western Meru, while Rafaeli came from the less populated east. Sylvanus won the elections, but while Davies saw the result as a triumph for 'tradition', the results were not nearly so clear. If anything, Sylvanus was the better educated and more successful farmer of the two. With little to separate them, the election had been fought largely on regional grounds and each had polled strongly in his home area. In

---

[53] Umoja wa Raia Meru to Governor, 29 Feb 1952; DC/AD to PC/NP, 27 March 1952; PC/NP to MLG, 31 March 1952 (all in TNA: 69/47/AR); Arusha District, Annual Report, 1952 (TNA: 472/ANR/1); H. Mason & M.J. Davies, 'The Meru Problem' in DC/AD to MLG, 12 March 1955 [OCRP: MSS. Afr.s. 1513(r)].

[54] Minutes and Papers of Constitutional Committee (TNA: 12844); Arusha District, Annual Report, 1953 (TNA: 19415); Mason & Davies, 'The Meru Problem'. The MCU members on the committee were: Rafaeli Mbise (Vice-Chairman), Afraeli Leena, Gotthelfu Manjeka, Kaburure Seiyala, Kirilo Zakaria, Kishili Ngoi-yaro, Kufise Namita, Mang'alo Kilienanga, Marko Mwenda, Martini Long'oswa, Mbaruku Oringai, Mose Sindela, Nathanaeli Suruve, Ndetaulwa Metuo, Petro Leena, and Ndetaulwa (Gamaliel) Sablak (Secretary). Rafaeli had led the movement at Engare Nanyuki; Afraeli, Marko, and Mbaruku had been deported in 1948; and Gamaliel was the Chairman of the Citizens' Union.

subsequent elections for the Council, members of the MCU took all the seats.[55]

The colonial administration's problems were not over, however, as Meru continued to refuse to co-operate with the administration. When an experienced Social Development Officer moved into Poli in 1953 to attempt to allay their suspicions of the government, people ignored his greetings, refused to sell him food, and physically threatened him and his servants. And when Anton Nelson, an American hired by Meru to help with their coffee, also moved into Meru at the end of 1954, the District Commissioner told him:

> The WaMeru are one of the most backward tribes in the whole territory. They have some of the best land and we have gone to great trouble to give them more, but they don't seem to appreciate all that we do for them. You can't trust them for one minute. They are sullen, impolite, ungrateful. When I drive through their country, I keep my car window rolled up or like as not somebody will spit in my face. At least I don't have to live among them. Good luck. You'll need it.[56]

The administration took a number of steps to gain Meru confidence. It had allocated £46,000 sterling in compensation due to the Meru for tsetse clearing, water supplies, schools, and health clinics in the new resettlement areas, but under pressure from the new Council, it redirected the money towards developing schools, roads and bridges, water supplies, and social services in central Meru. Over £60,000 was ultimately spent on development in Meru, 40 per cent of it in the central districts. The number of primary schools was nearly doubled, and the first two middle schools were opened. A Social Development Officer was appointed to facilitate the organization of women's clubs, adult literacy classes, sports clubs, a local newspaper, and self-help road construction.[57]

The administration also moved to resolve outstanding land disputes, such as the ongoing problem over Meru squatters on Focsaner's estate in Singisi Poli. Meru had been living on the farm since German times. Focsaner had first tried to evict them in 1948 so that he could sell the farm, but the administration had persuaded him to hold off in the light of Meru unrest over the Wilson Report. Focsaner tried again a year later, but Meru refused to leave or to pay him rent. A guerrilla struggle ensued, with Focsaner fencing off Meru land and blocking their cattle routes while Meru cut the fences and extended their occupation of the farm. The government finally bought the disputed 240 acres for Meru in the face of impending court action because it 'could not risk a judgment unfavourable to the tribe, in view of the Engare Nanyuki evictions', and when that did not solve the problem, it bought the remaining 760 acres as well.[58]

[55] Ironically, Davies actually preferred Rafaeli because of his moderating influence on the committee's deliberations. Yesterday's 'dangerous agitators' had become today's responsible leaders. APC/NP to MLG, 23 July 1953; DC/AD to PC/NP, 27 July 1953 (TNA:32593); Emanuel Kasengye N'nko (MHT 5); Arusha District, Annual Report, 1953 (TNA: 19415); Nelson, *Freemen of Meru*, 71-2.

[56] Nelson, *Freemen of Meru*, 91. See also Mason & Davies, 'Meru Problem', 21; James L. Brain, 'A Bridge in Meru', *Community Development Journal*, 4(1969), 17-18; Arusha District, Annual Report, 1954 (TNA: 472/ANR/1); Northern Province, Annual Reports, 1954-59 (TNA: 471/R.3/2).

[57] PC/NP to MLG, 29 July 1952 and subsequent correspondence (TNA: 42418); Arusha District, Annual Reports, 1952-3 (TNA: 472/- & 472/ANR/1); Northern Province, Annual Reports, 1952-5 (TNA: 19415); Mason & Davies, 'Meru Problem', 21-25; DC to District Team, 3 Nov 1956 (TNA; 9/8/2)

[58] Minutes, Meeting of District Reps, 8 April 1948 (TNA: 9/8/1); PC/NP to DC/AD, 17 May 1949 (TNA:

The climate of opinion slowly started to improve during the mid-1950s, but Meru continued their protests over Engare Nanyuki nonetheless. Kirilo threatened to re-occupy the lands in 1953, and the Council formally demanded their return a year later. Ironically, several of the European settlers who had taken up farms in the area became allies of the Meru when they protested to the UN Visiting Mission in 1954 that the land was unsuitable for European mixed farming or ranching and proposed exchanging it with Meru for land in Kingori. The cost of clearing land at Engare Nanyuki had proved prohibitive, the settlers complained, and it was too broken for large-scale mech-anized farming, while Meru nearby were able to produce excellent crops of maize using hand cultivation. Kingori, by contrast, was drier, but more open and better suited for European ranching. A government report issued the following year confirmed the set-tlers' claims. Of the six farms reallocated to Europeans, only two had been successfully occupied as the soil was too stony and shallow for mechanical cultivation, and the scrub and high floride content of the water made cattle ranching equally problematic. The report recommended that the southern 4,000 acres be returned to Meru farmers, who could better exploit its fertile pockets. The administration subsequently returned one of the farms it had been unable to lease to Meru; Meru purchased another two; and Engare Nanyuki itself was finally returned to the Meru, complete with a new church, which Meru dedicated on Easter Day 1962.[59]

The Co-operative, the Church, and New Forms of Farming

In the meantime, significant changes were occurring elsewhere in Meru as well. Kirilo had met an American Quaker and builder, Anton (Ax) Nelson, while he was in New York and invited him to work for the Meru to help with their coffee. Nelson arrived in 1954 and immediately negotiated lower brokers' commissions, comparable to those paid by Europeans, for Meru coffee. He encouraged Meru to start their own co-operative society as well, thus overcoming decades of Meru suspicion, and the Meru Growers' Co-operative Society (later Meru Co-operative Union) was formed the following year under the dynamic leadership of Bonifatio Urio and Sangito Kaaya. The co-operative was largely responsible for improving Meru cultivation techniques and quality control,

(58 cont.) 69/238); Arusha District, Annual Report, 1954 (TNA: 472/ANR/1); Northern Province, Annual Report, 1954 (TNA: 471/R.3/2); Mason & Davies, 'Meru Problem'; *United Nations Visiting Mission*, 58.

Focsaner himself was clearly less than sympathetic to Meru concerns, as he told the UN Visiting Mission in 1954:

... the Africans have got out of hand. They don't work, they are stealing day and night.... They are a bad lot. Ordinary punishment is not adequate for them. They get two or three months in prison – but the African doesn't mind that, he just laughs and says, 'I'm going to King George's hotel.'... We don't know what to do. We tried everything to come to peace with them. They say that the Government had no right to sell our properties because the land belonged to their grandfathers. But that's no business of ours.... Conditions are getting so bad that I don't go to bed without a firearm beside my bed. Not only myself, but all of the Europeans here. I hate to see so much land given back to the natives.... The world is getting so difficult now.

59 *United Nations Visiting Mission*, 57; Tanganyika, Legislative Council, *The Sanya Corridor* (Dar es Salaam, 1955); Nelson, *Freemen of Meru*, 153, 215-17.

and Meru incomes increased fourfold as a result. Over the following years, the Co-operative branched out to establish its own retail stores and credit union; it assessed its members to improve roads, transport, and education; and it imported new crop varieties and grade dairy cattle to improve Meru herds.[60]

At the same time, the local Lutheran Church was flourishing. Under the leadership of Zakariah Urio since 1939, it grew to 15,000 members and became fully independent of mission control in 1958. The number of parishes in Meru have continued to grow since then, and Meru has subsequently come to constitute a separate district and now diocese within the Evangelical Lutheran Church of Tanzania.[61]

Meru also began moving off the mountain during this period to pasture their cattle and establish farms for annual crops on the plains. While those evicted from Engare Nanyuki and Leguruki continued to refuse to settle in Kingori, other Meru did start to move there from the early 1950s. By 1954 several large farms had been staked out, including one by the former chief, Sante, after he had resigned as chief, and people were applying for loans to buy tractors to raise wheat. By the end of the decade, most of the area had been occupied and people were pushing south into Maji ya Chai and Ongadongishu. Many of those who had been in the forefront of the Land Case, the overhaul of local government and the establishment of the co-operative were also deeply involved in expansion. It became fairly common for successful coffee farmers on Meru to have a small coffee farm on the mountain and a larger farm raising maize and beans on the plain. Today Kirilo Japhet has a couple of acres of coffee and bananas on the mountain, 60 acres in Sakila where he raises maize with his sons, and another 100 acres at KIA (Kilimanjaro International Airport) where he grows seed beans.

Blood on the Land – Reprise

Meru had struggled tenaciously throughout the 1950s to regain their lands in Engare Nanyuki, bringing local administration in Meru to a standstill, calling Britain's good name as a trustee into question before the United Nations, and stirring the nationalist movement in Tanganyika into action. One could understand such militancy if *kihamba* land in the central coffee zone had been threatened, but Engare Nanyuki certainly did not seem like an auspicious site for triggering such a contentious political dispute. Wilson described it as 'this "bomb field" covered with the great and small hummocks of rock belched out in the final eruption of Mount Meru', and European agronomists generally considered it dry, barren and useless.[62]

Meru, however, viewed it differently. As bananas and coffee increasingly supplanted pastures and annual fields on the central slopes, Engare Nanyuki and Leguruki provided vital alternatives for pasturing cattle and raising annual crops. There were extensive grassland, water, and salt deposits for cattle; riverine plains for irrigated farming; scattered fertile pockets for rain-fed farming; and even some upland areas suitable for

[60] See Chapter 8.
[61] Danielson, *Forty Years with Christ*.
[62] *Arusha-Moshi Lands Commission*, 90.

bananas and coffee. The two areas were settled by elderly coffee farmers who sent their sons there to raise maize, beans, and cattle for the home market. They were thus closely integrated socially and economically with the densely populated central Meru area, and they played crucial roles in the overall process of coping with land shortage. When the colonial authorities proposed to realienate these areas, then, they threatened more than just Meru settled there; they threatened all Meru, not least the influential coffee farmers in central Meru.[63]

Meru had also taxed themselves heavily to buy the two farms' freehold, and they had been promised that the land would be legally theirs forever. They had then invested their time and labour in the land, converting it from bush to farms that belonged to the families who had domesticated them. Some even became *vihamba*. The Meru claim was thus not only economic; it was also legal and moral. Land 'bought' with one's labour could not simply be exchanged for other land, even if it was of equivalent value.

Land and production were not the only issues, however. The Wilson Report had come on the heels of a number of other issues, including controversies over chieftainship and the structure of local government, regulation and marketing of coffee, the crop cess, and the position of squatters on settlers' estates. Each was a potent issue in itself; together they contributed to a growing political consciousness and militancy among Meru which led to the breakdown of local government and the formation of the Citizens' Union.

The Union was organized by younger Christians and coffee farmers who combined traditional moral appeals with Christian and liberal ones to challenge colonial hegemony. They cited the responsibilities that went with wealth to criticize the chief or Meru investment in the land to prevent its alienation, on the one hand, and claimed consent of the governed and freehold ownership of land on the other. They charged their colonial rulers with violating the principles of 'trusteeship' embedded in the United Nations Charter and asserted that they were trying to impose South African-style 'apartheid'. No longer bound by the politics of pseudo-traditionalism, they usurped the role of the Native Authority and appealed directly to the colonial authorities in Dar es Salaam and London, and beyond them to the United Nations.

The issues for Meru were thus economic, political, and moral. Meru had fought for their land and their principles, resolutely avoiding compromise, while many of the Europeans involved in the case were punished for their sins. One of the settlers, Maj. S.E. du Toit, fell off a ladder and died, allegedly while climbing on to his roof to watch the church at Engare Nanyuki burn. Several other officials and settlers involved in the case died subsequently, provoking Fosbrooke and Mason to ask Rafaeli Mbise if Meru had caused their deaths. Rafaeli's response focused on the immorality of the officials:

> I asked them if they knew about sin, really knew about sin. They said yes. I asked if they had seen people praying before they had been evicted. They said yes. Then I said they had been praying to God for help since the Europeans were not going to help them. The Lord must have heard their prayers, because he made the Europeans pay for their sins. The whites had burned our houses, destroyed our crops, and arrested our people. Troup drove the people

---

[63] Japhet and Seaton, *Meru Land Case*, 11; Nelson, *Freemen of Meru*, 15–16; see also Chapter 7.

away and jailed them.... So he was paying for his sins for jailing and torturing people and throwing them off the land.[64]

Rafaeli's question echoes across 55 years of Arusha and Meru history. Then the warriors of Talala had killed the first two missionaries to settle on Mount Meru in order to cleanse the land of evil brought by the Germans. Now it was the Europeans who were paying for their own sins against the peoples of Mount Meru. The idiom had changed from witchcraft to sin, and Talala had actively combatted witchcraft by clubbing witches to death while the Europeans themselves suffered for their own sins. But had not Eliyahu likened Talala's moral crusades to those of the missionaries by calling them 'the Europeans of Arusha'? The language of discourse might have changed, but it remained a profoundly moral discourse nevertheless. The land was still afflicted with evil, evil that had to be purged if Meru and Arusha were to prosper.

Access to land remained the most potent issue in the Meru political lexicon, just as it had been 55 years before when, as Kirilo Japhet reminded the members of the United Nations, Arusha and Meru warriors killed the first missionaries because they threatened their land. The intervening years had only heightened the issue, as extensive land alienation and increasing population combined to create widespread shortage, threatening people's continued existence. There was, indeed, still 'Blood on our Land'.[65]

Land thus continued to be deeply embedded in Meru moral economy, but that morality was now grounded in Christian faith as well as in more traditional values. Meru Christians were deeply involved in the Land Case, and the Lutheran missionaries supported them as well. The Superintendent of the Mission, Elmer Danielson, expressed his concerns to the authorities before the evictions that the land issue would further exacerbate tensions between Europeans and Africans, and he reiterated them to the UN Visiting Mission afterwards. Shortage of land and the inability of people to provide for their families were acute personal problems in Meru. The evictions had been a serious political mistake, and he pleaded with the administration to mount a new inquiry to right the wrongs done to the Meru.[66]

---

[64] Rafaeli Mbise (MHT 3). See also Danielson, *Forty Years with Christ*, 147, who tends to agree with Rafaeli's interpretation.

[65] The title of I.R. Mbise's novel on the Meru Land Case (Dar es Salaam, 1974). The stories of the murder of the missionaries and of the evictions from Engare Nanyuki continue to feature prominently in Meru traditions and to resonate with Meru concerns today, as shown by Meru evoking them in the struggle against the formation and extension of the Arusha National Park. Roderick Neumann, 'The Social Origins of Natural Resource Conflict in Arusha National Park, Tanzania' (Ph.D., Berkeley, 1992).

[66] *United Nations Visiting Mission*, 59; Danielson, *Forty Years with Christ*, 138–49.

Conclusion

The colonial period in Arusha and Meru drew to a close much as it had begun, in a struggle over land and its meaning. But much had changed in the interim. The peoples of Mount Meru adopted increasingly intensive agricultural practices to cope with their growing populations and actively participated in an expanding market economy. New means of acquiring wealth by raising coffee and other cash crops supplanted cattle raiding, and a new class of educated Christian coffee farmers assumed political leadership as the values Meru and Arusha lived by became transformed by Christianity and Western education.

In the 1890s, a successful Meru or Arusha elder had based his reputation on having a substantial *kihamba* or *engisaka* on which he grew bananas, maize, and beans; a large family clustered around him; and a number of cattle which he exchanged with others or slaughtered for communal feasts. By 1960 his reputation was more likely to rest on his education and job; his roles in the Lutheran Church, Co-operative, and Citizens' Union; and his income from raising coffee on a small *kihamba/engisaka* surrounding his cement house and his production of annual food crops on the plains.

Dramatic as these changes were, however, many things remained the same. Rights to land continued to define people's social identities and be jealously guarded. Having one's own *kihamba* or *engisaka* and providing food for one's family took precedence over market factors, even as market conditions played an increasing role in family decisions regarding production. Expansion on to the plains divided family farms into specialized components for the production of bananas and coffee, annual crops, and milk, but far-flung fields remained integrated into family enterprises employing largely family labour. And exchange and distribution of wealth remained the hallmarks of responsible and effective leadership.

Christian elders gathered their sons around them on their shrinking plots and worried if there would be enough land for them all. Relations with others were as likely to be based on exchanges of cattle and wives as on fellow membership in the church or co-operative. Political appeals continued to be based as much on the responsibilities of those with power to ensure that their followers prospered as on their adherence to

democratic principles. And the peoples of Mount Meru continued to stress the importance of raising their own bananas, maize, beans, vegetables, and milk on their own
farms using family labour over that of growing coffee or running tractor farms on the
plains. Arusha and Meru may have become Christians and cash farmers, but Lutheran
Christianity had become Arusha and Meru religions; farming remained a family enterprise; and both peoples retained a profoundly moral sense of economic justice and communal responsibility. The historical path from the murder of the first missionaries to
the Meru Land Case had been long and tortuous, but land, one's relations with it, and
one's relations to others through it retained significant moral as well as economic value
throughout.

Socio-economic change on Mount Meru resulted from a complex array of factors,
including resource endowments; population growth; colonial policies regarding land,
labour, and authority; changes in the broader regional and national economies; and, not
least, the social values and practices of Arusha and Meru themselves. Meru and Arusha
largely shared environmental, economic, and political factors, along with similar conceptions of economic justice and social responsibility, and thus many of their responses
paralleled one another. Where they diverged was in the particular cultural understandings they each brought to their problems, the complex array of values and practices that
gave substance and meaning to their lives.

An example is their responses to increasing population. Population relative to available land expanded rapidly in both societies; both were similarly constrained by colonial
alienation of land and attempts to control land use; both exploited the same montane
environment; and both participated in the same regional economy. But there were significant differences in how people in the two societies responded. Population grew
more rapidly in Arusha due to their success in raiding their neighbours for cattle and
women in the late nineteenth century, and successive age-sets rapidly colonized the
slopes as each generation of warriors retired and settled down to clear new land to farm.
With the end of raiding and closure of the mountain frontiers in the early twentieth
century, however, Arusha turned inward to intensified mixed agricultural production
integrating cattle, bananas, and annual crops. Meru population, by contrast, grew more
slowly in the nineteenth century, and they expanded more evenly as lineages slowly
increased in numbers and filled existing land, forcing younger members to seek land
elsewhere. And in the twentieth century, Meru preferred coffee to mixed farming as a
means of meeting the needs of their increasing population. Both peoples thus expanded
across the mountain slopes and intensified their agricultural production in parallel but
different ways to bring about their own distinctive agricultural revolutions.

Meru and Arusha responded to political and economic changes occurring around
them in their own terms. They embraced the expanding market economy as agricultural
producers, but they were loath to enter it as workers, much to the frustration of the settlers and colonial administration, and they continued to invest market profits in cattle,
wives, feasts, and other social investments.

Their responses also reveal the multifaceted and contradictory nature of the historical context(s) in which they acted, including complex interactions among and
between local/indigenous *and* foreign/endogenous factors. The imposition of colonial

rule in 1900 imposed significant constraints on the expanding social and economic environment of the nineteenth century. The Germans, and later British, alienated vast tracts of land and clamped an 'iron ring' of settler estates around the mountain that foreclosed the possibilities of future Meru and Arusha expansion and dramatically affected local land use patterns. They fostered the development of a market economy and manipulated pseudo-traditional authorities to try to force people to pay taxes, work for Europeans, and change the ways they farmed. And they introduced new beliefs and social practices, including evangelical Christianity and education, to challenge local ones.

The colonial impact was not monolithic, however, and its hegemony was frequently ambiguous, contradictory, and contested. Administrators, settlers, and missionaries all entertained different goals and conflicting notions of their 'civilizing mission', of appropriate means of economic development, or of the proper exercise of political authority. While all believed in the innate superiority of European ways and shared a paternalistic approach to Africans, for example, each interpreted 'African interests' differently, often seeing themselves as protecting Africans from the others.

Important as colonial factors were, however, Arusha and Meru actually experienced such outside influences in the contexts of their own lives and historical experiences. New influences and ideas were perceived, interpreted, appropriated, and transformed in accord with local values, practices and needs. Thus colonial chiefs sought to employ the powers they enjoyed as members of the colonial administration to enhance their own positions at the same time as they sought to exercise those powers in socially responsible ways to ensure the well-being of others. Christian converts, initially estranged from their friends and relatives, subsequently sought to better the lives of others through developing churches, schools, co-operatives and political unions while simultaneously adapting Christian beliefs to local practices. And Arusha and Meru farmers responded to the shrinking availability of land by selectively adapting new crops, techniques, and land use patterns to existing social and agricultural practices. Meru and Arusha differed on how they perceived and interpreted the problems, influences, and opportunities facing them, however, and so they sought to appropriate them in different ways in accord with the lessons each drew from their own historical experience and tradition.

The concept of 'tradition' is a fraught one in Africa. Viewed by the British as both static and prescriptive, colonial administrators sought to enshrine 'tradition' as a rock against the tides of socio-economic change threatening to engulf African societies. But it proved more dynamic than they thought, as Arusha and Meru continued to deploy tradition creatively to meet their changing conditions and needs. What the British failed to appreciate was the dynamic interpretative role that tradition plays in society as people seek to understand and respond to problems of the present in terms of lessons drawn from their past. Tradition is thus both persistent and changing, a kind of historical running average, as the lessons of the past are continually reinterpreted in the context of a present that is itself in the process of being assimilated into the past. Those who focus narrowly on 'the invention of tradition' miss this point; 'tradition' is not simply invented to serve current interests, but is an endless dialogue between the past and the present in which people continually employ, debate, and reassess the relevance of past experience for the present.[1]

While tradition is thus fluid and dynamic, it can also be remarkably persistent, informing and guiding the terms of debate for long periods of time. Just as we speak of an ongoing Judaeo-Christian tradition, Jan Vansina has found deep undercurrents of thought persisting through two thousand years of Equatorial African history.[2] Tradition thus has real power to influence and control the terms of the debate as well as being influenced and transformed by them. We can thus speak of both the continuity of tradition *and* its transformation as part of a single unending process of renovation, innovation, and transformation.

Changing conceptions of ethnicity are a case in point. Meru and Arusha each had their own distinctive languages, forms of social organization, and ethnic identities, and they opposed one another bitterly through the late nineteenth century over control of cattle and land, as well as the people to work them. Such ethnic identities became heightened with Arusha successes, as many Meru were assimilated into Arusha society and Meru warriors joined their Arusha age-mates in raids elsewhere. Distinct Arusha and Meru identities were thus clearly formed by the time the Germans appeared on Mount Meru and first began to manipulate them to create pseudo-traditional chiefs and customary laws. Definitions of Arusha and Meru ethnicities slowly began to change, however, with the assimilation of new defining characteristics of identity in the twentieth century. Initially, for example, both peoples excluded Christians from the ranks of adult Meru and Arusha, but over time, membership in the Lutheran church, together with education and literacy, slowly came to be incorporated into their identities.

When Arusha or Meru evoked tradition, they did so in the form of stories that they felt encapsulated and conveyed enduring truths gained from their own historical experience, many of which we have generalized here as comprising a 'moral economy'. Every person had a right to land and the fruits of his or her own labour. Labour on the land conveyed rights in it. Hard work was rewarded with abundant crops, wealth, a large family, and the respect of others. Those who enjoyed wealth had an obligation to ensure the commonweal of others, since anti-social acts directed against others had the potential of bringing physical disaster on everyone. Together these comprised an 'Arusha' or 'Meru Ethic', in contrast to the colonialists' 'Protestant Ethic', and these were the terms in which they assessed and contested the changes brought by colonial rule. Thus, when German occupation seemed to threaten their very physical existence, they sought to purge their society of the evil responsible for the multiple disasters afflicting them by killing the first two missionaries to settle among them. Or, when the British evoked norms of private property to uphold settlers' rights, they responded with

---

[1] The basic text is T.O. Ranger & E.J. Hobsbawm (eds), *The Invention of Tradition* (Cambridge, 1992), but see Ranger's considered response to the often over-enthusiastic and naive endorsement the idea has received in T.O. Ranger & O. Vaughan (eds) *Legitimacy and the State in Twentieth Century Africa* (Houndmills, 1993). For parallel debates on ethnicity, see Leroy Vail (ed.), *The Creation of Tribalism in Southern Africa* (London, 1989) and Thomas Spear & Richard Waller (eds), *Being Maasai* (London, 1993).

[2] Jan Vansina, *Paths in the Rainforests* (Madison and London, 1990).

moral claims to subsistence and the duty of those in authority to assure prosperity. Their moral critique of colonialism was, then, as important as their political and economic ones.

Cultural values not only set Meru and Arusha apart from and against their German and British rulers; they also set them apart from one another. The first Meru to settle on Mount Meru in the seventeenth century found an environment similar to the one they had left on Mount Kilimanjaro, and so they were easily able to adapt their own agricultural practices, based on the irrigated cultivation of bananas, maize, and beans, and forms of social organization, based on descent, to the familiar environment. When pastoral Arusha Maasai first settled on Mount Meru in the early nineteenth century, however, they had to adapt to the radically new practice of mountain agriculture. Rather than simply adopting established Meru practices, Arusha adapted their own pastoral traditions to their new agricultural needs, transferring principles of ownership from cattle to land, evolving localized sections of the age-sets as a basis for local authority, and continuing to identify as Maasai.

Similarly, when both peoples were faced with increasing population and sharp limits on land in the twentieth century, Arusha initially favoured investments in cattle and more intensive forms of mixed farming, while Meru chose coffee as a means of intensifying their production. Such distinctions remain to this day, as Meru and Arusha have each chosen to pursue parallel patterns of development while developing their own religious, co-operative, and administrative institutions to achieve them. Thus each has developed its own diocese independent of the other within the Lutheran Church; the co-operative movement split into separate Meru and Arusha components; and attempts by the government to form a single local government remain a contentious issue. Similar as Arusha and Meru are to one another today, they continue to see themselves and their worlds in historically and culturally distinctive ways.

Explanations of socio-economic change in Africa usually focus either on diffusion of cultural practices from one people or area to another or on the determining role of material factors. Thus, when Arusha pastoralists first settled on Mount Meru in the early nineteenth century, one might have expected them either to adopt established Meru practices or to respond in a predictably similar manner to the common environment they shared, just as other Maasai refugees had done elsewhere. But economic factors were not the only ones determining Arusha responses and Meru exerted remarkably little influence on them, as they adapted their own cultural practices to the needs of mountain agriculture. Material factors may have determined that Arusha would change, but they did not prescribe how they should do so.

A similar situation developed in the twentieth century as both peoples faced increasing population pressure relative to available land. Capitalizing on common resource endowments of fertile volcanic soils, a rich variety of crops and micro-environments in which to raise them, and abundant rainfall and water supplies year round, both Meru and Arusha chose to intensify their agricultural production by expanding the cultivation of bananas in the central mountain districts, planting pastures in annual crops while moving cattle into stalls or on to the plains, pushing the margins of annual crop cultivation to the upper and lower reaches of the mountain and out on to the adjacent plains, and adopting new cash crops like coffee. There were, however, subtle but significant changes in how Arusha and Meru pursued these innovations, with more densely settled Arusha continuing to favour mixed farming over coffee.

Given the increasingly tight straits in which both peoples found themselves, it is not surprising that land and the values that it held for people should have been the focus of their ongoing conflicts with the colonial government. Even here, however, the two each pursued their own strategies. Meru favoured the development of coffee on the central mountain slopes, while shifting cattle and some annual crops into the northeast highlands around Engare Nanyuki. Thus, when the British threatened to expropriate the highlands in the late 1940s, Meru organized aggressively to keep land that had become a vital component of their overall economy. Arusha, by contrast, continued to cultivate their relations with pastoral Maasai, and exploited them to pasture cattle on the plains and to obtain additional farming land around Monduli. Their main conflicts with the government came over the continuing expulsions from Arusha town, the centre of early Arusha settlement, and over political control over access to new lands on Monduli and the plains.

The evictions from Engare Nanyuki symbolized the immorality of the wider colonial order for Meru, and they continue to evoke them today in continuing struggles with the Tanzanian government over the establishment of the Arusha National Park. At the same time, Arusha felt that a colonial chief, illegally imposed on them by the colonial authorities, had illegitimately allocated land newly available on Monduli to those who already possessed abundant land instead of to those who needed and deserved it. Similarly, they felt that the township authority had unjustly displaced Arusha from land cleared and settled by their ancestors, a dispute that continues to fester today in attempts by the government to allow people in the township to purchase Arusha land. Each people thus continues to act within the context of their own cultural values, historical experiences and traditions to the common problems facing them.

Bibliography

Abbreviations

AD	Arusha District
AHT	Arusha Historical Traditions
AO	Agricultural Officer
BRALUP	Bureau of Resource Assessment & Land Use Planning
CS	Chief Secretary
DC	District Commissioner
DO	District Officer
DSM	Dar es Salaam
ELMB	*Evangelisch-Lutherisches Missionsblatt*
(IJ)AHS	*(International Journal of) African Historical Studies*
JAH	*Journal of African History*
JRGS	*Journal of the Royal Geographical Society*
MHT	Meru Historical Traditions
NP	Northern Province
OCRP	Oxford Colonial Records Project, Rhodes House
PC	Provincial Commissioner
PRGS	*Proceedings of the Royal Geographical Society*
PRO	Public Record Office, London
SUGIA	*Sprache und Geschichte in Afrika*
TNA	Tanzania National Archives, Dar es Salaam
TNR	*Tanganyika/Tanzania Notes and Records*
UDSM	University of Dar es Salaam
UMFC	United Methodist Free Church
VO	Veterinary Officer

Archives and Libraries

Arusha Regional Resource Centre, Arusha
    Arusha Planning and Village Development Project
    reports and papers
    maps and aerial photos
Henry Fosbrooke Papers, Duluti

Lutheran Theological College, Makumira
    Evangelisch-Lutherisches Missionsblatt, Vols. 51–69(1896–1916)
    publications of the Leipzig Evangelical Lutheran Mission
    theses (listed individually below)
    R. Harjula, books and papers
Public Record Office (PRO), London
    CO 691, Tanganyika, Correspondence, 1916–1950
Rhodes House Library, Oxford Colonial Records Project (OCRP)
    Frances J. Bagshawe, Tribal Studies & Diaries
    L.B. Boyd-Moss, Diaries
    W.A. Forbes, Papers
    Clement Gilman, Tanganyika Diaries, 1905–43
    A.W.M. Griffiths, 'Land Tenure, Moshi District' & 'Report of the Land Use Survey Team
    on the Chagga Expansion Area South of Mt. Kilimanjaro'
    F.C. Hallier, Reports, Memorandum, & Diaries
    H. Mason & M.J. Davies, 'The Meru Problem'
    P.E. Mitchell, Diaries
    Basil J. Stubbins, Safari Diary & District Annual Reports
    Richard Thornton, Papers
    Sir Mark Wilson, Papers
Tanzania National Archives (TNA)
    German Records (series G31, G15)
    Secretariat
    Northern Province (series 69, 471)
    Arusha District (series 9, 439, 472)
    Kirilo Japhet papers
University of Dar es Salaam Library (UDSM)
    Province and District Books
    Hans Cory papers (includes papers by P.H. Gulliver & C.I. Meek)
    Bureau of Resource Assessment and Land Use Planning papers (BRALUP)
University of Dar es Salaam, Department of History
    Pangani Valley Historical Documents
    Economic History Research Papers

Official Publications

East African Statistical Department
    African Population of Tanganyika Territory, 1950, 1953
    Tanganyikan African Population Census, 1957
Evangelisch-Lutherisches Mission, Leipzig
    Evangelisch-Lutherisches Missionsblatt, Vols. 51–69 (1896–1916)
Tanganyika Territory
    Department of Agriculture, *Annual Reports*
    Provincial Commissioners, *Annual Reports*
    Blue Books
    Report on the Native Census, 1921
    Census of the Native Population of Tanganyika Territory, 1931

African Population of Tanganyika Territory, 1948
Report of the Arusha-Moshi Lands Commission, 1947
Arusha-Moshi Lands Commission, *Redistribution of Lands in the Arusha District*, 1949
Legislative Council, *The Meru Land Problem*, 1952
Legislative Council, *The Sanya Corridor*, 1955
Tanzania, Bureau of Statistics
Village Economic Surveys, 1961–62
1967 Population Census
Provisional Estimates of Fertility, Mortality, and Population Growth for Tanzania, 1968
Recorded Population Changes, 1948–1967
1978 Population Census
1978 Population Census, Preliminary Report
United Nations, Trusteeship Council
Official Records, 11th & 12th sessions
Petitions, T/Pet 2/99 and Add 1 to 7
Resolutions, 486(XI)
Report on the United Nations Visiting Mission to the Trust Territories of East Africa
United Nations, General Assembly, Fourth Committee
Official Records, 7th session
Resolutions, A/C.4/L242–245, A/2342
United Nations, General Assembly
Official Records, Plenary Meetings, 7th session

Interviews

Original tapes and translated transcripts are deposited at the University of Dar es Salaam Department of History and the Oral Data Archives, Indiana University. Copies of English translations are available from the author.

Arusha Historical Traditions (AHT)
1. Mosingo ole Meipusu, Kiranyi.
2. Yohanes ole Kauwenara, Kirevi.
3. Lodenaga Lotisia, Kirevi.
4. Ngole ole Njololoi, Sepeko.
5. Ngoilenya Wuapi, Kimunyak.
6. Loingoruaki Meshili, Sinon.
7. Jonathan Kidale, Sinon.
8. Eliyahu Lujas Meiliari, Olepolos.
9. Sabaya & Juma Nteipoi Loloiliang'a, Arusha Chini.

Meru Historical Traditions (MHT)
1. Anton Lukas Kaaya, Akeri.
2. Kirilo Japhet Ayo, Poli.
3. Rafaeli Mbise, Leguruki.
4. Japhet Ayo, Nkoaranga.
5. Emanuel Kasengye N'nko, Engare Nanyuki.

Books, Articles, Dissertations, and Papers

'Agro-Economic Zones of North Eastern Tanzania' (BRALUP Research Reports, No.16).

Acland, J.D., *East African Crops*. London: Longman, 1971.

Adams, W.M. & D.M. Anderson, 'Irrigation before Development: Indigenous and Induced Change in Agricultural Water Management in East Africa', *African Affairs*, 87 (1988), 519–35.

Adams, W.M. & R.C. Carter, 'Small Scale Irrigation in Sub-Saharan Africa', *Progress in Physical Geography*, 11 (1987), 1–27.

Ambler, Charles H., *Kenyan Communities in the Age of Imperialism: The Central Region in the Late Nineteenth Century*. New Haven: Yale, 1988.

Anderson, David M., 'Cultivating Pastoralists: Ecology and Economy among the Il Chamus of Baringo, 1840–1980' in D. Johnson & D.M. Anderson (eds), *The Ecology of Survival* (Boulder: Westview, 1988), 241–60.

—, 'Agriculture and Irrigation Technology at Lake Baringo in the Nineteenth Century', *Azania*, 24 (1989), 84–97.

Arens, William, 'Tribalism and the Poly-ethnic Rural Community', *Man*, ns 8 (1973), 441–50.

Baker, R.E.D. & N.W. Simmonds, 'Bananas in East Africa', *Empire J. of Experimental Agriculture*, 19 (1951), 283–90; 20 (1952), 66–76.

Baral, Bishnu, et al., 'In Search of Water: A Study of Farming Systems in the Lowlands of Arumeru District Tanzania' (Wageningen, ICRA, 1993).

Baroin, Catherine, 'Le conflit religieux de 1990–1993 chez les Rwa: sécession dans un diocèse luthérien de Tanzanie Nord' (Travaux et Documents, Institut Français de Recherche en Afrique, No. 15, 1994).

Bassett, T.J. & D.E. Crummey (eds), *Land in African Agrarian Systems*. Madison: Wisconsin, 1993.

Baumann, Oscar, *Usambara und seine Nachbargebiete*. Berlin: Dietrich Reimer, 1891.

—, *Durch Massailand zur Nilquelle*. Berlin: Dietrich Reimer, 1894.

—, *Die Kartographischen Ergebnisse den Massai-Expedition des Deutschen Antisklaverei Comités* (Ergänzungsheft 111, *Petermanns Mitteilungen*). Gotha: H. Haack, 1894.

Beidelman, T.O., 'The Baraguyu', *TNR*, 55 (1960), 245–78.

Benson, J. Stanley, 'A Study of the Religious Beliefs and Practices of the Maasai Tribe and Implications on the Work of the Evangelical Lutheran Church in Tanzania' (Master's thesis, Sacred Theology, Northwestern Lutheran Seminary, 1974).

Bernander, Gustav, *Lutheran Wartime Assistant to Tanzanian Churches, 1940–1945*. Lund: Gleerup, 1968.

Bernard, F.E., *East of Mount Kenya: Meru Agriculture in Transition*. Munich: Weltforum Verlag, 1972.

Berntsen, John L., 'The Maasai and their Neighbours: Variables of Interaction', *African Economic History*, 2 (1976), 1–11.

—, 'Maasai Expansion and Prophets' (seminar paper, SOAS, 1977).

—, 'Economic Variations among Maa-Speaking Peoples' in B.A. Ogot (ed.), *Ecology and History in East Africa (Hadith 7)* (Nairobi: 1979), 108–27.

—, 'Maasai Age-sets and Prophetic Leadership, 1850–1912', *Africa*, 49 (1979), 134–46.

—, 'Pastoralism, Raiding and Prophets: Maasailand in the 19th century' (Ph.D., Wisconsin, 1979).

—, 'The Enemy is Us: Eponymy in the Historiography of the Maasai', *History of Africa*, 7 (1980), 1–21.

Berry, L. & E., 'Land Use in Tanzania by Districts' (BRALUP Research Papers, No.6, 1968).

Berry, Sara, 'Social Institutions and Access to Resources', *Africa*, 59 (1989), 41–55.

—, *No Condition is Permanent: The Social Dynamics of Agrarian Change in Sub-Saharan Africa*. Madison: Wisconsin, 1993.

Bonte, Pierre & John Galaty (eds), *Herders, Warriors and Traders*. Boulder: Westview, 1991.

Boserup, Ester, *The Conditions for Agricultural Growth*. Chicago: Aldine, 1965.

Boyes, John, *The Company of Adventurers*. London: East Africa, 1928.

Brain, James Lewton, 'A Bridge in Meru', *Community Development Journal*, 4 (1969), 17–23.

Bravman, Bill, 'Becoming Taita: A Social History, 1850–1950' (Ph.D., Stanford, 1992).

Bunker, Steven, *Peasants Against the State: The Politics of Market Control in Bugisu, Uganda, 1900–1983*. Chicago: Chicago, 1987.

Burton, Richard F., *The Lake Regions of Central Africa*, 2 vols. London: Longmans, 1860.

—, *Zanzibar: City, Island and Coast*, 2 vols. London: Tinsley, 1872.

Chandler, M.T., 'Traditional Beekeeping among the Wameru of Northern Tanzania' (Tanzanian–Canadian Beekeeping Project, 1975).

Channock, Martin, *Law, Custom and Social Order*. Cambridge: Cambridge, 1985.

Christie, James, *Cholera Epidemics in East Africa*. London: Macmillan, 1876.

Claeson, C.F. & B. Egero, 'Movement to Towns in Tanzania' (BRALUP Resarch Notes, No.11, 1973).

Cliffe, Lionel & Paul Puritt, 'Arusha: Mixed Rural and Urban Communities' in L. Cliffe (ed.), *One Party Democracy* (Nairobi: East African Publishing House, 1967), 155–85.

Collett, David & Peter Robertshaw, 'Pottery Traditions of Early Pastoral Communities in Kenya', *Azania*, 18 (1983), 107–25.

Conyers, D., 'Agro-Economic Zones of Tanzania' (BRALUP Research Paper, No.25, 1973).

Cordell, D., J. Gregory, and V. Piché (eds), *African Population and Capitalism*, 2nd edition, Madison: Wisconsin, 1994.

Cory, Hans, 'Tribal Structure of the Arusha Tribe of Tanganyika' (UDSM, Hans Cory papers, 1948).

—, 'Arusha Land Tenure' (UDSM, Hans Cory Papers, 1953).

—, 'Arusha Law and Custom' (UDSM, Hans Cory papers, nd).

—, 'Proposals for the Adaptation of the Meru Age-grade System to Modern Requirements' (UDSM, Hans Cory papers, nd).

—, 'The Meru Problem' (UDSM, Hans Cory papers, nd).

—, 'Tribal Structure of the Meru, Tanganyika Territory' (UDSM, Hans Cory Papers, nd).

Coutouvidis, J., 'The Matsis Papers: A Greek Settler in Tanganyika', *Immigrants and Minorities*, 2 (1983), 171–84.

Cowen, M.P., 'Commodity Production in Kenya's Central Province' in J. Heyer, et al (eds), *Rural Development in Tropical Africa* (New York: St Martin's, 1981), 121–42.

Danielson, Elmer R., *Forty Years with Christ in Tanzania, 1928–1968*. New York: Lutheran Church in America, 1977.

—, 'Transition in Tanganyika' in J. Gould (ed.), *A Difficult Kind of Journey* (Helsinki: Finnish Anthropological Society, 1991), 28–41.

Dawson, E.C., *James Hannington*. New York: Anson D.F. Randolf, nd.

Doriye, Joshua S., 'The Effect of the Plantation Economy on Indigenous Agriculture in Northern Province, Tanzania, 1930–1960' (UDSM, Economic History Papers, 1973).

Dundas, C., *Kilimanjaro and its People*. London: H.F.& G. Witherby, 1924.

Ehret, Chris & Merrick Posnansky (eds), *The Archaeological and Linguistic Reconstruction of African History*. Berkeley: California, 1982.

Farler, J.P., 'The Usambara Country in East Africa', *PRGS*, 1(1879), 81–97.

—, 'Native Routes in East Africa from Pangani to the Masai Country and Victoria Nyanza', *PRGS*, 4(1882), 730–42, 776.

Feierman, Steven, *The Shambaa Kingdom: A History*. Madison: Wisconsin, 1974.

—, *Peasant Intellectuals: Anthropology and History in Tanzania*. Madison: Wisconsin, 1990.

Fischer, Gustav A., 'Dr. Fischer's Journal in the Masai Country', *PRGS*, 4(1884), 76–83.

Fischer, Gustav A., *Das Massailand*. Hamburg: L. Friederichsen, 1885.

Flatt, Donald C., *Man and Deity in an African Society: A Study of Religious Meaning and Value among the Ilarusa of Northern Tanzania*. Dubuque: Lutheran Church in America, 1980.

Fleuret, P., 'The Social Organization of Water Control in the Taita Hills, Kenya', *American Ethnologist*, 12 (1985), 103–18.

Fokken, H.A., 'Erzählungen und Märchen der Larusa', *Zeitschrift für Kolonialsprachen*, 7 (1916–17), 81–104, 193–211.

—, 'Gottesanschauungen und religiöse Uberlieferungen der Masai', *Archive für Anthropologie*, ns. 15 (1917), 137–52.

Fortmann, Louise, 'Development Prospects in Arumeru District' (USAID/Tanzania, 1977).

—, *Peasants, Officials and Participation in Rural Tanzania*. Ithaca: Cornell Rural Development Committee, 1980.

Fosbrooke, Henry A., 'An Administrative Survey of the Masai Social System', *TNR*, 26 (1948), 1–50.

—, 'Arusha Boma', *TNR*, 38 (1955), 51–2.

—, 'The Masai Age-Group System as a Guide to Tribal Chronology', *African Studies*, 15 (1956), 188–206.

French-Sheldon, M., *Sultan to Sultan*. London: 1892.

Frontera, Ann, *Persistence and Change: A History of Taveta*. Waltham: Crossroads, 1978.

Galaty, John G., 'Pollution and Pastoral Antipraxis: The Issue of Masai Inequality', *American Ethnologist*, 6 (1979), 803–16.

—, 'Being "Maasai": Being "People of Cattle": Ethnic Shifters in East Africa', *American Ethnologist*, 9 (1982), 1–20.

—, 'The Eye that Wants a Person, Where Can it not See? Inclusion, Exclusion and Boundary Shifters in Maasai Identity' in T. Spear & R. Waller (eds), *Being Maasai* (London: James Currey, 1993), 174–94.

—, 'Maasai Pastoral Ideology and Change' in P.C. Salzman (ed.), *Contemporary Nomadic and Pastoral Peoples* (Williamsburg: College of William and Mary, nd).

George, Mrs. John B., 'Meru Land and Politics', *Institute of Current World Affairs Newsletter*, 15 August 1953.

Giblin, James L., 'Famine, Authority and the Impact of Foreign Capital in Handeni District, Tanzania, 1840–1940' (Ph.D., Wisconsin, 1986).

—, 'East Coast Fever in Socio-Historical Context: A Case Study from Tanzania', *IJAHS*, 23 (1990), 401–21.

—, 'Trypanosomiasis Control in African History: An Evaded Issue?' *JAH*, 31 (1990), 59–80.

—, *The Politics of Environmental Control in Northeastern Tanzania, 1840–1940*. Philadelphia: Pennsylvania, 1992.

Glassman, Jonathon P., *Feasts and Riot: Revelry, Rebellion, and Popular Consciousness on the Swahili Coast, 1856–1888*. Portsmouth: Heinemann and London: James Currey, 1995.

Gray, Robert F., *The Sonjo of Tanganyika*. London: Oxford, 1963.

Green, Allen J., 'A Political Economy of Moshi Town, 1920–1960' (Ph.D., UCLA, 1986).

Gulliver, P. H., *Report on Land and Population in the Arusha Chiefdom*. Tanganyika Provincial Administration, 1957.

—, 'A History of Relations between the Arusha and the Masai' (EAISR Conference Papers, Kampala, 1957).

—, 'Memoranda on the Arusha Chiefdom: Arusha Chiefdom Population, 1948–57' (UDSM, Hans Cory Papers, 1957).

—, 'The Population of the Arusha Chiefdom: A High Density Area in East Africa', *Rhodes-Livingstone Journal*, 28 (1960), 1–22.

—, 'Land Shortage, Social Change, and Social Conflict in East Africa', *J. of Conflict Resolution*, 5 (1961), 16–26.

—, 'Structural Dichotomy and Jural Processes among the Arusha of Northern Tanganyika', *Africa*, 31 (1961), 19–35.

—, *Social Control in an African Society: A Study of the Arusha Agricultural Masai of Northern Tanganyika*. London: Routledge & Kegan Paul, 1963.

—, 'The Evolution of Arusha Trade' in P. Bohannan & G. Dalton (eds), *Markets in Africa* (1st ed., Evanston: Northwestern, 1962), 431–6.

—, 'The Arusha: Economic and Social Change' in P. Bohannan & G. Dalton (eds), *Markets in Africa* (2nd ed., New York : Natural History Library, 1965), 250–84.

—, 'The Arusha Family' in R.F. Gray & P.H. Gulliver (eds), *The Family Estate in Africa* (London: Routledge & Kegan Paul, 1965), 197–229.

—, 'The Conservative Commitment in Northern Tanzania: The Arusha and Masai' in P.H. Gulliver (ed.), *Tradition and Transition in East Africa* (London: Routledge & Kegan Paul, 1969), 223–42.

—, 'A Land Dispute in Arusha, Tanzania' in *African Dimensions* (Boston, 1975), 1–14.

Gulliver, P.H. & H.L. Snaith, 'Report on Constitutional Changes in the Local Government of Arusha Chiefdom' (UDSM, Hans Cory Papers, 1957).

Hakansson, Thomas, 'Social and Political Aspects of Intensive Agriculture in East Africa: Some Models from Cultural Anthropology', *Azania*, 24 (1989), 12–20.

Hamilton, A.C., *Environmental History of East Africa*. London: Academic, 1982.

Hanley, Gerald, *Warriors and Strangers*. London: Hamish Hamilton, 1961.

Hanson, Art & D. McMillan (eds), *Food in Sub-Saharan Africa*. Boulder: Lynne Rienner, 1986.

Harfort–Battersby, C.F., *Pilkington of Uganda*. New York: Fleming H. Revell, 1899.

Harjula, R., *God and Sun in Meru Thought*. Helsinki: Annals of the Finnish Society for Missiology & Ecumenics, 1969.

—, *Mirau and his Practice*. London: Tri-Med Books, 1980.

Harris, Grace C., *Casting Out Anger: Religion among the Taita of Kenya*. Cambridge: Cambridge, 1978.

Heine, B. and Rainer Vossen, 'Zur Stellung der Ongamo-Sprache (Kilimandsharo)', *Afrika und Übersee*, 59 (1975/76), 81–105.

Hinnebusch, Thomas & Derek Nurse, 'Spirantization in Chaga', *SUGIA*, 3 (1981), 51–78.

Hobley, C.W., 'Upon a Visit to Tsavo and the Taita Highlands', *Geographical Journal*, 5 (1895).

—, *Kenya: From Chartered Company to Crown Colony*. London: H.F. & G. Witherby, 1929.

Hodder, Ian, 'The Maintenance of Group Identities in the Baringo District, Western Kenya' in D. Green, et al. (eds), *Social Organization and Settlement* (British Archaeological Reports International Series, 47, 1978), 47–74.

Hohenberger, J., 'Comparative Masai Word List', *Africa*, 26 (1956), 281–7.

Hollis, A.C., *The Masai*. Oxford: Clarendon, 1905.

Höhnel, Ludwig von, *Discovery of Lakes Rudolf and Stefanie*, 2 vols. London: Longmans, Green & Co., 1894.

Hyden, Gören, *Beyond Ujamaa in Tanzania: Underdevelopment and an Uncaptured Peasantry*.

London: Heinemann, 1980.

Iliffe, John, *Tanganyika under German Rule, 1905–1912*. Cambridge: Cambridge, 1969.

—, *A Modern History of Tanganyika*. Cambridge: Cambridge, 1979.

—, *The African Poor*. Cambridge: Cambridge, 1987.

—, 'The Origins of African Population Growth', *JAH*, 30 (1989), 165–9.

Jackson, Frederick, *Early Days in East Africa*. London: Edward Arnold, 1930.

Jacobs, A.H., 'The Traditional Political Organization of the Pastoral Masai' (D.Phil., Oxford, 1965).

—, 'A Chronology of the Pastoral Maasai' in B.A. Ogot (ed.), *Hadith* I (Nairobi: 1968), 10–31.

—, 'The Irrigation Agricultural Maasai of Pagasi: A Case of Maasai-Sonjo Acculturation' (MISR, Social Science Research Conference Papers, 1968).

—, 'Maasai Intertribal Relations: Belligerent Herdsmen or Peaceable Pastoralists' in K. Fukui & D.Turton (eds), *Warfare among East African Herders* (Osaka: Senri Ethnological Studies No. 3, 1977), 33–52.

Jaeger, F., 'Der Meru', *Geographische Zeitschrift* (1906), 241–52.

Jaeschke,Ernst (ed.), *Zwischen Sansibar und Serengeti: Lutherische Kirche in Tansania*. Erlangen: Verlag der Evan.-Luth. Mission, 1968.

Japhet, Kirilo & Earle Seaton, *The Meru Land Case*. Nairobi: East African Publishing House, 1967.

Johnston, Alan, 'Population Profile of Arusha Region' (Arusha Regional Commissioner's Office, 1980).

Johnston, Erika, *The Other Side of Kilimanjaro*. London: Johnson, 1971.

Johnston, H.H., *The Kilima-Njaro Expedition*. London: Kegan, Paul, Trench & Co., 1886.

Johnston, P.H., 'Some Notes on Land Tenure on Kilimanjaro and the Vihamba of the Wachagga', *TNR*, 21 (1946), 1–20.

Kaaya, B., 'The Planting of Christianity in Meru: Its Conflicts and Similarities with the Traditional Culture of the Wameru' (Dipl. in Theology, Makerere, 1978).

Kamuzora, C.L., 'Monitoring Population Growth in Arusha Region' (Arusha Regional Commissioner's Office, 1981).

Kelly, Raymond, *The Nuer Conquest: The Structure and Development of an Expansionist System*. Ann Arbor: Michigan, 1985.

Kersten, Otto, *Carl Claus von der Decken's Reisen in Ost-Afrika in den Jahren 1859 bis 1865*, 4 vols. Leipzig: Winter'sche Verlagshandlung, 1869–79.

Kieran, J.A., 'The Origins of Commercial Arabica Coffee Production in East Africa', *AHS*, 2 (1969).

—, 'Christian Villages in Northeastern Tanzania', *Transafrican Journal of History*, 1 (1971), 24–38.

Kimambo, Isaria N., *A Political History of the Pare of Tanzania, c. 1500–1900*. Nairobi: East African Publishing House, 1969.

—, 'The East African Coast and Hinterland, 1845–1880' in J.F.A. Ajayi (ed.), *UNESCO General History of Africa*, Vol. 6, 234–69.

—, *Penetration and Protest in Tanzania: The Impact of the World Economy on the Pare, 1860–1960*. London: James Currey, 1991.

Kimirei, G., 'An Independent Religious Sect of Arusha' (thesis, Lutheran Theological College, Makumira, 1967).

Kisanga, E.J., 'The Colonial Mode of Articulation in Mwika Chiefdom, 1900–1961' (UDSM: Economic History Paper, 1975).

Kituyi, Mukhisa, *Becoming Kenyans: Socio-Economic Transformation of the Pastoral Maasai*.

Nairobi: ACTS Press, 1990.

Kjekshus, Helge, *Ecology Control and Economic Development in East African History*. London: Heinemann, 1977.

Koponen, Juhani, *People and Production in Late Precolonial Tanzania*. Helsinki: Finish Society for Development Studies, 1988.

Krapf, Johann Ludwig., *Vocabulary of the Engutuk Eloikob, or of the Language of the Wakuafi-nation in the Interior of Equatorial Africa*. Tübingen: L.F. Fues, 1854.

—, *Travels, Researches and Missionary Labours during Eighteen Years' Resident in Eastern Africa*. Boston: Ticknor & Fields, 1860.

Kratz, Corinne, 'Are the Okiek really Masai? Or Kipsigis? or Kikuyu?' *Cahiers d'études africaines*, 79 (1980), 355–68.

Kuney, Reuben ole, 'Pluralism and Ethnic Conflict in Tanzania's Arid Lands: The Case of the Maasai and the Waarusha' (13th International Congress of Anthropology and Ethnographic Sciences, Mexico City, 1993).

Lamphear, John, 'The Persistence of Hunting and Gathering in a "Pastoral World" ', *SUGIA*, 7 (1986), 227–65.

Larick, R., 'Iron Smelting and Interethnic Conflict among Precolonial Maa-speaking Pastoralists of North-Central Kenya', *African Archaeological Review*, 4 (1986), 165–76.

Last, J.T., 'A Journey into the Nguru Country from Mamboia, East Central Africa', *PRGS*, 4(1882), 148–57, 192.

—, 'The Masai People and Country', *PRGS*, 4(1882), 224–5.

—, 'A Visit to the Masai Living Beyond the Borders of the Nguru Country', *PRGS*, 5(1883), 517–43, 568.

Lema, A.A., 'The Lutheran Church's Contribution to Education in Kilimanjaro, 1893–1933', *TNR*, 68 (1968), 87–94.

—, 'The Impact of the Leipzig Lutheran Mission on the People of Kilimanjaro, 1893–1920' (Ph.D., Dar es Salaam, 1973).

Lemenye, Justin (H.A. Fosbrooke, trans. & ed.), 'The Life of Justin', *TNR*, 41 (1955), 31–57; 42 (1956), 19–30.

LeRoy, Alexandre, *Au KilimaNdjaro*. Paris: Sanard et Derangeon, [1893].

Levergood, Barbara Jo, 'Topics in Arusa Phonology and Morphology' (Ph.D., Texas, 1987).

Liebenow, J.G., 'Responses to Planned Political Change in a Tanganyika Tribal Group', *American Political Science Review*, 50 (1956), 442–61.

—, 'Some Problems in Introducing Local Government Reform in Tanganyika', *J. of African Administration*, 8 (1956), 132–9.

Lindquist, Ingmar, *Partners in Mission*. Åbo: Åbo Akademi, 1982.

Little, Peter D., 'Women as Ol Payian (Elder): The Status of Women among the Il Chamus (Njemps) of Kenya', *Ethnos*, 52 (1987), 81–102.

—, *The Elusive Granary: Herder, Farmer, and State in Northern Kenya*. Cambridge: Cambridge, 1992.

Lonsdale, John, 'The Moral Economy of Mau Mau: Wealth, Poverty and Civic Virtue in Kikuyu Political Thought' in B. Berman & J. Lonsdale, *Unhappy Valley*, Book Two (London: James Currey, 1992), 315–504.

Luanda, N.N., 'European Commercial Farming and its Impact on the Meru and Arusha Peoples of Tanzania, 1920–1955' (Ph.D., Cambridge, 1986).

Maddox, Gregory H., 'Leave Wagogo, You Have no Food: Famine and Survival in Ugogo, Tanzania, 1916–1961' (Ph.D., Northwestern, 1988).

Maddox, G., J.L. Giblin, & I.N. Kimambo (eds), *Custodians of the Land: Environment and Hunger in Tanzanian History*. London: James Currey, 1996.

Maeda, J.H.J., 'Popular Participation, Control, and Development: A Study of the Nature and Role of Popular Participation in Tanzania's Rural Development' (Ph.D., Yale, 1976).

Mandala, Elias, *Work and Control in a Peasant Economy: A History of the Lower Tchiri Valley in Malawi, 1859–1960*. Madison: Wisconsin, 1990.

Maro, Paul S., 'Population and Land Resources in Northern Tanzania: The Dynamics of Change, 1920–1970' (Ph.D., Minnesota, 1974).

—, 'Population Growth and Agricultural Change in Kilimanjaro, 1920–1970' (BRALUP Research Paper No. 40, 1975).

Marwick, M., 'Another Modern Anti-Witchcraft Movement in East Central Africa', *Africa*, 20 (1950), 110–12.

Masao, F.T., 'The Irrigation System in Uchagga: An Ethno-Historical Approach', *TNR*, 75 (1974), 1–8.

Mauritz, B. 'Über einige Gesteine des Vulkans Meru in Ostafrika', *Tschermaks Min. und Petrogr. Mitteilungen*, 27 (1908), 315–26.

Mbilinyi, Simon, *The Economics of Peasant Coffee Production*. Nairobi: Kenya Literature Bureau, 1976.

Mbise, A.S., 'The Evangelist: Matayo Leveriya Kaaya' in J. Iliffe (ed.), *Modern Tanzanians* (Nairobi: East African Publishing House, 1973), 27–41.

Mbise, I.R., *Blood on Our Land*. Dar es Salaam: Tanzania Publishing House, 1974.

Mbise, R. et al., 'Historia ya Kazi ya Injili Meru kuanzia mwaka 1895–1979 kwa Jubilii ya Miaka 75' (Akeri, 1979).

McCann, James, *People of the Plow: An Agricultural History of Ethiopia, 1800–1990*. Madison: Wisconsin, 1995.

McCarthy, Dennis, *Colonial Bureaucracy and Creating Underdevelopment*. Ames: Iowa, 1982.

McDonald, D.R., *Enemy Property in Tanganyika, Including a Catalogue of Enemy Properties*. Cape Town: 1946.

Mellinghoff, G., J. Kiwovele, & S. Kilowa (eds), *Lutherische Kirche Tanzania*. Erlangen: Verlag der Evan.-Luth. Mission, 1976.

Merker, M., *Die Masai*. Berlin: Dietrich Reimer, 1910.

Merritt, E.H., 'A History of the Taita of Kenya to 1900' (Ph.D., Indiana, 1975).

Methner, W., *Unter drei Gouverneuren*. Breslau: Wilh. Gottl. Korn, 1938.

Meyer, Hans, *Across East African Glaciers*. London: George Philip, 1891.

—, *Das Deutsche Kolonialreich*. Leipgiz: Verlag des Bibliographischen Instituts, 1909.

Miller, Charles, *Battle for the Bundu*. London: Macmillan, 1974.

Mlay, Wilfred, 'Assessment of Inter- and Intra-Regional Migrations in Arusha Region' (Arusha Regional Commissioner's Office, 1981).

—, 'Population Pressure in Arumeru District' (Arumeru District Commissioner's Office, 1982).

Mlay, Wilfred et al., 'Population Pressure in Arumeru District, Tanzania', *Pathpapers*, 12 (1985).

Mol, Frans, *Maa: A Dictionary of the Maasai Language and Folklore*. Nairobi: Marketing & Publishing Ltd, nd.

Moore, J.E., 'Rural Population Carrying Capacities of the Districts of Tanzania' (BRALUP Research Paper, No. 18, 1971).

Moore, Sally Falk & Paul Puritt, *The Chagga and Meru of Tanzania*. London: International African Institute, 1977.

Moore, Sally Falk, 'Politics, Procedures and Norms in Changing Chagga Law', *Africa*, 40 (1970), 321–43.

—, 'The Secret of Men: A Fiction of Chagga Initiation', *Africa*, 46 (1976), 357–70.

—, *Social Facts and Fabrications: 'Customary' Law on Kilimanjaro, 1880–1980*. Cambridge: Cambridge, 1986.

Mshana, B.Y., 'Arusha Synod, Tanzania: The Identity of the Church and its Ministry to Society' (M. of Sacred Theology, Wartburg Theological Seminar, 1976).

Mturi, Amani A., 'The Pastoral Neolithic of Western Kilimanjaro' *Azania*, 21 (1986), 53–64.

Murray-Rust, H., 'Soil Erosion and Sedimentation in Kisongo Catchment, Arusha Region' (BRALUP Research Paper, 317, 1971).

Mwase, N.R.L., 'Cooperatives and Ujamaa: A Case Study of the Arusha Region Cooperative Union Limited (ARCU)' in *Cooperatives in Tanzania* (Dar es Salaam, 1976), 78–90.

Nasari, C.T.S., 'The History of the Lutheran Church among the Wameru (Varwa) of Tanzania' (BD, Lutheran Theological College Makumira, 1980).

Ndagala, D.K., *Territory, Pastoralists, and Livestock: Resource Control among the Kisongo Maasai*. Uppsala: Acta Universitatis Upsaliensis, 1992.

Nelson, Anton, *The Freemen of Meru*. Nairobi: Oxford, 1967.

Neumann, Roderick P., 'The Social Origins of Natural Resource Conflict in Arusha National Park, Tanzania' (Ph.D., Berkeley, 1992).

New, Charles, *Life, Wanderings, and Labours in Eastern Africa*. London: Hodder & Stoughton, 1873.

Nkonya, E.M. et al., 'Arumeru District Diagnostic Survey' (Selian Agricultural Research Institute, 1991).

Nnko, S.E., 'The Interdenominational Conflicts with the Meru District of the ELCT Northern Diocese' (Dipl. in Theology, Makerere, 1980).

Nurse, Derek, *The Classification of the Chaga Dialects*. Hamburg: Helmut Buske, 1979.

—, 'Language Contact, Creolization and Genetic Linguistics: The Case of Mwiini' (African Studies Association, 1992).

Nurse, Derek & Gérard Philippson, 'The Bantu Languages of East Africa: A Lexicostatistical Survey' in E.C. Polomé & C.P. Hill (eds), *Language in Tanzania* (London: Oxford for the International African Institute, 1980), 26–67.

Nypan, A., 'Diffusion of Innovation and Community Leadership in East Africa' (Report No. 3, Section for Development Studies, University of Oslo, 1970).

Nypan, A. & M. Vaa, 'Leadership, Organizational Structure and Development' (Report No. 4, Section for Development Studies, University of Oslo, 1974).

—, 'Extension Theory and Local Theory' (Report No. 9, Section for Development Studies, University of Oslo, 1974).

Odner, Kurt, 'A Preliminary Report of an Archaeological Survey on the Slopes of Kilimanjaro', *Azania*, 6 (1971), 131–49.

Ogutu, M.A., 'The Cultivation of Coffee among the Chagga of Tanzania, 1919–1939', *Agricultural History*, 46 (1972), 279–90.

Oloya, J.J., *Coffee, Cotton, Sisal and Tea in the East African Economies, 1945–1962*. Nairobi: East African Literature Bureau, 1969.

Palangyo, P.K., *Dying in the Sun*. London: Heinemann, 1968.

Pätzig, Max, *Lasaros Laiser: Ein Leben für die Junge Kirche in Ostafrika*. Erlangen: Verlag der Evang.–Luth. Mission, 1959.

Phillipson, Gérard, 'Essai de phonologie comparé des dialectes chaga' in M.-F. Rombi (ed.), *Etudes sur le bantu oriental* (Paris: SELAF, 1983), 41–71.

—, *Gens des bananeraies: Contribution linguistique à l'histoire culturelle des Chaga du Kilimanjaro*. Paris: Editions Recherche sur les Civilisations, 1984.

Puritt, Paul, 'Systems of Authority among the Meru' (EAISR Conference Papers, 1966).

—, 'The Meru Land Case', *TNR*, 69 (1968), 53–7.

—, 'The Meru of Tanzania: A Study of their Social and Political Organization' (Ph.D., Illinois, 1970).

Ranger, T.O. & E.J. Hobsbawm (eds), *The Invention of Tradition*. Cambridge: Cambridge, 1992.

Ranger, T.O. & O. Vaughan (eds), *Legitimacy and the State in Twentieth Century Africa*. (Houndmills: Macmillan, 1993).

Rapp, A. et al. (eds), *Studies in Soil Erosion and Sedimentation in Tanzania*. Dar es Salaam: BRALUP, 1973.

Rebmann, J., 'Narrative of a Journey to Jagga, the Snow Country of Eastern Africa', *Church Missionary Intelligencer*, 1 (1849–50), 12–23.

—, 'Narrative of a Journey to Madjame, in Jagga', *Church Missionary Intelligencer*, 1 (1849–50), 272–6, 307–12.

—, 'Narrative of Journey to Madjame', *Church Missionary Intelligencer*, 1 (1849–50), 327–30, 376–81.

Richards, Audrey I., 'A Modern Movement of Witchfinders', *Africa*, 8 (1935), 448–61.

Richards, Paul, *Indigenous Agricultural Revolutions*. London: Hutchinson, 1985.

Rigby, Peter, *Persistent Pastoralists*. London: Zed, 1985.

Robertshaw, Peter, 'The Development of Pastoralism in East Africa' in J. Clutton-Brock (ed.), *The Walking Larder* (London: Unwin Hyman, 1989), 207–14.

— (ed.), *Early Pastoralists of South-Western Kenya*. Nairobi: British Institute in Eastern Africa, 1990.

Robertshaw, Peter & David Collett, 'A New Framework for the Study of Early Pastoral Communities in East Africa', *JAH*, 24 (1983), 289–301.

Rogers, Susan Geiger, 'The Search for Political Focus on Kilimanjaro' (Ph.D., Dar es Salaam, 1972).

Ruthenberg, Hans, *Smallholder Farming and Smallholder Development in Tanzania*. München: Weltforum Verlag, 1968.

Saibull, S. ole & R. Carr, *Herd and Spear*. London: Collins, 1981.

Sandgren, David P., *Christianity and the Kikuyu: Religious Divisions and Social Conflict*. New York: Peter Lang, 1989.

Sankan, S.S. ole, *The Maasai*. Nairobi: East African Literature Bureau, 1971.

Schanz, Johannes, *Am Füsse der Bergriesen OstAfrikas: Geschichte der Leipziger Mission am Kilimandjaro und in den Nachbergebirgen*. Leipzig: Verlag der Evan.-Luth. Mission, 1912.

Schoeller, Max, *Mitteilungen über meine Reise nach Äquatorial-Ostafrika und Uganda, 1896–1897*, 3 vols. Berlin: Dietrich, 1901, 1904.

Schwartz. Carl von, *Karl Segebrock and Ewald Ovir*. Leipzig: Evan.-Luth. Mission, 1897.

Scott, James, *The Moral Economy of the Peasant*. New Haven: Yale, 1976.

Shepherd, K., 'Banana Cultivars in East Africa', *Tropical Agriculture, Trinidad*, 34 (1957), 277–86.

Shio, Leonard, 'A Political Economy of the Plantation System in Arusha' (MA, Dar es Salaam, 1974).

Shipton, Parker, 'Land and Culture in Tropical Africa: Soils, Symbols, and the Metaphysics of the Mundane', *Annual Review of Anthropology*, 23 (1994), 347–77.

Shipton, Parker & Mitzi Goheen, 'Understanding African Land-Holding: Power, Wealth and Meaning', *Africa*, 62 (1992), 307–25.

Simmonds, N.W., *Bananas*. London: Longman, 1959.

Simonson, J. David, 'A Cultural Study of the Maasai to Determine an Effective Program of Evangelism' (M. Theology, Luther Theological Seminary, 1955).

Smedjebacka, Henrik, *Lutheran Church Autonomy in Northern Tanzania, 1940–1963*. Åbo: Åbo Akademi, 1973.

Sobania, Neal, 'Fishermen Herders: Subsistence, Survival and Cultural Change in Northern Kenya', *JAH*, 29 (1988), 41–56.

Soyinka, Wole, *Death and the King's Horseman*. New York: Hill & Wang, 1975.

Spear, Thomas, *The Kaya Complex: A History of the Mijikenda Peoples of the Kenya Coast to 1900*. Nairobi: Kenya Literature Bureau, 1978.

—, *Kenya's Past: An Introduction to Historical Method in Africa*. London: Longman, 1981.

—, *The Swahili: Reconstructing the History and Language of an African Society, 800–1500*. Philadelphia: Pennsyvania, 1985.

—, 'Introduction' in T. Spear & R. Waller (eds), *Being Maasai* (London: James Currey, 1993), 1–18.

—, '"Being Maasai" but not "People of Cattle": Arusha Agricultural Maasai in the Nineteenth century' in T. Spear & R. Waller (eds), *Being Maasai* (London: James Currey, 1993), 120–36.

—, 'Blood on the Land: Stories of Conquest' in R. Harms, J. Miller, D. Newbury & M. Wagner (eds), *Paths Toward the Past* (Atlanta: ASA Press, 1994), 113–22.

—, 'Land, Population, and Agricultural Development on Mount Meru' (Conference on the Growth of Farming in Africa, Cambridge, 1994).

—, 'Struggles for the Land: The Political and Moral Economies of Land on Mount Meru' in G. Maddox, J. Giblin, and I.N. Kimambo (eds), *Custodians of the Land: Environment and Hunger in Tanzanian History* (London: James Currey, 1996), 213–40.

—, 'Town and Country: Arusha and its Hinterland' (Conference on Africa's Urban Past, SOAS, London, 1996).

Spear, Thomas & Derek Nurse, 'Maasai Farmers: The Evolution of Arusha Agriculture', *IJAHS*, 25 (1992), 481–503.

Spear, Thomas & Richard Waller (eds), *Being Maasai: Ethnicity and Identity in East Africa*. London: James Currey, 1993.

Spear, Thomas (ed.), C. Michele & Timothy M. Murphy (trans.), *Evangelisch–Lutherisiches Missionsblatt*. Madison: African Studies Program, 1995.

Spencer, Paul, *Nomads in Alliance*. London: Oxford, 1973.

—, 'Opposing Streams and the Gerontocratic Ladder: Two Models of Age Organization in East Africa', *Man*, ns. 11 (1976), 153–75.

—, *The Maasai of Matapato*. Bloomington: Indiana, 1988.

—, 'Becoming Maasai: Being in Time' in T. Spear & R. Waller (eds) *Being Maasai* (London: James Currey, 1993), 140–56.

Stahl, K., *History of the Chagga Peoples of Kilimanjaro*. The Hague: Mouton, 1964.

Stock, Eugene, *The History of the Church Missionary Society*. London: Church Missionary Society, 1899–1916.

Sturdy, D., W.E. Carlton, & G. Milne, 'A Chemical Survey of the Waters of Mount Meru, Tanganyika, especially with regard to their qualities for irrigation', *J. of the East Africa & Uganda Natural History Society*, 45–6 (1932), 1–38.

Sutton, J.E.G., 'The Archaeology and Early Peoples of the Highlands of Kenya and Northern Tanzania', *Azania*, 1 (1966), 37–57.

—, *The Archaeology of the Western Highlands of Kenya*. Nairobi: British Institute in Eastern Africa, 1973.

—, 'Irrigation and Soil Conservation in African Agricultural History', *JAH*, 25 (1984), 25–41.

— (ed.), 'African Agriculture Technology and Field Systems', special issue of *Azania*, 24 (1989).

Swynnerton, R.J.M., 'Some Problems of the Chagga on Kilimanjaro', *East African Agricultural J.*,

14 (1949), 117–32.

Thomas, A., 'Notes on the Formal Education of Arusha "murren" at Circumcision,' *TNR*, 65 (1966), 81–90.

Thomas, Gary, 'Center and Periphery in Arusha Region' (Washington/Arusha: Development Alternatives, 1980).

Thomas, I.D., 'Population Density in Tanzania, 1967' (BRALUP Research Notes, No.5b).

Thompson, E.P., 'The Moral Economy of the English Crowd in the Eighteenth Century', *Past and Present*, 50 (1971), 76–136.

Thomson, Joseph, 'Through the Masai Country to Victoria Nyanza', *PRGS*, 6 (1884), 690–712, 758.

—, *Through Masailand*. London: Samson, Low, Marston, Searle & Rivington, 1885.

Thornton, Richard, 'Notes on a Journey to Kilimanjaro', *PRGS*, 35(1865), 15–21.

Thornton, R.J., *Space, Time and Culture among the Iraqw of Tanzania*. New York: Academic, 1980.

Turner, B.L., G. Hyden & R.W. Kates (eds), *Population Growth and Agricultural Change in Africa*. Gainesville: Florida, 1993.

Uhlig, C., 'Vom Kilimanjaro zum Meru', *Zeitschrift der Gesellschaft für Erdkunde zu Berlin* (1904), 692–718.

—, 'Die Tätigkeit des Vulkans Meru', *Geographische Zeitschrift*, 17 (1911), 278–81.

United States Department of State, 'Native Interests and Land Distribution in East Africa' (Intelligence Report No.5946, 1953).

Vail, Leroy (ed.), *The Creation of Tribalism in Southern Africa*. London: James Currey, 1989.

Vansina, Jan, *Paths in the Rainforests: Toward a History of Political Tradition in Equatorial Africa*. Madison: Wisconsin and London: James Currey, 1990.

Vickery, Kenneth, *Black and White in Southern Zambia*. New York: Greenwood, 1986.

Von Clemm, M.F.M., 'Trade Bead Economics in Nineteenth Century Chaggaland', *Man*, 63 (1963), 12–14.

—, 'Agricultural Productivity and Sentiment on Kilimanjaro', *Economic Botany*, 18 (1964), 99–121.

Von Loesecke, H.W., *Bananas*. New York: Interscience, 1950.

Vossen, Rainer, 'Linguistic Evidence Regarding the Territorial History of the Maa-speaking Peoples: Some Preliminary Remarks', *Kenya Historical Review*, 6 (1978), 34–52.

—, *The Eastern Nilotes*. Berlin: D. Reimer, 1982.

—, *Towards a Comparative Study of the Maa Dialects of Kenya and Tanzania*. Hamburg: Buske, 1988.

Vossen, Rainer & B. Heine, 'The Historical Reconstruction of Proto-Ongamo-Maa: Phonology and Vocabulary' in M. L. Bender (ed.), *Nilo-Saharan Linguistic Studies* (Hamburg: H. Buske 1989), 177–213.

Wakefield, E.S., *Thomas Wakefield: Missionary and Geographical Pioneer in East Equatorial Africa*. London: Religious Tract Society, 1904.

Wakefield, Thomas, 'Routes of Native Caravans from the Coast to the Interior of Eastern Africa...', *JRGS*, 40 (1870), 303–38.

—, 'Native Routes through the Masai Country', *PRGS*, 4 (1882), 742–3.

—, 'The Wakwavi Raid on the District near Mombasa', *PRGS*, 5(1883).

Waller, Richard D., 'The Maasai and the British, 1895–1905: The Origins of an Alliance', *JAH*, 17 (1976), 529–33.

—, 'The Lords of East Africa: The Maasai in the mid-Nineteenth Century' (Ph.D., Cambridge, 1979).

—, 'Interaction and Identity on the Periphery: The Trans-Mara Maasai', *IJAHS*, 17 (1984), 243–284.

—, 'Ecology, Migration and Expansion in East Africa', *African Affairs*, 84 (1985), 347–70.

—, 'Economic and Social Relations in the Central Rift Valley: The Maa-Speakers and their Neighbours in the Nineteenth Century' in B.A. Ogot (ed.), *Kenya in the 19th century* (*Hadith 8*) (Nairobi: Bookwise, 1985), 83–151.

—, '*Emutai*: Crisis and Response in Maasailand, 1883-1902' in D. Johnson & D.M. Anderson (eds), *Ecology of Survival* (Boulder: Westview, 1988), 73–113.

Weber, Max (H.H. Gerth & C.W. Mills, eds), *From Max Weber*. London: Routledge & Kegan Paul, 1948.

White, Landeg, *Magomero*. Cambridge: Cambridge, 1987.

Willoughby, J.C., *East Africa and its Big Game*. London: Longmans, Green & Co., 1889.

Winter, J.C., *Bruno Gutmann, 1876–1966*. Oxford: Clarendon, 1979.

Wood, P.J., 'The Forest Glades of West Kilimanjaro', *TNR*, 64 (1965), 108–11.

Wright, Ian, 'The Meru Land Case', *TNR*, 66 (1966).

Wrigley, C.C., 'Bananas in Buganda', *Azania*, 24 (1989), 64–70.

Index